'Cure, Comfort and Safe Custody'

'Cure, Comfort and Safe Custody'

PUBLIC LUNATIC ASYLUMS IN EARLY NINETEENTH-CENTURY ENGLAND

LEONARD D. SMITH

Leicester University Press
London and New York

First published 1999 by
Leicester University Press, *A Cassell imprint*
Wellington House, 125 Strand, London WC2R 0BB
370 Lexington Avenue, New York, NY 10017–6550

British Library Cataloguing-in-Publication Data

A catalogue record for this book is available from the British Library.

ISBN 0 7185 0094 6

Library of Congress Cataloging-in-Publication Data

Smith, Leonard D., 1947–
Cure, comfort, and safe custody : public lunatic asylums in early nineteenth century England / Leonard D. Smith.
p. cm.
Includes bibliographical references and index.
ISBN 0–7185–0094–6 (hardcover)
1. Psychiatric hospital care—England—History—19th century.
2. Psychiatric hospitals—England—History—19th century.
I. Title.

RC450.G7S63 1999
362.2′1′094209034—dc21 98–26009
CIP

Designed and typeset by Ben Cracknell Studios

Printed and bound in Great Britain by The Cromwell Press Ltd, Trowbridge, Wiltshire

Contents

	List of Illustrations	vi
	Acknowledgements	vii
	List of Abbreviations	ix
	Introduction	1
1	The Rise of the Public Asylum	12
2	Asylum Management	52
3	'Waste Stuff': Peopling the Asylum	93
4	'The Most Essential Instruments': From Keepers to Attendants	131
5	Inside the Asylum	159
6	Treatment and Care	187
7	Useful Occupation	227
8	With Due Restraint	247
	Conclusions: In Pursuit of Cure	284
	Bibliography	289
	Index	304

Illustrations

1 Nottinghamshire General Lunatic Asylum (1818)
2 Bedfordshire County Lunatic Asylum (1831)
3 Staffordshire General Lunatic Asylum (1834)
4 Norfolk County Lunatic Asylum (1825)
5 Lincoln Lunatic Asylum (1822)
6 Oxford (Radcliffe) Lunatic Asylum (1840)
7 Mechanical Restraint (1)
8 Mechanical Restraint (2)
9 Mechanical Restraint (3)
10 Mechanical Restraint (4)

Acknowledgements

I owe a considerable debt of gratitude to the Wellcome Trust, which has assisted me over several years with a research expenses grant. More importantly, the Trustees funded a Research Fellowship at the University of Birmingham for a year in 1994–5, which enabled me to take time out from the rigours of community mental health work and to make serious inroads into the archives.

The staff of several record offices have provided valuable assistance. Apart from the Public Record Office, these include the record offices of the counties of Bedfordshire, Cheshire, Cornwall, Devon, Dorset, Gloucestershire, Greater London, Kent, Lancashire, Leicestershire, Lincolnshire, Norfolk, Nottinghamshire, Staffordshire, Suffolk and the West Riding of Yorkshire. Other archive collections consulted include Chester City Record Office, Liverpool City Archives, Manchester Royal Infirmary Archives and the Warneford Hospital (Oxford) Archives.

The staff of various libraries have given much important help and advice. These include the central reference libraries of Birmingham, Chester, Gloucester, Lancaster, Lincoln, Maidstone, Norwich, Nottingham and Wakefield, the university libraries of Birmingham, Cambridge, Oxford and London, and the library of the Royal Cornwall Museum, Truro. Particular mention must go to the staff of the invaluable library collection of the Wellcome Institute. Thanks are also due to the librarian of the Royal College of Psychiatrists for enabling me to have access to copies of much of Dr C. Crommelinck's rare Belgian book.

The museum collections at St Bernard's Hospital (Hanwell), The Lawn (Lincoln) and Stanley Royd Hospital (Wakefield) provided important information and orientation. Particular gratitude is due to Lawrence Ashworth of the Stanley Royd Museum for his time and patience in allowing access to the museum's extensive archives, and for the benefit of his considerable knowledge.

A number of individuals have given assistance and support along the way. A special mention is due to Professor Roy Porter, who has always been prepared to offer encouragement as well as essential practical advice. He has given generously of his scarce time to read and comment on the earlier drafts of this book, and to give valuable suggestions. I would also like to thank Jonathan Andrews, David Wright and Mark Roseman for their work in reading and commenting on drafts.

For someone like myself who works mainly outside the academic field, interaction with other historians has been essential. In particular, fellow researchers in aspects of the history of psychiatry have provided invaluable expertise and stimulation – Professor Anne Digby, Peter Bartlett, Elizabeth Burrows, David Hurst, Pamela Michael, Akihito Suzuki, Elizabeth Malcolm, Joseph Melling, Richard Adair, Bill Forsythe, Professor Hugh Freeman, Ted Myers, Peter Nolan, Howard Purves, Professor Andrew Scull, Michael Neve, David Wright and Jonathan Andrews. The specialist seminars sponsored by the Wellcome Institute have provided excellent opportunities to broaden knowledge, and to explore and crystallize ideas.

I owe a large debt to Dorothy Thompson who encouraged me to pursue research in social history and showed the way. Professor Jim Boulton has offered personal encouragement, as well as enabling me to use the excellent facilities of the Institute for Advanced Research in the Humanities at the University of Birmingham. Professor Ian Brockington facilitated my irreplaceable year as a Research Fellow in the University's Department of Psychiatry. There are many others who deserve thanks for their encouragement. I will mention Anne Borsay, Stephen Roberts, Carl Chinn and Professor Martin Goodman, and hope that anyone omitted will forgive me.

A special thanks must go to my family – to Golda, Deborah, Daniel and Sonia Smith, for their patience, forbearance and encouragement, even though it meant that husband and father spent an inordinate amount of time elsewhere or upstairs.

Abbreviations

BCRO	Bedfordshire County Record Office/ Bedfordshire and Luton Archives
BPP	British Parliamentary Papers
CCRO	Cornwall County Record Office
CKS	Centre for Kentish Studies
DCRO	Dorset County Record Office
GCRO	Gloucestershire County Record Office
GLRO	Greater London Record Office
GRL	Gloucester Reference Library
LCRO	Lancashire County Record Office
LAO	Lincolnshire Archives Office
LPL	Lancaster Public Library
LLSL	Lincoln Local Studies Library
MRI	Manchester Royal Infirmary
NCRO	Nottinghamshire County Record Office/ Nottinghamshire Archives
NkCRO	Norfolk County Record Office
NRL	Nottingham Reference Library
SCRO	Staffordshire County Record Office
SuCRO	Suffolk County Record Office
WRCRO	West Riding County Record Office

Introduction

During the last two decades there has been growing attention to the history of provision for mentally disordered people in Britain. Interest has been stimulated in part by contemporary considerations. The significant pharmacological developments in the treatment of mental illness since the 1950s have been accompanied by profound changes in the ways in which sufferers are managed and looked after. In particular, we have witnessed a major shift in emphasis from institution-based management to care and treatment in the community. The most overt physical representation of new systems and altered priorities has been the relentless dismantling and demolition of our lunatic asylum heritage. The unseemly haste to turn these symbols of rejected ideas into rubble is bound to raise questions as to how we came to inherit the vast and imposing structures, and what sorts of ideals and principles led to their construction in the first place.

The narrative of the rise and fall of the lunatic asylum has engaged scholars emanating from more than one discipline. The established specialism of medical history has spawned an increasingly active and distinct sub-specialty in the history of psychiatry. Many of its recruits have turned to historical enquiry during or after distinguished careers in psychiatric practice.[1] This has provided them with perspectives rooted both in professional identity and in active attempts to relieve the victims of mental distress. The other significant contribution to the developing history of the asylum has come from social historians, drawn to consider the complex interactions of elements like societal change, deviance, professionalization and the growth of institutions. Andrew Scull's controversial *Museums of Madness* (1979), though not the first important work in the field, signalled a new interest among social historians.[2] The differing approaches between them and the psychiatric historians have brought tensions, which on occasions have erupted into conflict between the more outspoken advocates.[3] However, as calmer counsels have prevailed, both schools have come to acknowledge the validity of the other's contribution and have been able to incorporate the results of their scholarship.

This book focuses on the period of initial development in England of the system of state-sponsored institutional care for insane people. Although the provision of county lunatic asylums did not become mandatory until 1845, there was already by that date a network of public asylums in place, established through voluntary effort, county rate funding or a combination of the two. The voluntary lunatic hospitals of the later eighteenth century had provided the foundations. Their example informed the key legislation of 1808, which created the basic administrative machinery for the development of a comprehensive national system. Historians have tended to play down the significance of the 1808 County Asylums Act and its aftermath, because its clauses empowering justices to establish asylums were only adopted in a minority of counties.[4] A contrary and more positive interpretation has to acknowledge the remarkably early state intervention in social welfare provision that the legislation represented, and the relatively wide take-up of the Act's powers before 1845. It also recognizes that this was the first generation of lunatic asylums financed through the public purse and managed by the guidance of statute. These were true pioneer institutions, which offered a testing ground for the differing philosophies and sets of principles which coalesced in the care and treatment of the insane, as well as for the very practical administrative and managerial issues that had to be tackled.

The first half of the nineteenth century was a crucial period of transition in mental health care, reflecting the modernization and growing sophistication of political, economic and administrative structures.[5] It witnessed in microcosm phenomena which have been apparent throughout the last two centuries, down to the present time – the shifting balance between the ideals identified by Anne Digby of 'custody' and 'cure', and what Patricia Allderidge perceptively described as 'cycles' in the history of care of the insane.[6] In essence, the emphasis has been constantly changing between the promotion of recovery or rehabilitation and the protection of society and its members from the excesses of the unpredictable madman. Periods of progressive change have been followed by periods of restrictiveness, only to be succeeded again by greater relaxation. Never was this swinging pendulum exemplified more clearly than in the rejection of the old custodial regime and the emergence of the 'non-restraint' movement in the late 1830s and 1840s.

One of the more keenly argued debates in the history of psychiatry and of the asylum has been around whether the major and profound changes that occurred in the early part of the nineteenth century marked a clear break with the past.[7] The argument was, to an extent, created by later nineteenth-century writers intent on demonstrating the great progress that had been achieved, particularly since the emergence of 'moral treatment' and the subsequent triumph of 'non-restraint'.[8] The discrediting and castigation of earlier practices and practitioners served to provide a suitable contrast with those of a perceived enlightened and progressive liberal age. Twentieth-century writers have been prepared to readily subscribe to the idea of an earlier dark age of chains, darkness, filth and ill-treatment which lasted well into the nineteenth century.[9] This seductive picture has been exposed as too simplistic. The work of Roy Porter, in particular, has highlighted the extent of humane and innovative practice in some eighteenth-century institutions, public and private, whilst acknowledging the concurrent shortcomings elsewhere.[10] This book will further illustrate the clear continuities, rather than any fundamental breaks, between contrasting eras in the treatment of insanity.

At the heart of the debate has been the genesis, nature and progress of what became known as 'moral treatment'. The terminology had entered the vocabulary of the management of insanity during the later eighteenth century, and referred to means of treatment other than medical or physical interventions. It embraced methods of a psychological or interpersonal nature, or where aspects of the regime influenced or altered the patient's behaviour patterns. In practical terms, moral treatment came to incorporate occupation, organized leisure pursuits, religious participation and interactions between patients and medical men or staff. The term 'moral treatment' became widely used by practitioners in both private and public asylums; indeed, its application became an accepted element in any institution with even the slightest pretension toward enlightened or humane practice. Posterity has, however, tended to identify moral treatment with the particular practices of the York Retreat, which was established by the Quakers in 1794. The tendency was reinforced in the wake of the publication of Samuel Tuke's seminal *Description of the Retreat* in 1813, in which its much emulated methods were highlighted in the chapter on 'Moral Treatment'.[11]

A number of writers on insanity in the late eighteenth and early nineteenth centuries referred to the importance of 'management' in their treatment practices.[12] This alluded initially to the means whereby the mad-doctor gained influence, or even ascendancy, over the patient and made use of it to guide him toward restoration of the senses. Some of the elements of management coincided with aspects of moral treatment, and the hybrid term 'moral management' emerged.[13] As asylums grew steadily larger, the institution's operational system became increasingly important as an instrument of treatment, whilst attention to individual pathology and therapy receded. In the aftermath of the dissemination of 'non-restraint' among the largest asylums, this process was accelerated as management systems which embraced routine and structure became essential for the maintenance of order. By 1850, the connotations of 'moral management' were very far removed from those of the original terminology.

The reformers, local worthies and medical men involved in establishing the new generation of public asylums would proclaim their intention to provide moral treatment, alongside medical treatment, in the institution. 'Mad-doctors' or 'alienists' (the nineteenth-century term for psychiatrists), with varying degrees of enthusiasm, incorporated it into their armamentaria of therapy.[14] However, it proved extremely problematic in practice to match the aspirations. Real difficulties surrounded the implementation, in a relatively large asylum, of techniques that had been developed to suit smaller domestic-scale madhouses and a purpose-designed asylum like the Retreat. Genuine efforts were made, as at the West Riding Asylum with its strong Retreat influence, but the logistics and the realities of having to provide custodial care tended to defeat the attempts.

The nature of the asylum's regime, including the extent to which moral treatment ideals could be pursued, was not only determined by policy makers and managers. In an important essay, Michael Ignatieff emphasized the significant part that inmates' families and communities played in determining the nature of institutions. The 'dependent and dominated classes' were not merely victims of the mechanisms of the state, but contributed directly toward the development of the apparatus of social control.[15] Extending the argument, those consigned to institutions also helped to shape them. This is as true of asylum patients as of any other group. It must be borne in mind that, in the early part of the nineteenth century, the numbers admitted to asylums were still relatively small in comparison to the situation that developed over later decades.[16] Committal was only likely to occur in extreme circumstances where the behaviour associated with the individual's madness could no longer be safely contained by family or community. Those who did find their way into the asylum were likely to present a considerable challenge to the officers and staff who were expected to provide custody and an attempt to cure.

The realities of historical records, as regards both their content and their chancy survival rate, have inevitably tended to lead historians of the asylum to concentrate on the institutions themselves, and the prominent men at the helm. The voices of the most significant people, the insane patients, are notoriously hard to retrieve. Bill Luckin, in a valuable article, stressed the importance of using the available records to try to consider how individuals responded to the institution and its regime, routines, authority structures and so on.[17] Parts of the fourth and sixth chapters of this book represent such an attempt, though the limitations of the original data are clear enough.

Any interpretation of the lunatic asylum as essentially a monolithic instrument of social control does an injustice to many of its practitioners. Madness was (and is) rather more than a blatant manifestation of deviance. It constituted deep human suffering, likely to be accompanied by risk and danger both to the sufferer and to other people. The twin ideals of 'cure' and 'custody' were not impositions of those empowered to deal with the insane. On the contrary, they were the natural responses to the challenges presented by people who were, by turn, threatening and tormented. Treatment methods, arrangements for managing patients, and the environment within the institution have to be considered in this context.

The tensions between custody and cure form a constant underlying theme in this book.[18] The oscillations, usually gradual but occasionally sudden, are evident within individual institutions as well as within the asylum movement as a whole. Conditions inside the asylum reflected both therapeutic and custodial intent. There is a need for caution when considering those conditions. As Jonathan Andrews so expertly demonstrated in his study of eighteenth-century Bethlem Hospital, there are dangers inherent in retrospective surveys. Principal among these is the tendency to judge the performance of institutions and those who managed them, and the experiences of those who filled them, by current standards rather than those of the past.[19] In the mental health field, with its emphasis on constant advance, there has also long been a tendency to focus on and denigrate the limitations of past practices, as part of the process of extolling the virtues of the latest methods. Mythologies have been constructed, not least about Bethlem itself, which owe more to reflecting well on 'the march of progress' than on the true nature of early public asylums.

The historical development of the asylum during the early nineteenth century can be placed in some order by a series of key dates. By 1800, the principle of public responsibility for establishing asylums for the insane poor had been partially accepted, and found practical expression in the operation of charitable institutions in cities like London, Manchester, York, Liverpool and Exeter. Their example provided inspiration for the Gloucestershire magistrate and prison reformer Sir George Onesiphorus Paul, whose indefatigable efforts led to the appointment of the important Select Committee of 1807, and its selective consideration of evidence. Its report laid out the essential case for the state's acceptance of responsibility for the care of the insane.[20] The County Asylum Act, or Wynn's Act of 1808, which implemented some of the Select Committee's main recommendations, laid the legislative basis for the first generation of county lunatic asylums. It provided the necessary administrative infrastructure for their construction and management, as well as guidance on key standards. Despite its limitations, the Act provided the strategic and practical foundation for the English lunatic asylum system.[21] The first two county asylums built under the terms of the Act, in Bedford and Nottingham, were opened in 1812.

The years marking the culmination of the Napoleonic Wars were especially significant for the proponents of lunacy reform. The exposure of the scandals of the York Asylum, one of the prestigious eighteenth-century subscription asylums, demonstrated that poor conditions, corruption and cruelty were not confined to the maligned private madhouse sector.[22] The reformers' important achievement, the Select Committee on the State of Madhouses of 1815, produced evidence of extensive abuses not only at York, but also at Bethlem Hospital and various private establishments.[23] Meanwhile, the dissemination of Samuel Tuke's *Description of the Retreat* in 1813 presented a comprehensive prescription for an alternative approach to patient management.[24] The contrast between the old custodial and the new therapeutic methods was plain. The practical response both to the exposures and the new thinking was, however, limited. Attempts to bring in more effective legislation foundered, due in part to a reluctance to promote further centralizing measures.[25] The construction of county asylums did not accelerate. The reformers' clearest achievement was the opening of the West Riding Asylum at Wakefield in 1818, and the attempt to operate it on Tukean principles.

The extension of the public asylum system continued slowly but steadily through the 1820s. In 1820, the opening of the Cornwall County Asylum at Bodmin was followed by the Lincoln subscription asylum, later to attract considerable celebrity. The striking Gloucester Asylum, Sir Paul's much-delayed project, finally opened in 1823. By the middle of the decade, with most major developments having taken place in the provinces, the almost intractable problems of pauper lunacy in the metropolis were attracting the reformers' attention. London's shortcomings were highlighted by a Select Committee in 1827, leading directly to the projection and establishment of the massive showpiece Middlesex County Asylum at Hanwell three years later.[26] This was but one of five new county asylums opened between 1828 and 1833.[27]

Among the various far-reaching social reforms implemented by the Whig government of the 1830s, the Poor Law Amendment Act of 1834 was the most significant in its implications, not only for the relief of poverty, but also for the development of social services for people suffering from the consequences of deprivation and disability. Although pauper lunacy did not figure among its prime concerns, the Act contained an important clause which influenced the pattern of referral for admission to asylums. It required that lunatics and idiots who were deemed dangerous were not to be retained in the workhouse, but should be transferred to a lunatic asylum, whether public or private.[28] Although the aim was partly to seek appropriate treatment and management for mentally disordered people, a more significant motive was to divert from the workhouse those liable to be disruptive and disorderly. The effects of the clause varied in practice, as assessments of dangerousness were not consistent. However, it did promote a noticeable upward pressure on demand for places in most of the existing public asylums.

The issue of dangerous and other problematic behaviours, and how best to manage them within the asylum, was brought into sharp focus in the 1830s. The still dominant custodial and repressive system came under increasing attack from the liberal proponents of 'non-restraint'. The first declaration of 'total abolition' of mechanical restraint came at Lincoln in 1838, followed soon after by its highly symbolic abandonment at the Middlesex Asylum.[29] Non-restraint, with its accompanying environmental changes, came to dominate the philosophy of asylum management for much of the rest of the century. The lunacy reformers, led by Lord Ashley, had not at first embraced it completely. Some of their reservations were evident in the landmark *Report of the Metropolitan Commissioners in Lunacy* of 1844.[30] However, a new generation of apparently enlightened superintendents had demonstrated the practicality of running a large asylum as a liberal institution, where principles of 'moral management' might predominate. Although the case had not yet been proved, there was acceptance of the assumption that progressive practices in specialist asylums must lead to an improvement in the rates of 'cures' and recoveries. The evidence marshalled by the Metropolitan Commissioners provided the justification and impetus for major mandatory legislation. The Acts of 1845 marked the end of the period of *ad hoc* and piecemeal development by philanthropically inclined county activists. Now there was to be a great national system of asylums for pauper lunatics, backed by a central inspectorate to cover both public and private institutions.[31]

The essential premise of this book is that the group of lunatic asylums set up in the aftermath of the 1808 Act laid the foundation of the English asylum system. The purpose of the following chapters is to investigate and consider the operation of these pioneer institutions. To a large extent, the information cited has been gathered from primary source material, much of it held locally. As a consequence some of the detailed evidence may appear parochial and even idiosyncratic. However, the early asylums were much more the reflection of local endeavour than their later successor institutions. The local dimension is an important aspect of the overall picture.

There have already been a number of valuable studies of individual early county asylums.[32] Several of the key general works on the history of asylums or of psychiatry have included some consideration of the pre-1845 asylums, as part of the sequence of legislative, institutional or professional development. Their concentration, though, has been more on the later nineteenth century and the development of the vast lunatic warehouses that were passed down to the present generation for demolition.[33] There has hitherto not been a general study dedicated specifically to the public asylums of the first half of the nineteenth century. The intention here is to rectify the omission, and to construct a picture of the English lunatic asylum during a crucial period of transition and formation.

NOTES

1 R. Hunter and I. Macalpine, *Three Hundred Years of Psychiatry; 1535–1860* (Oxford, 1963); R. Hunter and I. Macalpine, *Psychiatry for the Poor. 1851 Colney Hatch Asylum. Friern Hospital 1973: A Medical and Social History* (London, 1974); W.L. Parry-Jones, *The Trade in Lunacy* (London, 1972); H. Freeman and G.E. Berrios (eds), *150 Years of British Psychiatry, 1841–1991* (London, 1991) and vol. II, *The Aftermath* (London, 1996); J.L. Crammer, *Asylum History; Buckinghamshire County Pauper Lunatic Asylum – St John's* (London, 1990); B. Cashman, *A Proper House: Bedford Lunatic Asylum, 1812–1860* (Bedford, 1992). Other psychiatrists have also published extensively on historical aspects, notably Alexander Walk and Trevor Turner.

2 A. Scull, *Museums of Madness: The Social Organisation of Insanity in Nineteenth-Century England* (London, 1979), revised and reprinted as *The Most Solitary of Afflictions: Madness and Society in Britain, 1700–1900* (London, 1993); A. Scull (ed.), *Madhouses, Mad-Doctors and Madmen: The Social History of Psychiatry in the Victorian Era* (London, 1981); R. Porter, *Mind-Forg'd Manacles: A History of Madness in England from the Restoration to the Regency* (Cambridge, 1987); D.J. Mellett, *The Prerogative of Asylumdom: Social, Cultural and Administrative Aspects of the Institutional Treatment of the Insane in Nineteenth Century Britain* (London, 1982); W.F. Bynum, R. Porter and M. Shepherd (eds), *The Anatomy of Madness: Essays in the History of Psychiatry* (3 vols) (London, 1985–8); A. Digby, *Madness, Morality and Medicine: A Study of the York Retreat, 1796–1914* (Cambridge, 1985); C. MacKenzie, *Psychiatry for the Rich: A History of Ticehurst Asylum, 1792–1917* (London, 1992).

3 T.E. Brown, 'The Mental Hospital and its Historians', *Bulletin of the History of Medicine*, vol. LVI (1982), pp. 109–14; A. Scull, 'Psychiatry and Social Control in the Nineteenth and Twentieth Centuries', *History of Psychiatry*, vol. II, no. 6 (June 1991), pp. 149–69; J.L. Crammer, 'English Asylums and English Doctors: Where Scull is Wrong', *History of Psychiatry*, vol. V, no. 17 (March 1994), pp. 103–15; Freeman and Berrios, *150 Years of British Psychiatry*, Introduction, x–xiii; K. Jones, *Asylums and After: A Revised History of the Mental Health Services: From the Early 18th Century to the 1990s* (London, 1993), pp. 39–40.

4 48 Geo. III, Cap. 96; K. Jones, *A History of the Mental Health Services* (London, 1972), p. 59.

5 H. Perkin, *The Origins of Modern English Society* (London, 1969); *The Cambridge Social History of Britain, 1750–1950*, vol. III, F.M.L. Thompson (ed.), *Social Agencies and Institutions* (Cambridge, 1990); J.C.D. Clark, *English Society, 1688–1832* (Cambridge, 1985); D. Fraser, *The Evolution of the British Welfare State* (London, 1984).

6 A. Digby, 'Changes in the Asylum: The Case of York, 1777–1815', *Economic History Review*, 2nd series, vol. XXXVI, no. 2 (May 1983), pp. 218–39; P. Allderidge, 'Hospitals, Madhouses and Asylums: Cycles in the Care of the Insane', in R.M. Murray and T. Turner (eds), *Lectures on the History of Psychiatry* (London, 1990), pp. 28–45.

7 A. Scull, 'The Domestication of Madness', *Medical History*, vol. XXVII, no. 3 (July 1983), pp. 233–48; A. Scull, 'Museums of Madness Revisited', *Social History of Medicine*, vol. VI, no. 1 (April 1993), pp. 3–23; Porter, *Mind-Forg'd Manacles*, pp. 2–12, 276–8.

8 D. Hack Tuke, *Chapters in the History of the Insane in the British Isles* (London, 1882).

9 M.S. Micale and R. Porter, 'Reflections on Psychiatry and its Histories', pp. 6–8, in Micale and Porter (eds), *Discovering the History of Psychiatry* (Oxford, 1994), pp. 3–36; W.F. Bynum, 'Psychiatry in its Historical Context', p. 24, in M. Shepherd and O.L. Zangwill (eds), *Handbook of Psychiatry*,

vol. I, *General Psychopathology* (Cambridge, 1983), pp. 11–38; N. Pevsner, *A History of Building Types* (London, 1976), p. 148 – 'Treatment in the early nineteenth century can hardly be distinguished from torture, even if the intention was often good. . .'.

10 Porter, *Mind-Forg'd Manacles*, chapters 3 and 4.

11 S. Tuke, *Description of the Retreat* (York, 1813), chapter 5; Digby, *Madness, Morality and Medicine*, chapter 3; Digby, 'Moral Treatment at the Retreat, 1796–1846', in Bynum, Porter and Shepherd (eds), *The Anatomy of Madness*, vol. II, pp. 52–72; Porter, *Mind-Forg'd Manacles*, pp. 187–212; M. Fears, *The 'Moral Treatment' of Insanity: A Study in the Social Construction of Human Nature* (University of Edinburgh, PhD, 1978); A. Scull, 'Moral Treatment Reconsidered', *Psychological Medicine*, vol. IX (1979), pp. 421–8.

12 W. Battie, *A Treatise on Madness* (London, 1758), pp. 68–9; J. Monro, *Remarks on Dr Battie's Treatise on Madness* (London, 1758), pp. 36–8; W. Pargeter, *Observations on Maniacal Disorders* (Reading, 1792), p. 49; J. Mason Cox, *Practical Observations on Insanity* (London, 1804), pp. 24–6.

13 J. Haslam, *Considerations on the Moral Management of Insane Persons* (London, 1817); A. Digby, *Madness, Morality and Medicine*, chapter 4; A. Digby, 'The Changing Profile of a Nineteenth-Century Asylum: the York Retreat', *Psychological Medicine*, vol. XIV (1984), pp. 739–48.

14 E.g. *Staffordshire Advertiser*, 26 September 1818 – the Committee responsible for establishing the new county asylum promised to provide 'the most approved system of medical and moral treatment'; W.F. Bynum, 'Rationales for Therapy in British Psychiatry: 1780–1835', *Medical History*, vol. XVIII (1974), pp. 317–34; A. Scull, 'From Madness to Mental Illness: Medical Men as Moral Entrepreneurs', *Archives Européennes de Sociologie*, vol. XVI (1975), pp. 218–51; N. Tomes, 'The Anglo-American Asylum in Historical Perspective', pp. 8–10, in C.J. Smith and J.A. Giggs (eds), *Location and Stigma: Contemporary Perspectives on Mental Health Care* (London, 1988).

15 M. Ignatieff, 'Total Institutions and Working Classes', *History Workshop*, vol. XV (Spring 1983), pp. 167–73.

16 Scull, *Most Solitary of Afflictions*, pp. 335–40.

17 B. Luckin, 'Towards a Social History of Institutionalisation', *Social History*, vol. VIII (January 1983), pp. 87–94.

18 The legislative reference to 'Cure, Comfort and Safe Custody', quoted in the title of this book, appeared in the preamble to the amending Act of 1811 – 51 Geo. III, Cap. 79.

19 J. Andrews, *Bedlam Revisited: A History of Bethlem Hospital c1634–1770* (PhD, University of London, 1991); J. Andrews, '"Hardly A Hospital, But a Charity for Pauper Lunatics" ? Therapeutics at Bethlem in the Seventeenth and Eighteenth Centuries', in J. Barry and C. Jones (eds), *Medicine and Charity Before the Welfare State* (London, 1991).

20 British Parliamentary Papers (BPP) 1807, vol. II, *Report of Select Committee on the State of Criminal and Pauper Lunatics*.

21 48 Geo. III, Cap. 96.

22 A. Digby, *From York Asylum to Bootham Park Hospital* (University of York, Borthwick Papers, 69, 1986), pp. 16–21; K. Jones, *History of the Mental Health Services* (London, 1972), pp. 66–74.
23 BPP 1814–15, vol. IV; BPP 1816, vol. VI.
24 Tuke, *Description of the Retreat;* K. Jones, *Lunacy, Law and Conscience, 1744–1845* (London, 1955), pp. 79–96.
25 Jones, *Mental Health Services*, pp. 86–7; Scull, *Most Solitary of Afflictions*, pp. 122–5.
26 BPP 1826–7, vol. VI, *Report of Select Committee on Pauper Lunatics in the County of Middlesex and on Lunatic Asylums.*
27 The others were for the counties of Cheshire, Suffolk, Dorset and Kent.
28 U. Henriques, *Before the Welfare State; Social Administration in Early Industrial Britain* (London, 1979); P. Bartlett, *The Poor Law of Lunacy: The Administration of Pauper Lunatics in Mid-Nineteenth Century England with Special Emphasis on Leicestershire and Rutland* (PhD, University of London, 1993), chapter 2; Jones, *Lunacy, Law and Conscience*, pp. 161–4; 4 and 5 Will. IV, Cap. 76, Section 45.
29 R.G. Hill, *Total Abolition of Personal Restraint in the Treatment of the Insane: A Lecture on the Management of Lunatic Asylums and the Treatment of the Insane* (London, 1839); J. Conolly, *The Treatment of the Insane Without Mechanical Restraints* (London, 1856).
30 *Report of the Metropolitan Commissioners in Lunacy to the Lord Chancellor* (London, 1844).
31 8 and 9 Vict., Cap. 100, Cap. 126.
32 A.L. Ashworth, *Stanley Royd Hospital, Wakefield: One Hundred and Fifty Years, A History* (London, 1975); J. Todd and L. Ashworth, *'The House': Wakefield Asylum, 1818....* (Bradford, undated, c. 1990); C.T. Andrews, *The Dark Awakening: A History of St Lawrence's Hospital, Bodmin* (Bodmin, 1978); Cashman, *A Proper House: Bedford Lunatic Asylum: 1812–1860;* J. Walton, 'The Treatment of Pauper Lunatics in Victorian England: The Case of Lancaster Asylum, 1816–70', in Scull (ed.), *Madhouses, Mad-doctors and Madmen*, pp. 166–97.
33 Scull, *Most Solitary of Afflictions;* Mellett, *The Prerogative of Asylumdom.*

1

The Rise of the Public Asylum

The foundations of the Victorian lunatic asylum system were laid during the eighteenth century. By 1800, developments in the private sector, the public sector and the voluntary sector had coalesced to create a 'mixed economy of care' for mentally disordered people. The private sector was represented by the growing number of madhouses, and by care at home of the individual lunatic. The public sector, in the guise of the parish authorities, was increasingly significant in several ways: the expansion of provision within the workhouse; the 'boarding out' of lunatics and idiots; the giving of outdoor relief to the insane and their families; and the placement of paupers in private madhouses and in public asylums. The voluntary sector was perhaps the key element in the developing fabric of institutional provision. The new public subscription asylums provided a genuine alternative to both the inadequate care of the workhouse and the profit-orientated care of the madhouse. They were, however, too few in number to make material inroads into the demand for specialist care and confinement. What they offered for the future, though, were practical examples, and also salutary lessons, as to what could be achieved by more direct public intervention. They gave those seeking the development of services a model, a precedent which could be used to demonstrate a practical means to achieve some control over the burgeoning problem of pauper lunacy.[1]

THE PUBLIC ASYLUMS OF THE EIGHTEENTH CENTURY

Historic Bethlem apart, the eighteenth-century public asylums were the direct offshoot of the voluntary subscription hospital, which formed one of the chief legacies of the Hanoverian and Georgian eras to the development of social welfare provision in Britain. From the 1730s onwards, hospitals or infirmaries were established in most of the main cities and county towns. By 1755 thirteen had opened in provincial cities or county towns, and five had opened in London; by the end of the century most major population centres and regional capitals had the benefit of a voluntary hospital. These were essentially a new type of charity, with most of their funds coming from pledged annual subscriptions, in addition to initial donations and bequests. The subscribers became governors of the institution by virtue of the level of their contributions, which gave both management responsibility and the right of nomination of patients. With their fine buildings in prominent positions, they were an important part of the social fabric of any town or city with pretensions to civilization, refinement or progressive ideals.[2]

The voluntary hospital movement, and the charitable action that supported it, developed out of a complex range of motivations. Commercial and industrial development was creating an expansion of the affluent middle classes, at the same time as reinforcing the fortunes of the more established landed classes. Prevailing religious and charitable principles fostered a more manifest philanthropy among those who had wealth to display, and who wished to be seen to use some of it for purposes other than the pursuit of pleasure and luxury. The hospital subscription list offered the opportunity to provide relief to the ailing poor, in a manner that was both conspicuous for the individual donor and ornamental to the town and county. The hospital's benefits could be seen to accord with progressive economic as well as social ideals. Whilst it aided those who could not be held responsible for the misfortune of illness or accident, it also offered the hope of curative treatment, which could return recovered patients to a capacity for productive labour or domestic management. If people were again able to support themselves and their families, they were less likely to be a burden to the poor relief system.[3]

The hospital for the sick poor, as an institution, required relatively little justification to the charitably disposed. However, a hospital or asylum for the victims of mental disorder appeared to be of less immediate necessity. Foucault's conception of a 'great confinement' of the deranged has been largely discounted as regards Britain. Nevertheless, the second half of the eighteenth century did witness a marked growth in the use of institutional solutions for dealing with people whose madness brought them into conflict with the norms and mores of family and community. In an era of conscious progressivism and 'reason', the possibility of taming unreason, even curing it, seemed increasingly attainable. The rise of the private madhouse, or at least the more reputable of them, was a practical expression of that optimism. The madhouse, however, was geared mainly to meet the needs of the wealthier classes, at least until necessity increasingly drove parishes to place insane paupers there in the later decades of the century. Provision for the latter, and for working members of the poorer strata of society, came to be viewed as an appopriate end for philanthropic activity.[4]

The perceived success of the subscription hospital model stimulated the development of other specialist facilities. Lunatics were often excluded from the hospitals. The existing charitable lunatic hospitals – Bethlem, a ward at Guy's in London, and the Bethel at Norwich (established in 1713), could meet no more than a small part of the demand. In a few cities, the leading citizens decided to promote lunatic hospitals or asylums, along comparable lines to the subscription hospitals. The means of raising funds tended to be similar; the subscribers were often the same people; indeed, the asylum was likely to be closely linked to the hospital, perhaps directly funded and managed by its subscribers and governors. Alliance with an established hospital was logical also on practical grounds. There was no doubt in the minds of the projectors that, whatever the limitations of contemporary physic and treatment, the care of the insane came clearly within the realms of medical treatment. Once that treatment was deemed to be appropriately administered in an institution, it followed that this was to be a hospital or an asylum, supervised by a physician, assisted by a surgeon and/or an apothecary. If the medical officers were shared with the infirmary, this not only maintained the unified structure, but also promised economical operation.[5]

Historiography has generally credited St Luke's Hospital in London, opened in 1751, with being the prototype for the group of public asylums which followed it. Five voluntary hospitals had already been established in the capital. The existence of Bethlem Hospital had no doubt delayed any attempt to make specific provision for the insane before 1750. It was concern over Bethlem's shortcomings, notably its inability to receive many of those referred, that led to the projection of an additional, alternative facility. St Luke's emerged from a meeting of interested parties in June 1750. The appeal for funds anticipated success, on the basis of the 'great spirit of charity' demonstrated in setting up 'other hospitals', thus clearly placing the venture in that tradition. Subscriptions did in fact flow in fairly readily, sufficient to enable the leasing of a small building, on the site of a former foundry, in November of the same year. The first patients were admitted in July 1751. By the beginning of 1753 there were 57 patients, rising to 70 in 1761.[6]

Although the successful establishment of St Luke's demonstrated the applicability of the subscription model to a lunatic hospital, it was several years before the precedent was adopted. The first provincial subscription lunatic hospital opened in 1765 in Newcastle, the English city whose distance gave it the least practical access to Bethlem and St Luke's. The Manchester 'Lunatick Hospital' followed in 1766, four years after the opening of the Royal Infirmary, whose trustees were responsible for its construction. It was built as an adjunct to the infirmary, its management and medical oversight being completely integrated with that of the parent institution. The infirmary trustees were governors of the asylum, the medical officers attended on it and the medicines were supplied directly.[7]

Several years elapsed before Yorkshire followed Lancashire. The York Lunatic Asylum was projected in 1772, and eventually opened in 1777. The York County Hospital dated back to 1740, but the asylum subscribers decided to adopt an independent model. The funds raised were sufficient to enable the asylum to be separately constituted, with its own governors. Its adoption of the title of 'lunatic asylum', rather than 'lunatic hospital' like its predecessors, was no doubt intended to emphasize its distinction from the hospital. A similar approach was adopted at Exeter, where the asylum proposed in 1795 opened in 1801. Its subscribers also decided on complete separation from the hospital, and this was enshrined in the asylum constitution. The decision appears to have been taken not so much for administrative considerations, but rather because of a concern that the pauper connotations of the hospital would deter middle-class people from sending their mad relatives to the asylum. Unlike York, and the other cities, the subscribers proceeded with limited funds and, rather than erect a splendid new building, they acquired a 'Gentleman's House' with two acres of land, for £700.[8]

The other subscription asylums were set up on the Manchester model. That at Liverpool was projected in 1789 and opened in 1792, immediately adjoining the infirmary. Its governors had considered the York model and rejected it, partly for financial reasons, in favour of combined management, unified finances and medical oversight from the infirmary. The Leicester Lunatic Asylum, built in 1781 but not opened until 1794, was also jointly governed with the Royal Infirmary, to which it was adjacent. The Hereford Lunatic Asylum, opened in 1799, was intended as 'an extension of the Plan of the Infirmary', whose governors launched the subscription fund in 1787. They became governors of the asylum, and physicians and surgeons were to be shared. The prestigious building, designed by John Nash, was erected within the infirmary grounds. The governors, however, became increasingly uneasy about the responsibility of asylum management, and in 1801 they leased it to one of the surgeons, at a nominal rental, to operate as a private asylum.[9]

The establishment of subscription asylums never became a 'movement' like the serial setting up of the hospitals that spawned them. Whether due to the stigma of lunacy and its consequent low public profile, or to the relative infrequency of its excesses attracting notice, most cities and counties did not take effective action. There were unsuccesful attempts in some county towns to establish asylums. The most notable of these was in Gloucester in the early 1790s, guided by the prison reformer Sir George Onesiphorus Paul. Sir George developed detailed plans for an asylum for the western counties. Having visited the asylums of Liverpool, Manchester and York, he and the Gloucester subscribers adopted the York prototype, with its separation from the hospital. However, his excessive caution at proceeding without substantial funds resulted in the project being shelved, until the Act of 1808 provided the means to bring in additional money. Even then, Gloucester had to wait until 1823 for its asylum.[10]

The motivations of the asylum promoters largely resembled those for the hospitals. The subscription list, published in county newspapers and in annual reports, offered further opportunity for conspicuous philanthropy and beneficence. The lunatic hospital or asylum was portrayed as providing for a particularly unfortunate and deserving group of people. The Manchester trustees spoke of 'unhappy Wretches' and 'miserable Objects'; no objects could be 'more truly deplorable'. The Exeter Asylum was intended 'to relieve the most helpless and pitiable Class of Mortals'. Dr James Currie, the Liverpool physician who piloted the establishment of the city's asylum, argued that men were subject to no evil 'so dreadful as insanity'. Appeals, such as that for St Luke's, stressed the uniqueness of the tragedy: 'The usefulness and necessity of hospitals for poor lunatics is evident, for there is no disease to which human nature is subject so terrible in its appearances or so fatal in its consequences.' For the city and county, an asylum was perhaps an even more potent representation of progressive ideals than an infirmary, for it relieved the most stigmatized of people.[11]

Part of the appeal for subscribers was the priority given to the admission of sufferers in circumstances construed as the most deserving – people of the 'middling rank' and non-pauper members of the poorer classes, without the means to purchase care. The St Luke's rules had stipulated only that proper objects of the charity should be 'poor and mad'. Some of its successors, though, were more specific. The Manchester Lunatic Hospital offered assistance to 'many Persons of middling

Fortunes' who had relations who were 'terribly afflicted'. Paupers were not, however, excluded from the charity asylums. The Leicester Asylum was established for the 'reception of pauper lunatics & others of the insane poor' whose relatives could not pay for private care. The provision of a cheaper alternative to the madhouse for people with limited means was seen as a proper object of charity. The Manchester trustees clearly expressed their purpose to preserve families 'from the impositions of those who keep private Mad-Houses', whilst their York counterparts sought to 'lessen the number of private mad-houses'. The madhouse proprietor was typified as more interested in the regular income from prolonged, neglectful incarceration than in promoting the cure of his patients. This was contrasted with the public asylum, depicted as offering humane and curative treatment. Moreover, the public asylum might not only relieve hard-pressed relatives, but also hold out the hope of recovery and of a return to productive labour or domestic responsibility.[12]

One essential difference between the management of lunatic asylums and that of the infirmaries was that residence in an asylum had to be paid for. The governors endeavoured to keep the charges low, in order to facilitate admission of the impecunious non-pauper. However, this posed problems of financial viability, and most public asylums began to accept higher paying private patients, using the profits to subsidize the poorer patients. Thus, at Manchester in the 1770s, the charges ranged from four shillings to one guinea per week, whilst at York in 1788 the patients were divided into eight classes, according to payments which ranged from six shillings to over one pound per week. Accommodation standards would vary in accordance both with the level of payments and with the social rank of the patient. The governors at Manchester, during the early 1780s, refined their arrangements by dividing the institution into two parts – the Lunatic Hospital, for the poorer classes, and the Asylum, for those who could pay more. The apartments for those of 'superior fortunes' offered: 'the greatest privacy, the best advice, the most tender treatment, and every comfort that can be afforded them in their unhappy situation'. The hospital was openly competing with the private madhouse sector, in trying to attract a wealthier clientele. The distinctions of rank, and the attempts to attract a better class of patient, characterized the operation of several of the early public asylums, and of some of their successors.[13]

There were motivations other than the charitable desire to relieve the afflicted. Lunatics and idiots were frequently the subject of fear, disgust and disgrace. A secure asylum offered the advantage of protecting the general public, and those who were more directly affected, from discomfort, disruption and worse. As the St Luke's appeal pointed out:

> those who are melancholy often do violence to themselves, and those who are raving, to others, and too often to their nearest relatives and friends, the only persons who can be expected to take the trouble of these unhappy objects upon them.

The York Asylum was intended to relieve those sufferers who were 'the objects of terror and compassion to all around them'. The threat of violence to others was not to be underplayed. In order to meet the exigency, the Manchester Lunatic Hospital offered 'a proper Place for their Reception, and a suitable Guard and Attendance upon their persons'. The frequently expressed curative ideal was clearly tempered by a strong element of practical control.[14]

The proclaimed intention of asylum managers to offer humane and curative treatment in an environment of secure control contained inherent conflicts. Asylums' management regimes were permeated by what might be styled the custody versus cure dynamic. The ongoing tension was both expressed and reinforced by the rules framed for each asylum. A key phrase contained in the original rules of the Manchester Lunatic Hospital, which was adopted and adapted by most of the others, encapsulated the dilemma. Patients were to be treated 'with all tenderness and indulgence compatible with the steady and effectual government of them'. The identical phrase was used at Hereford, whilst at Exeter it was amended to talk of the 'steady and effectual Government of the House'. The laying of boundaries to the legitimate use of force exercised asylum governors. Most rules contained the expectation that no 'unnecessary severity' should be employed. It is clear, however, that the use of physical power was anticipated and actively condoned. The Leicester rules referred to the 'necessary coercion' of some patients. The Manchester rules, as amended in 1777, spoke of a written order being required from the physician for the infliction of 'Stripes or Beatings', or of any coercion that was 'more than is necessary to restrain the Furious from hurting themselves or others'. The use of restraint by staff was further legitimated in the general requirement to examine regularly the extremities of chained patients, and to rub their feet each night and morning and cover them with flannel, in order to prevent mortification due to cold. Coercion, restraint and sometimes violent punishment were still essential elements in asylum management, not seriously questioned until the later exposures of abuses of power at the York Asylum and Bethlem.[15]

In framing their rules and regulations, asylum governors were influenced by those of other asylums, which accounts for their marked similarity. The asylums' overall management arrangements resembled one another, and were in turn influenced by those of the subscription hospitals. Governors were normally appointed on the basis of a specified level of subscription. Medical attendance was normally linked to the infirmary, and provided by its physicians and surgeons. A lay 'keeper' and matron would be employed to look after the patients and manage the house on a daily basis. In asylums without the infirmary link, routine management would be vested in a house apothecary. The authority of the physician was paramount, as made clear in the Exeter rules:

> That the Medical department of this Institution be under an attendant Physician and Surgeon, assisted by an Apothecary residing in the House, which Physician alone shall direct the Treatment and Management of the Patients, and possess a controul over the Officers and servants of the House, as far as regards their conduct towards them.

The extent of the physician's role in determining policy depended on how far he chose to involve himself in asylum affairs. William Battie at St Luke's had been the driving force behind the hospital, and achieved considerable recognition and wealth. Alexander Hunter at York adopted a particularly prominent role, and John Ferriar at Manchester, James Currie at Liverpool and Thomas Arnold at Leicester were all very active.[16]

The positions of the physicians were, in most cases, nominally honorary, but there was usually financial reward in the form of payments for the reception of private patients into the asylum, and for their ongoing care. In at least one case, however, that of Hunter at York, a substantial salary was paid. Several asylum physicians, including Battie, Hunter and Arnold, made use of their acquired status to open lucrative private madhouses, which inevitably reduced the level of their attention to asylum business. The particularly commercial orientation of the arrangements at York has been identified as a key factor in the propagation of the abuses in the asylum.[17]

Some of the problems associated with a later period were becoming apparent before 1800. The early public asylums were erected on a relatively small scale, compared to Bethlem Hospital. St Luke's initial capacity had been for about 70 patients. Manchester Lunatic Hospital was intended for 24 people; York Asylum began with twelve patients in 1777, and contained 28 by 1780. Others were even smaller; Leicester provided for ten and Exeter for fourteen. In most, however, and particularly in the larger cities, the original buildings soon proved inadequate and had to be adapted and extended, as numbers of chronic or 'incurable' patients accumulated. By 1787 Manchester had capacity for 80 people, rising to 100 by 1800. York's expansion was yet greater, its numbers growing to 66 in 1793, 137 in 1803 and 186 in 1808. Even at the later established Exeter, the numbers had grown from fourteen to 50 by 1812, with plans for further extensions. The problems in cities like Manchester were compounded by the asylum's location in a central, densely occupied area. The conception of the importance of a more spacious or rural location did not come until later.[18]

By 1800, ample evidence was available both of the possibilities offered by public asylums, and of the risks and problems associated with them. The small group of lunacy reformers, preoccupied with the shortcomings of private care and with the widespread neglect and mistreatment of many pauper lunatics, were seeking solutions. They were inclined to overlook some of the difficulties which had become apparent, particularly those associated with the need to reconcile the objective of therapeutic treatment, leading to cure, with the growing phenomenon of chronicity and incurability in the asylum. The development of ever larger institutions meant a lessening of personal attention, and the need for greater sophistication in methods of collective patient management. These posed a serious challenge to the already dubious effectiveness of asylum care. Nevertheless, the eighteenth-century public asylums offered a model which informed the legislators of 1808, much of which was replicated in the asylums built following the Act.

THE ACT OF 1808

One individual must be credited with providing much of the impetus toward the expansion of the public asylum system – Sir George Onesiphorus Paul. Sir George, born in 1746, was a prominent Gloucestershire magistrate and philanthropist of Whig-Radical inclinations. He became, after John Howard, the most influential prison reformer of the era, strongly influenced by Benthamite principles. Under his guidance, Gloucestershire surpassed all other counties in the development, by 1792, of modern custodial facilities, with five new houses of correction spread around the county and a new jail in the city of Gloucester. Gloucester Prison became the example to be emulated by others around the country. The system of management Paul promoted was designed to combine elements of deterrence, even terror, with humanity. His interest in the insane developed from a preoccupation with prison discipline. Mentally disordered inmates, often confined in prison or house of correction through lack of a suitable alternative, were unable to conform to discipline and order; their erratic behaviour threatened at times to disrupt the regime.[19]

In the aftermath of the completion of the prisons, and whilst still closely involved in their management, Paul embarked on a series of attempts to promote the development of a public susbcription asylum for the county and the surrounding region. After visiting the northern asylums and studying their operation and management, he drafted a set of detailed plans and rules for an independent asylum based on the York model. Many of his ideas were later adopted at other establishments. The collection of contributions began following a public meeting in Gloucester in September 1793. Nevertheless, despite the rapid increase of funds to a level that other counties might have envied (£4000 within a few months), the project did not proceed. Sir George considered the sum insufficient, and that more had to be raised before building could start. His stubborn insistence, and his dominance over the subscribers, served to block effective action for the foreseeable future.[20]

Interest in the Gloucester Asylum project revived after the turn of the century, though still with little concrete result. Paul remained preoccupied with the penal system, where there were continuing difficulties in trying to contain mentally disordered offenders in need of some specialist care. The issue had reached the public eye with the attempted assassination of the King by James Hadfield, and his subsequent acquittal on grounds of insanity. Legislation was passed in July 1800 to require that people acquitted of serious offences on such grounds should be held in safe custody at his Majesty's pleasure. With no alternative secure accommodation available, prison was the only recourse. In early 1805, with Gloucester Jail having put up for several years with two men detained under the Act, Paul protested to Lord Hawkesbury at the Home Office, complaining of the 'gross and dangerous impropriety' of confining 'outrageous lunatics' with ordinary prisoners. He received a sympathetic reply which was not, however, followed by any action. With a change of government a few months later, Sir George repeated his complaints to Lord Spencer, Secretary of State in the more reformist Ministry of 'All the Talents'. Spencer sought the benefit of Paul's acknowledged expertise on the subject, and Sir George responded with a lengthy and detailed letter in October 1806. This dealt with the state of both criminal and pauper lunatics, and was accompanied by specific proposals for reform.[21]

Much of Paul's submission considered the needs of criminal lunatics, before he went on to advocate the cause of 'the most degraded, the most ill used class of objects' that came to the attention of magistrates. His eloquent and evocative phraseology, later published in the Select Committee report, helped to galvanize influential opinion. He argued that the 'lunatic affection' was steadily increasing in the country, with serious consequences:

> I believe there is hardly a parish of any considerable extent, in which there may not be found some unfortunate human creature of this description, who, if his ill treatment has made him phrenetic, is chained in the cellar or garret of a workhouse, fastened to the leg of a table, tied to a post in an outhouse, or perhaps shut up in an uninhabited ruin; or, if his lunacy be inoffensive, left to ramble half naked and half starved through the streets and highways, teased by the scoff and jest of all that is vulgar, ignorant and unfeeling.

It was clear, though, that Sir George was not only concerned with the predicament of actual pauper lunatics, but perhaps even more with the non-pauper poor who could not afford the costs of private care. Though he commended the existing public asylums, particularly that at York, he considered their financial base to be generally not sufficiently strong to enable them to admit many poor people at rates they or their families could afford. His proposals centred round the development of institutions financed by subscription to provide this facility, supplemented by rate-supported provision for parish paupers. In effect, he was arguing for an extension of the public subscription asylum system, with state-sponsored subsidy to enable all sections of the poor to be catered for.[22]

Paul's analysis and proposals for reform were taken up by Charles Williams-Wynn, the Under-Secretary of State at the Home Office (and a nephew of Grenville, the Prime Minister). Through his efforts a Select Committee was established during 1807, composed of several reformers of either Benthamite or Evangelical leanings (including William Wilberforce, Samuel Romilly, George Rose and Samuel Whitbread). The Ministry, despite its Foxite reformist credentials, had in fact accomplished little of significance other than the abolition of the slave trade. The establishment of the Select Committee was one of what Harvey has called the 'overdue minor innovations' it brought about. Its comparative lack of perceived significance at the time is attested by its absence from the autobiographies or nineteenth-century biographies of any of the principal participants.[23]

The Select Committee called various witnesses, including the architect John Nash and Paul. It was Sir George's written submission, however, that formed the principal part of the published evidence, and was particularly influential in the formulation of the conclusions and proposals. These cited the benefits achieved by the subscription asylums and endorsed the idea of integrating them into the new arrangements. It was recommended that county magistrates should have the power to levy a rate to build an asylum, either on their own, or in combination with another county or counties. Where there was a subscription asylum in existence, 'great benefit' might result from combining with it. Where a new construction was envisaged, it would be desirable that it should include provision for 'persons of a superior class', paying their own expenses, as well as for those who were in a 'state of distress' but not paupers, and who might be supported by charitable subscription. The purpose would be not only to ensure the proper care and management of the inmates, but also to aim for 'their perfect cure'. The essential divergence, however, from Paul's propositions was that he had argued that it should be compulsory for county rates to be used to provide for the needs of pauper lunatics. The Committee was not prepared to advocate more than a permissive provision, arguing that public opinion was so favourable to the idea that compulsion was not necessary at that point. This apparent optimism facilitated a concession to political realism.[24]

Despite a change of administration, legislation followed a few months after the Select Committee. Historians, from different perspectives, like Kathleen Jones and Andrew Scull, have occupied many pages in trying to locate the work of the lunacy reformers in its philosophical, cultural and political contexts. The movement has been seen as having emerged from a coming together of the concerns of Benthamite Radicals and Evangelical Tories. Both groups adopted the imagery which characterized the eighteenth century as a period when the mad were treated as if akin to brutes, and madhouses were sinks of abuse and exploitation. The reformers sought to cleanse the worst excesses, whilst bringing about a system that was at the same time humane, conducive to the preservation of order and protective of the sensitivities of the wider public. More recently, Peter Bartlett has argued persuasively that the Act of 1808 came in the context of the developing Poor Law, and that its attempt to deal with pauper lunatics formed a clear element in that development. Although all these perspectives undoubtedly served to influence the activists, it is hard to escape the conclusion that the debate and the legislation carried little such meaning for the Government and most of Parliament. The lack of political interest in it, at the time and subsequently, seems to suggest that its enactment was almost accidental.[25]

'An Act for the Better Care and Maintenance of Lunatics, being Paupers or Criminals in England', better known as 'Wynn's Act' (after Charles Wynn, who piloted it through Parliament), received the Royal Assent on 23 June 1808, after a comparatively easy passage through Parliament.[26] The Act was remarkable in a number of ways, not least because it signified, whether by design or by accident, an unusually direct intervention by the state in health and welfare provision. Although informed by a concern for the insane poor, the legislation was not solely altruistic, for it embraced considerations of economy and of local public order as well as those related to social amelioration. The provision spread beyond pauper lunatics, for the legislation took account of Paul's concerns with the needs of the non-pauper by making the option of care in a public asylum, as opposed to a private madhouse, more accessible. There was no intent to supersede the charitably-funded public asylums of the later eighteenth century. On the contrary, the model on which they had developed was integrated into the new arrangements.

The Act itself was quite wide-ranging and comprehensive, demonstrating that its framers had studied the issues carefully. It dealt with the processes by which an asylum project might be set on foot, the initial and ongoing management arrangements, the financial mechanisms, the building work, arrangements for admissions and discharges of patients, the legal powers of justices of the peace and the requirements on overseers of the poor. The most significant part was perhaps the brief clause that outlined standards for the siting of the asylum and the accommodation to be provided. The buildings, whether newly erected or adapted, were to be in 'an airy and healthy situation', with a good water supply. Whilst this inferred that the asylum should be away from the town centre, the requirement that there should be the 'Probability of the Vicinity of constant Medical Assistance' had the opposite implication. Thus it was that siting on the edge of the county town was to become the norm for the early group of county asylums. The expectation was that the building would provide not only for separation of the sexes, but also for separate wards for 'Convalescents and Incurables'. There were to be distinct day rooms and airing grounds for convalescents. Individual lunatics 'of every description' were to be accommodated in 'dry and airy Cells'. The Act thus attempted to balance the custodial with the therapeutic elements, and to reinforce the developing orthodoxy of classification and separation according to the nature of the patient's condition.[27]

The key limitation of the Act was its essentially permissive nature. County justices were empowered to provide a county asylum, and to levy a rate for the purpose. The complacent, though pragmatic, view of the Select Committee that this was all that was required had been accepted. The voluntarism was qualified, however. Parish overseers, in counties where an asylum was provided, were required to ensure that any 'Lunatic, insane Person, or dangerous Idiot' of whose existence they were informed, and who was chargeable to the Parish, had to be conveyed to the asylum 'until he or she shall be duly discharged'. The Parish was to be responsible for paying their maintenance in the asylum. Failure to comply with the requirements entailed the risk of a fine on the overseer. The significance of the clause was not only in the element of compulsion, but perhaps even more in the blanket requirement to consign mentally disordered paupers to the asylum, without apparent consideration as to the likelihood of either curability or chronicity. There was a strong inference here that removal of inconvenience and discomfort from the community was at least as important an objective as the promotion of relief for the individual sufferer.[28]

In acknowledgement that county justices might be hesitant about taking such a major step, the Act promoted options which were designed to render it easier. It firstly gave the justices authority to unite with those of neighbouring counties to provide an asylum, thus sharing the expense. This was based on a proposition of Paul's to the Select Committee that an asylum for each region should be sufficient, and that counties might be grouped accordingly (as in his own earlier plan for an asylum for the western counties at Gloucester). Detailed arrangements were laid out as to the manner in which negotiations were to take place, and a form of agreement was provided, which suggests an expectation that the provision might be quite widely adopted. In the event, the take-up was rather limited, although the Nottinghamshire justices, among the first to mobilize under the Act, did make use of the facility in a limited way.[29]

More significant than providing the machinery for counties to act together were the provisions to enable county justices to unite with the subscribers of existing or projected voluntary asylums. The legislation followed Paul in explicitly acknowledging the advantages of the existing subscription asylums, which provided for 'Lunatics of all Descriptions', and were able to utilize the higher payments of the better-off to subsidize the poorer patients. It was 'fit and expedient to support and encourage such laudable institutions', and might be 'of great advantage' if asylums to be erected under the Act were connected with a voluntary susbcription asylum. Detailed guidance was given on how justices might enter into agreement with committees of subscribers, so underlining that this was the favoured method of proceeding to build an asylum. An arrangement like this could bring benefits to all parties. It offered the advantages of bringing in funds from the voluntary sector, so lessening the likely burden on county rate-payers, whilst at the same time offering a means of subsidizing the favoured subscription-based schemes which could not come to fruition due to insufficient funds.[30]

In essence the Act of 1808 did not mark a completely radical departure. It ensured the integration, maintenance and further stimulation of existing institutional practice, and gave it greater public legitimacy. The extension of the system of eighteenth-century-style public asylums was fostered, with added scope for experimentation with pauper-only facilities. The outcome of the Act, in terms of new buildings, was not insignificant. Eight asylums had been opened by 1825 (Nottinghamshire and Bedfordshire, 1812; Norfolk, 1814; Lancashire, 1816; Staffordshire and West Riding of Yorkshire, 1818; Cornwall, 1820; Gloucestershire, 1823). The importance, however, of this new generation of asylums, with the others that followed in the late 1820s and 1830s (Cheshire and Suffolk, 1829; Middlesex, 1831; Dorset, 1832; Kent, 1833; and Leicestershire, 1837), goes beyond their numbers. They represented a solid testimony to the acceptance of state responsibility for management of the mentally disordered poor, perhaps second only to that which had been accepted for the criminal poor. The precedent having been made, there could be no reversal. The new institutions were also to provide, with all their serious limitations, a testing ground for new ideas of institutional management and the practical reconciliation of ideals of cure and of custody.[31]

A MONUMENT TO MUNIFICENCE – THE FOUNDATION OF AN ASYLUM

The optimism of the Select Committee and the framers of the Act as to its likely general adoption was not borne out. The response was patchy among the county magistracy who were called upon to implement it. Resistance or inaction were hardly surprising on a number of grounds. Primarily, the projection and construction of a lunatic asylum was a costly business, particularly in a time of war and disrupted trade. Many counties, such as Gloucestershire and Oxfordshire, were already burdened with expenditure on other public projects, such as gaols, bridges and civic halls.[32] A further burden on the county rates to pay the cost of a mortgage loan, as well as other ongoing costs, was not to be taken on lightly. Added to this, there were often serious qualms about the whole principle of a publicly-financed provision. Although the idea had now received legislative sanction, there were still some scarcely acceptable implications of centralization and state intervention to be overcome.

On the other hand, however, the Act had much to offer the county magistracy. It gave them the opportunity to take on additional powers and to enhance their authority at a time when this was coming under some threat from the prospect of political upheaval.[33] The tangible powers, of commissioning and erecting a prominent building, of levying a rate, of requiring returns from overseers, and of compelling parishes to send people to the asylum, were themselves quite significant. To these were added the more intangible extension and consolidation of the web of paternalistic control, whereby the county gentry and clergy conspicuously ministered to the poor and unfortunate. Where county justices acted together with voluntary subscribers these considerations were further enhanced, for it tended to be the same figures who dominated both groups.

In the months following the passage of the 1808 Act, there were deliberations in a number of county Quarter Sessions as to whether to proceed. In some the matter was deferred, or no further action was taken. Where there was a decision to go forward, this was usually driven by the efforts of influential individuals, as in the first two counties to proceed – Bedfordshire and Nottinghamshire. Much of the impetus in Bedfordshire came from its radical Whig MP Samuel Whitbread, one of the members of the Select Committee. His influence in the county was considerable; he had been largely responsible for the development of the key civic buildings in Bedford – the infirmary, the county gaol and the house of industry. A lunatic asylum was the next logical segment in the local fabric of control tempered with benevolence. Under his guidance, an early decision was taken in January 1809 and a committee of visiting justices formed which included himself and the Duke of Bedford. Within a few months, plans were drawn up and a site acquired from the Duke. Whitbread organized the purchase of all the necessary equipment and the appointment of a governor and matron. The Bedford Asylum opened to receive its first patients in May 1812.[34]

In Nottinghamshire, plans for a subscription asylum were well advanced before the passage of the Act. Money had been accumulating since 1789, and the funds had reached over £5000 by October 1803, when the subscribers started taking tentative steps to proceed. Agreement had actually been reached in July 1808 on the purchase of land in Nottingham. However, the new legislation radically altered the situation, with the opportunity presented for a financial injection from the county. Matters moved fairly rapidly, under the influence of Dr John Storer, a prominent Nottingham physician who had a close involvement with the infirmary, and Reverend J.T. Becher of Southwell, a leading prison reformer who was already identified with various philanthropic projects in the county. Agreement was reached on a tripartite union of the county of Nottinghamshire, the county of the city of Nottingham and the existing subscribers. Storer, previously chairman of the subscribers, became chairman of the joint committee. He provided the intellectual and philosophical lead, eloquently speaking and writing in support of the scheme. Becher took on the more administrative aspects, drawing up the Articles of Union between magistrates and subscribers, as well as extremely detailed rules and regulations for the management and practice of the institution. The asylum opened in February 1812, the first under the Act, to the considerable pride of Storer (now elevated to Vice-President), who expressed the hope that it would serve as an example to other counties.[35]

The individual efforts of the energetic and single-minded Yorkshire magistrate Godfrey Higgins were particularly influential in the projection and realization of the West Riding Pauper Lunatic Asylum, which opened at Wakefield in 1818. The county had not immediately taken up the opportunities offered by the 1808 Act. Higgins, however, became deeply embroiled in the exposure of the abuses of the York Lunatic Asylum from 1813 onwards, after being confronted with evidence of ill-treatment of a pauper lunatic whom he had committed. He worked closely with Samuel Tuke, the grandson of the founder of the York Retreat and author of the influential *Description of the Retreat*. They campaigned with letters to prominent people and to the press, with pamphlets and by direct attacks in governors' meetings. Higgins and Tuke succeeded in gaining first an investigation, and then a full consideration by the Select Committee on Madhouses in 1815. In the wake of the exposures, Higgins was able to mobilize his fellow magistrates to undertake a large-scale venture, despite an expense totalling more than £23,000. The influence of Tuke's ideas had been considerable, and he was commissioned to prepare detailed guidance on the design and plan of the asylum, with a view to its being established on progressive principles. This was published as part of Tuke's *Practical Hints on the Construction and Economy of Pauper Lunatic Asylums*. Higgins himself prepared and published the rules and regulations for the new asylum. He also was instrumental in the recruitment of William Ellis to be the first director of the asylum, having satisfied himself that Ellis was sufficiently imbued with a Tukean philosophy. Higgins continued to exert a dominant influence over asylum affairs for more than a decade.[36]

The Lancashire Asylum, also intended to cater almost exclusively for paupers, had opened in 1816 in Lancaster. The county magistrates, headed by Lord Stanley, had agreed to proceed as early as July 1809. A site was purchased near Liverpool, at Bootle, but abandoned due largely to objections raised by an influential group of Lancashire physicians. Various other locations were considered before a gratuitous offer in 1811 by the Corporation of Lancaster of a parcel of land was accepted. As in Yorkshire, there were already public asylums in existence (at Manchester and Liverpool), but these were unable to meet the growing demand for the admission of pauper lunatics. The circumstances were similar in the county of Norfolk, where the Norwich Bethel had been in operation since the 1720s. A proposal for a county asylum had been agreed by 1811; it opened in May 1814, in the village of Thorpe St Andrew, three miles outside Norwich.[37]

As Andrew Scull has observed, the early county asylums were not particularly a phenomenon of counties at the forefront of industrialization and urbanization. This is illustrated by the early commitment not only of Bedfordshire and Norfolk, but also shortly afterwards of Cornwall. Its magistrates were fairly quick to react to the 1808 Act. Action was initiated at a prestigious public meeting headed by the High Sheriff in August 1810. A subscription fund, headed by a large donation of £500 from the Prince Regent, who became the asylum's patron, accumulated fairly rapidly. However, it took until October 1815 for the mechanics of union between county and subscribers to be finally agreed. Further delays ensued in locating a suitable site, in raising loans, in disputes with the person appointed as governor and as a result of the frequent failure of sufficient visiting justices to attend meetings. The asylum eventually received its first patients in August 1820, ten years after the initial proposal.[38]

The Staffordshire General Lunatic Asylum, the fifth to open, was also the victim of delays. The magistrates had decided in 1810 to proceed under the 1808 Act. A small fund was already in existence, following a bequest of £1000 to the General Infirmary in 1803 for an asylum ward. This was augmented by a further £1000 in 1810, and the infirmary trustees then agreed to make the money available for a joint asylum. Agreement between trustees and magistrates proved difficult to achieve, owing to the trustees' desire to retain a high degree of independence. However, their funds were too limited to allow them to act alone and the obstacles to union were overcome in March 1812. Further delays then followed owing to local opposition and the unwillingness of the infirmary governors to have the asylum built adjacent to it. An alternative site beside the county gaol was acquired in 1815, and the asylum finally opened for patients in October 1818.[39]

In Gloucestershire the tortuous route to providing what Paul had meticulously planned in the 1790s eventually ended in 1823. As early as 1802, the subscribers decided to proceed to build a small-scale asylum, with the £5000 they had available, only to be persuaded against the idea by Sir George. Further moves in 1806 again proved abortive. The Act which Sir George had promoted, with the county's circumstances in mind, gave the required stimulus. The magistrates agreed in October 1810 to progress, and began to take steps accordingly. Sir George himself had meanwhile not been inactive; he embarked on a tour of northern and Scottish asylums, and returned particularly impressed with the Newcastle and York subscription asylums (apparently oblivious of the shortcomings of the latter, which were soon to be exposed). His support for the idea of a joint asylum was now at best equivocal. However, the subscribers, whose funds in 1811 stood at over £8000, were not prepared to delay further. William Stark, the architect of the Glasgow Asylum, on Sir George's recommendation, was engaged to design the building. The precedent of joint action in Nottingham gave practical inspiration, and after several months of detailed negotiations a three-way union between the subscribers and the counties of Gloucestershire and the city of Gloucester was finalized at the end of 1812, and ratified by a narrow majority at the Quarter Sessions in January 1813.[40]

Paul remained far from satisfied, having various reservations and objections to the arrangements. He asserted that the burden of expenditure was not equitably divided, with the county bearing more than its fair share. His arguments were, however, set aside and he, evidently piqued, declined any further involvement with the project. A series of further obstacles led to more delay. William Stark died in November 1813, with the implementation of his plans just begun. Part of the building had been completed by July 1816, when work had to be suspended due to the money having run out. In February 1817, the surveyor responsible for the project died. Little then happened for four years, until eventually work was resumed by early 1822, based on scaled-down estimates. The saga ended in July 1823 when the Gloucester Asylum finally opened, though still with part of the building left to be finished when the funds allowed.[41]

In at least two counties, groups of subscribers opted to go it alone. This occurred in Paul's neighbouring county, Oxfordshire, partly under his influence. The magistrates had considered adopting the 1808 Act, but concluded that the county could not afford the expenditure, with all the other public works currently under way. The impetus came in 1812 from the governors of the Radcliffe Infirmary, who determined on providing a subscription asylum to cater primarily for impoverished non-paupers. Overtures were made to the county to establish a joint asylum, without success. As a result, a conscious decision was taken to exclude those for whom the Act had made provision, i.e. parish paupers. The asylum, known initially as the Radcliffe Lunatic Asylum (later the Warneford Asylum), opened on the outskirts of the town in 1826. With its selective admission policy and prestigious connections, it was able to establish itself as something of a model institution.[42]

No such selectivity characterized the Lincoln Lunatic Asylum. Indeed, its predominantly pauper clientele may have led some writers, notably Kathleen Jones and Andrew Scull, mistakenly to classify it as a county asylum. A subscription fund had been established early in the century, closely linked to the County Hospital; by July 1807 it had reached over £3000. An energetic fund-raising campaign had increased this to nearly £7000 by April 1809, and a site was purchased. Richard Ingleman, the architect of the Nottingham Asylum, was engaged. The subscribers, however, feared that their funds were not sufficient and little happened for a few years. Following the much-praised example of neighbouring Nottinghamshire, the county magistrates in August 1813 proposed a union to build a joint asylum. The negotiations proved fruitless, owing to an inability to agree on the financial arrangements or the admissions policy. Evidently, neither magistrates nor subscribers were prepared to sacrifice sufficient independence of action to work together – a trait that became endemic in public life, and particularly in medical circles, in the city. The subscribers, after much prevarication, resolved in 1817 to proceed alone and, with support from the cathedral-dominated clerical establishment, the local gentry and the physicians, the Lincoln Lunatic Asylum was finally ready to admit patients in April 1820.[43]

In determining location of their asylums the committees of visiting justices, or of justices and subscribers, were influenced partly by established practice, but also by the guidance of the 1808 Act to situate them in an 'airy and healthy situation', near to available medical attendance. This usually steered them toward the outskirts of a large town or city, to a position slightly less central than the earlier public asylums. In virtually every case, as in Nottingham, Bedford, Lancaster, Stafford, Wakefield and Gloucester, these considerations, combined with those of administrative convenience, the requirements of subscribers and civic prestige, drew the asylum to the county town, Norfolk being the only exception. Depending on the size of the town, the sites tended to be about a mile from the centre, with an outlook onto open fields; inevitably, within a few years, most of them were to become urban asylums.[44]

Generally, the sites were purchased from local landowners, themselves sometimes members of the committee of visiting justices. In Lancashire, five acres of waste land on Lancaster Moor was donated by the Corporation as an inducement, after the committee had unsuccessfully tried to acquire a site in a more central part of Lancashire. A piece of waste ground, totalling nine acres, was similarly provided by the burgesses of Bodmin for the Cornwall Asylum. Like the Stafford Asylum, this was next to the county gaol, though the grounds of Bodmin Asylum incorporated the additional attraction of the gibbet used for public executions. In several instances, particularly among the earliest to be built (Bedford, Nottingham, Lancaster and Lincoln), the urban location meant that they only had relatively small acreages of land attached, which later proved problematic both as regards expansion of the building and the provision of recreation and employment opportunities for the patients. The more far-sighted committees of the Stafford, Wakefield and Gloucester Asylums acquired sites with ample amounts of land.[45]

The design and architecture of the new generation of asylums mirrored the developing stylistic influences of Georgian public buildings. The architects commissioned were, in most cases, local men who had gained experience from a range of public projects, like John Foulston in Cornwall, John Wing in Bedfordshire and W. Cole Junior in Cheshire. Alternatively, they were men with an established reputation in institutional architecture, like Richard Ingleman who had designed prisons and houses of correction, or William Stark who had produced the impressive Glasgow Asylum and had published a book on asylum construction. Designs reflected the twin strands of custody and of cure, combining elements of both the penitentiary and the infirmary. Externally, asylum architecture superficially bore more resemblance to a hospital. The desire for the reality and the impression of security, however, was evident in features like solid brick outer walls, ten to fifteen feet in height, and small high windows. Behind the imposing facade, the emphasis in internal design was clearly more toward the penal institution.[46]

In projecting their buildings, visiting committees turned to the managers or medical officers of existing institutions for guidance. The

Nottingham subscribers took early advice, in 1803, from Dr Alexander Hunter, the physician to the York Asylum, and from its architect. Dr John Storer, in launching his proposals to the Infirmary Governors in 1808, had consulted those running the asylums at York, Manchester, Liverpool and Exeter. In 1809, advice was sought from the unlikely source of Edward Long Fox, the proprietor of Brislington House, a private asylum near Bristol. Fox, despite his clear antagonism to the 1808 Act, offered detailed suggestions on aspects of the building and its internal arrangements. These included the accommodation of the 'filthy and noisy' in cells separate from the main building. He was well aware of the need to reconcile custody and cure in the new asylums:

> Another object of attention is not to construct the asylum, by deviating materially from mens ordinary habitations so as to impress with painful & gloomy ideas, but to consult their comfortable feelings as much as safety will allow. The Bed Steads Tables & Chairs ought to be secured to the Floor, or the Wall, to prevent their employment as means of scaling the Walls or offensive Weapons, the fires ought to have guards before them light but strong and the Fire Utensils should be chained to the grates.

After receiving Fox's advice, Nottingham Asylum's surveyor was despatched to see Brislington at first hand, which resulted in some alterations to Richard Ingleman's plans.[47]

Samuel Whitbread, the driving force behind the Bedford Asylum, had been impressed with the evidence given by Thomas Dunston of St Luke's to the Select Committee of 1807. Consequently, much of the early design, planning and equipment of the asylum was based on that of St Luke's. The first governor, a man with little previous experience, was appointed on Dunston's recommendation. The visiting committee of the Stafford Asylum took wider advice, seeking information and literature from all the existing public asylums; responses were received from Manchester, Liverpool, Leicester and Exeter. From the last came suggestions on fund-raising, staffing and social class separation, as well as advice to have no less than two acres of land, to provide for airing grounds and to include a garden for patients to work in. In selecting their first superintendent, the Stafford magistrates turned to the traditional recruiting ground of Bethlem for the young surgeon/apothecary John Garrett.[48]

The West Riding magistrates gave the most thorough consideration to the essential elements of their undertaking. Godfrey Higgins visited Bethlem, St Luke's and the Leicester and Nottingham Asylums. He consulted extensively with Samuel Tuke, who was commissioned to prepare detailed guidance for prospective architects. A competition, with a first prize of 100 guineas, was launched. The winning design, that of Watson and Pritchett of York, encompassed an 'H' block principle, with identical wings for each sex. Tuke's *Practical Hints* delineated four 'primary objects', of paramount importance to the 'welfare and comfort of lunatics':

> 1st, The complete separation of male and female patients.
>
> 2nd, The separation of patients in proper numbers, and in distinct apartments, according to the state of their minds.
>
> 3rd, A system of easy and constant superintendence over the patients, by their attendants, and over both, by their superior officers.
>
> 4th, That the accommodation for the patients should be cheerful, and afford as much opportunity for voluntary change of place and variety of scene, as is compatible with security.

Tuke's principles became standard asylum practice, not only at Wakefield, but in most public asylums. His emphasis on the importance of security, of inspection and of classification and separation of patients according to mental condition, gave added legitimacy to the more custodial approaches to asylum practice. This aspect of his ideas has been accorded rather less historical prominence than the more gently humanitarian elements of 'moral management'.[49]

The architect of the Cornwall Asylum, John Foulston, evidently took his inspiration from William Stark's Glasgow Asylum and James Bevans's design for the proposed London asylum, illustrated in the Select Committee reports of 1815–16. Bodmin was the only early English asylum erected on a radial design, based on the 'panopticon' principle expounded by Jeremy Bentham. Five galleries branched out of the asylum's circular central portion. Foulston himself was extremely conscious of the symbolic aspects of his building:

> The entrance gateway is designed in the character of an approach to a private park, for there is a partial sagacity in madness which requires consideration, and several patients have been induced to pass through this entrance under an idea that they were about to visit some person of distinction.

The intention of the radial design, used in several prisons, was to maximize the facilities for observation and inspection. The floor levels were carefully arranged 'so as to admit of inspecting, at the same time both the upper and lower floors of the wing of the buildings'. All the doors and windows were of cast iron, transported from Broseley in Shropshire, at a cost of £2000. The only external advice taken appears to have been from Bethlem Hospital, on 'the different securities necessary for the patients'. The custodial aspect of the asylum was no doubt enhanced by its location next to the prison.[50]

William Stark's design for the Gloucester Asylum was almost equally unique, and incorporated some of the features he had recommended in his influential book. Its centrepiece was a crescent, with wings leading off to the rear. After Stark's decease, the committee had to seek detailed guidance from elsewhere. The initial inspiration was drawn from Bethlem, from whence were recruited the surgeon George Poynder as superintendent, the matron and the head keepers. After this, Gloucester appears to have been the first to learn lessons from another county asylum, that of Stafford. Once in post, Poynder worked closely with John Garrett, who came down from Stafford to help with preparations. The furniture and equipment were ordered and fitted 'as near as may be to the Stafford plan', including the iron fireguards and the 'instruments of restraint'. Garrett even sent his chief carpenter to help for several days. In drawing up rules and regulations, the committee of visitors made enquiries from other asylums, but in the end opted to copy those of Stafford. Once the asylum was ready to open, Garrett was invited to go round and inspect; several of his practical suggestions were adopted.[51]

The sources of guidance varied for the other asylums of the 1820s. The Lincoln governors characteristically appear to have taken little advice, though their architect, Richard Ingleman, was able to utilize his experience in designing the Nottingham Asylum. The Radcliffe (Oxford) governors consulted the other subscription asylums, including particularly Exeter, but also St Luke's, Manchester and Lincoln; they also received personal advice from Paul and from Thomas Warburton, the proprietor of the Bethnal Green madhouses. The architect commissioned was Ingleman, whose plan closely followed that of Lincoln Asylum. Interestingly, he was given initial instructions by Thomas Warburton, who vetted the plans before approval by the governors. The committee of the Suffolk County Asylum, opened in 1829 in an adapted former house of industry (workhouse) at Melton near Woodbridge, had their architect's plans perused by the medical staff of Bethlem and St Luke's. They followed precedent by appointing as governor George Wallett, a former apothecary and superintendent at Bethlem. Some advice was taken from the neighbouring Norfolk Asylum, but the Suffolk magistrates were largely oblivious to available information and experience from other county asylums. Indeed, up to the planning of the Middlesex Asylum, more than fifteen years after that at Nottingham had opened, the amount of information gathering and experience sharing between county asylums was remarkably small, excepting the exchange between Stafford and Gloucester. The examples of the longer established subscription asylums, and even of discredited Bethlem, remained the more powerful influences.[52]

Continuities with the earlier subscription asylums were extremely marked. The practice was maintained of erecting imposing buildings, which served as an adornment to the county and a symbol of the beneficence and progressive spirit of its privileged and wealthy elite. At the Staffordshire Quarter Sessions in July 1818, with the asylum about to open, George Chetwynd called on every friend to humanity to rejoice 'in the establishment of so noble an Institution'. He declared that, in a few years:

> we shall, I have no doubt, under the blessing of Providence, look upon this Establishment as the brightest ornament of our native County, and we shall leave it to posterity an enviable monument of the humanity and liberality of the present enlightened age.

With its grand facade and extensive, well-laid-out grounds, Stafford Asylum was indeed an impressive edifice. The pioneering Nottingham Asylum had been considered a 'large and handsome building'. The 'spacious and handsome' white brick Norfolk Asylum was fronted by a Grecian portico, supported by four columns. The 'handsome' front of the Lancaster Asylum was set off by Doric pillars. The Gloucester Asylum, with its Cheltenham-style crescent, was aptly described on opening as 'a most substantial, commodious, and elegant Pile of Building'; a foreign visitor later likened it to a nobleman's country mansion. The subscription asylums at Lincoln and Oxford were equally striking. Lincoln was fronted with a classical Ionic portico; its position near the castle, on top of a hill overlooking the surrounding region, has made it one of the landmarks of the city. The Radcliffe Asylum, though more modest in design, and away from the city centre, was also clearly intended to impress spectators.[53]

Having embarked on the projection and construction of an asylum, subscribers and county magistrates had no intention of letting it slip into secluded anonymity. These new buildings, with their striking, elegant designs and their prominent location, acquired all the trappings of a prestigious undertaking. Their well-publicized subscription lists, and the well-connected names which dominated the committees of management, emphasized their arrival among the foremost institutions of their city, county and region. Whilst it was true that the 1808 Act had not stimulated universal action, the response was sufficient to ensure the growing ascendancy of the public asylum as a visible symbol of the ability of a benevolent ruling elite to control and manage the manifestations and ravages of mental disorder.

EARLY DAYS

Behind the grandeur of their exteriors, the new buildings contained the same sort of custodial features that had characterized public asylums from Bethlem and St Luke's onwards. The more progressive thinking exemplified in some of the better-run private madhouses, and in the practices of the York Retreat, were only beginning to become influential before the Select Committee of 1815.[54] Architects, justices, house committees, medical officers and asylum superintendents naturally opted for the accepted methods of patient management. The prevalent philosophy determining the physical nature of the institution was to combine reasonable comfort and the pursuit of 'cure' with the maintenance of adequate security for the staff and for the public at large. The resolution of these conflicting objectives remained problematic. The creation of a forbidding environment, though perhaps not the deliberate intent, was the frequent consequence.

Prison-orientated architecture, with its ordered pattern of galleries, cells, airing courts, high walls, high windows, stone-flagged floors, iron doors and iron gates, continued to exercise a dominating influence on the nature of most parts of the building behind the grand facade. Asylum patients were mostly housed in single cells, which opened into galleries. These galleries served not only as corridors, but also as day-rooms or recreation areas in time of inclement weather. In some cases, such as the Chester Asylum opened in 1828, there were cells on both sides of the gallery, which severely limited the amount of light and air reaching the narrow gallery. In others, such as Gloucester and Lancaster, the cells were back to back, opening into a gallery, which meant that there was no direct light and air coming into the cells. The use of iron in doors and windows was general. Thomas Allis of the York Retreat visited Gloucester Asylum before its opening in 1823 and, though 'much pleased with the general Aspect of the Institution', disliked the appearance of the iron doors and wire gratings at the windows; he thought these gave it 'too much of a Prison like appearance'. Another influential visitor, George Man Burrows, criticized the corridors into which the cells opened as being 'dangerously narrow'. Several of the early county asylums were later condemned as appearing too much like prisons. Their airing courts, often confined and bare, and surrounded by high walls, served to confirm this impression.[55]

An imposing and intimidating building was consistent with the still prevalent idea that madness and the madman were to be controlled and managed as a prelude to bringing about a cure. However, such ideas were difficult to express openly as a rationale for an institution that was portrayed as an exemplification of public benevolence and compassion. Indeed, much of the rhetoric employed in the early publicity stressed the humane approaches which were to be upheld. The Stafford Asylum promised to provide 'the care and protection of the unfortunate Sufferers, on the most approved system of medical and moral treatment, by kindness, attention, and humanity'. The committee of the Gloucester Asylum similarly assured the public that it would be conducted with 'the most tender solicitude for the welfare and recovery of the Patients'. These phrases were not intended to be empty, or to be pious aspirations. There was a genuine hope and belief that humanity could co-exist with authoritative control.[56]

With the publication of Tuke's *Description of the Retreat* in 1813, and then of the Select Committee reports, the new current of progressive ideas steered some asylum managers toward the adoption of more liberal approaches to patient management. The Retreat's teachings gained some influence on the flagship Nottingham Asylum. Nottingham's first director and matron, Thomas Morris and his wife, stayed at the Retreat for a period in late 1811 to study 'the proper mode of treatment', prior to commencing their duties; Samuel Tuke was gratified at the 'prospect of doing some good beyond our own sphere'. Morris found the information he had learnt 'of the greatest use to me'. He remained in regular correspondence with George Jepson, the Retreat's superintendent, and told him he considered the Retreat to be 'the best in the kingdom or in the whole World'. Dr Charles Pennington, the asylum's first physician, later told Tuke that the Morrises had closely imitated the Retreat's 'admirable system' of mild and humane management. The Nottingham Asylum, three years after opening, was held up as an example of good practice by the Select Committee, with Reverend John Becher, one of its governors and guiding activists, giving detailed evidence. The application and continuance of Tukean methods was, however, far from easy in an asylum which was required to accept a wide range of patients. Becher advised the Committee that the aim was to pursue a 'system of mildness' like that of the Retreat. However, with the most 'outrageous' patients there was little alternative other than to have recourse to handcuffs and chains.[57]

The Retreat also received visits from magistrates or officers associated with other county asylums, including Bedford, Lancaster and Cornwall. The degree of influence of its philosophy on their practices, however, was at best limited. Apart from Nottingham, the only other early county asylum where there was a serious attempt to adopt the new thinking was at Wakefield. The close association of Samuel Tuke with the design and construction of the asylum was a declaration of intent by Godfrey Higgins and the magistrates as to the principles upon which they expected it to operate. Its first director, William Ellis, had laid out his own progressive credentials, as well as his praise of Tuke, in a pamphlet published in 1815. He first visited the Retreat in 1816; and, following his appointment to Wakefield in December 1817, he visited the Retreat twice more before the first patients were admitted. Clearly the influence of the Retreat's approach was very significant at Wakefield, though Daniel Hack Tuke's later opinion that it was the Retreat's 'legitimate child' was an overstatement. Ellis and his wife concentrated on particular elements of the approach, notably the promotion of the centrality of work, both as a therapeutic tool and as part of the development of a communitarian philosophy. They also, by contrast, instituted a programme of rigid economy, which pandered to the aspirations of the Yorkshire magistrates as careful guardians of the county rates.[58]

The new asylums were not universally welcomed. As well as direct public criticism, there was more insidious resistance demonstrated by parishes and their officers who chose to ignore the requirements of the 1808 Act. The opening of the asylum would be accompanied by circulars and by newspaper advertisements stating the requirement for all pauper and criminal lunatics and dangerous idiots in the county to be committed there. The numbers of places provided had been based on projections taken from the returns sent by parishes of the numbers of mentally disordered people chargeable to them. In the event, the numbers of patients forthcoming were usually far short of what had been anticipated. In Gloucestershire, for example, the returns had indicated that there were 150 paupers deemed eligible for the asylum, which had 120 places, 60 of which were for paupers. However, by January 1824, six months after opening, only 31 paupers had been sent in.[59]

The reticence of parish officers and local magistrates was doubtless due in part to a resentment of the power of the county justices which the asylum represented. Beyond this, and perhaps even more importantly, overseers were attempting to avoid the expense of paying asylum fees. The immediate consequence was to increase the anticipated costs per head for each pauper patient, or at least make it difficult for charges to be reduced sufficiently to attract more patients. In most of the affected counties, the magistrates were having to issue exhortations to parishes to fulfil their obligations and send their lunatics to the asylum. In Gloucestershire there was a note of desperation as the visiting committee urged the borough magistrates 'to aid them in filling the Wards . . . with such Pauper Patients . . . as are eligible by law for admission into it; and the Committee earnestly call upon the supporters and well-wishers of the Institution, to recommend to it Patients of all descriptions'. Where such appeals failed, threats were sent out to invoke the provisions of the Act to prosecute and fine overseers who overlooked or reneged on their responsibilities.[60]

There were also early problems, in some of the mixed-class asylums, in attracting private patients. Although there were continuing attacks on the reputation and motivation of private madhouse proprietors, for many wealthier people the public asylum did not yet represent a suitable alternative. The perceived stigma of a public institution, and particularly one where people of all social classes were admitted, was a serious obstacle. William Stark, architect of the Glasgow Asylum, had referred in 1810 to the 'common receptacles' of lunacy, where 'persons of liberal education, and of respectable rank in society, are unavoidably mixed with those of the lowest rank, of the most brutal manners, and of the most profligate habits'. His building designs, like those of his rival Robert Reid (architect of the Edinburgh Asylum), were intended to promote a strict separation of the classes within the asylum. However, despite its class segregation, the Gloucester Asylum experienced considerable difficulty in enticing the lucrative private patients who, it was anticipated, would subsidize the costs of charity patients. The committee of visitors attributed the problem to 'very false notions' prevailing about the asylum and the treatment of people within it. It took several years for the better-off to be sufficiently convinced to submit their relatives in any significant numbers.[61]

Direct opposition to the new county asylums was based on two distinct grounds – excessive cost and a questioning of their whole premise. In some counties, concern at the likely expenditure was expressed in concerted local campaigns of petitions and protests. In Suffolk, these methods achieved a postponement, and were responsible for a revised, cheaper scheme entailing the purchase of an existing building rather than a new construction. In Middlesex, several parishes lodged objections on grounds of cost. The directly affected parishioners of Hanwell marshalled additional arguments; the asylum would be 'painfully conspicuous' to people in the area, some of whom would be driven away, leading to raised poor-rates and reduced land values. One of their supporters, Alderman Bridges, suggested that the 'cries and noises of the unhappy inmates' would be distressing to those in the vicinity. The protests barely served to delay proceedings.[62]

The fiercest opposition was in Staffordshire, where the madhouse proprietor Thomas Bakewell began a campaign as soon as the asylum was on the drawing board. With the asylum about to open in 1818, others joined in. An anonymous critic condemned the 'immense and unprecedented expence' to which the county had been subjected. The magistrates had acted with 'offensive egotism' in forcing a 'mighty bedlam' on the ratepayers, at a time of severe agricultural distress. Their asylum was a monument of 'parade, profligacy, and extravagance'; the 'ruinous expence' would itself turn people into paupers and desperate lunatics, who would fill it. He scorned the outward magnificence of the asylum and its surroundings, upon which the magistrates had evidently prided themselves, with its 'double flight of steps – an artificial serpentine river . . . a sweeping and tasty carriage-road, lined with shrubberies, winding through the gay foliage, and a fine bridge bestriding a *made* river, ornamented by a *jet d'eau*'. All this 'pomp and shew' was in stark contrast to the 'abode of misery, humiliation and wretchedness indescribable' inside. The whole enterprise was merely a source of jobbery and patronage for the county's 'great men'. In a subsequent, and even more forthright, outburst he questioned the whole basis of public asylums, suggesting that pauper lunacy was no more a public concern than the education of the poor.[63]

These rather hysterical attacks were suitably refuted by supporters of the enterprise. The ongoing campaign of Thomas Bakewell proved more difficult to deflect, however, as it took on dimensions far wider than Staffordshire. Bakewell had made his views known well before the Stafford Asylum opened, initially by letters to the press and to leading politicians. His attempts to influence public figures led to his being invited as a witness before the Select Committee on Madhouses, where he was questioned about his practices at his private asylum at Spring Vale. He used the opportunity to promulgate his case against public asylums, and county asylums in particular. He considered them fatally flawed, because of the Act's requirement to accept all pauper and criminal lunatics and dangerous idiots. In his view, it was essential to have a complete separation of new, curable cases from the incurable. A large public asylum which admitted all was 'a great deal more calculated to prevent recovery than to promote it, under the best regulations possible', for the necessary separation could not be effected.[64]

Bakewell elaborated his views in a lengthy pamphlet, published after his appearance before the Select Committee, declaring that:

> Large Public Asylums for the Insane, are certainly wrong, upon system; for nothing can be more calculated to prevent recovery, from a state of Insanity, than the horrors of a large Mad House, close confinement, and a state of idleness in the company of incurable Lunatics nor can any medical treatment compensate for the defect of the system & the few that do recover is no argument in their favor for some will recover in spite of the worst treatment possible.

His perception was that county asylums' admission policies would render them primarily receptacles for the accumulation of chronic patients. Those admitted in the first stages of an acute disorder would, when mixed with people of severely deteriorated condition, have their chances of recovery reduced. The curative means necessary for acute patients would be impossible to apply, in a regime geared toward the management of people exhibiting the most deteriorated behaviours. By the very nature of the needs of many of the patients, the regime would be one of 'close confinement', more appropriate to a prison. The large size of these institutions could only serve to aggravate the problem. Bakewell's proposed solution was not an abolition of the public asylum, but rather the creation of a network of state-sponsored small receiving hospitals, which would accept only those people recently affected, with a concentration on methods to achieve a rapid recovery.[65]

Bakewell's criticisms ruffled some of the advocates of county asylums. The Staffordshire magistrates went so far as to offer him the superintendence of their asylum, which he declined. Several prominent figures took issue with his criticisms. William Ellis questioned the idea of separate hospitals for curables, contending that curable and incurable patients only needed to be separated within the same building. A house that contained none but those considered incurable 'would paralyse all efforts to amend them'. Samuel Tuke expressed similar reservations, styling Bakewell's objections as 'either chimerical or unfounded', for proper classification within the asylum, according to state of mind, should be sufficient. He considered the limitation of numbers to those who could be properly observed by the superintendent as far more important than the provision of separate asylums for acute and chronic cases. Godfrey Higgins adopted a more defensive position, conceding that Bakewell's idea of small asylums for recent cases might be superior to the plans for Wakefield. He pointed out, however, that when these were drawn up there had been no doubt but that the systems adopted by St

Luke's or the Retreat were the most appropriate. Bakewell's dissenting challenge was largely discounted.[66]

Bakewell, however, remained undaunted. He continued for another fifteen years to agitate for his approach through numerous articles in popular literary journals, as well as by periodic lobbying of politicians and of county magistrates, such as those of Middlesex, who were planning asylums. His argument persisted that insanity was among the most curable of diseases if treated when recently presented, and that if his model were adopted there would be a large financial saving to the authorities caused by a diminution of the numbers going on to become chronic cases. He remained, though, something of a lone voice, and little more than an irritant to the proponents of public asylums. His repeated representations were to little avail, and by 1830 he had reached the point where he conceded defeat in his attempts to convince influential opinion.[67] Nevertheless, the scenarios that Bakewell had laid out proved not to be inaccurate. The new generation of public asylums did indeed develop into large custodial institutions, dominated and largely shaped by their increasing saturation with the irredeemably chronic.

NOTES

1 R. Porter, *Mind-Forg'd Manacles: A History of Madness in England from the Restoration to the Regency* (Cambridge, 1987), chapter 3.

2 J. Woodward, *To Do The Sick No Harm: A Study of the British Voluntary Hospital System To 1875* (London, 1974), pp. 8–20, 147–8.

3 R. Porter, 'The Gift Relation: Philanthropy and Provincial Hospitals in Eighteenth-Century England', in L. Granshaw and R. Porter (eds), *The Hospital in History* (London, 1989), pp. 149–78; A. Borsay, 'Cash and Conscience: Financing the General Hospital at Bath, c.1738–1750', *Social History of Medicine*, vol. IV, no. 1 (August 1991), pp. 207–229; M.E. Fissell, '"The Sick and Drooping Poor" in Eighteenth-Century Bristol and its Region', *Social History of Medicine*, vol. II, no. 1 (April 1989), pp. 35–58 (see especially p. 36); Woodward, *To Do The Sick No Harm*, pp. 17–21.

4 Porter, *Mind-Forg'd Manacles*, chapter 3; A. Scull, *The Most Solitary of Afflictions: Madness and Society in Britain 1700–1900* (London, 1993), chapters 1–2.

5 Porter, *Mind-Forg'd Manacles*, pp. 129–33; Scull, *Most Solitary of Afflictions*, pp. 17–18; M. Winston, 'The Bethel at Norwich: An Eighteenth Century Hospital for Lunatics', *Medical History*, vol. XXXVIII, no. 1 (January 1994), pp. 27–51.

6 Porter, *Mind-Forg'd Manacles*, pp. 130–2; K. Jones, *A History of the Mental Health Services* (London, 1972), pp. 40–1; Scull, *Most Solitary of Afflictions*,

p. 18; Woodward, *To Do The Sick No Harm*, pp. 147–8; C.N. French, *The Story of St Luke's Hospital* (London, 1951), pp. 4–12 (quote, p. 5), 18–20.

7 Manchester Royal Infirmary (MRI) Archives, 'An Account of the Proceedings of the Trustees of the Public Infirmary in Manchester, in Regard to the Admission of Lunaticks into that Hospital' (c.1763), 'Lunatick Hospital, in Manchester, December 10, 1766'; Porter, *Mind-Forg'd Manacles*, p. 132; N. Roberts, *Cheadle Royal Hospital: A Bicentenary History* (Altrincham, 1967), pp. 4–12.

8 A. Digby, 'Changes in the Asylum: The Case of York, 1777– 1815', *Economic History Review*, 2nd series, vol. XXXVI, no. 2 (May 1983) pp. 218–39; A. Digby, *From York Lunatic Asylum to Bootham Park Hospital* (University of York, Borthwick Papers, 1986), pp. 1–5; R. Hunter and I. Macalpine, 'Introduction' to S. Tuke, *Description of the Retreat* (London, 1964), p. 6; Staffordshire County Record Office (SCRO), Q/AIc, Box I: Letter, 10 March 1812, Reverend James Manning, Exeter to C. Aylesbury; Devon County Record Office, 3992/F/H13, Sixth Report of Exeter Lunatic Asylum (1807), 3992/F/H26, 16 March 1795, 16 July 1800.

9 Liverpool Record Office, 614 INF 1/1, Minutes of Board of Trustees of Liverpool Infirmary, 17 August, 7 September, 7 December 1789, 614 INF 5/2, Liverpool Infirmary, *Annual Reports*, 1789–93; *Liverpool Advertiser*, 29 August, 15 October 1789; SCRO, Q/AIc, Box I: Letter, 11 March 1812, J. Squires, Liverpool Asylum to C. Aylesbury, Letter, 13 March 1812, Secretary of Leicester Asylum to C. Aylesbury, 'Statutes, Laws or Rules for the Government of the Leicester Lunatic Asylum' (15 August 1794), pp. 3–6; E.R. Frizelle, *The Life and Times of the Royal Infirmary at Leicester* (Leicester, 1988), pp. 63, 66; H.G. Orme and W.H. Brock, *Leicestershire's Lunatics: The Institutional Care of Leicestershire's Lunatics During the Nineteenth Century* (Leicester, 1987), p. 6; J. Throsby, *Select Views in Leicestershire* (Leicester, 1789), vol. II, p. 35; J. Throsby, *The History and Antiquities of the Ancient Town of Leicester* (Leicester, 1791), p. 314; Hereford and Worcester County Record Office (Hereford), 560/8, Hereford Infirmary, *Annual Report*, 1799, 560/25, Hereford Infirmary, Governors' Meetings, 17 August 1815, 560/26, Minutes of Governors of Hereford Infirmary, 30 October 1823; *Rules for the Government of the Lunatic Asylum in Hereford* (Hereford, 1799; copy in Hereford City Library), p. 3. The Newcastle Lunatic Hospital had also been 'privatized' some years before (Porter, *Mind-Forg'd Manacles*, p. 132).

10 A. Bailey, 'The Founding of the Gloucestershire County Asylum, now Horton Road Hospital Gloucester, 1792–1823', *Trans. Bristol and Gloucestershire Archaeological Society*, vol. XC (1971), pp. 178–91 (especially pp. 178–81); G.O. Paul, *A Scheme of an Institution and a Description of a Plan for a General Lunatic Asylum for the Western Counties to be Built in or Near the City of Gloucester* (Gloucester, 1796); Sir G.O. Paul, *Observations on the Subject of Lunatic Asylums, Addressed to a General Meeting of Subscribers to a Fund for Building and Establishing a General Lunatic Asylum Near Gloucester*

(Gloucester, 1812), pp. 11–24; Gloucester Reference Library (GRL), J7.22, 'An Abstract of Proceedings Relative to the Institution of a General Lunatic Asylum in or Near the City of Gloucester' (Gloucester, 1794).

11 MRI Archives, 'An Account of the Proceedings', 'The Auditor's Report of the Present State of the Public Infirmary in Manchester', vol. XIII (1764–5); Liverpool Record Office, 614 INF 5/2, 3 March to 31 December 1796; *Liverpool Advertiser*, 29 August 1789; French, *Story of St Luke's*, p. 5; Devon County Record Office, 3992/F/H26, 'Outline of a Plan for a Lunatic Asylum', 16 March 1795.

12 French, *Story of St Luke's*, p. 15; Digby, *From York Lunatic Asylum*, pp. 2, 5–9; MRI Archives, 'An Account of the Proceedings'; SCRO, Q/AIc, Box I: Letter, 13 March 1812.

13 Roberts, *Cheadle Royal Hospital*, pp. 28–9; Digby, *From York Lunatic Asylum*, p. 6; MRI Archives, 'State of the Public Infirmary', no. XXXI (1782–3); SCRO, Q/AIc, Box I: Letter, 7 March 1812; Warneford Hospital Archives, WP5, xv, 7 April 1818, Letter from Mr Taylor, Manchester Infirmary.

14 MRI Archives, 'An Account of the Proceedings', 'Lunatick Hospital in Manchester, December 10, 1766'; French, *Story of St Luke's*, p. 5; Digby, 'Changes in the Asylum', p. 223.

15 Roberts, *Cheadle Royal Hospital*, pp. 22, 27; *Rules of the Lunatic Asylum in Hereford*, pp. 7–8; SCRO, Q/AIc, Box I: 'Statutes and Constitution of the Lunatic Asylum near Exeter', pp. 19, 22, 'Rules for the Government of the Lunatic Hospital and Asylum in Manchester' (1791), p. 13, 'Rules for the Government of the Leicester Lunatic Asylum', pp. 10–11; Digby, 'Changes in the Asylum', pp. 222–9; J. Andrews, *Bedlam Revisited: A History of Bethlem Hospital, c1634–1770* (PhD, University of London, 1991), chapters 3–4; K. Jones, *History of the Mental Health Services* (London, 1972), pp. 75–8.

16 SCRO, Q/AIc, Box I: Manchester Rules (1791), Leicester Rules, pp. 3–6, Exeter Rules, p. 10; *Rules of the Lunatic Asylum in Hereford*, pp. 3–13; Paul, *Scheme of an Institution*, p. 12; Digby, *From York Lunatic Asylum*, pp. 1–13; Porter, *Mind-Forg'd Manacles*, pp. 131–3; R. Hunter and I. Macalpine, *Three Hundred Years of Psychiatry, 1535–1860* (Oxford, 1963), pp. 402–5, 467–9, 517–19, 543–6; P. Carpenter, 'Thomas Arnold: A Provincial Psychiatrist in Georgian England', *Medical History*, vol. XXXIII (April 1989), pp. 199–216; Frizelle, *Royal Infirmary at Leicester*, pp. 63–6; Orme and Brock, *Leicestershire's Lunatics*, p. 6; G. McLoughlin, *A Short History of the First Liverpool Infirmary* (London, 1978), pp. 47–53, 106–15; J.A. Shepherd, *A History of the Liverpool Medical Institution* (Liverpool, 1979), pp. 18, 37–44, 64–7.

17 Porter, *Mind-Forg'd Manacles*, pp. 131, 134–5; Digby, *From York Lunatic Asylum*, pp. 8–11; Carpenter, 'Thomas Arnold', pp. 204–10; SCRO, Q/AIc, Box I: Exeter Rules, p. 20; Paul, *Scheme of an Institution*, pp. 4, 12.

18 French, *Story of St Luke's*, p. 20; Roberts, *Cheadle Royal Hospital*, p. 5; Digby, *From York Lunatic Asylum*, p. 17; Frizelle, *Royal Infirmary at Leicester*, p. 66; C.P. Philo, *The Space Reserved for Insanity: Studies in the Historical Geography*

of the Mad-Business in England and Wales (PhD, St David's University College, Lampeter, 1992), pp. 108–30; SCRO, Q/AIc, Box I: Letter, 10 March 1812.

19 M. Ignatieff, *A Just Measure of Pain: The Penitentiary in the Industrial Revolution 1750–1850* (London, 1989 edn), pp. 98–102; E.A.L. Moir, 'Sir George Onesiphorus Paul', in H.P.R. Finberg (ed.), *Gloucestershire Studies* (Leicester, 1957), pp. 195–224.

20 *An Abstract of Proceedings Relative to the Institution of a General Lunatic Asylum in or Near the City of Gloucester* (Gloucester, 1794); Paul, *Scheme of an Institution*; Paul, *Observations on the Subject of Lunatic Asylums*, pp. 10–12; *Gloucester Journal*, 22 July, 16 September, 11 November, 9 December 1793, 17 March 1794, 13 September 1802; Bailey, 'The Founding of the Gloucestershire County Asylum', pp. 178–80.

21 Paul, *Observations on the Subject of Lunatic Asylums*, pp. 15–17; Jones, *History of the Mental Health Services*, pp. 55–6; A.D. Harvey, *Britain in the Early Nineteenth Century* (London, 1978), chapter 3.

22 BPP 1807, vol. II, *Report of Select Committee on the State of Criminal and Pauper Lunatics*, pp. 17–19.

23 *Journal of the House of Commons*, vol. 62 (1807), pp. 606, 715; Paul, *Observations on the Subject of Lunatic Asylums*, pp. 17–18; Jones, *History of the Mental Health Services*, pp. 55–8; *The Life of Samuel Romilly, Written by Himself* (London, 1842); R. & S. Wilberforce, *Life of William Wilberforce*, vol. III (London, 1838).

24 *Select Committee on the State of Criminal and Pauper Lunatics*, pp. 6–7, 19.

25 Scull, *Most Solitary of Afflictions*, chapter 2; Jones, *History of the Mental Health Services*, pp. 54–9; M. Donnelly, *Managing the Mind: A Study of Medical Psychology in Early Nineteenth Century Britain* (London, 1983), pp. 18–29; P. Bartlett, *The Poor Law of Lunacy: The Administration of Pauper Lunatics in Mid-Nineteenth Century England with Special Emphasis on Leicestershire and Rutland* (PhD, University of London, 1993), pp. 42–9.

26 *Journal of the House of Commons*, vol. 63 (1808), pp. 248, 307, 336, 340, 351, 382, 394, 445, 453, 464; 48 Geo. III, Cap. 96.

27 Section XVI.

28 Sections I–II, XVII–XVIII.

29 Sections III–V; *Select Committee on the State of Criminal and Pauper Lunatics*, p. 19; Paul, *Scheme of an Institution*.

30 *Select Committee on the State of Criminal and Pauper Lunatics*, p. 19; 48 Geo. III, Cap. 96, Section XXII; Paul, *Observations on the Subject of Lunatic Asylums*, pp. 46–7.

31 Since the early writings of Kathleen Jones, there has been a tendency to downplay the numerical significance of the post-1808 asylums, emphasizing the number of counties that did not take up the Act rather than those that did – *Lunacy, Law and Conscience, 1744–1845: the Social History of the Care of the Insane* (London, 1955), pp. 73–6.

32 Sir G.O. Paul, *Doubts Concerning the Expediency and Propriety of Immediately Proceeding to Provide a Lunatic Asylum, or, House for the Reception of Lunatics, for the County of Gloucester* (Gloucester, 1813), pp. 34–44.

33 Bartlett, *Poor Law of Lunacy*, pp. 22–3.

34 A. Foss and K. Trick, *St Andrew's Hospital Northampton: The First One Hundred and Fifty Years (1838–1988)* (Cambridge, 1989), pp. 11–12; Bedfordshire County Record Office/Bedfordshire and Luton Archives (BCRO), OGE/1, 'Minutes and Proceedings Respecting the County Gaol, House of Correction, and Lunatic Asylum', 5 October 1808, 11 January, 12 April, 20 May 1809, 8, 27 April 1812; Cashman, *A Proper House: Bedford Lunatic Asylum, 1812–1860* (North Bedfordshire Health Authority, 1992), pp. ix–xi, 5–7, 15–25.

35 Nottingham County Record Office/Nottinghamshire Archives (NCRO), SO/HO/1/1/1, 1 November 1803, 12 July 1808, 14 September, 5, 12 October 1808, 23 August, 15, 29 November 1809, 4 October 1810, SO/HO/1/2/1, 12 December 1810; *Nottingham Journal*, 8 October 1803, 15 October 1808, 26 September, 14 October, 25 November 1809, 30 March, 1 June 1811, 11 January, 15 February 1812; Nottingham Reference Library (NRL), qL3648, 'Nottinghamshire General Lunatic Asylum, First Annual Report' (1813); *Articles of Union for the General Lunatic Asylum Near Nottingham, with the By-Laws, Rules, Orders, and Regulations* (Nottingham, 1825); *An Address to the Public Concerning the General Lunatic Asylum Near Nottingham* (Nottingham, 1811); R. Evans, *The Fabrication of V irtue: English Prison Architecture, 1750–1840* (Cambridge, 1982), pp. 243–4, 282.

36 Digby, *Madness, Morality and Medicine: A Study of the York Retreat, 1796–1914* (Cambridge, 1985), pp. 239–245; Digby, 'Changes in the Asylum', pp. 224–9; Jones, *History of the Mental Health Services*, pp. 67–74; BPP 1814–15, vol. IV, *Select Committee on Madhouses, with Minutes of Evidence* (1814–15), pp. 1–9; Stanley Royd Hospital (Wakefield), 'Order Book – Pauper Lunatic Asylum', 20 October, 30 November 1814, 1 March, 26 December 1816, 16 October 1818; S. Tuke, *Description of the Retreat* (London, 1813); S. Tuke, *Practical Hints on the Construction and Economy of Pauper Lunatic Asylums: Including Instructions to the Architects Who Offered Plans for the Wakefield Asylum* (York, 1815); G. Higgins, *Rules for the Management of the Pauper Lunatic Asylum for the West Riding of the County of York, Erected at Wakefield* (Wakefield, 1821); W.C. Ellis, *A Letter to Thomas Thompson, M.P.* (Hull, 1815), pp. 9, 14, 18; C. Crowther, *Some Observations Respecting the Management of the Pauper Lunatic Asylum at Wakefield* (Wakefield, 1830), pp. 5–11; C. Crowther, *Some Observations on the Management of Madhouses: Illustrated by Occurrences at the West Riding and Middlesex Asylums* (London, 1838), pp. 44, 50.

37 E. Baines, *History, Directory and Gazetteer of the County Palatine of Lancaster*, vol. II (Liverpool, 1825), p. 18; *An Address to the Magistrates of the County of Lancaster on the Situation Proposed for the Intended County Lunatic Asylum*

(Liverpool, 1810); Lancaster Public Library (LPL), B886, 11 July 1809, MS2545, 30 July 1811; W. White, *History, Gazetteer, and Directory of Norfolk* (Sheffield, 1845), p. 690; Norfolk County Record Office (NkCRO), SAH 2, 28 April, 29 August 1814; Winston, 'The Bethel at Norwich', pp. 38, 49.

38 Scull, *Most Solitary of Afflictions*, p. 29; C.T. Andrews, *The Dark Awakening: A History of St Lawrence's Hospital Bodmin* (Bodmin, 1978), pp. 24–36; Cornwall County Record Office (CCRO), DDX97/1, 18 October 1815, 17 October 1820; *West Briton*, 24 August 1810; J. Maclean, *Parochial and Family History of the Parish and Borough of Bodmin in the County of Cornwall* (London and Bodmin, 1870), p. 4. The Cornwall magistrates were largely instrumental in securing the amending Act of 1811 (51 Geo. III, Cap. 79), which gave justices more discretion over admissions to county asylums, empowering them to refuse admission where the person was not dangerous – Andrews, *The Dark Awakening*, p. 28; Paul, *Doubts Concerning the Expediency*, p. 14.

39 *Staffordshire Advertiser*, 25 January, 21 March 1812, 26 September 1818; SCRO, D550/1, pp. 1–3, 16 November 1815, 1 October 1818, Q/AIc, 'Considerations on the Lunatic Asylum Intended to be Erected in the County of Stafford' (25 March 1812); *Ninth Report of the Commissioners in Lunacy* (1855), Appendix B, p. 65.

40 Paul, *Observations on the Subject of Lunatic Asylums*, pp. 20–36, 43–55; Gloucester County Record Office (GCRO), HO22/26/9, 'Gloucester Lunatic Asylum' (7 January 1840), pp. 6–17; *Gloucester Journal*, 13 September 1802, 7 July 1806, 8 October 1810, 30 March, 20 July, 28 September 1812; Bailey, 'The Founding of the Gloucestershire County Asylum', pp. 180–3.

41 GCRO, HO22/1/1, 26 November 1813, 5 July 1816, 1 February, 7 June 1822, 26 July 1823, HO22/3/1, p. 1; *Gloucester Journal*, 30 June, 18 August 1823; Bailey, 'The Founding of the Gloucestershire County Asylum', pp. 185–6; Moir, 'Sir George Onesiphorus Paul', p. 217.

42 Brenda Parry-Jones, *The Warneford Hospital, Oxford, 1826–1976* (Oxford, 1976), pp. 7–11; *An Account of the Origin, Nature and Objects of the Asylum on Headington Hill, Near Oxford* (Oxford, 1827), pp. 1–6; *Useful Information Concerning the Origin, Nature and Purpose of the Radcliffe Lunatic Asylum* (Oxford, 1840), pp. 3–8.

43 Jones, *History of the Mental Health Services*, p. 89; Scull, *Most Solitary of Afflictions*, p. 29; Sir Francis Hill, *Georgian Lincoln* (Cambridge, 1966); Sir Francis Hill, *Victorian Lincoln* (Cambridge, 1974); Lincolnshire Archives Office (LAO), LAWN 1/1/1, 17 June, 8 July 1807, 6 April, 21 September 1809, 5 August, 13 October 1813, 12 March 1817, 18 February, 10 April 1820, 6 April 1829; *Nottingham Journal*, 14 October 1809.

44 48 Geo. III, Cap. 96, Section XVI; Philo, *The Space Reserved for Insanity*, pp. 160–86; SCRO, Q/AIc, 'Considerations on the Lunatic Asylum', 25 March 1812; BCRO, OGE/1, 20 May 1809.

45 NCRO, SO/HO/1/1/1, 1 November 1803–12 July 1808; Stanley Royd Hospital, 'Order Book, Pauper Lunatic Asylum', 30 November 1814; BCRO, OGE/1, 20 May 1809; E. Baines, *History, Directory and Gazeteer of the County Palatine of Lancaster*, vol. II, pp. 17–18; LPL, B886/MS2545; CCRO, DDX 97/1, 27 July 1816; Maclean, *History of the Parish and Borough of Bodmin*, p. 5; *Report of the Metropolitan Commissioners in Lunacy to the Lord Chancellor* (1844), pp. 15–16, 131–3.

46 N. Pevsner, *A History of Building Types* (London, 1976); A.D. King (ed.), *Buildings and Society* (London, 1980); T.A. Markus, *Buildings and Power; Freedom and Control in the Origins of Modern Building Types* (London, 1993), pp. 95–6, 130–40; Evans, *The Fabrication of Virtue*; J. Taylor, *Hospital and Asylum Architecture in England, 1840–1914* (London, 1991), pp. 11, 25, 134–7; J.A.S. Forsyth, *The County Lunatic Asylums, 1808–1845; A Study of the Way in Which a Building Type was Developed* (BA Architecture Dissertation, University of Newcastle, 1969); W. Stark, *Remarks on Public Hospitals for the Cure of Mental Derangement* (Glasgow, 1810); R. Reid, *Observations on the Structure of Hospitals for the Treatment of Lunatics* (Edinburgh, 1809); J. Foulston, *The Public Buildings, Erected in the West of England by John Foulston, F.R.I.B.A.* (London, 1838); Cashman, *A Proper House*, pp. 11, 15; J. Hemingway, *History of the City of Chester*, vol. II (Chester, 1831), p. 227.

47 NCRO, SO/HO/1/1/1, 1 November 1803, 12 October 1808, 22 March, 29 April, 24 May 1809.

48 Cashman, *A Proper House*, pp. xi, 18, 23; BCRO, OGE/1, 8, 27 April 1812; GLRO, MA/A/J/1, 7 February 1828; SCRO, Q/AIc, D550/1, 13 April 1818; *Staffordshire Advertiser*, 26 September 1818.

49 Stanley Royal Hospital, 'Order Book – Pauper Lunatic Asylum', 30 November 1814, 9 March 1815; *Wakefield and Halifax Journal*, 15 December 1815; Tuke, *Practical Hints*, pp. 10–11, 47, 51–4; Scull, *Most Solitary of Afflictions*, pp. 96–103; Jones, *History of the Mental Health Services*, pp. 48–53; Hunter and Macalpine, 'Introduction' to Tuke, *Description of the Retreat*; University of York, Borthwick Institute, L/3/2, Higgins to Tuke, 11 January, 10 February, 24, 26 October, November 1814, April, September, 21 December 1815, Tuke to Higgins, 12 April, 9, 23 December 1815.

50 Foulston, *Public Buildings, Erected in the West of England*, pp. 67–9, 106 (quote, p. 67); CCRO, DDX 97/1, 15 October 1816, 23 February 1819; *Select Committe on Madhouses* (1814–15), Minutes of Evidence, Plate II; *Select Committe on Madhouses* (1816), 3rd Report, p. 6; *The Builder*, 25 July 1846, p. 349.

51 Stark, *Remarks on Public Hospitals*; T.A. Markus, 'Buildings for the Sad, the Mad, and the Bad in Urban Scotland 1780–1830', in Markus (ed.), *Order in Space and Society: Architectural Form and its Context in the Scottish Enlightenment* (Edinburgh, 1982), pp. 91, 97; GCRO, HO22/1/1, 5 July, 22 August, 4 October, 6 December 1822, 23, 30 January, 8, 13 February, 4 April, 22 May, 26 June 1823.

52 LAO, LAWN 1/1/1; Warneford Hospital Archives, W.P.5, 2, 16 March, 17 April 1816, 27 February, 5, 7, 20 April 1818, 20 April 1820, 15 March 1821; Suffolk County Record Office (SuCRO), Acc 2697, 25 January, 12 March, 3 December 1827, 27 June, 6 November 1828; GLRO, MA/A/J/1, 28 November, 19 December 1827, 14 January, 7, 14 February 1828. George Wallett had given evidence regarding Bethlem to the Select Committee on Madhouses.

53 *Staffordshire Advertiser*, 18 July, 26 September, 2 October 1818; W. White, *History, Gazetteer, and Directory of Nottinghamshire* (Sheffield, 1832), p. 173; W. White, *History, Gazeteer, and Directory of Norfolk* (Sheffield, 1845), p. 690; Baines, *History, Directory and Gazeteer of Lancaster*, p. 17; *Gloucester Journal*, 18 August 1823; C. Crommelinck, *Rapport sur les Hospices d'Aliénés de l'Angleterre, de la France, et de l'Allemagne* (Courtrai, 1842), pp. 98, 108; *Lincoln and Lincolnshire Cabinet for 1828* (Lincoln, 1828), pp. 30–1; A.B. Granville, *The Spas of England; Midland Spas* (London, 1841), p. 84; *An Account of. . .the Asylum. . .Near Oxford*, pp. 10–11. For similar developments in asylum architecture in continental Europe, see Christine Stevenson, 'Madness and the Picturesque in the Kingdom of Denmark', in W.F. Bynum, R. Porter and M. Shepherd (eds), *The Anatomy of Madness*, vol. III, *The Asylum and Its Psychiatry* (London, 1988), pp. 13–47.

54 Digby, *Madness, Morality and Medicine*; W.L. Parry-Jones, *The Trade in Lunacy* (London, 1972), chapter 7; L.D. Smith, 'To Cure Those Afflicted with the Disease of Insanity; Thomas Bakewell and Spring Vale Asylum', *History of Psychiatry*, vol. IV (1993), pp. 107–27; *Select Committee on Madhouses* (1814–15), pp. 50– 2, evidence of W. Finch.

55 Ignatieff, *A Just Measure of Pain*, chapters 4, 6; Taylor, *Hospital and Asylum Architecture*, p. 135; *Report of the Metropolitan Commissioners in Lunacy* (1844), pp. 12–14, 21–3; Chester City Record Office, HW 356; Baines, *History, Directory and Gazeteer of Lancaster*, p. 17; LPL, *Report of the Medical Officers of the Lunatic Asylum for the County of Lancaster* (Lancaster, 1842), pp. 4–6; SuCRO, Acc 2697, 11, 25 January 1828, 7 July 1829; GCRO, HO22/1/1, 31 March 1813, 27 February, 29 May 1823, HO22/50/1, 15 March 1823, 17 August 1826; Crommelinck, *Rapport sur les Hospices*, pp. 108–9; LAO, LAWN 1/1/1, 29 October 1821, LAWN 1/1/2, 1 September 1823; *Eighth Report of the Commissioners in Lunacy* (1854), Appendix G, p. 137.

56 *Staffordshire Advertiser*, 26 September 1818; *Gloucester Journal*, 18 August 1823.

57 Digby, *Madness, Morality and Medicine*, p. 247; Borthwick Institute, C/1, Morris to Jepson, 6 December 1811, 24 October 1812, 10 July 1814; S. Tuke, *Memoirs of Samuel Tuke*, vol. I (London, 1840), p. 166; *Select Committee on Madhouses* (1814–15), pp. 178–9; NCRO, SO/HO/1/3/1, 4 December 1811.

58 Digby, *Madness, Morality and Medicine*, pp. 244–6; Ellis, *Letter to Thomas Thompson, M.P.*, pp. 9, 14–15, 18, 45; Stanley Royd Hospital, 'Order Book –

Pauper Lunatic Asylum', 11 December 1817, 4 January 1819. For further discussion of Ellis's work at Wakefield, see chapter 7.

59 Stanley Royd Hospital, 'Order Book – Pauper Lunatic Asylum', 24 July, 24 December 1818; CCRO, DDX 97/1, 17 October 1820; GCRO, HO 22/1/1, 20 March 1823, 19 January 1824; SuCRO, Acc 2697, 12 January, 21, 27 April 1829; *Nottingham Journal*, 11, 18, 25 January 1812; *Wolverhampton Chronicle*, 7, 28 October 1818; *Wakefield and Halifax Journal*, 23 October 1818; *Gloucester Journal*, 18 August 1823.

60 CCRO, DDX 97/1, 14 November 1820; GCRO, HO 22/1/1, 20 September, 13 November 1823, 1, 29 January 1824; *Gloucester Journal*, 18 August, 3 November 1823, 9 February 1824.

61 Stark, *Remarks on Public Hospitals*, pp. 14, 19; Reid, *Observations on Structure of Hospitals for Treatment of Lunatics*; GCRO, HO 22/8/1, Gloucester Asylum, *Annual Reports*, 1826, 1829.

62 SuCRO, Acc 2697, 29 March, 10 April, 20 October 1826; GLRO, MA/A/J/1, 28 November 1827; *The Times*, 16 November 1827, 19, 29 April, 2 May 1828.

63 *Lichfield Mercury*, 2, 30 October 1818.

64 *Staffordshire Advertiser*, 29 October 1814, 3 February 1816, 2, 19, 26 December 1818; *Lichfield Mercury*, 2, 30 October 1818; *Select Committee on Madhouses* (1814–15), p. 125. For full discussion of Bakewell's campaign, see L.D. Smith, 'Close Confinement in a Mighty Prison: Thomas Bakewell's Campaign Against Public Asylums, 1810–1830', *History of Psychiatry*, vol. V (1994), pp. 191–214.

65 T. Bakewell, *A Letter Addressed to the Chairman of the Select Committee of the House of Commons Appointed to Enquire into the State of Madhouses* (Stafford, 1815), pp. 7–9, 16–26 (quote, p. 9); Borthwick Institute, L/3/2, Higgins to Tuke, 21 December 1815, Tuke to Higgins, 23 December 1815.

66 Smith, 'Close Confinement in a Mighty Prison', p. 203; *Staffordshire Advertiser*, 19 December 1818; Ellis, *Letter to Thomas Thompson*, pp. 43–8; *Monthly Magazine*, April 1816, p. 223, May 1816, pp. 318–9, July 1816, pp. 481–3; *Imperial Magazine*, June 1826, cols. 513–4.

67 Smith, 'Close Confinement in a Mighty Prison', pp. 201–10; *Monthly Magazine* (June 1822–April 1830), May 1828, cols. 407–8, July 1828, cols. 621–2, March 1830, col. 260; Greater London Record Office (GLRO), MA/A/J/1, 24 April 1828.

2

Asylum Management

The movement to develop more public asylums continued steadily through the later 1820s and 1830s, though not at the pace sought by the advocates of lunacy reform. New county asylums were opened for Suffolk and Cheshire in 1829, Middlesex in 1831, Dorset in 1832, Kent in 1833 and Surrey in 1841. These were primarily pauper asylums, but those in Chester and Forston (Dorset) also made provision for private patients. Another joint county and subscription asylum opened in Leicester in 1837. Asylums funded only by public subscription were established near Oxford in 1826, and at Northampton in 1838. Although still only a minority of counties were covered, by the time of the Metropolitan Commissioners' report in 1844 there were fifteen county asylums, and a further five counties had a charitable asylum within their borders. Some had access to more than one institution, if containing one of the earlier public asylums or lunatic hospitals of Manchester, Liverpool, York, Norwich and London.[1]

The newer asylums were generally set up on similar lines to their predecessors, their projectors having sought advice and made observation visits. Local circumstances did ensure, though, that there were some differences. In several instances (Suffolk, Middlesex, Dorset, Surrey), the earlier practice of building in close proximity to the county town was abandoned. Financial stringency precluded the magistrates of Suffolk and Dorset from erecting fine new buildings. In Suffolk, they opted to convert a disused house of industry, and in Dorset a substantial donation was used to adapt and extend a country house a few miles from Dorchester. In Middlesex, with its teeming metropolitan catchment area, the whole enterprise at Hanwell had to be conducted on a scale far greater than anything hitherto undertaken.[2]

The similarities and differences between the institutions also characterized their management arrangements. Before the legislation of 1845, there was limited guidance on how an asylum should be organized and administered. Lay and medical managers had to develop their own strategies and systems. They tended initially to follow the precedents of St Luke's and its successors. Where the asylum's foundation had been closely linked with a hospital, the existing structures of the parent institution were influential. As the new institution became established, and its officers more confident, the arrangements became increasingly individualized. In each asylum a balance had to be struck between the influence of lay and professional control. It was often a difficult balance, affected by local or parochial factors as well as the inherent tensions between ambitious or zealous officers, and committees of justices or governors who considered themselves responsible for protecting both the interests of the public and those of the patients.

THE ADMINISTRATIVE FRAMEWORK

Lay Leadership

The eighteenth-century public asylums had been managed on similar lines to the subscription hospitals. They were administered by a board of governors or trustees, who were members either by virtue of being an infirmary governor or by a specified level of donation or annual subscription. Later subscription asylums followed similar models, though with local variations. At Lincoln Asylum, membership of the board of governors was gained through a benefaction of twenty guineas, or an annual subscription of three guineas. There was no limit on the number of governors, which later became a source of great difficulties. Although the asylum's origins were bound up with the County Hospital, its management was kept distinct and independent. In the subscription asylum at Oxford, the lay management was closely integrated with the Radcliffe Infirmary, whose governors' role was extended to cover the asylum.[3]

The county asylums required mechanisms for the exercise of official control. The Act of 1808 vested this in the only local government body remotely qualified – county justices, acting through the Quarter Sessions, who already had a key role in prison administration. The original decision to proceed had to be taken on a majority of at least seven justices at the sessions. They were then to appoint a committee of visiting justices to superintend the construction and then the management of the asylum. The visiting justices were empowered to appoint a clerk and a surveyor and to make contracts for the erection of the building, with a requirement to report periodically to the Quarter Sessions. Once the asylum was operational, at least five had to be present at meetings for decisions to be taken. They could make regulations for the 'Management and Conduct' of the institution, including setting the responsibilities for officers and staff, whom they were able to appoint and dismiss. They were to set payment rates for patients, and the salaries and wages of officers and staff. They were also responsible for supervising and paying for ongoing repairs and maintenance. In relation to patients, they could order the discharge of people deemed no longer to require detention. The powers were, therefore, quite considerable, with a degree of discretion as to how they were exercised.[4]

One of the Act's key objectives had been to stimulate the efforts of voluntary subscribers. It laid down the mechanisms whereby justices and subscribers could negotiate and unite to provide a joint asylum. It did not prescribe the composition of an ongoing management body, leaving scope for arrangements according to local circumstances. These normally reflected the relative proportions of the initial capital invested. Thus, at Nottingham, there was a President and 32 visiting governors, seventeen elected by the subscribers and benefactors, twelve by the county magistrates and the remaining three by the magistrates of the City of Nottingham. At Stafford, where the subscribers had only raised a relatively small sum, they were represented by three trustees on the committee of visitors, to work with the twelve visiting justices. At Gloucester, with a long-established group of subscribers, the proportions were more even, with eighteen county justices, two city justices and fourteen subscribers. This later proved a source of friction, as the subscribers increasingly came to feel that they had insufficient control and were not receiving benefits commensurate with their contribution to the original construction costs.[5]

Committees of visitors were drawn largely from members of the aristocracy or the local gentry, following the composition of the county bench (and also, generally, of voluntary subscribers). Clerics were becoming increasingly prominent, reflecting both their growing temporal involvement as magistrates and the perception that the care of the troubled was within their legitimate sphere. It was not uncommon for a minister to chair the committee and to take an active role in the determination of policy, like Reverend J.T. Becher at Nottingham and Reverend Charles Crawley at Gloucester, and both the Dean and the Precentor at Lincoln. The president of the asylum would be an aristocratic landowner, or possibly a bishop. The Duke of Newcastle, the Lord

Lieutenant of the county, took the presidency of Nottingham Asylum prior to its opening. The Earl of Harrowby was president at Stafford, Lord Stanley at Lancaster and the Bishop of Gloucester at his county's asylum. At Lincoln, the Earl of Yarborough presided over the governors; when he died in 1824, his son was accorded the presidency shortly after he assumed the title. Some of these men were little more than figureheads. Others, like Harrowby or Yarborough, took a fairly active role in asylum affairs, particularly at critical points.[6]

The level of direct involvement of committees of visitors varied. Frequency of meetings was related to the extent to which they participated in the policy direction and ongoing business of the institution. They would normally meet quarterly, prior to or after the Quarter Sessions. At Wakefield it was merely specified that the visiting justices would meet on the first Mondays of January, April, July and October, primarily for the purpose of making contracts. At Gloucester, on the other hand, where the designated role of the committee was to 'superintend the direction of the House', additional meetings were arranged to enable them to carry out their obligations. Most committees of visitors were prepared to call special meetings according to need.[7]

In practice, most committee members did not have the time, the knowledge or the inclination to immerse themselves in the detailed oversight of asylum affairs. Much of the more routine work was generally delegated to a house committee, a smaller group of justices, or justices and subscribers, who met weekly to transact business and make decisions on practical daily issues. Their responsibilities could be extensive and wide-ranging. At Nottingham, the house committee met each Thursday, and were empowered to admit and discharge the non-pauper patients, to determine weekly charges, to superintend the condition of the house and its furniture, to hire and dismiss the junior staff, to inspect and pay bills, to deal with complaints and to correct abuses. At Gloucester, the duties were similar, but also included regular examination of the wards and bedding, and an inspection of the provisions. At Suffolk, the house committee had authority to oversee discharges of patients and to exercise, in general, the 'management of the house'. There were, therefore, differences in the extent of delegated power. House committees would, however, report regularly to their committee of visitors, who retained the power to consider and ratify the more significant decisions which had policy implications. In some asylums, notably those for Bedford, Cornwall, Norfolk and Dorset, the visitors operated without a house committee, thus retaining direct responsibility for routine management.[8]

In the subscription asylum at Lincoln, the management model comprised a similar division between an overall supervisory body and a sub-committee that dealt with more routine business. The main decision-making forum, the General Board, convened quarterly, its meetings becoming known as Quarterly Boards. Participation was open to all governors who chose to attend. The Weekly Boards required a minimum of three governors present to proceed with most business, or five if it concerned the suspension of officers or the dismissal of keepers and nurses. Their powers resembled those of the house committees of a county asylum, with rather greater emphasis on the inspection and monitoring functions. The fluid nature of membership of Weekly Boards meant that any governor who made the commitment to attend regularly could exercise considerable influence over both practice and policy in the asylum. One diligent individual, Dr E.P. Charlesworth, was able to avail himself of Lincoln's unusual constitution to dominate the institution's development over a period of three decades.[9]

Rules and Regulations

A major early responsibility of committees of visitors or governors was to produce rules and regulations for the asylum's management. The task might be delegated to a sub-committee, to an individual member deemed to have the knowledge and experience or possibly to the superintendent if appointed in advance of opening. Normally, copies of the rules of predecessor institutions would be acquired, and then adapted to meet the local circumstances. At Nottingham, the detailed rules or 'by-laws' were drafted by the indefatigable Reverend Becher, and at Wakefield the work was undertaken by Godfrey Higgins. At Gloucester, the visitors largely adopted the rules of the Stafford Asylum, which were themselves based on those of earlier subscription asylums. At Suffolk, the justices called on the new superintendent, George Wallett, to draft the rules, but they were not fully satisfied with his handiwork and had to re-write them. The variation in drafting methods, and the consequent differences in content, underlined the strong parochial element in asylum administration.[10]

Rules and regulations contained a mixture of principle, directive, obligation, guidance and exhortation. They were intended to prescribe management and staff responsibilities and to protect the interests of patients, as well as those of rate-payers and subscribers. The rules for the first county asylum, at Nottingham, were among the most comprehensive, as its governors needed assurance and stability in their venture. They detailed the roles and responsibilities of visiting governors, the treasurer, the physician and surgeon, the director and matron, and the 'assistants and servants'. They specified admission procedures, and the manner in which patients were to be treated. The Gloucester Asylum rules were yet more extensive, particularly as related to the duties of officers and staff, and the handling of patients. They also detailed the arrangements of the subscription fund, and laid out visiting restrictions. The Wakefield rules, in accordance with Higgins' reforming orientation, placed more weight on the protection of patients' interests and the prevention of abuses by the staff. The rules of the later asylums also differed in emphasis. Both Suffolk and Dorset detailed the duties, responsibilities and practice of the keepers or 'inferior officers'. At Suffolk there was a section on the rights of patients, particularly regarding employment.[11]

Asylum rules served primarily as a frame of reference rather than as a body of requirements to be strictly upheld. Allusion could be made to them when there was a dispute as to their proper fulfilment, but attitudes could not be prescribed. Rules at least provided a focus for the vigilant visitor or diligent officer. However, they could also provide a cover for poor practice or inaction. At Lincoln, which as a subscription asylum may have accepted a more flexible adherence to standards, the limitations of the initial rules and their failure to prevent abuses became evident by the late 1820s. The consequence was, in 1832, their complete replacement with a very detailed set which altered the emphasis from listing the roles and responsibilities of governors, officers and staff, to covering the important aspects of daily life in the asylum and laying down how patients were to be dealt with and how their interests were to be upheld. This exemplified how the rules might be used not just as a means of setting and reinforcing standards, but as a means of influencing the overall asylum culture; Lincoln's example, however, was not followed elsewhere.[12]

Medical Management

After the visitors, the physician occupied the most prominent place in the early asylum hierarchy. The leading role taken by prominent physicians in the development of the subscription asylums was continued by men such as Dr John Storer at Nottingham, Dr Hardwick Shute at Gloucester, Dr E.P. Charlesworth and Dr Alfred Cookson at Lincoln, and Dr Caleb Crowther and Dr Disney Alexander at Wakefield. They were, invariably, well established in the locality and already acting as physicians to the infirmary and other medical institutions. It was a natural extension of their remit to take on a comparable role in relation to the asylum. Crowther and Alexander followed earlier practice and waived any fees for their work at Wakefield Asylum; their counterparts at Lincoln followed suit in regard to pauper patients. However, the voluntary principle was increasingly on the decline, and most asylum physicians were being appointed as salaried officers; even Wakefield succumbed in 1829. Those attached to joint asylums like Stafford or Gloucester could also earn significant additional sums from attendance on charitable and private patients.[13]

The physician retained responsibility for medical supervision of the asylum and for determining and prescribing individual treatment regimes. He was required to visit, examine and attend to all the patients on a weekly or twice-weekly basis, and to maintain case-books. In some asylums, his oversight was extended by an expectation to regularly inspect the house and monitor the conduct of staff, to ensure that treatment plans and standards of care were maintained. This potentially gave him the lead role in shaping policy and practice. At Wakefield, it was enjoined that every officer and servant was to pay attention to the physicians' orders and treat them with 'the most marked respect'. The physicians' professional credibility, deserved or otherwise, and their standing in the locality, gave them scope also to wield considerable influence over the lay visitors or governors. The role continued to be a powerful one; how powerful depended largely on the ability, the commitment and the ambition of the individual physician.[14]

The other key management role was held by the salaried resident head of the establishment, variously entitled Director (Nottingham, Wakefield and Lincoln), Governor (Bedford, Norfolk and Cornwall), Superintendent (Suffolk, Middlesex and Dorset), House Surgeon and Superintendent (Lancaster, Stafford and Gloucester) or Surgeon Apothecary (Oxford). The titles had some significance, not only in regard to their implied level of authority, but also in regard to the required qualifications. The early appointments as 'Governor' at Bedford and Norfolk, for example, were seen not to require a medical qualification, but rather the qualities needed to manage a custodial institution. The questionable manner in which both asylums developed was thus probably not merely the result of an accidental train of circumstances, but symptomatic of how their counties' visiting justices viewed asylum administration. In time, management titles converged, with Superintendent or Medical Superintendent becoming the most common by

1840. By this time, as Andrew Scull has shown, the medical dominance of public asylum management had become the generally accepted norm.[15]

The powers of the superintendent centred round his supervisory responsibility for the staff, the building and the care of the patients. The phrase commonly used to encapsulate the role stated that he was to 'superintend the general economy' of the house. He was required to be fully resident and not to be engaged in any business outside the asylum. The administrative duties included purchases of goods and equipment, payment of bills and account keeping, maintenance of inventories, keeping registers of patients and of admissions and discharges, the preparation of annual accounts and reports, and acting as secretary to the committee of visitors and house committee, to whom he was directly responsible. They could also include the calculation and setting of the weekly charges for patients, and the ensuring that payments were received from parishes or boards of guardians.[16]

The superintendent's practical authority was mainly exercised by his management of the staff. He was responsible for hiring them, directing their duties, laying down and monitoring standards, and for reporting misconduct to the house committee; in certain circumstances he could order instant dismissal. His duties with regard to patient care included at least daily contact with all of them. He was responsible for the organization of the wards and their order and cleanliness, the dietary arrangements, and safety and security. The degree of responsibility for individual treatment was, however, constrained. The superintendent had to ensure the implementation of the treatment, and the administration of medicines, prescribed by the physician, to whom he was expected to report regularly on patients' progress. There was more than an implication of subordination, which mirrored the lingering hierarchical divisions between physicians and surgeons, from whose ranks most superintendents were drawn.[17]

Local idiosyncracies led to variations in the nature and extent of the superintendent's responsibilities. Where he was not medically qualified, as at Bedford and Norfolk, there could be no role in the implementation of treatment, which fell instead to the physician or a visiting surgeon. In some later asylums, like Suffolk and Dorset, no physician was appointed, probably to save the expense. This inevitably meant greater powers for the superintendent. At Dorset Asylum, he was responsible for the management of 'every part thereof', including the direction of individual treatment and the prescription of medicine. This unusual arrangement was partially regularized after a few years by the appointment of a physician, Dr George Button, as superintendent.[18]

The most singular conditions attached to the role of superintendent were developed in the early years of the Cornwall Asylum. The visitors were clearly uneasy about taking on the setting up and management of the asylum, and contracted it out to one James Duck as its 'Governor and Surgeon'. He was to be responsible for the employment and payment of staff and the purchase of equipment, in return for which he would receive fourteen shillings for each pauper patient and a sum set by himself for subscription patients. The arrangement broke down in acrimony before the asylum opened. Undaunted, the visitors came to a similar arrangement in early 1820 with a Dr Kingdon, designated the 'contractor', and also permitted him to engage in private practice outside the asylum. By the time he resigned in 1824, however, the visitors had evidently had second thoughts about medical private enterprise, and replaced him with a salaried superintendent.[19]

Although the superintendent had overall responsibility for house management, some aspects fell to the matron. She would have delegated responsibility for oversight of the care of the female patients, the supervision of the female staff and the management of the domestic aspects of asylum life, such as food preparation, cleaning and laundry.[20] If the matron was the superintendent's wife, as was often the case, his position was further enhanced. Even without this, his authority could be considerable. Its extent was constrained not so much by the rules, which could always be interpreted with some elasticity, as by the discretion which the committee of visitors was prepared to grant, which in turn depended on their own knowledge and level of commitment. Superintendents like Samuel Hitch at Gloucester, William Ellis at Wakefield and later at Hanwell, and John Kirkman at Suffolk acquired a degree of dominance by virtue of the experience, skill and organizational ability which they were able to demonstrate.

An effective superintendent needed a range of qualities, skills and abilities to fulfil his varied responsibilities. Paul Slade Knight of Lancaster Asylum suggested in 1821 that the post required 'the exertions of men greatly superior in acquirements and intellect to the general order of mankind'. This remarkable person also needed great powers of self-control, so as to 'contemplate with compassion' the insults and aspersions of the patients, and to master his 'malevolent passions'. Most of all, he should not be a 'shuffler' in his dealings with patients; a lack of firmness would only excite contempt. John Conolly, 25 years later, maintained that, to effectively manage patients, the superintendent's character and deportment should influence everyone in the establishment, so that their 'manners and language' reflected his. He had to be 'naturally benevolent', with inexhaustible patience. Conolly's greater emphasis on a tolerant and gentle approach echoed the changes in patient management that had occurred in the wake of the non-restraint movement. His priorities also underlined how he, like other leading alienists, still considered the care and treatment aspects of the role to take precedence over the more administrative aspects.[21]

The salaries of superintendents varied markedly, being often commensurate more with the perceived low status of the post than with the degree of responsibility. Where no qualification was required the lowest salaries were paid. At Bedford, the first governor, William Pither, received only 60 guineas per annum, whilst at Norfolk Asylum Mr Caryl received £125. At Nottingham, where the first director was only expected to hold an apothecary's qualification, the salary was also relatively modest at £140. As it became the norm to appoint a qualified surgeon, a higher salary had to be paid. The best remunerated posts were at Stafford, Wakefield and Gloucester where John Garrett, William Ellis and George Poynder respectively were appointed at £200 per annum. Economy, however, remained a key factor for visiting committees. George Wallett and his wife, appointed as superintendent and matron to the Suffolk Asylum in 1828, received only £150 between them. The governors of subscription asylums were also not particularly generous. Thomas Fisher at Lincoln, a qualified surgeon, was appointed at £100 per annum in 1820; the post had initially been advertised at £60 but nobody applied. Basic salaries were augmented by the provision of accommodation and full board, and by various perquisites, such as an allowance for children or for keeping a horse and chaise. They could also be enhanced in joint appointments; matrons' salaries could range from £25 to as much as £50 per annum.[22]

The superintendent's numerous responsibilities, together with the constraints on his personal life, became increasingly onerous with the asylum's steady expansion. A progressive rise in salaries was implemented, in recognition of the additional work and of the need for a higher calibre of post-holder. John Garrett's salary at Stafford rose from £200 in 1818 to £300 in 1824, and £400 in 1830. At Suffolk, John Kirkman and his wife were appointed in 1831 on £175; their joint salary steadily increased, reaching £250 in 1838, £300 in 1841 and £450 in 1845. Similar increases occurred elsewhere, as a pay structure developed that reflected patient numbers and some comparability between asylums. It was perhaps also a reflection of a gradual improvement in the status of medical ministration to the insane, which accompanied the profession's increasing claims to expertise in the developing models of moral treatment, alongside their more traditional medically-based territory.[23]

Financial recognition, however, could not in itself resolve the problem of the superintendent's growing workload. From the beginning, they were seen as medical men, administrators, clerks and supervisors. George Poynder at Gloucester, for example, was described as 'House Surgeon, Apothecary, Superintendent, and Secretary'.[24] It became increasingly impractical, however, for one man effectively to carry out all the required roles and tasks. To maintain the efficient working of the institution, there had to be some delegation of responsibilities. An administrative structure was developed in most asylums by the appointment of officers such as secretary, clerk and house steward, whose duties might include purchasing, management of the stores and equipment, and the keeping of accounts. At Gloucester, several attempts were made to provide Samuel Hitch with suitable administrative support, beginning in 1836 with the appointment of a house steward and secretary, at £50 per annum. Two years later, a separate post of clerk was established, at 20 guineas. However, there was difficulty in sorting out responsibilities and, after the steward resigned in April 1840 over a salary dispute, the visitors tried appointing a chief accountant, assisted by a first-class (private) patient as sub-accountant. When this arrangement collapsed a few months later, Hitch was given back some of his former duties, with an accompanying salary increase. However, the problem remained that this was too much even for the ablest man. Various other changes followed over the ensuing years, largely to facilitate Hitch's continuance in post.[25]

As numbers of patients grew, superintendents found the requirement for daily attention to the condition of each patient an ever more unmanageable burden, particularly if there was an intention to promote recovery. One means to tackle this was by providing medical assistance. At Nottingham, Bodmin and Melton (Suffolk), the superintendents were permitted to take on an apprentice. At Wakefield William Ellis was given an assistant in 1825, at a salary of 50 guineas, and in 1842 an additional post of 'clinical clerk and apothecary' was created. After Ellis moved to the new Middlesex Asylum in 1831, its sheer scale rendered it essential for him to have an assistant. Both Thomas Quick and George Button used the post as resident surgeon/apothecary at Hanwell as a means of preparation and training to take on, successively, the superintendence of the Dorset Asylum. At Gloucester, the asylum's smaller scale and thrift-conscious visitors precluded a salaried assistant. Undaunted, Samuel Hitch arranged in 1841 to bring in assistant medical officers, who would pay for the privilege of training with him whilst taking on some case-work. These sorts of arrangements, though relatively crude, provided precedents for the more sophisticated medical bureaucracies that developed in the post-1845 asylums.[26]

The process occurred later in the other key area of the superintendent's responsibility, management of staff, as their numbers increased more slowly than those of the patients. In several asylums, like Bodmin, Wakefield, Lancaster and Hanwell, a supervisory structure was established by the mid-1840s. This entailed the elevation of a male attendant to head attendant, with a higher salary and responsibilities which included the day-to-day direction and monitoring of the other attendants. A similar arrangement was adopted at the Lincoln subscription asylum in 1840, where both a head keeper and a head nurse were appointed; its peculiar circumstances after the abolition of restraint in the late 1830s required a greater level of staff surveillance of patients. At Lancaster, the chief attendant's duties included some of a more administrative nature, like keeping inventories and administering medicines, and some related to patient care, such as the daily recording of individual patients' activities and state of health. On administrative matters he reported to the house steward, thus creating an emergent managerial chain of command.[27]

The accompaniment of a developing managerial establishment was the increasing remoteness of the superintendent. This had a certain inevitability as asylums became ever larger. An idealistic William Ellis had suggested in 1815 that 100 to 120 was the maximum number of patients that could effectively be supervised in one asylum. However, he as much as anyone was responsible for a pragmatic acceptance of numbers growing far beyond that, first at Wakefield and then at Hanwell. By 1844, Hanwell Asylum contained almost 1000 patients, followed by Lancaster with 600, Wakefield with 430 and Surrey with 380. The Stafford, Gloucester and Kent Asylums each had around 250. Samuel Tuke argued in 1841 that numbers should not exceed 200, and that there was increasing danger of mismanagement and abuse if all aspects of the institution's management were kept within the hands of one man. By then, however, the point had been passed in several asylums where a superintendent could effectively keep in close contact with the patients, or be familiar with the essentials of their daily management. The processes of delegation and consequent bureaucratization were virtually unavoidable. The situation that Scull and others noted as having developed by the 1860s was already becoming all too evident well before the legislation of 1845 gave the seal of approval to the large county asylum.[28]

MEDICAL AND LAY MANAGEMENT: A FORUM FOR CONFLICT?

The identification of the real nature of power within the asylum system, of the sources of the power and of the premises upon which it was exercised, has become a preoccupation of some historians of the institution and of psychiatry. Theories of social control, of deviancy and of 'labelling' have been particularly influential following the critiques of continental writers such as Michel Foucault, Klaus Doerner and Robert Castel. Andrew Scull, in particular, has sought to build on their challenging perspective in his interpretation of the evidence on the development of asylumdom. His emphasis on the professionalization of asylum management, and particularly on the emerging hegemony of the medical profession, accords with an approach which places the asylum and its officers squarely within the apparatus of state and bourgeois control of deviancy. By this analysis, the alienists' sincerely proclaimed humanitarian concern for their patients rendered them unwitting participants in the process.[29]

Scull has managed to attract the anger, and even the fury, of some commentators, particularly psychiatrists offended by his perceived attacks on the achievements of their predecessors. Ultimately, though, their criticisms are probably of less moment than the challenges raised as a result of historical scholarship. In particular, recent work calls into question the pre-eminence of medical men in shaping both asylum affairs and wider administrative policy. Akihito Suzuki has shown the dominant role of a politically motivated Middlesex magistracy in shaping key aspects of policy in the Hanwell Asylum; a superintendent of the stature of (Sir) William Ellis was sacrificed largely for falling foul of magisterial aspirations. Peter Bartlett has also argued, in relation to the Leicestershire Asylum, that the power of the justices has been underestimated and that the medical men were a rather less important part of the asylum's administrative network. For the justices, it was important to retain responsibility for the commissioning and running of a county asylum, at a time when other sources of authority and prestige, like poor relief and highway management, were being removed.[30]

The exercise of control of the asylum, its policy and its daily management, was a complex process. The balances of power between justices and salaried officials, between laymen and medical men, and even between the different types of medical men, were invariably delicate. These balances were essentially determined locally, and reflected the local and county social and political scene, as well as the influence of interest groups or of powerful and determined individuals. Where the greatest conflicts occurred, as at Middlesex, Wakefield and Lincoln, these were in a context of either a wider political volatility in the area, or of clashes between the ambitions of influential local personalities. To attempt a more global analysis of power, control or hegemony in the pre-1845 asylum is probably to read too much into the available evidence.

The divisions of management responsibilities between justices or visitors, superintendent and physician, when effective, provided a system of checks and balances against the inappropriate or mistaken use of power by any of the parties. The divisions could also, at least in theory, produce a dynamic tension which led to progressive change and creativity in the asylum. In practice, however, the lack of clarity as to the boundaries of role and responsibility was more likely to lead to rivalry, conflict and soured relations, which only served to inhibit the effective functioning of the institution.

A powerful superintendent was always likely to be the focus of dispute with magistrates who took their management role seriously. For example, Samuel Hitch, who took up post at Gloucester in 1828, became increasingly assertive as he grew in experience. He periodically took issue with the visitors over inadequate facilities, and other areas of practice and policy. He generally, however, maintained good working relations with the successive chairmen, Reverend Charles Bathurst and Reverend Charles Crawley, by regular consultation and exchange of letters. Hitch was apparently prepared to put up with the imperious tone of Bathurst's letters and with Crawley's attempts to dominate most aspects of asylum affairs, provided they consulted him fully. Eventually, however, his professional ambition and his pursuit of high standards of practice brought him into increasing conflict with the visitors. His qualification as a physician in 1842 signalled a growing self-confidence. He and his wife (the matron) openly challenged the magistrates over issues of overcrowding and the poor conditions in the pauper quarters. Their frustrations contributed to their resignation in the summer of 1845, though Hitch continued uneasily as consulting physician for a further two years.[31]

A conscientious medical superintendent, with a humanitarian approach to patient care, might find himself in conflict with magistrates interested in the vigilant pursuit of economy. The Suffolk magistrates had demonstrated their intent to minimize initial outlay by adapting a disused workhouse rather than following neighbouring Norfolk in building a striking edifice. They sought to keep their charges as low as possible by restricting expenditure on staffing and provisions. The first governor, George Wallett, resigned after serious disagreements in September 1831. His successor, John Kirkman, had to contend with magistrates intent on reducing costs to the levels of the Norfolk Asylum, with its unusually meagre staffing and parsimonious dietary provision. When Suffolk Asylum began publishing annual reports in 1839, Kirkman used these to highlight the sparseness of his patients' diet, suggesting that this was a false economy, which hampered patients' recovery. He drew particularly unfavourable comparisons with what patients received elsewhere. He protested also about conditions, such as the cold stone floors in the basement rooms. His remonstrances did bring about some improvements, for his growing prestige (he too had obtained his MD in 1839) rendered it difficult for the magistrates to ignore him or to dispense with his services. Dr George Button of the Dorset Asylum also successfully confronted the visitors in 1844, on the issue of overcrowding, making outspoken representations about the ill-effects of contaminated air.[32]

Some of the most damaging asylum conflicts occurred where professional pride supervened in the overlapping roles of the house surgeon/superintendent and the physician. The lingering status differentials between physicians and surgeons, or surgeon-apothecaries, could lead to added complications. This proved the case at Lincoln, where three attached physicians served for a month at a time in rotation. Their authority was consolidated by the purchase of governorships. The most prominent and influential, Dr Charlesworth, immersed himself in all aspects of the asylum's affairs, bringing him into damaging conflict with the resentful first director, Thomas Fisher. The quarrel eventually flared into open public hostilities before Fisher was forced to resign in some disgrace. Subsequent house surgeons (the change of title was deliberate) were young, newly qualified men to whom Charlesworth could act as patron and mentor, like the celebrated Robert Gardiner Hill, appointed in 1835. The reforms in treatment methods instituted by Charlesworth and Hill brought fame to Lincoln Asylum. They also brought years of destructive conflict and factional in-fighting between the medical men associated with it.[33]

The eventful confrontations which occurred at the Wakefield Asylum comprised a series of role conflicts, involving magistrates, physicians and resident officers. They illustrated the possible consequences of the presence of several powerful men (and a resolute woman). The material for ignition was present from the asylum's inception. Godfrey Higgins, the single-minded and outspoken magistrate, led the movement to set up the asylum. He recruited William Ellis as director, a man with a strong belief in his own abilities and in his Christian mission to alleviate the suffering of the unfortunate. Ellis was joined by his wife Mildred as matron, who was to prove formidable in her own right. Two prominent and influential Wakefield physicians, Dr Richardson and Dr Caleb Crowther, who had offered their services gratis to further the great endeavour, formed another powerful element. Crowther, in particular, was a strong and determined character, unwilling to brook opposition and firm in his belief in the pre-eminence of the physician.[34]

The problems at Wakefield were essentially about authority and control, and began soon after the asylum opened in 1818. Ellis had clear ideas on how to run an asylum, and was fully supported by Higgins. Qualified as a surgeon and an apothecary, he quickly enhanced his status by securing a qualification as a physician, the first director of a public asylum to do so. His position was further strengthened by the magistrates' decision in July 1821 to revise the rules, reducing the duties and responsibilities of the two physicians and effectively giving Ellis 'the general responsibility of a Medical Superintendent'. The flamboyant Dr Crowther had already taken against Ellis, and regarded him as an upstart attempting to usurp the physicians' authority. A few months after the asylum opened, he had complained to the magistrates about a decision to allow Ellis to take on some private practice outside the asylum, arguing reasonably that this was contrary to the asylum's rules. Apart from the principle, he was also naturally concerned about the possible damage to his own custom. His protests resulted in the revocation of the arrangement, which increased the enmity between Crowther and both Higgins and Ellis.[35]

Matters became fraught as a consequence of a dispute which Crowther probably engineered. The background lay in an early arrangement that Crowther would be responsible for the male patients and Richardson for the females, and that every three years they might change over. Richardson withdrew after a few months and was succeeded by Dr Disney Alexander. Alexander developed a close working relationship with Mrs Ellis, the matron, who appreciated his sympathetic approach to the female patients, which accorded with her own gentle, maternal style. He became regarded by the patients as their 'friend and benefactor'. Mrs Ellis had already angered Crowther by unsuccessfully seeking to involve herself in the care of the male patients. He now attempted, in 1825, to invoke the original agreement, to exchange responsibilities with Dr Alexander, and to become physician to the females.[36]

The ambitious Crowther was evidently seeking case material for a book on mental disorder. For greater credibility, he needed to cite female as well as male cases. Mrs Ellis was horrified at the prospect of him taking over the female patients and working closely with her. She enlisted Alexander's support and threatened to resign. Crowther was outraged at the prospect of being thwarted by 'inferior officers' like Dr Ellis (the 'Apothecary') and his wife. He considered that Ellis wanted to be 'sole lord and master' over physicians and magistrates, and that the usurpation of power had to be resisted. Crowther demanded that Alexander accede to his wishes, threatening him with exposure and professional ostracism. Alexander went public to defend himself and to predict that irreparable damage would be caused by the sacrifice of Mrs Ellis. Ultimately, the destructive affair was resolved by two of the magistrates persuading Crowther to withdraw his claim in the best interests of the asylum.[37]

Crowther remained an embittered man, with a simmering resentment against the Ellises and Higgins. Relations between them continued uneasily until the final break in 1828. Following criticism by Higgins of his practice during a dysentery epidemic in the asylum, Crowther resigned. He sought to vindicate his position by a published attack on both Higgins and William Ellis, in which he characterized Ellis as an autocrat who had thwarted the legitimate rights of the physicians, and condemned Higgins and the other magistrates for having taken his part. Crowther continued to be a powerful and influential figure in Wakefield.[38]

Perhaps due partly to weariness from the conflict, as well as his personal ambition, William Ellis moved in early 1831 to become resident physician and superintendent of the new Middlesex Asylum at Hanwell. Higgins had strongly supported his candidature and recommended him to the Middlesex magistrates. As an experienced and highly regarded superintendent, taking over a showpiece institution under the auspices of magistrates inexperienced in asylum management, Ellis was in a strong position. They were prepared to delegate a great deal of responsibility to him. He, in turn, was able to consolidate his position by writing rules which gave no significant role to a visiting physician, and vesting all the real authority in the resident physician/superintendent.[39]

Ellis's move to Hanwell did not, however, shake off Crowther. Hostilities were renewed after Ellis (now *Sir* William) went into print in 1838 with his *Treatise on Insanity*, in which he attacked management arrangements at county asylums which left little discretionary power for the medical superintendent, 'nominally' the head of the establishment:

> One or two of the physicians residing in the neighbourhood, and who are expected to visit the patients once or twice a week, have in many of them, the entire discretion; the superintendent and matron having little more to do, than to carry their orders into execution.

The consequence of this, he argued, was a division of responsibility and ineffective management. Crowther could not let the veiled criticism pass, and responded in his own polemic. He turned his ire initially on the inadequacies of management by magistrates – jurisdiction by a 'Star Chamber' composed of 'a set of ignorant and irresponsible justices', totally unfit to govern asylums. He launched scurrilous personal attacks on the Ellises and on Dr Corsellis, the current superintendent at Wakefield, claiming that they were self-seeking, overpaid and incompetent. He repeated his earlier theme that the work of the director of a pauper asylum was of an 'inferior order', compared to the skill and responsibility of the physicians. The violence of Crowther's invective probably reduced the impact of his more valid arguments. In more reasoned vein, for example, he contended that the amalgamation of medical and management roles in one post meant too much work for one man, which, particularly in the cases of large asylums like Wakefield or Hanwell, was almost certainly true, as Samuel Tuke averred three years later.[40]

Ellis was no innocent party in the transactions. Crowther's characterization of him as seeking overall control of asylum affairs was not without truth. He had a strong belief in the correctness of his paternalist approach and in his therapeutic system built around the twin philosophies of the work ethic and religious devotion. Ultimately, his single-mindedness brought him into conflict with sections of the Middlesex magistrates. Increasingly he was viewed as the ally of those who sought to promote a rigid and inflexible economy. He came under growing criticism for the poor rations received by patients. With a change in the political dominance of the county magistracy, Ellis was sacrificed, despite his considerable reputation and the prestige associated with the grant of his knighthood.[41]

Relations between the key people involved in asylum management did not usually sink to such depths. The potential for tensions was, however, always present due to the nature of the divided and overlapping responsibilities of magistrates, superintendents and physicians. The locus of power and control was unclear, often deliberately so. It resided among status-ridden professionals and zealous or parsimonious amateurs. The care of the insane perhaps attracted certain personalities – the crusading, or the idiosyncratic, as well as those who had been unable to make their mark in more attractive branches of the medical profession. With these different and unpredictable elements, hegemony in the asylum was fluid. It was ultimately down to the strength of character or the charisma of the individual superintendent, physician or chairman of the visitors to determine where the balance of influence and control lay.

POLICY AND PRACTICE – MANAGEMENT IN ACTION

The operation of a large institution like an asylum was a complex enterprise. Professional and lay managers had to concern themselves with a range of matters other than the essentials of patient care and staff management. These included the maintenance of the building's fabric, control of its finances and interactions with other bodies such as parish officers, boards of guardians, local magistrates and central government. This section concentrates on some important particular aspects of asylum administration – admissions and discharges, financial management, and building development. Among the detail of practical decision-making and implementation, each of these areas had important connections with policy issues.

Admission and Discharge

County justices did not work to explicit admissions policies. They were faced with the need not only to reconcile the conflicting objectives of custody and cure, but also to ensure occupancy levels conducive to financial viability. The accumulation of a growing body of chronic patients was one consequence. Visitors, superintendents and medical officers, however, did not wish to accept the responsibility for this, with all its implications of failure of the asylum ideal. They responded by conducting a sustained campaign against parish overseers or boards of guardians who avoided expenditure, and their responsibilities, by keeping people out of the asylum until they were beyond the reach of effective medical intervention. They remonstrated in letters and in published annual reports, and cajoled and threatened in newspaper appeals.[42]

Some visitors did attempt to take more practical steps to alter, or postpone, the asylum's fate. The Gloucester visitors expressed an intention from the beginning to be selective, by rejecting those cases that were deemed hopeless and not dangerous. At Nottingham also there were early attempts to refuse people who appeared harmless and incurable. As the asylums filled up, justices and visitors became more prepared to exercise their discretion in order to prevent further overcrowding. By 1827, with more applicants than they could receive, the Nottingham visitors were proclaiming and practising a policy of selection. At Gloucester in January 1839 Charles Bathurst, the chairman of the visitors, suggested to Samuel Hitch that the time had come to impose restrictions:

> There must be a point at which we should say, to admit to be crowded on floors, to admit to be disturbed by unseparated noisy cases, is not to admit to cure. The point at which we might in strictness say we are full, is arrived at already. For if the having a separate cell is not the limit, where is one to be found?

At Wakefield also, from the late 1830s onwards, with a major problem of overcrowding, there was little alternative but to refuse large numbers of admissions.[43]

Although the visitors' powers to select the people admitted were limited, they could attempt to influence the manner of admission. Cases were not infrequent of people arriving in a deteriorated physical condition, as a result of their treatment before or during the journey. Visitors and superintendents would use the opportunity to attack referring agencies for the unenlightened and parsimonious policies which such episodes illustrated. The Cornwall Asylum visitors in May 1825 tackled the magistrates of Trigg about the case of John Tucker, brought in with two black eyes and 'in a most offensively dirty state', by an overseer and an attendant who were both drunk. There had been improper delay in sending Tucker 'till he was in a decaying state of bodily health'; he died within a few days of admission. Another case in 1845 attracted the attention of *The Times;* an inquest on a man who died at Cornwall Asylum was highly critical of the Falmouth guardians owing to the neglect and the ill-treatment he had suffered, first during a prolonged stay in the Penryn workhouse and then en route to the asylum.[44]

Visiting justices had a much clearer role in the implementation of discharge, emanating from the Act of 1808. At some asylums, particularly in the early years when justices were inclined to take their responsibilities more seriously, they involved themselves directly by interviewing patients put forward for discharge. At the Norfolk Asylum, patients were called before the committee and addressed by the chairman, who would advise them to 'be circumspect in their conduct so as to guard against a return of their disorder'. More generally, though, visitors would act on the recommendation of the medical officers as to whether the person had recovered sufficiently, whether they had ceased to be dangerous or whether they were an 'improper object' for detention.[45]

The amending legislation of 1811 enabled justices, based on medical recommendation, to discharge those no longer considered 'fit objects', and to replace them with the 'fittest objects for immediate Reception'. They could use these powers to influence the composition of the asylum population. When there was pressure on beds, or a greater emphasis on curability and turnover, space might be cleared for those in more pressing need by discharge of the harmless and incurable back to their parishes or union workhouses. The Stafford Asylum managers, for example, sought the steady removal of significant numbers from 1839 onwards, culminating in requests to unions to remove 21 'unfit objects' in February 1842. William Ellis reported sixteen such people discharged from Wakefield during 1828, to make room for more urgent cases. His successor C.C. Corsellis supported the justices in a similar policy; during 1843, 21 'harmless and idiotic' people were removed to their parishes, to be replaced by others who were dangerous and more amenable to treatment. The governors at Lincoln adopted similar measures, though a concerted attempt to weed out idiots and incurables, in September 1838, foundered when the physicians would not identify more than three as suitable for discharge, fearing the consequences of replacing them with more dangerous patients.[46]

Asylum managers' measures to alleviate overcrowding or free space for more suitable candidates were not always welcomed. Attempts to accelerate discharges were sometimes resisted by parish officials, guardians or relatives, unwilling to accept responsibility for people who, though deemed 'harmless and incurable', might still be awkward and difficult to manage. Disputes could arise, as between Cirencester Union and Gloucester Asylum in January 1840, regarding a man called Hughes. His discharge was sought by Samuel Hitch, but the clerk to the union retorted that there was 'no possibility' of accommodating him in the workhouse, that he was as bad as any of their other patients in the asylum and that if he were sent out they would have 'no Alteration' but to place him in another asylum. In a subscription asylum, the governors had more leeway to enforce their views. Thus when, in November 1830, the parish of Long Sutton sought to stall the discharge from Lincoln Asylum of Robert Bratt, regarded by the governors as 'cured', the decision was to send him home 'forthwith' accompanied by a keeper. In 1844 the Lincoln governors had a series of disputes with the Boston Union, who complained both about premature discharges and patients being retained too long; the result was the peremptory removal by the guardians of all Boston patients from Lincoln to Haydock Lodge private asylum.[47]

Most frequently, however, disputes arose because of the desire of parishes or guardians to remove people prematurely, to save on the expenses. George Button of Dorset Asylum, in 1843, deprecated that removal was misguidedly sought 'on the first appearance of recovery', which could lead to a speedy relapse and so 'ultimately increase the dreaded expense'. Some visitors used their authority to withhold discharge if they considered the person not to be in a fit state, or if the facilities in the community for their care were inadequate. In the early years of the Norfolk Asylum, the visitors were scrupulous in scrutinizing requests for discharge, motivated partly by a desire to keep occupancy rates up. In November 1815 applications were refused from two parishes for the discharge of female patients, despite offers by both husbands to provide a woman to take care of them. In one case, the committee accepted the medical officers' view that 'she was one of the worst patients in the house and if discharged would most probably destroy herself'; in the other case they did not consider the man's earnings sufficient. In March 1840 they would not discharge two patients unless the relatives entered into an agreement that 'every precaution will be taken to prevent self destruction and a proper person be constantly in attendance'. The Nottingham visitors in September 1842, following medical advice, refused to discharge John Ogden to Matlock Union; they considered him not fit to be at large or in a workhouse, 'his temper being irascible & when excited he becomes dangerous'. Visitors were clearly prepared to take their responsibilities seriously.[48]

Financial Management

The control of the institution's finances, and the need to ensure solvency, continually preoccupied magistrates, visitors, governors and salaried officers. Essential expenditure on staffing, heating, maintenance and provisions had to be covered by income received from parishes or guardians, from voluntary subscribers, or from patients or their relatives. A great deal of time and effort was spent in considering and setting the weekly charges. The aim usually became to fix them at as low a level as possible, in order to encourage referral of appropriate patients, and to dissuade parochial authorities from keeping insane people in the workhouse. There was also a clear intent to compete on price with private asylums, based on the principle that public asylum care was motivated by humanitarian considerations and inherently more desirable.

At Nottingham Asylum, the weekly charges for county paupers were set in 1812 at 9 shillings. This was comparatively low; in most asylums the initial charges were higher, to cover the costs consequent on a full staff establishment dealing with relatively low numbers of patients. At Norfolk Asylum, the charges were first set at 14 shillings, and the same at Cornwall Asylum when it opened in 1820. The careful West Riding magistrates fixed their charges at 10s.6d in 1818, still seen as high by most parishes. The committee of the new Suffolk Asylum publicly apologized for the necessity to charge 12s.2d per week in January 1829, promising to reduce the rate as soon as possible. These high levels of maintenance payments deterred already reluctant parish officials from sending their lunatics to the asylum, which served to keep occupancy low and restricted the scope for reductions in price.[49]

With maintenance costs in the workhouse several shillings less, asylum managers were forced to review charging policies. Norfolk Asylum's rates were quickly slashed to 9 shillings, and then steadily reduced over subsequent months and years, until in March 1835 they were down to 4s.9d; in 1844, with them standing at 5s.9d, the justices prided themselves on having consistently had the lowest charges in the country. A similar process was repeated elsewhere. The rates at Suffolk Asylum more than halved within two years of opening, down to 5s.3d; they fell as low as 4s.8d in 1835, and then continued to hover between 5 and 7 shillings. The Cheshire Asylum's rates, initially 10 shillings in 1829, fell as low as 4 shillings in 1836. Visiting justices competed to demonstrate the attractiveness of their institutions to hard-pressed parishes. William Ellis at Wakefield, who placed great store on his economical management, worked for a steady reduction in the maintenance charges. The initial 10s.6d was reduced to 9 shillings in 1821, 8 in 1822, 7 in 1824, 6s.6d in 1828, and 6 shillings in 1830. His successor C.C. Corsellis managed to reduce the charge to 5s.6d in 1843. Ellis himself relentlessly pursued a similar policy at Hanwell, gradually lowering the charges from 9 shillings down to 5s.3d.[50]

Charging arrangements could be rather more complicated than merely setting a rate for parish paupers. In the mixed-class asylums, like Nottingham, Stafford and Gloucester, and in the subscription asylums, rates had also to be set for private and charity patients. Provision for the latter, the impoverished non-pauper, whose family could not afford private madhouse care, was considered a primary function of the asylum. As the committee of the Stafford Asylum told the public in September 1818, people with insufficient means to avail themselves of its benefit, and who were ineligible for parish support, were 'objects of peculiar pity', who might remain a 'hopeless burden' on their families. Visitors or governors sought, as far as possible, to assist this deserving group. The charges for charity patients varied considerably, partly according to the number and generosity of contributors to the subscription fund. Where the fund was sufficient, they could exercise discretion in charging according to the means of the patient and his family. Charity patients might pay amounts similar to paupers, or perhaps even lower, whilst receiving standards of food and accommodation comparable to private patients.[51]

The admission of private patients brought public asylums into direct competition with the private sector. Asylum managers, arguing that the mentally disordered should not be subjected to the depredations of private madhouse keepers, sought to compete on price as well as on standards of care and comfort. 'First-class' patients were usually charged on a sliding scale, according to their means and the facilities offered. At Stafford in 1819, the first-class patients were divided into three ranks; those of the 'inferior rank' were to pay at least 12 shillings per week, the 'middling ranks' no less than £1, and the 'highest rank' from 2 guineas upwards. The arrangements were refined the following year: if wine was required, the charges were £3 per week; for a personal servant, with additional accommodation, they rose to 3½ guineas. By October 1820, the asylum contained eighteen first-class patients; by October 1829 there were 39, with 24 in the second rank and eight in the first. In similar arrangements at Gloucester, first-class patients paid from 1½ to 2 guineas; for separate rooms and a personal servant, they paid 2½ to 3 guineas. The most lavish arrangements were at the Radcliffe subscription asylum, where 'parlour patients' were offered the 'shield of good faith, honourable feeling and christian compassion', as compared to the 'ill usage' of private madhouses, for up to 4 guineas per week. The expressed intention was always to use the profits earned from private patients to subsidize the charity patients.[52]

A legislative amendment in 1815 allowed asylums funded entirely by the county to accept private patients, if they had spare capacity. Several took up the option, including Bedford, Lancaster, Norfolk and Suffolk. The Bedford visitors, so alarmed at the costs of low occupancy, had agreed to admit up to ten in October 1812, three years before legal clearance. Similar concerns actuated the Norfolk magistrates in December 1815; they advertised for private patients in the county press, offering to admit them at 13s.6d per week, a rate scarcely more than the pauper charge, though discretionary charges were later introduced. They were referred to as 'boarders', a description also adopted at the Suffolk Asylum, where there were fourteen in April 1834. The Cheshire Asylum, designed for 90 patients, was constructed to provide for twenty of the better classes, favouring them with comfortable accommodation at the front of the house and the best airing grounds. The aim in admitting private patients to county-funded asylums was hardly altruistic, but was to earn additional income and subsidize the costs of pauper patients. As the demand for space for pauper lunatics spiralled in the 1830s, the numbers of private patients had to be run down and the income forfeited.[53]

The admission of private patients was not the only aspect of the county asylums' growing participation in the 'trade in lunacy'. They also actively attracted custom from adjoining counties without a public asylum. Naturally, paupers from another county's parishes were received at higher rates, though these were still cheaper than the charges that would have been incurred at alternative private asylums. Bedford agreed to accept people from neighbouring counties in 1815 at 16 shillings, about a third more than for their own county paupers. The ever-entrepreneurial Norfolk magistrates advertised in 1816 in the Ipswich and Bury St Edmunds newspapers for Suffolk paupers. The Cornwall Asylum managers recognized the potential market in Devon; in 1828 they negotiated discount rates with the Devonport guardians, charging them 12s.6d a week each for five to ten patients, 11s.6d for eleven to fifteen and 10s.6d for sixteen or more. The expense of placement at Bodmin did not go unnoticed in west Devon, and by the late 1830s, the more stringent financial housekeeping of its new poor law unions led to a decline in referrals, as more lunatics were accommodated in special wards in the workhouses.[54]

The Stafford Asylum visitors were particularly industrious, attracting clientele from across the Midlands. In late 1818, two months after opening, the visitors agreed to admit up to 30 paupers from Birmingham, at 12 shillings per week for curables, and 10 shillings a week for incurables, rates only fractionally higher than those for county paupers. In July 1821, an agreement was made to accept Worcestershire paupers. By 1825, out-county paupers were paying 20 shillings, as compared to 9 shillings for Staffordshire's. A significant commercial arrangement in July 1828 transferred 37 Birmingham paupers from the private Droitwich Asylum. Stafford now had pauper patients from Warwickshire, Worcestershire, Shropshire, Leicestershire, Cheshire and Derbyshire, as well as private and charitable patients. Of its 187 patients in early April 1829, only 69 were Staffordshire paupers. However, economic incentive eventually had to give way to demographics; by 1833 the press of demand for accommodation for county paupers was restricting entry of those from elsewhere.[55]

On occasions, the commercial interests of the asylum might conflict with the philanthropic ideal. The Suffolk visitors ascertained in 1838 that their charges for 'boarders' were comparatively low and resolved to raise the weekly minimum to 20 shillings. The Bury St Edmunds magistrates protested that 'small shopkeepers and mechanics. . .just above the description of paupers', whose income might only be 25 shillings or less, were now effectively excluded. The visitors made a volte-face, restoring preferential rates for these classes, and granting them precedence over paupers from outside the county or from boroughs that did not contribute to the county rate, who were all now to be excluded from the asylum due to overcrowding.[56]

The usual corollary to admissions policies that aimed to maximize income was a pursuit of strict economy in the asylum's expenditure. Nowhere was this approach more strenuously adopted than in East Anglia, where the visitors of the Norfolk and Suffolk Asylums vied with one another in pursuit of the lowest costs. The Norfolk justices, having constructed an expensive building, went to the other extreme with minimal staffing, low wages and salaries, and a poor standard and quantity of diet for the patients. The Suffolk justices, concerned in 1835 that their expenses per head at Melton were higher than Norfolk's at Thorpe, ignored protests and attempted to match their neighbour by reducing the numbers and wages of staff, as well as the already meagre bread and meat rations of the patients (except for the 'boarders'). John Kirkman, the superintendent, successfully agitated for some amelioration of the policy, but at the Thorpe Asylum a harsh regime based on financial stringency was perpetuated, culminating eventually in the public exposure of serious abuses.[57]

The performance of superintendents tended to be largely judged by their success in controlling expenditure. One of the most effective was William Ellis, whose 'most strenuous exertions' to limit all areas of spending brought savings which facilitated ever lower charges at Wakefield, and later at Hanwell. In 1825, he told the Yorkshire magistrates what they wanted to hear regarding the cautious use of ratepayers' money:

> The Institution being intended for the reception of none but Paupers, the strictest economy consistent with the welfare of the Patients, has been practised, in every department.[58]

Ellis's implicit acceptance that pauperism meant an entitlement only to basic standards highlighted one of the essential dilemmas in public asylum provision. Whilst the pursuit of the curative and the philanthropic ideals was seen to merit a generous material provision, to counteract the deprivation which many patients had suffered prior to admission, there was no scope for undue lavishness toward the pauper lunatic.

Stringent financial management brought a risk of accusations of parsimony at the expense of vulnerable people. Claims about the achievement of economy would have to be offset by suitable declarations as to comfort and consideration toward the patients. The dilemma was clear to the Kent justices in 1839, when they responded to complaints about high charges. Their 'first consideration' was that the asylum should be well conducted and the 'suffering inmates' properly treated, but at the same time they were 'very desirous that a well regulated economy should be observed throughout every department'. In 1830, the Suffolk visitors had reported to Quarter Sessions their 'unqualified approbation' of the asylum's management, and in particular 'the strict attention paid to the comfort of the Patients with at the same time the utmost regard to economy in every department of expenditure'. In October 1821, the Nottingham Asylum governors expressed their approval of the 'kindness, attention, and economy' shown by the director and the matron in the performance of their duties. A similar mixture of principles informed them in extending the asylum in 1829, upon a plan combining 'every possible comfort to the inmates, with a regard to the strictest economy'. In the event, economy prevailed, for the new wings remained unopened for almost five years because of an inability or unwillingness to pay for the necessary additional staff.[59]

Building Development

The decision to extend the asylum, followed by the planning and completion of the work, was usually the most significant project that managers would have to undertake. All the first generation of county asylums, like the earlier subscription asylums, outgrew their original buildings and had to be enlarged, some of them several times, before 1850. With an absence of any forward planning, backed by a reluctance to undertake further expensive capital investment, justices and governors would eventually be faced with a critical overcrowding problem which required a prompt response. Where possible they would attempt to deal with it by relatively inexpensive expedient measures, by internal rearrangements and by minor building alterations. It was only when such measures had been exhausted that money was found for construction ventures.

The onset of the problem of lack of capacity to meet a growing demand was initially met by pragmatic means. At the Norfolk Asylum in 1821 the visitors first converted a small hospital ward into sleeping rooms for eight of the 'quietest male patients' (at a cost of only £5), and then adapted the waiting room and the physicians' room to receive more patients. At the Suffolk Asylum, in 1832, space for eight 'dirty patients' was created by converting two bathrooms. At Gloucester, in the same year, Samuel Hitch was concerned at the excessive number of water closets; the visitors welcomed the opportunity to convert some into four additional sleeping rooms for paupers. Elsewhere, other expedients were adopted. At Wakefield in 1835, where earlier major extensions had proved insufficient, the hospital, some staff rooms and the basement were requisitioned for patients. A series of measures were taken in the 1830s and the early 1840s at Stafford, with the infirmaries being taken over, day rooms being adapted as sleeping rooms and beds being placed in the gallery corridors. At Lancaster, the drastic step was taken in 1841 of converting the chapel into a dormitory, leaving the religious services to be held in a shed. Measures like these could only temporarily relieve the pressure until some more substantial steps were taken.[60]

An inherent resistance to expenditure led to prevarication over proposals to extend overcrowded buildings or to build new ones. In the mixed-class asylums, the funding of capital projects was further complicated by attempts to share out fairly the potential liabilities of county and subscribers. Convoluted negotiations might be required, producing delay and inaction. At Gloucester, the whole issue of the respective entitlements and responsibilities of subscribers and justices became the subject of a long-running, at times acrimonious, dispute which hampered the asylum's proper development. The difficulties emanated partly from the tensions involved in catering for pauper, charity and private patients within the same institution. At Stafford, the means to resolve both the social class problem and the overcrowding problem were finally agreed in 1847; a new asylum was to be built for the first- and second-class patients, freeing up all of the original asylum for the growing numbers of paupers. Coton Hill Asylum eventually opened in 1854. The subscribers at Nottingham followed suit in 1855, removing their private and charitable patients to a new asylum, and the Gloucester disputes were similarly resolved not long afterwards.[61]

In each asylum the time eventually came when opportunistic adjustments to the building were inadequate and major work had to be undertaken. The Lancashire justices, faced with the consequences of a burgeoning industrial population, bowed to the inevitable relatively quickly. The original building at Lancaster, opened in 1816, provided for 250 patients; as early as 1825, they added an extension for a further 50. The Nottingham governors also took action in the 1820s. In 1825 they added five new cells for 'turbulent' patients, and then made a number of internal rearrangements and changes in classification to provide more capacity. In 1829 they built two new wings for twenty incurables of each sex, which eventually opened in 1834. At neighbouring Lincoln, in 1828, over £1500 raised from subscribers was spent on extensions and a complete internal reorganization, to provide for a further twenty patients, making a total capacity of 78. At Gloucester, where additional accommodation was badly needed by 1830, plans were drafted but the justices and subscribers were unable to raise the money. Fortuitously, a major fire at the asylum in May 1832 produced enough insurance money to provide extra room for paupers and 'noisy' patients.[62]

Other counties managed to hold out until the 1840s. Cornwall, also constrained by the need for justices and subscribers to work jointly, provided a substantial new building in early 1844. A chronic and desperate overcrowding situation at Dorset's asylum forced the prevaricating justices to agree to construct two new wings in 1844. With their original debt paid off, the equally reluctant Suffolk justices finally succumbed to the pleadings of John Kirkman in 1843, and agreed to spend £5000 on new wings to accommodate 30 patients of each sex. They could console themselves with Kirkman's observation that the buildings 'could not lay much claim to an imposing appearance' but met the basic needs of pauper patients as economically as was feasible.[63]

In the more populous counties, the justices had to accept reality and mount programmes of periodic expansion of their asylums. At Lancaster in 1841, large new wings, each for 70 patients, were added to earlier extensions; when completed they were already insufficient. At Wakefield, the first new wing was added in 1830, accommodating an additional 70 patients. A further large building was added in 1841; its formal opening in July was marked by a tea-party attended by 300 patients, 'many of whom expressed a strong desire to be in the list of occupants', after being conducted round 'the various apartments'. The already very large Hanwell Asylum repeatedly outgrew itself after its opening in 1831, and extensions had to be added every few years. The Kent Asylum, near Maidstone, had to be extended within three years of its opening in 1833. Originally designed for 168 people, new sections were added in 1836, 1837, 1842, 1845, and 1847, by which time its capacity had reached 443.[64]

There was by now a recognition that the demand for public asylum accommodation was growing inexorably, and could be met only by more institutions or by expansion of those already in existence. As John Kirkman commented wryly in 1838, it was a 'melancholy truth' that 'Asylums are no sooner built than it is found necessary to enlarge them, and no sooner are they enlarged than they are filled.' The phenomenon of expansion by successively adding wings had become established. In the process, the principle that asylums should be relatively small in order to maximize therapeutic effectiveness was abandoned. William Ellis, when young and idealistic in 1815, argued that 100 to 120 should be the maximum number of patients, to ensure proper attendance to individual cases. The Wakefield Asylum, based on his mentor Samuel Tuke's design notes, was built to accommodate 150. Yet, under Ellis's superintendence, principle was soon sacrificed to expediency; by December 1823, there were 231 patients, and Ellis was saying that the building could reasonably accept up to 250. Wakefield's expansion continued, to the evident despair of Samuel Tuke, who re-stated his conviction in 1841 that the maximum number should be 200. By the time Ellis moved to Hanwell, he had clearly jettisoned ideas of the desirability of small-scale asylums, and went on to preside over its steady expansion toward massive proportions.[65]

Humanitarian superintendents (and visitors) were caught in a predicament. Without funds to build a second asylum, the alternatives were to refuse admission to those who needed it or who might be susceptible to 'cure', to condone overcrowding, or to extend the building. John Kirkman faced the predicament at Suffolk in the 1840s. Whilst stating a view that 250 was the most an asylum should hold, he pressed for new buildings to take the numbers higher, in order to reduce severe overcrowding. Lord Ashley and the Metropolitan Commissioners in Lunacy in 1844 were perturbed at the situation in the larger asylums. They argued that no asylum for curable lunatics should contain more than 250 patients, with perhaps 200 being the largest number that could be beneficially managed. They were critical of the situation in Kent, Surrey, the West Riding, Lancashire and particularly Middlesex, where numbers had gone far beyond the optimum. Commissioners, however, could only exhort. Across the country, the exigencies of the situation, and fear of the cost implications of the original principle, led to the development of a rationale for asylum growth. What had earlier been resisted was now becoming accepted policy.[66]

By 1844, most of the asylums had more than doubled in size since their opening (see Table 1). By the very nature of these changes in size and scale of operation, the asylums had become quite different institutions from what their projectors had envisaged. The whole management task had significantly altered, and was now concerned mainly with the logistics and practicalities of the organization of a large aggregation of incapacitated and highly dependent people. The lay gentlemen of the visitors and governors, who had undertaken their task for a range of reasons connected with patronage, duty, status and philanthropy, found themselves increasingly detached from the realities of the routine management of the growing numbers of patients within the institution. Inevitably, the professional medical managers, people like John Conolly, Samuel Hitch and John Kirkman, were able to step in and consolidate their positions within a developing bureaucracy. They attained a growing dominance within the management structure, utilizing their perceived medical expertise to buttress their administrative powers.

Table 1 Growth in size of county asylums, 1812–1845[67]

Asylum	*Year of opening*	*Initial capacity*	*Numbers in 1844**	*Numbers in 1845***
Nottingham	1812	80	125	206
Bedford	1812	40	139	
Norfolk	1814	80	164	182
Lancaster	1816	250	600	
Stafford	1818	120	243	
West Riding	1818	150	432	
Cornwall	1820	112	133	
Gloucester	1823	110	257	273
Chester	1828	90	164	
Suffolk	1829	130	206	238
Middlesex	1831	600	975	
Dorset	1832	60	153	
Kent	1833	168	249	443***

* The numbers for 1844 are taken from figures published in the *Report of the Metropolitan Commissioners in Lunacy*. In some instances these appear to understate patient numbers, notably for the Nottingham Asylum.

** The numbers for 1845 have been extracted from local sources.

*** This figure relates to 1846–7.

The context for medical ascendancy was the new approach to the treatment of mental disorder which accompanied the 'non-restraint' movement of the late 1830s and 1840s. Although the 'moral management' methods emanating from the York Retreat had not been widely influential in the early county asylums, there was a profound change in the wake of the developments at the Lincoln and Hanwell Asylums. Their example spread quickly throughout the public asylum network. The revolution in patient management involved considerably more than the removal of coercion. It brought with it new methods of organization of activities within the institution, different types of relationship between staff and patient and a significant change in the role of keepers or attendants. The role of the medical superintendents became paramount. The new system appeared to offer the promise of a curative resurgence, by means largely of organization and management, and medical superintendents were the only men who could be trusted by justices or governors to have sufficient expertise to implement it. As medical men adopted this new incarnation of 'moral management' and incorporated it into their treatment armoury, so their position within asylumdom became unassailable.[68]

NOTES

1 *Report of the Metropolitan Commissioners in Lunacy to the Lord Chancellor* (1844), pp. 9, 189 – in addition to the purpose-designed county asylums, workhouse facilities in Hull and Bristol had been declared county asylums under special Acts of Parliament; J. Hemingway, *History of the City of Chester* (Chester, 1831), pp. 226–8; Dorset County Record Office (DCRO), Dorset Quarter Sessions records, Lunatic Asylums, Forston House, (3), 15 July 1828; A. Foss and K. Trick, *St Andrew's Hospital, Northampton: The First One Hundred and Fifty Years (1838–1988)* (Cambridge, 1989).

2 DCRO, Forston House, 1(a), 2; Suffolk County Record Office (SuCRO), Acc 2697, 10 April, 20 October 1826.

3 Lincoln Local Studies Library (LLSL), 'Rules for the Lunatic Asylum at Lincoln' (Lincoln, 1819), p. 3; B. Parry-Jones, *The Warneford Hospital, Oxford, 1826–1976* (Oxford, 1976), p. 7.

4 48 Geo. III, Cap. 96, Sections II, VI, XXIV, XXV.

5 Nottinghamshire County Record Office/Nottinghamshire Archives (NCRO), SO/HO/1/1/1, hand-bill dated 4 October 1810; J.T. Becher, *Resolutions Concerning the Intended General Lunatic Asylum Near Nottingham* (Newark, 1810), p. 9; Staffordshire County Record Office (SCRO), D550/1, 1812, p. 1; Gloucester Reference Library (GRL), J7.26, 'Rules and Regulations for the Government of the General Lunatic Asylum of the County and City of Gloucester' (1823), Preface; Gloucestershire County Record Office (GCRO), HO22/26/9, pamphlet, 'Gloucester Lunatic Asylum', 7 January 1840.

6 F.M.L. Thompson, *English Landed Society in the Eighteenth Century* (London, 1963), pp. 110–11, 287–8; A.H. Doyle, *Clergy of the Church of England as Justices of the Peace, 1750–1850* (University of Birmingham, MA thesis, 1986), pp. 45, 134; NCRO, SO/HO/1/2/1, 4 October 1810; SCRO, D550/1, p. 3; W. White, *History, Gazetteer, and Directory of Staffordshire* (Sheffield, 1834), p. 136; GCRO, HO22/1/1, HO22/3/1–2; Lincolnshire Archives Office (LAO), LAWN 1/1/2–4. For Lord Yarborough's role at a crisis in the affairs of the Lincoln Asylum, see *Proceedings of the Quarterly Board of the Lincoln Lunatic Asylum, Held on October 13, 1830* (Lincoln, 1830 – copy in Cambridge University Library, Hunter Collection).

7 Godfrey Higgins, *Rules for the Management of the Pauper Lunatic Asylum for the West Riding of the County of York, Erected at Wakefield* (Wakefield, 1821), p. 26; GRL, Gloucester Asylum, Rules and Regulations, p. 8; Nottinghamshire County Asylum, *Articles of Union for the General Lunatic Asylum Near Nottingham with the By-Laws, Rules, Orders and Regulations* (1825), pp. 28–32; SuCRO, B106/10/4.2, 'Rules and Regulations for the Government of the Pauper Lunatic Asylum Erected at Melton, near Woodbridge, for the County of Suffolk' (Bury, 1828), p. 3; DCRO, 'Rules and Regulations for the Management of the Pauper Lunatic Asylum for the County of Dorset' (Dorchester, 1833), p. 3.

8 GRL, Gloucester Asylum, Rules and Regulations, p. 8; Nottingham Asylum, *By-Laws, Rules, Orders and Regulations*, pp. 32–4; SuCRO, Suffolk Asylum, Rules and Regulations, p. 5; SCRO, D550/2–6. GCRO, HO22/3/1–2; NCRO, SO/HO/1/3/2–3. The Rules of the Dorset Asylum (found in DCRO) make no mention of a house committee. Rules do not appear to have been published for the Norfolk and Cornwall Asylums; there are no other records to indicate the existence of a house committee.

9 LLSL, Lincoln Asylum, Rules, pp. 4–5. For Charlesworth, see chapter 8.

10 NCRO, SO/HO/1/2/1, 12 December 1810; GCRO, HO22/1/1, 4 April 1823; Nottingham Asylum, *By-Laws, Rules, Orders and Regulations*, Preface; G. Higgins, *Rules for Management of the Pauper Lunatic Asylum for the West Riding of the County of York, Erected at Wakefield* (Wakefield, 1821); Stanley Royd Hospital, 'Order Book – Pauper Lunatic Asylum, 1814–27', 15 September 1817; SuCRO, Acc 2697, 11, 25 January, 31 March, 25 August 1828.

11 Nottingham Asylum, *By-Laws, Rules, Orders and Regulations*; GRL, Gloucester Asylum, Rules and Regulations; Higgins, *Rules of the Pauper Lunatic Asylum for the West Riding*; SuCRO, Suffolk Asylum, Rules and Regulations, pp. 12–17; DCRO, Dorset Asylum, Rules and Regulations, pp. 18–22.

12 LLSL, Lincoln Asylum, Rules (1819); *Rules of the Lincoln Lunatic Asylum* (Lincoln, 1832).

13 For Dr Crowther and Dr Alexander, see H. Marland, *Medicine and Industrial Society in Wakefield and Huddersfield, 1780–1870* (Cambridge, 1987), pp. 125, 169–70, 262, 292–3, 308, 320–1, 351–5; Stanley Royd Hospital, Order Book –

Pauper Lunatic Asylum, 2 November 1814, Diary of Dr Gettings – Transcript of extracts from Minutes of Visitors, October 1829; LAO, LAWN 1/1/1, 4 March 1822. At Gloucester Asylum, the physician was paid a salary of £100 per annum. He received between 2 and 5 guineas on admission of every private patient, repeated annually (GRL, Rules, p. 9).

14 Nottingham Asylum, *By-Laws, Rules, Orders and Regulations*, pp. 43–8; GRL, Gloucester Asylum, Rules and Regulations, pp. 9–11; Higgins, *Rules of the Pauper Lunatic Asylum for the West Riding*, pp. 27–8; LLSL, Lincoln Asylum, Rules (1819), p. 11. At Cheshire Asylum, the unusual power of Dr Llewelyn Jones was expressed in the dual title of 'physician and director' – British Parliamentary Papers (BPP) 1836, vol. XLI, *County Lunatic Asylums, Returns*, p. 5.

15 Lancaster Public Library (LPL), MS 34, 21 May 1836; Warneford Hospital Archives, W.P. 68(x), *Rules and Orders of the Radcliffe Asylum* (1836), p. 14; A. Scull, *The Most Solitary of Afflictions: Madness and Society in Britain, 1700–1900* (London, 1993), chapter 4; A. Scull, C. Mackenzie and N. Hervey, *Masters of Bedlam: The Transformation of the Mad-Doctoring Trade* (Princeton, 1996), chapter 1. At Lincoln Asylum, the title Director was abandoned in 1832 in favour of that of 'House Surgeon', in an apparent move to lessen the power of the post – see L.D. Smith, 'The "Great Experiment": The Place of Lincoln in the History of Psychiatry', p. 57, in *Lincolnshire History and Archaeology*, vol. XXX (1995), pp. 55–62. At Norfolk Asylum, the Governor was also frequently referred to as the 'Master'.

16 Nottingham Asylum, *By-laws, Rules, Orders and Regulations*, pp. 51–5; GRL, Gloucester Asylum, Rules and Regulations, pp. 11–15; Higgins, *Rules of the Pauper Lunatic Asylum for the West Riding*, pp. 5–10; SuCRO, Suffolk Asylum, Rules and Regulations, pp. 7–10; DCRO, Dorset Asylum, Rules and Regulations, pp. 7–12; LLSL, Lincoln Asylum, Rules (1819), pp. 12–13.

17 Ibid.; I. Waddington, *The Medical Profession in the Industrial Revolution* (Dublin, 1984), pp. 1–8, 20–1; I. Loudon, *Medical Care and the General Practitioner*, 1750–1850 (Oxford, 1986), pp. 19–27. Surgeons were appointed to the posts at the asylums for Nottinghamshire, Lancashire, Staffordshire, Cornwall, Gloucestershire, Suffolk and Dorset. Only at Wakefield was a physician initially appointed as superintendent. The rather complex arrangements at Chester were illustrated by the presence of an 'apothecary and superintendent', who was clearly subordinate to the 'physician and director' (BPP 1836, vol. XLI, *County Lunatic Asylums, Returns*, p. 5.)

18 B. Cashman, *A Proper House: Bedford Lunatic Asylum, 1812–1860* (North Bedfordshire Health Authority, 1992), chapter 3; DCRO, Dorset Asylum, Rules and Regulations, p. 7; DCRO, Forston House (3), 13 October 1840.

19 C.T. Andrews, *The Dark Awakening: A History of St Lawrence's Hospital Bodmin* (Bodmin, 1978), pp. 32–4, 47; Cornwall County Record Office (CCRO), DDX 97/1, 16 November 1818, 11 October 1819, 1 February 1820, 9 April 1822, 31 August 1824. There were precedents for contracting out the running of public asylums – at Newcastle in the eighteenth century, and at

Hereford in 1802 (see R. Porter, *Mind-Forg'd Manacles: A History of Madness in England from the Restoration to the Regency* (Cambridge, 1987), pp. 132, 134, and L.D. Smith, 'The Pauper Lunatic Problem in the West Midlands, 1815–1850', p. 102, in *Midland History*, vol. XXI (1996), pp. 101–18.

20 Nottingham Asylum, *By-laws, Rules, Orders and Regulations*, p. 57; GRL, Gloucester Asylum, Rules and Regulations, p. 17; Higgins, *Rules of the Pauper Lunatic Asylum for the West Riding*, pp. 10–12; LLSL, Lincoln Asylum, Rules (1819), pp. 13–14.

21 *Lonsdale Magazine*, February 1821, pp. 45–6; J. Conolly, *The Construction and Government of Lunatic Asylums* (London, 1847), pp. 140–2.

22 Cashman, *A Proper House*, pp. 18–19; Norfolk County Record Office (NkCRO), SAH 2, 28 April 1814; NCRO, SO/HO/1/3/2, 17 November 1831; SCRO, D550/1, 12 January 1818; GCRO, HO22/1/1, 5 July 1822; SuCRO, Acc 2697, 3 December 1828; LAO, LAWN 1/1/1, 15 November 1819, 7 January, 18 February 1820; Higgins, *Rules of the Pauper Lunatic Asylum for the West Riding*, p. 5.

23 SCRO, D550/1, 14 July 1824, 14 July 1830; SuCRO, Acc 2697, 1 November 1832, 7 October 1834, 5 October 1841, 23 December 1845; Scull, *Most Solitary of Afflictions*, pp. 217–25; A. Scull, 'From Madness to Mental Illness: Medical Men as Moral Entrepreneurs', *Archives Européennes de Sociologie*, vol. XVI (1975), pp. 218–51; A. Scull, 'Mad-Doctors and Magistrates: English Psychiatry's Struggle for Professional Autonomy in the Nineteenth Century', *Archives Européennes de Sociologie*, vol. XVII (1976), pp. 279–305.

24 SCRO, D550/1, 12 January 1818; GRL, Gloucester Asylum, Rules and Regulations, p. 11.

25 GCRO, HO22/1/1, 6 October, 12 December 1836, 8 October 1838, 7 October 1839, 6 April, 12 October 1840, 13 May, 1 October 1841, 4 March 1844, 2 April 1845, HO22/3/2, 2 November 1835; GRL, (H) G1.6, '13th Report of the Visitors of the Gloucestershire Lunatic Asylum' (1836); LPL, 'Report of the Medical Officers of the Lunatic Asylum for the County of Lancaster' (1841), p. 15; L.D. Smith, '"A Worthy Feeling Gentleman": Samuel Hitch at Gloucester Asylum, 1828–1847', in H. Freeman and G. Berrios (eds.), *150 Years of British Psychiatry*, vol. II, *The Aftermath* (London, 1996), pp. 479–99.

26 Nottingham Asylum, *By-laws, Rules, Orders and Regulations*, p. 54; CCRO, DDX 97/1, 20 March 1826; SuCRO, Suffolk Asylum, Rules and Regulations, p. 10; Stanley Royd Hospital, Diary of Dr Gettings, Extracts from Minutes, 27 October 1825, January 1842; DCRO, Forston House, 1(a), 4 January 1836, Michaelmas 1840; GCRO, HO22/1/1, 11 October 1841, 12 October 1842.

27 CCRO, DDX 97/1, 31 August 1824, 25 October 1842, 1 April 1845; LPL, 'Report of the Medical Officers of the Lunatic Asylum for the County of Lancaster' (1841), pp. 15–16; LLSL, '17th Report of Lincoln Lunatic Asylum' (1841), pp. 4–6.

28 William Ellis, *A Letter to Thomas Thompson, M.P.* (Hull, 1815), p. 17; *Report of the Metropolitan Commissioners in Lunacy to the Lord Chancellor* (1844), p. 85; S. Tuke, 'Introductory Observations' to M. Jacobi, *On the Construction and Management of Hospitals for the Insane* (London, 1841), pp. x–xv; Scull, *Most Solitary of Afflictions*, chapter 6; P. McCandless, '"Build! Build!" The Controversy Over the Care of the Chronically Insane in England, 1855–1870', *Bulletin of the History of Medicine*, vol. LIII (1979), pp. 533–74.

29 M. Foucault, *Madness and Civilization* (London, 1971); K. Doerner, *Madmen and the Bourgeoisie: A Social History of Insanity and Psychiatry* (Oxford, 1981); R. Castel, *The Regulation of Madness: The Origins of Incarceration in France* (Oxford, 1988); Scull, *The Most Solitary of Afflictions*.

30 J.L. Crammer, 'English Asylums and English Doctors: Where Scull is Wrong', *History of Psychiatry*, vol. V, no. 17 (March 1994), pp. 103–15; K. Jones, *Asylums and After: A Revised History of the Mental Health Services from the Early Eighteenth Century to the 1990s* (London, 1993), pp. 39–40; A. Suzuki, 'The Politics and Ideology of Non-Restraint: The Case of the Hanwell Asylum', *Medical History*, vol. XXXIX (1995), pp. 1–17; P. Bartlett, *The Poor Law of Lunacy: The Administration of Pauper Lunatics in Mid-Nineteenth Century England With Special Emphasis on Leicestershire and Rutland*, pp. 13–28. Scull has probably partially rescued his reputation with his psychiatric critics following his recent collaborative volume, *Masters of Bedlam* (with co-authors Mackenzie and Harvey). Other recent studies have further confirmed Bartlett's emphasis on the continuing strong position of the justices: B. Forsythe, J. Melling and R. Adair, 'The New Poor Law and the County Pauper Lunatic Asylum – the Devon Experience 1834–1884', *Social History of Medicine*, vol. IX, no. 3 (December 1996), pp. 335–56; D. Wright, 'Getting Out of the Asylum: Understanding the Confinement of the Insane in the Nineteenth Century', *Social History of Medicine*, vol. X, no. 1 (April 1997), pp. 137–55.

31 GCRO, HO22/1/1, 28, 29 May 1830, 17 October 1834, 14 April, 19 October 1835, 19, 24 March 1845, HO22/3/2, 16 January 1845; C. Crommelinck, *Rapport sur les Hospices d'Aliénés de l'Angleterre, de la France et de l'Allemagne* (Courtrai, 1842), p. 109. For a fuller examination of Hitch's work at Gloucester, see Smith, '"A Worthy Feeling Gentleman"', in Freeman and Berrios (eds), *150 Years of British Psychiatry*, vol. II.

32 SuCRO, Acc 2697, 20 October 1826, 18 October 1830, 20 September 1831, 31 March, 21 June 1835; B 106/10/4.4 (1–4), Reports of the Suffolk Lunatic Asylum, 1839–42; DCRO, Forston House (4), Easter 1844.

33 For the professional differences and difficulties between physicians, surgeons and apothecaries, see Loudon, *Medical Care and the General Practitioner 1750–1850*, pp. 19–25. For a more detailed consideration of events at Lincoln Asylum, see Smith, '"The Great Experiment": The Place of Lincoln in the History of Psychiatry', pp. 55–62. L.J. Ray, referring to the later Victorian asylum, perceptively noted the structural tensions that arose owing to the conflict between the role of physician as healer and the role of

superintendent as custodian ('Models of Madness in Victorian Asylum Practice', pp. 230–1, in *Archives Européennes de Sociologie*, vol. XXII (1981), pp. 229–64).

34 Ellis, *Letter to Thomas Thompson*; H. Warner Ellis, *'Our Doctor': Memorials of Sir William Charles Ellis, M.D., of Southall Park, Middlesex* (London, 1868), pp. 1–15; Marland, *Medicine and Industrial Society in Wakefield and Huddersfield*, pp. 262, 292, 320.

35 C. Crowther, *Observations on the Management of Madhouses: Illustrated by Occurrences at the West Riding and Middlesex Asylums* (London, 1838), pp. 49–50; C. Crowther, *Some Observations Respecting the Management of the Pauper Lunatic Asylum at Wakefield* (Wakefield, 1830), p. 4; Higgins, *Rules of the Pauper Lunatic Asylum for the West Riding*, pp. 5, 9; Stanley Royd Hospital, Diary of Dr Gettings, Extracts from Visitors' Minutes, 30 July 1821.

36 D. Alexander, *An Impartial Statement of the Question Recently Agitated Between Dr Crowther and Dr Alexander Respecting the Visiting Department of the Pauper Lunatic Asylum* (Wakefield, 1825), pp. 5–23.

37 Ibid., pp. 7, 13–20; Crowther, *Some Observations Respecting the Management of the Pauper Lunatic Asylum*, pp. 5–7.

38 Ibid, pp. 6–11; Marland, *Medicine and Industrial Society*, pp. 292–3, 320–1, 353–4.

39 Crowther, *Observations on the Management of Madhouses*, p. 50; Greater London Record Office (GLRO), MA/A/J/1, 7, 23 February, 2 March 1831.

40 William C. Ellis, *A Treatise on the Nature, Symptoms, Causes, and Treatment of Insanity With Practical Observations on Lunatic Asylums* (London, 1838), pp. 209–10; Crowther in *Observations on the Management of Madhouses* (1838) – pp. 3, 27–9, 41–4, 49, 66, 71–2, 84–6 – refers disparagingly to Ellis as the 'Knight of Hanwell'; Tuke, 'Introductory Observations', p. xv; Marland, *Medicine and Industrial Society*, p. 321.

41 Suzuki, 'The Politics and Ideology of Non-Restraint', pp. 8–9.

42 For example, the Nottinghamshire magistrates warned overseers of the poor that, if they 'shall wilfully delay, or neglect to give Information' to a justice of the peace regarding every insane pauper, they were liable to a fine of £10 (*Nottingham Journal*, 11, 18, 25 January, 1 February 1812); the Staffordshire magistrates issued similar warnings (*Wolverhampton Chronicle*, 7 October 1818).

43 *Gloucester Journal*, 18 August 1823; *Nottingham Journal*, 10 November 1827; NCRO, SO/HO/1/3/1, 19 February 1812, 5 December 1816, SO/HO/1/3/2, 8 November, 27 December 1827; GCRO, D3848/1/1, no. 45, 25 January 1839; West Riding County Record Office (WRCRO), C85/107, 16th Report of West Riding Pauper Lunatic Asylum (December 1834), 17th Report (December 1835), C85/114, 26th Report (1844), p. 3.

44 CCRO, DDX 97/1, 9 May 1825, DDX 97/2, 7, 28 January 1845; *The Times*, 11 February 1845. An instance at the Norfolk Asylum in January 1826 led to indictments for manslaughter after the visiting justices took up the case of

a woman in frail health who died shortly after arrival at the asylum, having been brought in an open cart with little protection against the cold and inclement weather (NkCRO, SAH 3, 30 January, 7 February 1826).

45 48 Geo. III, Cap. 96, Section XXIII; NkCRO, SAH 2, 27 February, 4 August 1815; SCRO, D550/62, 11 June 1842.

46 51 Geo. III, Cap. 79, Section V; GCRO, HO 22/3/1, 25 June 1832; NCRO, SO/HO/1/3/2, 27 December 1821, 2, 16 March, 16 November 1826, 19 August 1830; CCRO, DDX 97/2, 27 April 1841; SCRO, D550/5; WRCRO, C85/107, 8th Report of West Riding Asylum (December 1826), 10th Report (December 1828), C85/108, 15th Report (1834), pp. 3–4, C85/114, 24th Report (1843), p. 3; LAO, LAWN 1/1/3, 30 March 1835, LAWN 1/1/4, 21 April, 9, 16 September 1838; *Nottingham Journal*, 10 November 1827, 31 October 1829.

47 GCRO, D3848/1/1, 11 January 1840; LAO, LAWN 1/1/3, 15 November 1830, LAWN 1/1/5, 7, 14, 28 October 1844.

48 DCRO, 2nd Report of the Superintending Physician (Epiphany 1844), p. 17; NkCRO, SAH 2, 27 November 1815, SAH 6, 30 March 1840; NCRO, SO/HO/1/3/3, 14 September 1842.

49 NCRO, SO/HO/1/3/1, 12 February 1812; CCRO, DDX 97/1, 16 November 1818, 1 February 1820; NkCRO, SAH 2, 28 April 1814; WRCRO, C85/107, 2nd Report of West Riding Asylum (31 December 1820); SuCRO, Acc 2697, 21, 27 April 1829.

50 NkCRO, SAH 2, 28 April 1814, SAH 3, 30 March 1818, 27 June 1821, SAH 4, 26 March 1827, SAH 5, 27 March 1835; Cambridge University Library, Hunter Collection, *Report of the Visiting Justices of the Norfolk Lunatic Asylum* (1844), pp. 5, 8; SuCRO, Acc 2697, 18 October 1830, 13 October 1835, 27 March 1838, 8 April 1839; Cheshire County Record Office, QJB/4/5, 13 July 1829, QJB/4/9, 18 October 1834, QJB/4/12, 7 October 1836; LAO, LAWN 3/1, 5th, 6th, 7th Reports of the West Riding Asylum (1822–4); WRCRO, C85/107, 10th Report of the West Riding Asylum (31 December 1828), 12th Report (31 December 1830), C85/114, 25th Report (1844), p. 23; Suzuki, 'The Politics and Ideology of Non-Restraint', p. 9.

51 *Staffordshire Advertiser*, 26 September 1818; NCRO, SO/HO/1/3/2, 11 April, 9 May 1822, 1 January 1824, 10 March 1825; GCRO, HO22/1/1, 4 April, 10 July 1823, HO22/8/1, Gloucester Asylum, *Annual Reports*, 1824, 1825, 1829, 1830, 1840; *Nottingham Journal*, 6 November 1824; L.D. Smith, '"Levelled to the Same Common Standard": Social Class in the Lunatic Asylum, 1780–1860', pp. 146–7, in O. Ashton, R. Fyson and S. Roberts (eds), *The Duty of Discontent: Essays for Dorothy Thompson* (London, 1995), pp. 142–66.

52 SCRO, D550/1, 13 July 1820; D550/2, 27 March 1819, D550/62, 17 October 1829; GCRO, HO22/8/1, Gloucester Asylum, 1st Report (1824); GRL, Gloucester Asylum, Rules and Regulations, p. 31; *An Account of the Origin, Nature and Objects of the Asylum on Headington Hill, Near Oxford* (Oxford, 1827), p. 19; Nottingham Asylum, Articles of Union, p. 6.

53 55 Geo. III, Cap. 46, Section XII; BCRO, LB/1/1, 3 October 1812, LB/1/8, 3 June 1815, 14 October 1828; *Lonsdale Magazine*, February 1821, p. 45; J. Hemingway, *History of the City of Chester* (Chester, 1831), vol. II, pp. 226–8; NkCRO, SAH 2, 20 March, 23 December 1815, SAH 3, 29 July 1816, 27 October 1817, SAH 5, 25 April 1836; SuCRO, Acc 2697, 1 April 1834, B106/10/4.4 (5–6), 5th Report of Suffolk Asylum (1843), pp. 6–7, 6th Report (1844), p. 5; LPL, MS 34, 21 April 1836, 28 May, 12 September 1836.

54 BCRO, LB/1/8, 3 June 1815; NkCRO, SAH 3, 28 October 1816; CCRO, DDX 97/1, 26 May 1828; R.M. Barton (ed.), *Life in Cornwall in the Mid-Nineteenth Century* (Truro, 1971), p. 45; BPP 1834, vol. XXVIII, *Report of Commissioners on the Administration and Practical Operation of the Poor Laws in England and Wales* (1834), evidence of Captain Chapman, pp. 429–30; BPP 1836, vol. XLI, *County Lunatic Asylums Returns*, pp. 5, 6, 9, 11, 22, 29 – these returns show considerable differentials between charges to paupers from within the county and to those from other counties.

55 SCRO, D550/1, 31 December 1818, 18 October 1820, 11 July 1821, 13 July 1825, 17 October 1827, 16 July 1828, 3 July 1833. For the growing commercialization of the market for the care of pauper lunatics, see Smith, 'The Pauper Lunatic Problem in the West Midlands, 1815–1850'.

56 SuCRO, Acc 2697, 22 June, 5 October 1838, 8 April, 21 June, 26 July, 4 October 1839.

57 NkCRO, SAH 2, 8 July 1815 (the total cost of Thorpe Asylum was over £35,000), SAH 5, 27 March 1835, 25 April 1836; SuCRO, Acc 2697, 23 June, 13 October 1835, B 106/ 10/4.4 (1–3), Suffolk Asylum, 1st Report (1839), pp. 7–9, 2nd Report (1840), pp. 3–6, 3rd Report (1841), p. 11; *Journal of Mental Science*, no. 7, 15 April 1854, pp. 99–102, 'Misgovernment of the Norfolk County Asylum'.

58 Andrews, *The Dark Awakening*, p. 55. In appointing a new superintendent to Cornwall Asylum in 1828, prime importance was given to the 'economic management' of the institution; LAO, LAWN 3/1, 4th Report of West Riding Asylum (1822); WRCRO, C85/107, 7th Report of West Riding Asylum (31 December 1825); Suzuki, 'The Politics and Ideology of Non-Restraint', p. 9.

59 CKS (Centre for Kentish Studies), Q/GCL/1, 16 April 1839; SuCRO, Acc 2697, 19 April 1830; *Nottingham Journal*, 13 October 1821, 31 October 1829, 5 November 1831, 10 October 1834.

60 NkCRO, SAH 3, 20 April, 25 July 1821; SuCRO, Acc 2697, 3 January 1832; GCRO, HO 22/1/1, 12 May, 5 July 1832; WRCRO, C85/107, 17th Report of West Riding Asylum (31 December 1835); SCRO, D550/1, 3 July 1833, 10 March 1841, Staffordshire County Asylum, *Report on Proposed Extensions and Alterations* (1847–8), D550/5, 31 August 1837; *Report of Metropolitan Commissioners in Lunacy* (1844), p. 12; LPL, *Report of the Medical Officers of the Lunatic Asylum for the County of Lancaster* (1841), p. 13.

61 GCRO, HO22/26/8, hand-bill dated 9 April 1838, reporting a Subscriber Committee meeting, HO22/26/9, pamphlet 7 January 1840 – 'Gloucester

Lunatic Asylum'; SCRO, D550/1, *Report on Proposed Extensions and Alterations* (1847–8); *Charitable Institution for the Insane of the Middle Classes: Proceedings at a Public Meeting* (Stafford, 1851 – copy in William Salt Library, Stafford); *Ninth Report of the Commissioners in Lunacy* (1855), Appendix B, p. 67; D. Hunter, *A History of the Coppice, Nottingham, 1788–1918* (Nottingham, 1918), p. 24.

62 E. Baines, *History, Directory and Gazetteer of the County Palatine of Lancaster* (Liverpool, 1825), vol. II, p. 17; Hunter, *History of the Coppice*, pp. 19–20; NCRO, SO/HO/1/2, 5 February, 5 March 1829; *Nottingham Journal*, 31 October 1829; LAO, LAWN 1/1/2, 27 March, 28 April, 5 October 1827; E.P. Charlesworth, *Remarks on the Treatment of the Insane and the Management of Lunatic Asylums Being the Substance of a Return from the Lincoln Lunatic Asylum, etc.* (London, 1828), pp. 5–13; GCRO, HO22/1/1, 25 September 1829, 29 July 1831, 12 May 1832, 2 January 1833.

63 CCRO, DDX 97/2, 25 January 1842, 27 February 1844; J. Maclean, *Parochial and Family History of the Parish and Borough of Bodmin in the County of Cornwall* (London and Bodmin, 1870), p. 5; DCRO, Forston House (4), Michaelmas 1843, Easter 1844, Michaelmas 1844, Reports of Visiting Justices, Epiphany 1844, p. 5; SuCRO, Acc 2697, 4 April, 19 August, 21 November 1843, B106/10/4.4 (6–8), 6th Report (1844), p. 12, 7th Report (1845), pp. 5–6, 8th Report (1846), p. 5.

64 LPL, *Report of the Medical Officers of the Lunatic Asylum for the County of Lancaster* (1841), p. 14; WRCRO, C85/107, 11th Report of West Riding Asylum (31 December 1829), 13th Report (31 December 1831), 23rd Report (31 December 1841); Scull, *Most Solitary of Afflictions*, p. 168; J.E. Huxley, 'History and Description of the Kent Asylum', *Asylum Journal of Mental Science*, no. 3, 15 February 1854, pp. 39–45 (especially p. 40).

65 SuCRO, B106/10/4.4 (1), Report of the Suffolk Lunatic Asylum (1839), p. 4; Scull, *Most Solitary of Afflictions*, pp. 167–9; Ellis, *Letter to Thomas Thompson*, pp. 14, 17; LAO, LAWN 3/1, 5th Report of West Riding Asylum (1823); Tuke, 'Introductory Observations', p. x.

66 SuCRO, B106/10/4.4 (7,8), 7th Report of Suffolk Asylum (1845), p. 4, 8th Report (1846), p. 5; *Metropolitan Commissioners in Lunacy* (1844), p. 23; D. Hack Tuke, *Chapters in the History of the Insane* (London, 1882), pp. 179–80.

67 *Metropolitan Commissioners in Lunacy* (1844), p. 85; BPP 1814–15, IV, *Select Committee On Madhouses*, p. 177; NCRO, SO/HO/1/3/3, 17 May 1845; BCRO, OGE/1, 20 May 1809; NkCRO, SAH 2, 28 April 1814, SAH 6, 26 August 1845; Baines, *History of Lancaster*, p. 17; *Staffordshire Advertiser*, 26 September 1818; LAO, LAWN 3/1, West Riding Asylum, 5th Report; CCRO, DDX 97/1, 1 February 1820; GCRO, HO22/26/8, 9 April 1838; GRL, (H) G1.6, Gloucester Asylum, 22nd Report (1845); Hemingway, *History of Chester*, vol. II, p. 227; SuCRO, B106/10/4.4 (1), p. 4, (7), p. 6, (8), p. 6; DCRO, Forston House (3), 14 October 1828; Huxley, 'History and Description of Kent Asylum', p. 40.

68 See Scull, 'Mad-Doctors and Magistrates: English Psychiatry's Struggle for Professional Autonomy in the Nineteenth Century', and 'From Madness to Mental Illness: Medical Men as Moral Entrepreneurs'. Scull stresses the emergence of medical supremacy in the second half of the nineteenth century. The process would appear to have been well under way before 1845. Other writers have also emphasized the growing medical dominance over asylum management in the wake of 'moral management' and non-restraint – P. McCandless, *Insanity and Society: A Study of the English Lunacy Reform Movement, 1815–1870* (PhD, University of Wisconsin, 1974), pp. 103–6; N. Tomes, 'The Anglo-American Asylum in Historical Perspective' in C.J. Smith and J.A. Giggs (eds), *Location and Stigma: Contemporary Perspectives on Mental Health Care* (London, 1988), pp. 7–10; A. Digby, *Madness, Morality and Medicine: A Study of the York Retreat, 1796–1914* (Cambridge, 1985), chapter 6.

3

'Waste Stuff': Peopling the Asylum

In an era when the 'user' movement has a growing contribution to make in determining the nature and style of service provision, we are clearly reminded of the proper focus of mental health services. Historians of the nineteenth-century asylum have tended to overlook study of the patients who filled the institutions and have largely relied upon generalizations or reproduction of statistics from annual reports. This can partly be accounted for by the sparsity of evidence. Parliamentary and commissioners' reports, asylum reports and minutes of managing committees largely dwelt on general issues of institutional management, rather than on the minutiae of ongoing practice and the experiences of those on the receiving end of it. The consequence has been a historiography which, though not exactly distorted, has often lacked a clear perspective on the people who entered the asylum and contributed so materially to the way it was shaped.

Several social historians of insanity have sought to investigate patterns of committal, and to discern underlying trends. There has been a search for explanations related to the processes of urbanization and industrialization, or to the more overt imposition of the mechanisms of social control. Such analyses have tended to focus on the mid- and late-Victorian periods, when the asylum population expanded quite dramatically. Andrew Scull has argued that this expansion was at least partly related to widening definitions of insanity, which encompassed conditions and behaviour patterns not previously considered to necessitate asylum treatment. A number of recent studies of post-1845 asylums have made use of computer-based analysis of case-records and admission papers to develop a detailed profile of asylum populations. It is anticipated that their publication will underline the variations and the complexities of the relationships between families, communities and the asylum.[1]

For the first half of the century, with smaller patient numbers and less comprehensive available data, there are difficulties in drawing definitive conclusions about any patterns of admission. The weight of the evidence indicates no significant shift in the parameters of committal. People admitted to public lunatic asylums were those who exhibited high levels of mental abnormality and social dysfunction. The study by John Walton of admissions to the Lancaster Asylum tends to confirm this impression. Levels of admission were seen to relate to the ability and preparedness of families to cope with their disordered and disturbed members. In socially cohesive small towns, the ability to tolerate aberrant and inconvenient behaviour appeared greater than in the larger and rapidly growing urban centres. Admission to a public asylum was generally very much a matter of last resort, when the resources of family and community were no longer sufficient to contain the insane person.[2] A recent important essay by David Wright has underlined the central role of families in initiating the confinement of their uncontainable disturbed members.[3]

'FIT OBJECTS' – ASYLUM ADMISSIONS

> Since the opening of the Asylum, in 1816, almost every possible variety of mental disease has been brought under inspection here, from the raving maniac, with incessant exertion, to the melancholy hypochondriac, obstinately silent, and refusing the food necessary for his subsistence; and from such as do not utter a sensible sentence, to those whose minds are only erroneous on a single subject.[4]

This 1825 synopsis of the Lancaster Asylum's population, by the historian and journalist Edward Baines, could equally have encapsulated the range of patients in any of the post-1808 public asylums. He was describing people with conditions nowadays deemed psychotic, or manifestations of severe mental illness. The early nineteenth-century asylum was not a receptacle for those who were merely deviant, odd, eccentric or socially unacceptable. It catered largely for people who manifested a serious psychological disturbance or major intellectual deficit. Their condition and behaviour would have reached the point where the apparent risk of harm to the sufferer, to other people, or to property meant that their presence within family or community could not be sustained without an unacceptable level of discomfort or stress.

The 1808 Act had, however, created a somewhat complicated situation, by requiring that all pauper and criminal lunatics and dangerous idiots were sent to the county asylum. People newly presenting as insane would be referred alongside others whose condition had long been apparent. The consequence was that the new asylums simultaneously accepted acute and chronic patients, whose management and treatment needs and objectives could be markedly different. The 'catch-all' element was further stimulated initially by the need to fill the institution rapidly, in order to reduce the per capita costs incurred by staffing, provisions and other fixed expenditure.

Many of the early admissions were from other institutions, notably private madhouses. Within three months of the Stafford Asylum's opening in September 1818, 21 patients were transferred from private establishments, including twelve from Bakewell's at Spring Vale, four from Proud's at Bilston and three from Ricketts's at Droitwich. A similar pattern was apparent at the Gloucester Asylum. Of its first 36 admissions in 1823, fourteen were transferred from private madhouses – including seven from Droitwich and four from Harris's at Hook Norton. After the Kent Asylum opened at Maidstone in 1833, 29 patients were moved from Rix's madhouse at Malling, in addition to 27 from metropolitan madhouses at Hoxton, Peckham and Bethnal Green. Some of these people had already been confined for several years. Their removal was dictated partly by economic motives, but also by 'political' considerations which sought to demonstrate disapproval of the alleged abuses of private madhouses. The acrimonious and accusatory exchanges between Thomas Bakewell and the Staffordshire magistrates and John Garrett, the new asylum's superintendent, exposed the tensions that were present.[5]

Among the first group of admissions were some who had spent periods in madhouses, but were subsequently removed to a workhouse or to be maintained by the parish at home. Emmanuel Johnson (57), a Wombourn nailer, had been two years at Proud's house in Bilston when first declared insane, only to be removed as no benefit had been perceived; after six years 'confined to a wall in his wife's house', he was admitted to Stafford. Dorothy Birch (44) had spent a year at Spring Vale, but not having improved was removed to the workhouse until the new asylum opened. Other patients had experienced more than one madhouse, like Hannah Cox (54), admitted to Gloucester in September 1823, after earlier spells at houses in Henley-in-Arden and Hook Norton. For the parishes of people like these, the new asylum, with its optimistic fanfare, offered new opportunity to bring about amendment of their condition and, perhaps, future financial savings.[6]

Many others among the first wave of county asylum patients were moved from parish workhouses, particularly in counties where there had been little private madhouse provision. Thus, within a few months of Lancaster Asylum's opening in 1816, batches of patients were transferred from the workhouses of the county's main towns, notably Manchester, Liverpool and Oldham. Even in counties which did contain madhouses accepting paupers, like Staffordshire and Gloucestershire, some people were admitted after many years spent in the workhouse.[7] They were not necessarily any less disturbed than those who had earlier been sent to a madhouse. Prior to the opening of the county asylum, it had been parochial circumstances which determined whether such people were contained in the workhouse or offered the, however unsatisfactory, specialist care of a madhouse. Recent research on provision in Devon has underlined the significance of local political differences in determining the type of placement offered to pauper lunatics.[8]

In the asylums' first months, only a minority of patients were admitted directly from their own homes. However, once the initial influx from madhouses and workhouses had been absorbed, most admissions were direct from the community, perhaps after a brief sojourn in the workhouse. This continued to be the case until the time asylums became full, when guardians had again to resort to the workhouse. The people admitted were those whose behaviours could no longer be tolerated or comprehended by their local community or their family. In many cases, attempts had been made to contain them at home by bringing in medical assistance. The usual failure of such interventions, combined with a growing adherence to the principle that effective treatment required removal from familiar surroundings, precipitated committal to the asylum.[9]

The Path to Committal

The behaviours most likely to lead to admission were those which posed real or apparent risk, particularly if arousing the attention of the authorities by a public display of violence and threat. William Harper (31), a butcher with a prison record, was committed to Gloucester in 1826 after violence in Coleford in the Forest of Dean. Believing he was a king, he broke windows, attacked passers-by and pulled a gentleman's footman from his horse and kicked him. A 50-year-old farmer, six feet tall and of 'athletic form', was readmitted to Lincoln Asylum in June 1832 after breaking windows in the village rectory, attacking several of his neighbours and attempting to kill his wife with a garden fork kept in his bedroom along with a gun and other weapons. Thomas Taylor (68) was admitted to Norfolk Asylum in December 1822, his parish being unable to manage him: 'he having such a pretencely to bite, and women in particulor, so that all persons where fearfull of going near him'. In some cases, there was evident risk to local social order. Joseph Yeates (46), a recently dismissed agricultural labourer, was admitted to Gloucester in 1823, after three months of confused, abusive and violent behaviour, during which he struck several people and threatened to kill all the farmers in his parish. The violent conduct of John Gilverthorpe (35) of Wakefield, convinced that his mother had usurped his property, brought committal in 1821 after his delusions led to a written threat, delivered to the curate of his parish of Burgwallis, that 'he would burn down the Corn stacks'.[10]

Most of the violence or threat which led to admission did not occur in a public arena, however, but within the family. Samuel Stephens (36), a Gloucester gas works employee admitted in September 1823, had become incoherent and threatening, then attacked his wife and child with a poker and smashed everything within reach. Thomas Stagwood of South Burgh was admitted to Norfolk Asylum in April 1823 after being restrained from killing his wife and child with a hatchet. Ann Platts (32) of Radford, suffering a first episode of insanity, was admitted to Nottingham in 1826, after she had 'repeatedly attempted mischief to her children'. For these sorts of attacks to lead to the asylum rather than prosecution, there would be observable evidence of mental disorder, often in the form of delusional ideas. Alexander Welstead (55), a Gloucester sawyer with ten children, believed that God was speaking to him through the wall; he attacked his wife and children and turned them out of the house, before his removal to the asylum in May 1826. George Shepherd (54), a Woolwich clerk, convinced that a dwarf was suffocating him, would walk the streets for hours to get away from it; things then became more serious: 'Threatened to cut his Wife up for dogs meat if she did not get rid of it. Threatened his neighbours life in whose house he fancied this Dwarf was.' Admission to the Kent Asylum followed in December 1836. John Wills (28), a Cheltenham butcher, had tried to hit his child with a cleaver, after running about in the street naked saying that the Devil had got him; he was taken to Gloucester in November 1827. Delusions, particularly if bizarre and incomprehensible, gave rise to apprehension of dangerously unpredictable behaviour.[11]

Serious attempts at self-harm, particularly when of a dramatic nature, were common precipitants of committal. Hanging or throat-cutting appear to have been the most frequent means employed in the early nineteenth century. Benjamin Buckborough (68), an agricultural worker with a history of insanity, was admitted to Wakefield in August 1823 after several attempts to hang himself, as was Mary Berry (41), of Skipton, the mother of ten children, in November. Mary Harris (44) of Westbury on

Severn, a mother of five, tried to hang herself and threatened to kill her children before being committed to Gloucester Asylum in 1824. George Taylor (55) of Halifax was admitted to Wakefield in December 1822 after an attempt to cut his throat; he died within three weeks from physical complications. Joseph Clapham (29), a gentleman's cook, tried to cut his throat whilst in a 'paroxysm of rage', imagining that people around him had taken against him, and was admitted to Gloucester as a charity patient in January 1825. Esther Taylor (40), a mantua maker from Deerhurst Walton, sought to make doubly sure by attempting both to hang herself and to cut her throat; admission to Gloucester followed in August 1823. What these and other cases had in common was the sheer violence and desperation of the suicidal behaviour.[12]

There were, of course, other means of attempting suicide. Lucy Garrett (48), who kept a small shop and a school in Cheltenham, depressed after the death of her husband, almost succeeded in drowning herself; determined to try again, she was taken to Gloucester in 1824 as a charity patient. Charlotte Cooper of Gainsborough was admitted to Lincoln in February 1838 after attempting 'self destruction' at home; en route to the asylum she threw herself into the Fossdike (a ship canal). Similar intent was shown by a 17-year-old Lincolnshire girl admitted in 1835 after jumping into a stone pit, and by Robert Greenwood (26), a Yorkshire weaver, taken to Wakefield (uninjured) after throwing himself out of a twenty-feet-high window. Few cases, though, were as graphic as that of William Mortimer (66) from Headingley, whose third attempt at suicide brought him to Wakefield in July 1823 with 'a very large protrusion of intestines &c contained in a bag which was occasioned by his ripping his body open with a knife'.[13]

A serious risk factor for mentally disordered people in the community was the liability to neglect or abuse. Eventually situations might come to the attention of the authorities. Matters had become critical for Mary Ann Yeates, of unknown age, of no fixed address and unable to account for herself, admitted to Wakefield in March 1821 after being found on the road 'nearly starved to death & almost naked', with parts of two toes having fallen off through mortification. This was perhaps a case of benign neglect. The attentions of other people could be more actively neglectful. A woman of 50 admitted to Dorset Asylum in March 1838 had been 'confined for a period of 17 years in a dark cellar, fastened to the wall by a chain passed round her waist', provided with a trough from which she ate her food. On admission she was a 'miserable object', with legs and arms 'so contracted as to be perfectly useless'.[14]

The sensational revelations associated with some cases aroused wider public interest. A notorious example was that of William Buckley (42), a former woollen manufacturer, admitted to Wakefield in July 1823. Insane for eleven years, it was ascertained that his father 'has kept him these many years in a situation so low he could not stand upright & almost in a state of nakedness'. He was unshaven and his limbs had become almost unusable. A similar case in Staffordshire in 1826, that of the 'Mucclestone Idiot', caused some local sensation. George Smith had been looked after by his father, whose death left him in the care of a brother and sister, who kept him for fifteen years locked up in a small room. He was discovered by a local magistrate living among filth and straw, virtually nude, with long beard and finger nails, body emaciated and limbs contracted. After being taken to Stafford Asylum, he survived for three years. Extreme cases these may have been, but they highlight the possible consequences of a general ignorance, fear and apprehension of mental disorder.[15]

Behaviours deemed to signify mental illness differ between cultures and over time. In nineteenth-century Britain, one of the more common aberrant behaviours presented, both prior to admission and inside the asylum, was the tearing of clothes. It was interpreted as a primary indication of insanity, or otherwise one of several elements in a pattern of disturbed behaviour. Gloucester Asylum received numerous cases during the 1820s. Leah Sims (40), a Radborough clothing worker suffering from a puerperal disorder, refused food, would not respond to questions and tore her clothes. Catherine Millard (34), a wool picker and spinner of Avening, tore her clothes, broke windows, threw stones and used threatening and abusive language. Anne Sayer (55) of Tibberton, an unusually elderly victim of a post-natal psychosis, was tearing her clothes, laughing and singing, six days after delivery. In several cases, there were associated delusional experiences. Hester Clark (32), a domestic servant, imagined that 'her soul is lost & she is doomed to everlasting torment'; on hearing she was to about be taken to the asylum she tried to hang herself. Significantly, it was mostly among female patients that clothes tearing was regarded as a major element in the psychopathology. The act had evident biblical connotations, whereby people in distress rent their garments. For the poor, clothing was a valuable commodity; its destruction was a gesture expressing a degree of desperation close to suicide.[16]

Male sufferers were more likely to remove their clothes than to destroy them. Stripping, particularly in public, led to committal in many instances. Anthony Hands (32), a Cheltenham painter, was admitted to Gloucester in 1827, after a rapid onset of symptoms when he became 'quite outrageous', noisy and incoherent, and was then found on the road 'quite naked with his clothes tied up in a bundle'. A few months before, William Goodwin (46) of Gloucester had been admitted after having 'ran into the street with nothing but his shirt on'. Both men had previous histories of episodic insanity, as did William Cooke (27), a Tewkesbury stocking weaver, who abandoned work and set off wandering round the country; undressing in public precipitated his admission to Gloucester in March 1824. A journey to Gloucester was also the consequence for Thomas Cook (32), an agricultural labourer with no history of mental disorder, who ran about Wotton under Edge without his clothes and was 'very wild & incoherent', in the spring of 1826.[17]

Whilst anti-social or dangerous behaviours were those most likely to ensure committal, the expression of delusional ideas was a frequent accompaniment in the train of events that preceded certification. Delusions with grandiose content most often excited attention, and a likely diagnosis of 'mania'. A common presentation was a poor person with ideas of possessing great wealth, like Sarah Briggs (66) of Wakefield, moved from workhouse to asylum in 1821, having been 'very troublesome' because of her belief that she was the owner of Sir William Pilkington's estate. Samuel Hanks (39), a Dursley stocking weaver admitted to Gloucester in 1824, had been raving incoherently, with 'high notions of his wealth' and convinced that he was Colonel Berkeley. Robert Thorne (60), a coachman from Clifton, admitted in 1823, believed that he was 'Lord Clifton' and very wealthy. Others also assumed the persona of famous or prominent personages. Mary Wilcock (43), a Preston house servant, admitted to Lancaster in 1817, claimed that she was Lady Stanley, wife of the great county magnate. Evan Probert (60), an unemployed teacher from Worcester, admitted to Gloucester in 1826, had announced that he was the Archbishop of Canterbury.[18]

Other grandiose delusions centred around the potential for great achievement. Mary Anne Berry (29) of Cheltenham, whose plasterer husband had failed in business and left town in a hurry, started preaching, praying and swearing, and expressed 'extravagant opinions of her own greatness', resulting in admission to Gloucester in 1828. John Bradley (26), a clerk from Cheltenham admitted in 1829, had various 'high notions', including a scheme to pay off the national debt in eight months. More ambitious was Edward Day, taken to Norfolk Asylum in November 1822; in his incoherence he claimed that 'he his a going to purches the world, and suchlike'. Stephen Ingram (30), a Clifton cabinet maker, was admitted to Gloucester in 1829 after he had set off wandering round the country with a conviction that 'all the ladies are in love with him', but he would wed none other than a virgin, and had vainly walked 1000 miles in search of one! Jacob Scott (35), a Cheltenham bill-hanger subject to particularly florid ideas, concluding in 1824 that the nation's affairs were in disarray and that he had an important part to perform, took a post-chaise to London and attempted to go to the House of Lords. In 1828, believing himself the only prophet on earth, he wandered the streets collecting crowds, preaching and then swearing at them. He told his wife that he 'was Lackington Hill & had Cheltenham on his head'. Attempts to amend his thinking by bleeding and purging failed, and the inevitable admission followed.[19]

In contrast, many presented with delusions of a morbid or distressing character. The unfortunate Sarah Dawson (50) from Manchester, admitted to Lancaster in 1818, was preoccupied with the idea that she had a hedgehog or rats in her insides, and would speak of little else. Another Lancaster patient, Henry Williams, was convinced that he was a fatted sheep; he would cower in terror at the sight of 'every jolly rosy-faced man' who visited the asylum, expecting this to mean that he was to be taken to the slaughterhouse. Henry Lloyd (40), a Bristol druggist admitted to Gloucester in 1824, refused food in the belief that there was 'no passage' for it, and that he was 'doomed to eternal torments'. Benjamin Clarke (53), a farmer from Kirkby-in-Ashfield, was admitted to Nottingham twice in a severely depressed frame of mind during 1826; on the first occasion his mind was 'entertaining perverted notions of his affairs', and on the second he was in 'despair of his affairs & apprehensions of poverty'. These sorts of presentations generally resulted in a diagnosis of 'melancholia'.[20]

Ideas of persecution or of other external interference were widely evident among those admitted. A young man from Stafford, Edward Fouke, expressed suspicion for several months that his food and drink were being poisoned; his fears culminated in a 'burst of excitement', leading to admission in March 1842. The belief of Charlotte Margarette (30) of Deerhurst in Gloucestershire, in 1829, that she had been bewitched by a travelling tinker led to the admission that had not been brought about by her restlessness, incessant talking and destructiveness. In the Dorset Asylum, serving a poverty-stricken rural population, patients' most prevalent delusions centred around being 'overlooked', beliefs that supernatural powers were being exerted over or by the individual. This was powerfully based in the popular culture of the region, and exemplified the period-specific and culture-specific nature of the psychopathology of delusional thinking.[21]

The complex relationship between religion and insanity influenced many admissions. Religious zeal was socially acceptable to a point, but when construed as excessive the descent into madness was feared, manifested in gross over-activity or in deluded ideas. References to figures like the Devil, the Holy Ghost or the Virgin Mary were common. Mary White (33), a Tetbury schoolteacher, in August 1828 started wandering the streets, singing carols, preaching sermons and proclaiming herself the Virgin Mary, a prophetess and 'the Judge of the World'; she was violent, threatening, noisy and abusive, and admission to Gloucester followed. The conversation of Benjamin Wiles (29), a 'steady and industrious' Cheltenham carpenter, became incoherent and religiose, with 'most ridiculous ideas' regarding the Devil; public preaching and his violent manner led to his committal. Elizabeth Pulham (40) of Winchcombe, an impoverished mother of seven, believed that she would never die, but that she had 'sinned against the Holy Ghost & that the devil has got her in hell'; after trying to strangle herself she was admitted to Gloucester in 1827. It was where religious over-indulgence led to apprehensions of serious risk that the authorities would intervene. Their anxiety was heightened when groups or sects deemed extreme or undesirable were involved, for this was likely to be viewed as not only symptomatic, but also causal, of insanity.[22]

THE 'CAUSES' OF INSANITY

> While there are very many, of course, in pauper life, as *our inmates* are, where the cause is decidedly *physical*, there are many also where it is *moral*, or perhaps more correctly, *immoral*. Here, amongst our men, the drunkard may see enough (one would think) to check the headlong career of his desperate indulgence; and amongst our women, the heartless seducer may behold no fewer than thirteen remnants of a fatal wreck. The Splitting Sectarian may here witness *some* sad effects of his endeavours to proselytize, and the wild fanatic may look at *one* end of his *condemnatory* ravings.[23]

John Kirkman, the devoutly religious superintendent of the Suffolk County Asylum, writing in late 1839, was anxious to point some moral lessons in considering the factors that had propelled people into his asylum. His distinction of 'physical' and 'moral' (or psychological) causes highlighted two key elements in the orthodox approach to the origin of individual insanity. First, asylum doctors and writers on mental disorder had universally embraced the concept of causality. There had to be a definite cause for a person's mental collapse, capable of discovery. Secondly, the cause was normally identified as a singular one, either physical or moral, rather than the product of a range of contributory factors. Faced with the chaos and confusion of insanity, the 'alienist' sought to retrieve some clarity, even certainty. Conceivably, the extraction of a clear cause might steer him toward the key to curative treatment. This appears to have been the ideological basis of the search for the cause in each case of admission to a public asylum.[24]

By the first decade of the nineteenth century, written works on insanity were automatically including sections on causality.[25] The influential Bethlem apothecary, John Haslam, in 1798 reinforced the separation of physical and moral causes. He identified several physical causes of insanity, including heredity, blows to the head, intoxication and fever. The various moral causes he put forward became widely accepted and familiar over the subsequent decades: grief; unsatisfied desires; religious terror; disappointment of pride; fright; misfortune. He was careful to link the physical and the moral, by allowing that the changes in the brain that occurred in insanity might be either cause or effect of the disease. Thus, whilst the origins of the disorder might be moral, there would be a physical component in the presentation.[26]

Other writers, like the lay madhouse keeper Thomas Bakewell, also carefully separated the moral from the physical. He stressed the primacy of physical factors, considering insanity as essentially a physical disease, whose 'immediate cause' was a 'diseased state of the brain'. The social factors generally regarded as causes, such as relationship difficulties, excess study, religion or alcohol abuse, were acting on a physical predisposition. They might even directly precipitate the action of the physical cause, due to the neglect or misuse of essential bodily functions. Like Haslam, Bakewell conceded that some of the apparent moral precipitants may be effect rather than cause. His chief conviction was that bowel complaints lay at the heart of mental disorder. He was not alone in this idea. William Ricketts, surgeon and proprietor of the large Droitwich Asylum, told the Select Committee on Madhouses in 1815 that he believed the disease 'to proceed most frequently from a derangement of the digestive organs'. This emphasis on the physical basis of insanity remained central for many commentators. Sir Andrew Halliday declared in 1828 that madness 'is found to proceed in all cases from some real tangible bodily ailment'. John Conolly two years later registered his agreement with other medical authorities in 'ascribing mental disorders to corporeal disease'.[27]

At the time Halliday and Conolly were writing, most asylum medical officers were painstakingly seeking to identify the moral or physical causes behind each admission. This was apparent in the published work of the two county asylum superintendents sufficiently confident to lay their views before the public. The first to do so was Paul Slade Knight, for several years house surgeon and superintendent of Lancaster Asylum, though he had departed some time before the publication of his book in 1827. Knight drew his observations from case-records kept at the asylum. He carefully distinguished moral cause – 'an affection of the mind' – from physical – 'a disorder of the body'. He had concluded, however, that the 'moral impulses' rarely produced insanity, but rather that manifestations like religious zeal or 'the passions' were the 'inevitable result of the corporeal affections'. He advocated a careful examination of the patient, with a view to discovering the underlying disease:

> No symptom should escape the severest scrutiny; and by a cautious induction, it is probable, that the true cause of all this frightful disturbance may be ascertained.[28]

This emphasis on 'corporeal diseases' in the production of madness, and the relegation of social or environmental factors to precipitants or consequences, would ensure the recognition of insanity as a medical condition which could only be treated and managed by medical officers using medical treatments.[29]

Sir William Ellis, writing ten years later, drew on his experience as superintendent of two county asylums, Wakefield and Hanwell. In his *Treatise* he dwelt at length on the causation of mental disorder, citing case examples. He too regarded insanity in all its forms as 'in reality a disease of the brain and nervous system', but it could be precipitated by either physical or moral causes. The physical causes might include a trauma such as a blow on the head, or the effects of illness like fever or lung disease. Developmental factors such as old age, or pregnancy and childbirth in women, were common in the origin of insanity. Ellis highlighted the importance of material deprivation. The consequences of severe poverty could include lack of food and over-exposure to cold, to which he identified agricultural labourers as particularly prone. The physical effects were compounded by the emotional distress associated with the inability to escape from poverty. With a body 'emaciated from want', the brain could not endure the pressure of the person's anxiety about their situation.[30]

Ellis also gave prominence to 'moral' or social causality. Poverty and distress were, he concluded, responsible for more admissions to Wakefield and Hanwell than any other moral cause. Most cases occurred among married people who not only had to contend with their own deprivations, but also were powerless to meet their children's basic needs. Ellis acknowledged that moral causes might differ between social groups and between different parts of the country. Intense study, for example, was not a frequent cause of admissions to pauper asylums. Like most alienists, he frequently ascribed insanity to religious excess:

> Too intense thought upon religious subjects is the moral cause, which, next to distressed circumstances and grief, has produced, as far as we have been able to ascertain, the greatest number of cases in the institution at Wakefield.

Among other significant moral causes Ellis singled out grief, particularly among women 'deranged from the loss of their children'. Terror or fright were identified specifically, as were mortified pride, disappointed love and jealousy. He clearly linked the moral and the physical, contending like Thomas Bakewell that these psychological stresses excited the brain and generated a physiological disorder.[31]

Ellis acknowledged that some causes straddled the boundary between the moral and the physical. Inebriety was one of these. As a devout Methodist, he adopted a condemnatory tone toward all forms of 'vice'. These, he believed, weakened the person's constitution and produced insanity as a result of general debility. For Ellis, there was one particular vice whose 'secret and unsuspected indulgence' both weakened the person's general powers and directly affected the brain and the nervous system. He could hardly bring himself to write the word 'masturbation', but he claimed that its 'awful consequences' were evident on his daily rounds, where might be seen: 'those, gifted by nature with high talents, and fitted to be an ornament and a benefit to society, sunk into such a state of physical and moral degradation as wrings the heart to witness'. Ellis had no doubt that this 'fertile source of insanity' was the main cause of madness 'in a very large number of patients in all public asylums'. It was also often a consequence of a mental disorder, where 'venereal desires' resulted from a high state of excitement in the cerebellum.[32]

Surviving case-material from the early county asylums provides background for the conclusions of Ellis, Knight and other writers on causation. The nature of the information gathered on admission from overseers, medical officers and relatives illustrates the concentration on the search for individual cause. A wide range were identified, physical and moral. By the end of the 1830s, some superintendents had started to utilize their case-material to develop an analysis of attributed causes. C.C. Corsellis of Wakefield, drawing on twenty years of admissions, produced a table in 1838 which detailed 55 distinct causes. His physical causes ranged from 'inflammation of brain' and 'injuries on the head' to 'suppressed catamenia' and 'atmospheric exposure'. Moral causes comprised stresses as diverse as 'misfortunes in business', 'religious anxiety', 'studying astrology' and 'political excitement'.[33]

The process of detection usually started with heredity; questions about family history of mental disorder were invariably asked on admission. Affirmative answers would be taken as virtually explanatory of the disorder, as with several Gloucester admissions in 1824–5. The father of Joseph Clapham (29) had been 'afflicted with Insanity & believed to have died in a Lunatic Asylum'; Mary Harris (44) had a grandmother and two uncles who 'laboured under insanity'; Hester Clark (32) had a sister 'at this time labouring under melancholia'. The Nottingham records did not usually specify the relative, but identified patients having a hereditary predisposition. For George Glover (60), an attorney admitted in 1826, it was reported that 'the disease is hereditary, affecting many parts of his family'. In the notable case of Sarah Ward (31), a suicidal patient admitted in 1827, the illness was considered 'strongly hereditary', her mother, grandmother and grandfather all having killed themselves. At Wakefield, Corsellis commented particularly on the hereditary element in admissions, noting in 1837 that it was becoming increasingly apparent:

> In some instances, three successive generations have been inmates of this establishment at the same time. There are now five mothers and their daughters; and in one instance, the father, mother, and daughter, were admitted patients within a short period of each other.

He observed, tellingly, that the 'hereditary taint' was much more noticeable in females.[34]

Female patients' disorders were frequently identified as linked to childbirth. Corsellis's table included 34 cases. Joanna Burke (26) of Westbury upon Trym, admitted to Gloucester in 1824, became unwell the day after her third child was born; she was noisy, violent and deluded, and attempted to get up the chimney. Elizabeth Dalby (33), a dressmaker, became 'deeply melancholic' following a birth and was admitted to Nottingham in November 1824. The circumstances sometimes aggravated the disorder; Sarah Moseley (28) of Keighley was re-admitted to Wakefield in September 1821 with a violent relapse after giving birth to a child fathered by a man of 72. Where cause was hard to identify, it was often deemed puerperal even though evidence was lacking. Causality was occasionally ascribed to another feminine physiological stress, described for Hannah Ploughright (42) of Radford, admitted to Nottingham in 1825, as 'change of constitution'. The first admission of Mary Smith (49), in 1827, was attributed to 'constitutional derangement from the period of life'. It was the physical change, rather than any emotional accompaniment, that was deemed the significant factor.[35]

Direct damage to the head has long been regarded as a self-evident cause of derangement. Corsellis identified 32 cases of head injury, mainly among men. A quiet mother of nine, admitted to Gloucester in May 1827, Elizabeth Neath (40), had become wild and incoherent, praying, singing and swearing, after a fall and violent blow to her head. A head injury or fall carried less stigma than some other causes, particularly for a private patient such as George Hawkesley Cartwright (30), a solicitor admitted to Nottingham in 1826. The certifying medical man attributed his ten-year history to a fall, but was unable to elaborate about 'in what manner it happened, or what its immediate effects were'. Exposure of the head to excessive heat also figured as a cause. The disorder of a domestic servant admitted to Gloucester in 1825 was attributed to effects of the heat of the cooking fire. The sun also attracted blame. Dorothy Musgrove, re-admitted to Nottingham in August 1826, had relapsed due to 'outdoor labour during the hot weather'. A Gloucestershire agricultural worker, Elizabeth Poole (63), admitted in 1828, had a long history of mental illness, which proved difficult to explain until it was revealed that 'she reap'd in the full sunshine without a bonnet on' the day before her first attack.[36]

The deprivation of basic necessities was regarded by most practitioners as a key causative factor. Dr Charlesworth of Lincoln considered insanity to be 'always a disease of debility'. John Conolly argued that it was 'the frequent result of half starvation, going on for years or for generations'. Superintendents regularly commented on the very poor physical state of many of those admitted. Samuel Gaskell and Dr Edward de Vitrie of Lancaster wrote in 1841 that many on admission presented 'such strong features of abject want' as to suppose this the main cause of their malady, a conclusion reinforced by their speedy recovery after receiving a good diet. A typical situation was that of Isabella Millard (33), a Stroud mantua maker, admitted to Gloucester in 1827, having had her goods seized for debt and her family evicted for non-payment of rent; she had been 'unable to procure food & often fasted 28 hours at a time'. The frequency of these cases in industrial West Yorkshire, particularly during trade slumps, led

C.C. Corsellis to conclude in 1845 that poverty was the most prolific cause of admission to a pauper asylum:

> Where the general health is impaired by unremitting labour, and insufficient food, domestic calamities, and those vexations incident to human nature, which in health would be successfully contended with, prey on the mind with an irresistible power.

His 1838 table showed 75 cases caused by poverty and distress, in addition to 42 ascribed to 'pecuniary disappointment' and nineteen to 'misfortunes in business'.[37]

Poverty, as William Ellis argued, also constituted a 'moral' cause, because of the overwhelming social stresses associated with the inability to earn a subsistence. The fear of poverty, linked with financial losses or unemployment, was frequently identified as a distinct factor. Joseph Yeales (44), a Gloucestershire agricultural labourer, became 'depressed in his spirits' after dismissal, leading to admission in 1823. Thomas Jones (35), a Cheltenham shoemaker admitted in 1824, had reacted to his goods being seized for debt. Nathaniel Gee (46), a Lenton hosier admitted to Nottingham in 1825, had taken to drink and threatened to drown himself after 'disappointment in his business'. The malady of Alfred Mosley (21), a Basford lace manufacturer, was attributed to 'great disappointment in his trading pursuits'. A Sheffield cutler, George Fowler (44), became a charity patient at Nottingham in 1826, after 'anxiety of mind produced by want of work'. Admissions related to poverty reflected the economic structure of the districts – lace and hosiery workers were strongly represented at Nottingham Asylum; weavers and other textile workers at Gloucester and Wakefield; agricultural workers at Dorset.[38]

Corsellis and his predecessor William Ellis both computed the largest single moral cause at Wakefield to be intemperance, accounting for no less than 342 cases (303 males) in Corsellis's 1838 table. Both men, strongly religious in inclination, may have been inclined to blame drinking or other dissipated behaviour in order to draw salutary lessons for the poor. Corsellis was especially concerned at the consequences of their moral condition, their over-indulgence in 'ardent spirits', and the 'calamitous effects' of the ubiquitous beer-houses. Drink was identified as the cause behind many a descent into insanity and the asylum. There was a recognition in some cases, though, that drinking might be symptom rather than cause. Even the moralistic Corsellis, with the benefit of fourteen years' experience, had come to this position by 1844:

Intemperance in the use of stimulating drinks, which is so commonly assigned as the proximate cause of insanity amongst the working classes, is but too frequently had recourse to, in the futile hope of removing unwonted depression, but with the real effect of facilitating the intended attack.

He had been forced to acknowledge that alcohol abuse was often a response to poverty, and only an indirect cause of admissions to his asylum.[39]

The excessive use of alcohol was an element in that demoralization often attributed to the labouring poor. John Kirkman of Suffolk Asylum had little doubt that 'moral depravity' was the essential cause of insanity, and that its real sources were guilt and sin. Corsellis blamed the deterioration in the moral condition of the West Riding poor on the 'pernicious effects' of the masses crowded into the 'houses, yards, and factories of our manufacturing towns', as well as on drink. Caleb Crowther, the colourful physician to the West Riding Asylum, partly agreed about the origins of insanity in the district. The manufacturing towns and adjacent villages, he claimed, supplied most of the deranged patients, but it was not poverty that drove them to degradation:

The men residing there earn high wages, indulge in drunkenness, and wear out their constitutions by excesses of every kind. Derangement occurs, as the last link in a chain of diseases resulting from such excesses.

Not all asylum medical officers accepted this simple causative link. Dr George Button of Dorset Asylum was very aware that the circumstances of his rural catchment population differed from those of other areas. He recognized intemperance to be the 'most fruitful cause' of insanity in some counties, but noted with some pride in 1842 that it had not accounted for a single admission to his asylum in the previous year. He naturally hoped that this indicated some improvement in the moral state of the county.[40]

The antithesis of drunkenness and dissipation, for men like Ellis and Kirkman, was a strict adherence to religious principle. However, religious activity also attracted much attention in determining the aetiology of mental disorder, in the same way that religious manifestations were commonly noted in symptomatology. Corsellis gave 'religious anxiety' as the cause for over a hundred cases in Wakefield's first twenty years. Practices deemed erroneous, misguided or excessive were likely to be blamed for insanity's onset. John Conolly, from his experience at Hanwell, concluded that among educated people and women nearly half the cases of derangement arose from the 'perversion of religion' alone:

Exciting meetings, enthusiastic exhortations, false reports of wild missions, foolish biographies of sickly and delirious children, incoherent tracts, and books of unfruitful controversy, constitute all the intellectual exercises of these sincere and misguided persons.

Other authorities, however, were less convinced. George Button, a former pupil of Conolly's at Hanwell, used his analysis of Dorset admissions to dismiss as 'unfounded and erroneous' the popular idea that religion was a fruitful source of madness. Admission and case-records, however, suggest that most medical officers adopted a position similar to Conolly, viewing religion as causal among people of both sexes and all levels of intellect.[41]

The attribution of insanity to religion was often couched in judgemental language. The admission to Gloucester of Elizabeth Marshall (36) of Temple Guiting in 1828 originated in her attendance at 'a Chapel of Methodist Dissenters of low stamp', where she listened to 'discourses of damnatory kind'. Matthew Munton (22), admitted to Nottingham in 1824, became insane after a meeting of the 'Methodists Ranters'. Sarah Willers (56) of South Searle, admitted in 1828, had developed delusions of great wealth after having been 'annoyed & alarmed by the Methodists'. Several admissions to Norfolk Asylum in the 1820s and 1830s were linked to Methodism. The insanity of Mary Rose of Ashmanhaugh in 1824 'came upon her, in consequence of her giving herself over to the Ranters'. The popular enthusiasm widely aroused by Methodism, and its apparent association with political dissent, was seen as fertile breeding territory for madness. Other fundamentalist sects also attracted attention. Hannah Richardson, admitted to Lancaster in 1816, became insane after having been 'dipped in a Well near Kendal as an Anabaptist'. In other cases, the religious influence was less specific. The disorder of William Avann (44), a 'sober and industrious' travelling brush salesman from Gloucester, admitted in 1824, was ascribed to fanaticism; he was 'fond of frequenting places of worship and reading religious books'. Intense religious activity was usually viewed by medical officers as anything other than a healing agent.[42]

Loss, in various guises, was a commonly identified source of mental disorder. Bereavement or grief were often the 'exciting cause' which initiated the steps toward the asylum. Mary Berry (41) of Skipton, victim of three previous episodes of insanity, had her worst attack after her brother was killed in a fall from his horse, and was admitted to Wakefield in November 1823. William Hind (25), a Derbyshire framework knitter, admitted to Nottingham in 1828, was allegedly rendered vulnerable by associating with the Methodists, but it was the sudden death of his mother which precipitated his mania. George Monks (28), admitted to Nottingham in a filthy and neglected state in 1827, had become deranged after his father had hung himself. The death of a loved one was an easily identifiable explanation among the chaos of events leading to admission.[43]

The failure of relationships was blamed for many a derangement. The admission of Harriet Thompson (27) of Attercliff to Wakefield in July 1823 was simply explained by her 'disappointment in love'. The re-admission to Nottingham in 1827 of Elizabeth Freeling (22) of Derby, resulted, according to her family, from 'disappointed affection'. Elaboration was hardly necessary, as emotional vulnerability was self-evident. When Sarah Buttle of Carleton was admitted to Norfolk Asylum in October 1815, Mr Caryl, the asylum master, recorded meaningfully that 'her Insanity came up on her through Love'. There were instances when men were seen to succumb, like Luke Fletcher (40), a Derbyshire blacksmith admitted to Nottingham in 1826. However, as Anne Digby has suggested, this was considered primarily a cause which took women to the asylum. Corsellis's 1838 table attributed 62 admissions to 'Disappointed Love', 40 of them women. In addition, it linked 26 cases to 'Unkindness of husband'. Cruelty or ill-treatment by spouses were also represented as causes in several cases admitted to Gloucester and Nottingham.[44]

Exhaustion due to intellectual activity periodically figured as a precipitant. Richard Parsons (44), a Mansfield solicitor admitted to Nottingham as a private patient in 1825, had become insane because of 'intensity of application and overexertion'; he recovered within a fortnight. John Birks (29), a Mansfield tanner, was admitted in a 'maniacal condition' in April 1826, following 'intense study'. John Green (26), a Newent plumber and glazier, went in to Gloucester as a charity patient in 1826 after 'too close application to business'. This particular cause was associated more with middle than poorer class patients. Another private patient, John Gardner (34) of Painswick, a proctor admitted to Gloucester in 1826, was thought by his relatives to have fallen victim to 'Intense application to business – dining late without taking nourishment between breakfast & dinner & sitting up late at night, his constitution not being strong. . .'. Interestingly, their conclusion was accepted; his frequenting of public houses and free indulgence in 'spirituous liquors' were deemed only symptomatic. Had he been a pauper, the emphasis might have been different. Corsellis's 1838 figures also suggest that 'study' as a cause was viewed as strongly gender-related; it had accounted for 21 male admissions and only three female admissions since 1818.[45]

Corsellis and his predecessor Ellis had identified numerous other causes which each brought about a few admissions, like jealousy (34), pride (9), studying astrology (7), quarrels with neighbours (4) and political excitement (4). Four women had become deranged after 'consulting with men', and three men as a result of 'onanism'. The value-laden attributions were clear enough, as was the moral message for the maintenance of mental health. Incidental case-records also contain examples where those defining the cause were influenced by ideas of propriety. The aptly named John Daft (22), a Lenton gardener admitted to Nottingham in 1827, had been, according to his father, 'sober and industrious' until 'the reading of Carlisle's works' made his mind morbid. The unfortunate Sarah Oakey (20), a Cheltenham laundress also previously 'sober and industrious', was admitted to Gloucester in 1826 with melancholia, brought on allegedly by 'reading novels'. Here were salutary lessons on the dangers of deviant behaviour.[46]

This survey of 'exciting causes' is far from exhaustive. Contemporary psychiatry might view the attempts of parish officials and of alienists in the early nineteenth century to locate causality, particularly uni-causality, as crude and simplistic. This may well be so. The relevant consideration, however, is not that these were the true causes of an individual's disorder, but that they were determined to be. Clarity in diagnosing cause produced some semblance of order amid the chaos of madness, by explaining the otherwise inexplicable. The exposition of a cause, particularly a 'moral' cause, provided the intellectual justification for removal to the asylum from the environment that nurtured it. By receiving treatment in the sequestered asylum, the sufferer could be insulated from that cause and placed back on the road to recovery.

CHANGING PATTERNS OF COMMITTAL

Whilst risk, behaviour and symptomatology determined committal in individual cases, patterns of admission were greatly affected by developments in policy and practice. From the county asylums' inception, there was an ongoing discourse and debate as to their essential purpose. Notions of the asylum's role as a vehicle for 'cure' conflicted with what some in the county hierarchy perceived as its purpose: to provide a refuge for all suffering mental disorder and to remove them from the liability to inconvenience others. The provisions of the Act of 1808 had weighted the argument toward the asylum being viewed as a general receptacle for all lunatics or 'dangerous' idiots in the county, even though the amending Act of 1811 had given some discretion on admission to local justices.[47] The very presence of a large, expensive and symbolic building provided an impetus towards its full utilization. The consequence was the referral and acceptance, initially, of all types of sufferer.

The asylums were, to an extent, victims of their own success. Families who had struggled to cope with the ravages of an incapacitated member were presented with a more acceptable option than the workhouse or the parish-sponsored place in a dubious private madhouse. Parish authorities, earlier reluctant to make use of the asylum, could see an alternative for some of the disruptive and disagreeable people who posed management difficulties in the workhouse. Consequently, by the early 1820s, increasing numbers of people whose disorders were of long standing, but who had previously not received specialist care were being referred to county asylums. These new chronic admissions were added to those who had become chronic within the asylum to influence fundamentally the composition of its population. Superintendents and committees of management came increasingly to lament the accumulation of hopeless and 'incurable' patients, many of whom were elderly. The concept of the asylum as a primarily curative institution was steadily being eroded.

In the earliest of the new asylums, the problem had become apparent within a few years. This arose partly because of miscalculations as to the likely level of referrals. It had been anticipated that a rapid influx of admissions would follow the opening of an asylum, particularly people transferred from workhouses or from parish relief in the community. When the clamour did not materialize, as after Nottingham Asylum opened in 1812, a policy not to admit incurable people was quickly rescinded. Stafford Asylum was also faced, in 1818–19, with an initially slow accumulation of patients. The admittance and retention of incurable pauper patients was then actively fostered there by charging lower maintenance rates than for those deemed curable. Financial pressures to maximize occupancy had started to take precedence over any residual ideas of the asylum as a place for the promotion of cure.[48]

These considerations operated on top of the legislative requirements. Although magistrates had more discretion on committal after 1811, all lunatics and idiots considered dangerous were still expected to be sent to the county asylum, once it had opened. Dangerousness was always a difficult concept. Its interpretation might vary greatly between localities, but it did not encompass a distinction between curability and incurability. Economy influenced the decisions taken in most parishes; an asylum place was relatively expensive and this could colour the assessment of danger, or at least postpone it for as long as possible. The Nottingham Asylum managers were acknowledging by 1815 that most incurable pauper patients sent in by magistrates were 'turbulent' or dangerous lunatics, who had been disordered for many years. Paul Slade Knight of Lancaster Asylum complained bitterly in 1822 that many insane people were kept for long periods grossly neglected or worse in the county's workhouses. Transfer to the asylum came only when they were completely unmanageable, or when someone threatened a prosecution (under the 1808 Act) against the parish overseer. By that time, Knight contended, their condition had deteriorated to the stage where any possibility of curative treatment had disappeared completely – an argument that was to become extremely familiar over the next few years.[49]

These concerns were voiced by the Cornwall Asylum visitors in 1822. With only 50 people admitted in almost two years since opening, they bemoaned parishes that avoided their responsibilities. Most people sent were 'old and incurable, and dangerous cases', not those susceptible of cure. The situation was comparable at Wakefield. William Ellis was, however, under no illusions about the expected clientele. Being a purely pauper asylum, there was not the discretion available to the managers of some other public asylums:

> Patients must be admitted under every form and complication of the disease: – incurables of many years standing; cases of extreme emaciation of body, from want of food and previous care, insanity joined with epilepsy, and the furious idiot; all these must take up their abode there, until death relieves them from their sufferings.

Of the 138 people admitted in the first year, 95 were 'old cases', some brought almost in a dying state. Small wonder, therefore, that he called for early attention to the onset of insanity and to 'the duty of sending the Paupers immediately on its being discovered'. His pleas, largely unheeded, had to be regularly repeated. Even the fining of overseers for neglect of their responsibilities hardly affected the tendency to withold suitable candidates and to submit only those whose condition had become 'irremediable'. One insightful patient told her nurse in 1822 that she might have become quite well if sent a few months sooner; however, she now was nothing more than 'a piece of waste stuff put out of sight'.[50]

Throughout the 1820s and early 1830s the testimony of superintendents was that they were not receiving enough of the right type of patients. The blame fell largely on parsimonious parish officials, who chose to ignore their advice that the costs of early intervention would be more than offset by great savings from prevention of the descent into chronicity. C.C. Corsellis was scathing in his condemnation of overseers in 1833, after another had been fined by the magistrates:

> It is a circumstance much to be lamented, that a sense of Duty generally operates little with these persons, when the consequence of Pounds, shillings and pence is concerned.

This was, he insisted, a false saving, as the family of the person kept in the workhouse was likely to become pauperized. The railing against the dominance of chronic admissions was not, however, universal. The 'incurables' had their advocates. The Nottingham Asylum visitors, in appealing for funds in 1826, were not ashamed to claim that the asylum received patients 'whether capable of cure, or past recovery'. If the latter, the asylum had a clear role to provide them with 'the means of passing their hapless existence under the greatest alleviations that such dread maladies will admit'. Within a few months, however, growing congestion in the asylum led the Nottingham managers to modify their welcoming policy.[51]

The passage of the Poor Law Amendment Act in 1834 has been cited by several writers as being particularly influential in determining the nature of subsequent asylum admissions. The significant clause, section 45, stipulated that dangerous lunatics or idiots should not be kept in a workhouse for longer than two weeks; they were to be transferred to a county or public asylum, or to a licensed private establishment. The intention of the section had been to put pressure on poor law unions to ensure the diversion of mentally disordered people to appropriate facilities. However, its emphasis on dangerousness was influential in diverse ways, promoting some admissions whilst discouraging others. The term 'dangerous' remained undefined, and was interpreted differently between unions. At one extreme, the flexibility served the interests of unions reluctant to pay for asylum care, giving a justification to retain in the workhouse people experiencing an acute or florid episode where there was no perceived threat to anyone. Alternatively, where the union adhered to the letter of the law, or where pressurized by the Poor Law Commissioners, the new emphasis led to the transfer of some awkward or difficult people previously managed in the workhouse, some for long periods. The overall effects on asylum admissions were to both increase their levels of problematic behaviour and reinforce their tendency toward chronicity.[52]

The new Poor Law largely accentuated existing patterns of committal. An initial surge of admissions to some asylums followed implementation. The Gloucester Asylum visitors noted in 1836 that many paupers had been sent 'who had been improperly detained in their respective Parishes'. They observed not only the increased numbers, but also

the unfavourable character, of the several cases admitted during the last and present year; a good proportion of such cases consisting of confirmed and incurable Idiots, or involving a combination of epilepsy or palsy in the insanity, highly unfavourable to future recovery, or even relief.

They anticipated, however, that this short-term effect of the new law would soon be exhausted, and that in future it would ensure early admissions. These hopes proved to be too optimistic, as financial considerations continued to dominate much decision-making. Frustrated superintendents continued to have little influence over who entered their asylums. John Garrett, the Stafford superintendent, wrote in 1841 in exasperation to the prime minister Sir Robert Peel, a vice-president of the asylum, calling the situation 'a perfect lottery' which gave little idea of how many admissions to anticipate:

One Poor Law Union sends in all cases of every description; another, to save expense, only sends some, or none; at one time the discharge of harmless cases is solicited from the Committee; and then frequently these very cases are sent back again under fresh warrants of Commitment. . . .

The character of county asylums as receptacles for people with poor prognosis and bleak prospects, instead of curative hospitals, had by now become the reality.[53]

By the early 1840s, literature emanating from asylum medical officers contained frequent reference to the chronic state of many of the patients they were required to receive. George Button of Dorset Asylum complained in 1840 that, of 28 admitted during the year, only six were 'recent cases' with any prospect of recovery. His subsequent reports contained a similar refrain. By the end of 1842 John Kirkman of Suffolk Asylum was lamenting that his ideal of asylums as 'Hospitals for the Insane', places of cure, was in jeopardy. The nature of the people being sent meant that asylums were increasingly becoming places of detention. He followed the orthodox line on how this arose:

Persons are kept back from various causes, till that which was originally functional disturbance, becomes organic disease, and the patient, after having been afflicted for years, is sent to the Asylum, to remain, and end his days, in a place of safe keeping.

The situation, he contended, was getting worse, and admissions had 'a more unfavourable aspect than has appeared since the opening of the Asylum'. He too had to keep repeating his protests, as the asylum became desperately overcrowded with people whose cases were deemed hopeless.[54]

The theme was taken up in November 1841 by the influential asylum superintendents and physicians who attended the inaugural meeting of the Association of Medical Officers of Hospitals for the Insane. They vented their indignation at the prevalent delays by poor law officials in sending people to their asylums. The position received official endorsement when adopted by the Metropolitan Commissioners in Lunacy in their seminal Report of 1844. Although their intention was to promote the general erection of county asylums, they had to acknowledge that many admitted to those already in existence were not of the most promising material. Admission appeared mostly to be 'either indiscriminate or [a] matter of accidental arrangement', without reference to urgency. All asylums were becoming ever more crowded with chronic cases whose prospects were extremely poor. The Commissioners still insisted that the main object of a county asylum should be the 'cure' of insanity. They consequently emphasized what had become almost axiomatic, and what Andrew Scull has characterized as an 'article of faith', that patients had to be sent as early as possible after the appearance of their insanity, if asylum therapy was to be effective. Despite the Commissioners' powerful endorsement of the stream of protest and exhortation, however, the situation altered little and the asylum population continued to disappoint the hopes and expectations of medical officers and committees of visitors.[55]

'A MELANCHOLY SPECTACLE': THE ASYLUM WARD

To appreciate properly the task that faced house committes, boards of governors, superintendents and particularly the 'keepers', there must be some attempt to consider the nature of the congregation of people they were attempting to manage. This is not a particularly straightforward proposition, in the absence of detailed contemporary descriptions of the asylum population or the reality of life on a ward. Observers would naturally comment on the more extreme illustrations of mad behaviour that they witnessed. Thus the Reverend Charles

Higgins, visiting Bedford Asylum in September 1836, was faced with some 'most distressing and appalling objects'. William Ellis was making a point about the prolonged neglect suffered by most patients before admission to Wakefield when he described the majority as a 'melancholy spectacle' in 1829. His successor Corsellis tried to be more positive, referring to his new charges in 1832 as 'unfortunate and interesting individuals'. For most observers, however, it was instances of violent or socially inappropriate behaviour, conforming to preconceived expectations, that aroused comment.[56]

The reality of the patient population was, though, rather more complex. The institution contained people who exhibited all manner of symptomatology, ranging from the profoundly depressed and immobile to the grossly deluded and hyperactive. Those with chronic disorders were accommodated alongside others whose aberrant and deviant symptoms had only recently appeared. The aggregation of all these different types of patient might have been expected to produce a permanent, almost unmanageable, state of chaos on the wards. However, this was not generally the case, for wards and galleries were controlled by relatively few staff. Patients' idiosyncracies to an extent cancelled each other out. Paul Slade Knight's comment in 1827 that the 'characteristic deportment' of the mass of the patients at Lancaster was 'tranquil' was probably not based on any particular merits of that asylum, but was linked to the nature of the interaction of a large assembly of disordered people in a controlled environment.[57]

The apparent tranquillity of most parts of the asylum, for much of the time, was due in part to the presence of the substantial proportion of chronic, 'incurable' patients, many elderly and physically deteriorated. They helped to create a culture permeated by apathy, lethargy and resignation. The relative calm and order was furthered by the mechanisms of control and discipline employed in public asylums since well before the Act of 1808, and which the new thinking promoted by the York Retreat and its spokesman Samuel Tuke had hardly yet altered. Before the 1840s, the display of the means and practice of restraint and coercion acted as powerful determinants of patient behaviour, and deterrents to many of the more overt manifestations of disturbance or excess.[58] The prevalence of order and conformity is, however, not to be overstated. The lunatic asylums, after all, were receiving people who had conducted themselves in ways that were seriously anti-social or that posed risk or threat. The system could contain or repress the worst excesses, but it could not of itself eradicate the symptoms of mental disorder and their associated behaviours.

Some patients were prone to neglect themselves and to act in ways incompatible with meeting basic needs. Food refusal was a commonly reported phenomenon, stemming from depressive apathy or perhaps an active hostility to the asylum regime. In the extreme it proved fatal, as for Thomas Pattinson (45), a Derbyshire man who died three months after admission to Nottingham in 1826; persistent efforts to get him to take food and medicine had failed, as he 'pertinaciously resists all nourishment'. In the case of George Monks (28), admitted the following year, there was an evident protest element; he silently and obstinately refused asylum fare, but persisted in eating grass as an apparently more acceptable alternative. More pervasive than refusal of food, however, was unrestrained consumption. Paul Slade Knight remarked that patients in the worst state ate voraciously, consuming twice as much as sane people. Robert Gardiner Hill, in 1857, recalled that:

> Not many years ago they used to swallow food after the fashion of wild animals; sometimes they were very voracious, and would cram as much into their mouths as possible, and were in danger of being choked.

The Belgian Dr Crommelinck noted in 1841 that lunatics in the asylums he had visited often swallowed their food without chewing it. Although seen as a sign of disinhibited or uncouth behaviour, eating habits were probably not unrelated to the manner of meal provision. Until the late 1830s, food was often provided in tin cans or 'trenchers', without the benefit of potentially dangerous cutlery.[59]

In the prevailing mythology of mental derangement, lunatics were indifferent to, or did not actually feel, the cold. The tendency of patients to discard or destroy footwear, clothing and bedding appeared to confirm an unnatural tolerance of discomfort. Slade Knight, writing about Lancaster Asylum in 1820, explained that:

> many of the unhappy patients cannot be induced, either by persuasion, admonition, or any gentle coercion, to wear their shoes and stockings when up, or their clothing when in bed, and were therefore liable to suffer much from cold in their feet.[60]

Case-notes refer frequently to patients tearing their clothing,[61] usually as symptomatic of their continuing disorder, and often as justification for the imposition of mechanical restraint. In the early months of Norfolk Asylum, the destruction of clothes or bedding was a frequent occurrence. The 'master', Mr Caryl, saw it as defiant behaviour to be dealt with severely, both for prevention and deterrence, as is illustrated by extracts from his Journal in 1814–15:

6 May. John Nudd. Completely distroyed his shirt and rent another so I was under the necessity of Locking him down to his bed.

6 June. Mrs Lincoln. Distroyed her rugg and blanketts for which I keep her lockd in the day chair of the day time and Cross lockd for nights.

6 August. Abraham Ling. Became very violent and distroyed his shirt and Breeches, for which I ordered him to be kept constantly with the Straight westcoat upon him till he behaved better.

Even the most drastic measures could not thwart the really determined patient:

20 February. Robert Russell. Distroy'd his coat all tho chained by both his Hands & Legs, and to the chair – for which I orderd him to his bed and there lockd all day & Night – he also destroys a part of his beding every night.[62]

Despite a vigorous approach, the problem remained endemic. In 1842, Samuel Gaskell reported to the Lancashire magistrates that many of his patients destroyed or refused to wear shoes. He and his colleague De Vitrie were forced to try new solutions. They introduced cloth boots and, to deal with the destruction of clothes, a new garment that combined jacket and trousers, that could only be buttoned from behind.[63]

Indifference to personal hygiene, or inability to maintain it, characterized a large number of patients, particularly among the 'incurables'. A Wakefield doctor noted in 1830 that 70 out of the 260 patients in the West Riding Asylum soiled their beds every night. Sir Edward Bromhead, a vice president of Lincoln Asylum, in 1839 described indifference to the 'calls of nature' as 'the great Blot of our own & other Institutions'. In most larger asylums, separate provision was made for 'dirty' patients, but in several this was not possible. They would be placed either with the refractory patients, or with the 'insensible' or chronic, depending on the behavioural context of the incontinence. At Lancaster, a novel and drastic solution was implemented – specific 'warm rooms' in which incontinent patients were strapped or chained all day in rows of special chairs that doubled as water closets, with direct outlets into the sewage system. Some patients' habits went beyond incontinence. Dr Crommelinck graphically referred to patients who ate their own excrement; the inventive director of Nottingham Asylum, Thomas Powell, contrived a special attachment for latrines to prevent the practice.[64]

Visitors to public asylums could expect to experience disinhibited and socially inappropriate behaviours. Some patients were noisy – shouting, singing or talking wildly. The cumulative effect could be what Slade Knight called in 1820 a 'babble'. There was much bad language, described by the Reverend Charles Higgins as 'frequently too disgusting & demoralizing' for the ears of young female staff at Bedford Asylum in 1836. William Ellis had in mind actions as well as language when he regretted that the conduct of many of his patients at Wakefield was 'depraved and abandoned'. Patients often had few social inhibitions; strangers, like the American Pliny Earle visiting Wakefield in 1841, might be importuned by people begging for tobacco, or money to purchase it. Their behaviour patterns were not solely the consequence of mental disorders, but were aggravated by the rigours, discomforts and restrictions of institutional life.[65]

Although relative tranquillity prevailed in the asylum, violence among patients was not uncommon, directed toward their peers, to staff or to themselves. Every asylum had its core of violent patients, episodic and habitual, of both sexes. Case-notes frequently referred to the behaviour of particular people as violent, wild or furious. Their anger was taken out on furniture and equipment, particularly windows, as well as on other people. Precautionary measures had to be implemented to minimize the effects. William Ellis, before starting office at Hanwell in 1831, called for additional cell accommodation in case the patients should be as 'violent and refractory' as at Wakefield. In part, patients were responding to their circumstances. The incidence of violence was noticeably greater at times of particular stress in the institution, as at Lincoln when the non-restraint system was being exposed to hostile scrutiny in 1840–1, or in the early months of the Norfolk Asylum in 1814.[66]

Violence in the asylum was not a male preserve. Indeed, Paul Slade Knight reckoned in 1827 that, at Lancaster, there had been twice as many women as men who had been 'noisy, violent, and unruly'. The journal of the inexperienced and harassed Mr Caryl at Norfolk Asylum illustrates that he and his small group of staff were having to contain problematic behaviour from women as well as men, as this entry from 1815 shows:

> 29 September. Amy Harris became very violent and broke four panes of Glass in the womens Hospital and 6 in the small Laundry by throwing stones in the womens Convalescent yard. I therefore ordered her to bed, she then broke three panes of Glass in her Cell by throwing her Jordon at the window.. . .

Examples of violent women could be found in all asylums, like Susan Cox (26) of Grantham, admitted to Nottingham in early 1827. Variously described as 'very wild', 'furious', 'very furious' and 'very violent', she had to be placed in a strait waistcoat in a darkened room in an attempt to control her. The experience of Robert Gardiner Hill at Lincoln, in 1840 and 1841 when his non-restraint system was under attack, was that it was in the female refractory North Gallery where the most serious and violent breakdowns of order occurred. Evidence that female asylum patients were more prone to violence is, however, little more than circumstantial, and Slade Knight's bold assertions cannot be verified.[67]

Instances of violence between patients could hardly be unexpected, considering the association of assorted disordered people in a constricted environment. Sometimes random and unpredictable, at others violence occurred in the context of a grudge, as in this incident recorded at Lincoln in 1824:

> 29 October. Robinson, Mr continues very cross, and violent requiring confinement, he flew furiously at Wallis yesterday and struck him over the eye before the Keeper was able to prevent it; some time (more than a month) ago, Wallis struck Robinson which he promised to pay him for, and tho apparently so inanimate has ever borne it in mind since.

Fighting became a serious problem at Lincoln in the early 1840s, when a demoralized staff group, precluded from using even the threat of mechanical restraint, were unable to maintain order. In the volatile atmosphere of Norfolk Asylum in 1815, fights occurred frequently, sometimes involving several people, as illustrated in a report from the master:

> 29 October. I ordered John Batley to be let walk about the yard. He had not been so long before He was Falling out with some of the other Patients and had his face marked and his Leg kicked by some one, who I could not make out. I therefore drest his Leg and ordered him to be Kept with both his Legs Locked to Prevent him from Kicking at others.

Conflicts at times became extremely serious, even fatal. At Norfolk in April 1818, a patient called Bailey was killed by another in a fight. In December 1816, two patients at Nottingham, Thomas Clark and Joseph Taylor, had been killed on successive days by sudden blows from other patients. The house committee responded belatedly by appointing an additional keeper, to ensure there was a keeper for each gallery and that patients were no longer left unsupervised.[68]

Aggression would often be directed toward the staff, who had to be resilient in sustaining assaults of varying magnitude. The tendency was to blame such attacks on the individual and collective pathology of the patients. The incidence of such attacks, however, was clearly related to the nature of the asylum's regime, and the numbers and the level of experience of the staff. The low numbers, poor quality, low pay and inexperience of management and staff help to explain the particular frequency of assaults at Norfolk Asylum in late 1814 and early 1815, where staff were beaten, kicked and even stoned.[69]

Patients' aggression was at times directed inwards. Suicidal attempts, some violent in nature, were not infrequent and were sometimes successful. In 1818, a desperate Nottingham patient, whose known intent led to one of his hands being secured to his bed, managed to strangle himself with the other hand, by twisting a torn sheet round his neck. Hanging or strangulation proved the most common means of suicide. At Norfolk Asylum, Samuel Vincent hanged himself in the lavatory in 1815, using a knotted handkerchief; in 1821, Ann Pierson used her apron suspended from a door. A Lincoln patient, Elizabeth Sewards, managed to strangle herself in August 1821. Self-injury with sharp instruments could be more dramatic. At Norfolk in 1823, Robert King cut a vein in his thigh with a piece of glass; Sarah Fenton's third suicide attempt was by 'cuting her Tongue in two places with an old pair of scissors'. Others chose direct blows to the head. William Goodburn (45) died from a fractured skull after throwing himself over the bannisters at Nottingham in 1825. John Slack (50), whose attempt to hang himself had failed in March 1828, tried to kill himself the next time by striking his head on the wall and the ground. At Norfolk in 1824, Lydia Williams sustained serious facial injuries when she 'attempted to distroy herself by dashing out her braines' against a restraint chair.[70]

In a closed asylum community suicidal behaviour could become contagious. At Lancaster in 1841–2, four patients hanged themselves from the iron window bars within a few months: of these, one used a plaited bed sheet, one a piece of blanket, another a pair of braces. Gaskell and De Vitrie had to implement special precautions to prevent further imitations. C.C. Corsellis observed in 1841 that Wakefield Asylum's history showed that, if word got out about a suicide attempt, it 'generally leads to others of the same nature'.[71]

Patients did not always accept confinement passively. Damage to property and attacks on staff were, in part, signs of protest at both the reality of incarceration and the conditions in the asylum. An institutional counter-culture emerged, particularly under the more custodial regimes. At Norfolk Asylum during 1841, an identified group of disaffected male patients were systematically destroying clothing and equipment, soiling their rooms, attacking other patients and intimidating and defying the 'porters' and the governor. Dr Crommelinck found an insidious undercurrent of simmering resentment in the older part of Lancaster Asylum when he visited in 1841. The patients were sullen and dejected, contemplating vengeance:

his countenance inspires fear, he swears, speaks constantly with anger, insults the visitor as well as the doctor, and is seized with the instinct of injustice, he protests against his sojourn in this prison, and his protestations are always accompanied by very disagreeable gestures and words for the person who must endure them or be afraid of them.

The advocates of 'non-restraint', like Hill and Conolly, argued that it was the whole nature of the environment in the unreformed asylum that promoted disaffection among the patients. With the new system from the late 1830s onwards, their demeanour and character improved accordingly.[72]

Dissent found its most practical and enterprising expression in escape attempts. These occurred quite frequently at all public asylums, and a proportion succeeded. Many were straightforward attempts to scale the perimeter wall. Several escapes occurred among patients working in the grounds or in adjoining fields. Others clearly involved a certain amount of planning. One Gloucester patient in 1841 bolted from a supervised walk. At Stafford, in 1823, a patient ingeniously stole his keeper's keys; in 1830, another escaped from the asylum brewery where he was trusted to assist. At Norfolk Asylum in 1821, a conspiracy by three patients to steal the keeper's keys was thwarted; in 1822 Chas Palmer managed to get away by climbing out through the privy, despite his hands being chained. Escapes were often a source of public alarm, leading to a hue and cry. Rewards for recapture might be offered, as for two men who bolted from Nottingham in 1832; one of them, Valentine Jessopp, was colourfully depicted:

fustian jacket, waistcoat and trousers, ribbed worsted stockings, a black Hat irregularly cut around the brim, with a broad white band, he talks incoherently of his being a son of Napoleon Buonaparte and occasionally sings hymns in a loud tone.

Some even left intending to return, like the seaman John Phillips who escaped from Gloucester in 1843. He wrote to Samuel Hitch to tell him what had happened:

Sir when i left your Astablishment i left with the intenshon Of coming back again but i whent home to Bristol and i got Drinking so i did not like To come back and i left Bristol and whent To Portsmouth to get a ship. . .and i listed thinging i shod not pas the Doctor but he passed me. . .

Phillips clearly had at least some of his wits about him! Others also eluded their pursuers and remained free. Some were recaptured, perhaps to try again another day.[73]

The patients who passed through, or remained in, the asylum made up an amorphous populace. There is little doubt that the level of disturbance or impairment of most was considerable. If they were paupers it had to be so, in order for the parish or the guardians to commit scarce resources. Although growing shortages of space, and the new Poor Law of 1834, had some effects on the asylum population's composition, it did not alter significantly. The 1808 Act and subsequent legislation had reflected the public's desire for protection from the excesses of the deranged, and this continued to be a prime motivator of committal. The pursuit of the curative ideal by reformers and by medical officers usually took second place. The asylums, therefore, had to attempt to contain and care for quite disparate groups of people, whose needs and capacities were frequently incompatible. The emergent regime and environment of the asylum were largely shaped by the capabilities and characteristics of the most disadvantaged and disabled people who entered. Yet, there were many who retained sufficient integrity of personality, or regained it, to ensure that individuality and diversity continued to be features of the asylum population.

NOTES

1 A. Scull, *The Most Solitary of Afflictions: Madness and Society in Britain, 1700–1900* (London, 1993), chapter 7; A. Scull, *Social Order, Mental Disorder* (London, 1989), pp. 239–47; A. Scull, 'Psychiatry and Social Control in the Nineteenth and Twentieth Centuries', *History of Psychiatry*, vol. II, no. 6 (June 1991), pp. 149–69; M. Donnelly, *Managing the Mind: A Study of Medical Psychology in Early Nineteenth Century Britain* (London, 1983), pp. 95–7; David J. Mellett, *The Prerogative of Asylumdom: Social, Cultural and Administrative Aspects of the Institutional Treatment of the Insane in Nineteenth Century Britain* (London, 1982), pp. 8–11. Publications are forthcoming by David Wright on the Buckinghamshire Asylum, Jo Melling, Richard Adair and Bill Forsythe on the Devon Asylum, and Pamela Michael and David Hurst on the North Wales Asylum.

2 J. Walton, 'Lunacy in the Industrial Revolution: A Study of Asylum Admissions, 1848–50', *Journal of Social History*, vol. XIII, no. 1 (Fall 1979),

pp. 1–22; J. Walton, 'Casting Out and Bringing Back in Victorian England: Pauper Lunatics, 1840–70', in W.F. Bynum, R. Porter and M. Shepherd (eds), *The Anatomy of Madness: Essays in the History of Psychiatry* (3 vols, London, 1985–8), vol. II, *Institutions and Society*, pp. 132–46.

3 D. Wright, 'Getting Out of the Asylum: Understanding the Confinement of the Insane in the Nineteenth Century', *Social History of Medicine*, vol. X (April 1997), pp. 137–55.

4 E. Baines, *History, Directory and Gazetteer of the County Palatine of Lancashire* (Liverpool, 1829), vol. II, p. 17.

5 SCRO, D550/65, 'Apothecaries' Day Book' (1818–19), 29 September 1818–21 December 1818; GCRO, HO22/70/1, nos. 5–36; *Staffordshire Advertiser*, 19 December 1818, 16 January 1819; CKS, MH/Md/2/Ap1, 1833–4; L.D. Smith, 'Close Confinement in a Mighty Prison: Thomas Bakewell and his Campaign Against Public Asylums, 1815–1830', *History of Psychiatry*, vol. V (1994), pp. 191–214, pp. 203–5.

6 SCRO, D550/65, 11, 21 November 1818; GCRO, HO22/70/1, no. 18.

7 Lancashire County Record Office (LCRO), QAM 1/30/11, 'Report of Female Patients Admitted into the Lancashire Lunatic Asylum', 1816–17; SCRO, D550/65, 2, 8, 19 October 1818; GCRO, HO22/70/1, 1823–4.

8 B. Forsythe, J. Melling and R. Adair, 'The New Poor Law and the County Pauper Lunatic Asylum – the Devon Experience 1834–1884', *Social History of Medicine*, vol. IX, no. 3 (December 1996), pp. 335–56.

9 R. Porter, *Mind-Forg'd Manacles: A History of Madness in England from the Restoration to the Regency* (Cambridge, 1987), p. 155; Scull, *The Most Solitary of Afflictions*, p. 14; Donnelly, *Managing the Mind*, p. 97.

10 GCRO, HO22/70/1, nos. 3, 156, 218; R.G. Hill, *Total Abolition of Personal Restraint in the Treatment of the Insane: A Lecture on the Management of Lunatic Asylums and the Treatment of the Insane, Delivered at the Mechanics Institution, Lincoln, on the 21st June, 1838* (London, 1839), pp. 31–5; NkCRO, SAH 126, 22 February, 1 March 1822; WRCRO, C85/936.

11 GCRO, HO22/70/1, nos. 20, 23, 47, 149, 210; NCRO, SO/HO/1/9/1, no. 692; NkCRO, SAH 126, 18 February, 20 April 1823; CKS, MH/Md2/Ap1, no. 309.

12 WRCRO, C85/936; GCRO, HO22/70/1, nos. 73, 87, 135.

13 GCRO, HO22/70/1, no. 42; LAO, LAWN 1/1/4, 19 February 1838; Hill, *Total Abolition*, pp. 25–6; WRCRO, C85/936.

14 WRCRO, C85/842; DCRO, *Report of the Visiting Justices of the County Lunatic Asylum* (Epiphany 1842), Obituary Table, no. 11.

15 WRCRO, C85/936; LAO, LAWN 3/1, West Riding Asylum, 5th Report (1823); William Salt Library, Stafford (scrapbook), 'Remarkable Case of the Mucclestone Idiot'.

16 GCRO, HO22/70/1, nos. 4, 5, 14, 25, 32, 38, 79, 96.

17 GCRO, HO22/70/1, nos. 45, 51, 143, 175, 208.

18 WRCRO, C85/842; LCRO, QAM 1/3/11, p. 17; GCRO, HO22/70/1, nos. 26, 64, 65, 168.

19 GCRO, HO22/70/1, no. 219; HO22/70/2, nos. 272, 301, 309; NkCRO, SAH 126, 30 November 1822.

20 LCRO, QAM 1/3/11, p. 127; P. Slade Knight, *Observations on the Causes, Symptoms and Treatment of Derangement of the Mind* (London, 1827), p. 8; GCRO, HO22/70/1, no. 60; NCRO, SO/HO/1/9/1, no. 664.

21 GCRO, D3848/1/1, Hitch Papers, 10 July 1843, U. Fowke to Samuel Hitch, HO22/70/2, no. 292; DCRO, *Report of Visiting Justices* (Epiphany 1842), p. 13.

22 GCRO, HO22/70/1, no. 234, HO22/70/2, nos. 247, 248.

23 SuCRO, B106/10/4.4(2), Suffolk Asylum, 2nd Annual Report (1840), p. 14.

24 Questionnaires which were completed prior to admission normally included a question on cause: e.g. that for the Gloucester Asylum asked for 'Causes and Previous Appearances', GCRO, HO22/70/1.

25 T. Arnold, *Observations on the Nature, Kinds, Causes and Prevention of Insanity* (Leicester, 1782–6); J. Mason Cox, *Practical Observations on Insanity* (London, 1804); J. Haslam, *Observations on Insanity* (London, 1798); T. Bakewell, *The Domestic Guide in Cases of Insanity* (Stafford, 1805); W.S. Hallaran, *An Enquiry into the Causes Producing the Extraordinary Addition to the Numbers of the Insane, Together with extended Observations on the Cure of Insanity* (Cork, 1810).

26 Haslam, *Observations on Insanity*, pp. 99–103.

27 T. Bakewell, *Domestic Guide in Cases of Insanity*, pp. 9–16; T. Bakewell, *A Letter Addressed to the Chairman of the Select Committee of the House of Commons Appointed to Enquire into the State of Mad-Houses: to Which is Subjoined, Remarks on the Nature, Causes, and Cure of Mental Derangement* (Stafford, 1815), pp. 28, 48–50; L.D. Smith, 'To Cure Those Afflicted with the Disease of Insanity: Thomas Bakewell and Spring Vale Asylum', *History of Psychiatry*, vol. IV (1993), pp. 119–20; BPP 1816, vol. VI, *Report of Select Committee on Madhouses, with Minutes of Evidence* (1816), p. 51; Sir A. Halliday, *A General View of the Present State of Lunatics and Lunatic Asylums in Great Britain* (London, 1828), p. 4; J. Conolly, *An Inquiry Concerning the Indications of Insanity* (London, 1830), pp. 14–15.

28 Paul Slade Knight, *Observations on the Causes, Symptoms and Treatment of Derangement of the Mind* (London, 1827), pp. 21–40 (main quote, p. 40).

29 Scull, *Most Solitary of Afflictions*, chapters 4–5.

30 Sir W.C. Ellis, *A Treatise on the Nature, Symptoms, Causes and Treatment of Insanity, With Practical Observations on Lunatic Asylums* (London, 1838), pp. 41, 46, 60–5, 86–93, 100.

31 Ibid., pp. 60–82 (main quote, p. 67).

32 Ibid., pp. 96–7, 335.

33 WRCRO, C85/107, 20th Report of West Riding Asylum (31 December 1838); Table reproduced in A.L. Ashworth, *Stanley Royd Hospital, Wakefield, One Hundred and Fifty Years: A History* (London, 1975), p. 59, and J. Todd and L. Ashworth, *'The House': Wakefield Asylum 1818...* (Wakefield Health Authority, 1993), p. 55.

34 GCRO, HO22/70/1, nos. 73, 79, 87, 96; NCRO, SO/HO/1/9/1, nos. 594, 610–2, 658, 669, 676, 681, 683, 692, 696, 708, 712, 722, 725; WRCRO, C85/107, 19th Report of West Riding Asylum (31 December 1837).

35 GCRO, HO/22/70/1, no. 64; NCRO, SO/HO/1/9/1, nos. 583, 632, 668, 718; WRCRO, C85/842; E. Showalter, *The Female Malady: Women, Madness and English Culture* (London, 1985), pp. 59–61.

36 NCRO, SO/HO/1/9/1, nos. 647, 673; GCRO, HO22/70/1, no. 191, HO22/70/2, nos. 239, 242.

37 J. Conolly, *The Construction and Government of Lunatic Asylums* (London, 1847), p. 66; WRCRO, C85/107, 20th Report of West Riding Asylum (31 December 1838), C85/114, 27th Report (1846), p. 4; LPL, *Report of the Medical Officers of the Lunatic Asylum for the County of Lancaster* (1841), p. 11; GCRO, HO22/70/1, no. 204.

38 GCRO, HO22/70/1, nos. 3, 62; NCRO, SO/HO/1/9/1, nos. 613, 627; DCRO, Report of Visiting Justices (Epiphany 1844), p. 37.

39 WRCRO, C85/114, West Riding Asylum, 20th Report (1839), p. 7, 26th Report (1845), p. 5, 27th Report (1846), p. 4 (main quote); GCRO, HO22/70/1, nos. 40, 62, 149, 150, 151, 156, 175, 196; NCRO, SO/HO/1/9/1, nos. 595, 607, 614, 644, 662, 690, 724.

40 SuCRO, B106/10/4.4 (3), Suffolk Asylum, 3rd Report (1841), p. 13; WRCRO, C85/114, West Riding Asylum, 20th Report (1839), p. 7; Caleb Crowther, *Some Observations Respecting the Management of the Pauper Lunatic Asylum at Wakefield* (Wakefield, 1830), p. 14; DCRO, *Report of Visiting Justices* (Epiphany 1842), p. 10.

41 Conolly, *Construction and Government of Lunatic Asylums*, p. 123; DCRO, Report of Visiting Justices (Epiphany 1844), p. 35.

42 GCRO, HO22/70/1, nos. 70, 219, 234, HO22/70/2, nos. 246, 248; NCRO, SO/HO/1/9/1, nos. 582, 590, 708, 718, 768, 769, 772, 804, 811; NkCRO, SAH 126, 1 June 1822, 8 September, 2 December 1824, SAH 127, 8 August 1832, 7 January 1833; LCRO, QAM 1/30/11, p. 9; D. Hempton, *The Religion of the People: Methodism and Popular Religion c.1750–1900* (London, 1996), pp. 150–9; E.P. Thompson, *The Making of the English Working Class* (Harmondsworth, 1968), pp. 400–30, shows the profound emotional effects that Wesleyan Methodism might have on vulnerable individuals.

43 WRCRO, C85/842, 3 November 1823; NCRO, SO/HO/1/9/1, nos. 722, 769.

44 NCRO, SO/HO/1/9/1, nos. 589, 623, 671, 705; NkCRO, SAH 125, 11 October 1815; WRCRO, C85/842, 21 April, 30 July 1821, 30 July 1823, C85/107, West Riding Asylum, 20th Report; GCRO, HO22/70/1, nos. 2, 142, HO22/70/2, no. 250; A. Digby, *Madness, Morality and Medicine: A Study of the York Retreat, 1796–1914* (Cambridge, 1985), p. 212.

45 NCRO, SO/HO/1/9/1, nos. 634, 652; GCRO, HO22/70/1, nos. 133, 138; WRCRO, West Riding Asylum, 20th Report.

46 WRCRO, C85/107, West Riding Asylum, 20th Report; NCRO, SO/HO/1/9/1, no. 737; GCRO, HO22/7/1, no. 170.

47 48 Geo. III, Cap. 96, Section XVII; 51 Geo. III, Cap. 79, Section I.

48 NCRO, SO/HO/1/3/1, 19 February, 25 March 1812; SCRO, D550/1, 2 November, 31 December 1818.

49 NCRO, QS/CA/358, Annual Reports, 24 June 1815, 30 June 1816; Paul Slade Knight, *A Letter to the Right Honourable Lord Stanley, and the Other Visiting Justices of the Lunatic Asylum for the County of Lancaster* (Lancaster, 1822), pp. 11–15.

50 *West Briton*, 20 September 1822; WRCRO, C85/107, West Riding Asylum, 1st Report (31 December 1819), 2nd Report (31 December 1820), 3rd Report (31 December 1821), 7th Report (31 December 1825); LAO, LAWN 3/1, West Riding Asylum, 4th Report (31 December 1822).

51 GCRO, HO22/8/1, Gloucester Asylum, Annual Reports, 1825, 1827, 1828; WRCRO, C85/107, West Riding Asylum, 11th Report (31 December 1829), 14th Report (2 January 1833); *Nottingham Journal*, 21 October 1826, 10 November 1827; NCRO, SO/HO/1/3/2, 12 April, 12 July, 16 August 1827.

52 K. Jones, *A History of the Mental Health Services* (London, 1972), pp. 124–6; R.G. Hodgkinson, 'Provision for Pauper Lunatics 1834–1871', *Medical History*, vol. X (1966), pp. 138–54; W.L. Parry-Jones, *The Trade in Lunacy* (London, 1972), p. 19; Donnelly, *Managing the Mind*, pp. 13–15; Mellett, *The Prerogative of Asylumdom*, pp. 134–7; P. Bartlett, *The Poor Law of Lunacy: The Administration of Pauper Lunatics in Mid-Nineteenth Century England With Special Emphasis on Leicestershire and Rutland* (PhD, University of London, 1993), pp. 145–6.

53 GRL, (H) G1.6, Gloucester Asylum, 13th Report (1836); British Museum Add. MSS, 40,429, Peel Papers, vol. CCXLIX, fos. 108–11, 114–15 (quote).

54 DCRO, *Report of the Visiting Justices* (Epiphany 1840), p. 4; Report of the Visiting Justices (Epiphany 1842), p. 9; Report of the Visiting Justices (Epiphany 1844), p. 11; SuCRO, B106/10/4.4, Suffolk Asylum, 5th Report (1843), pp. 5–6 (containing quotes), 6th Report (1844), pp. 5–6, 7th Report (1845), pp. 5–7; see also I. Lodge Patch, 'The Surrey County Lunatic Asylum (Springfield): Early Years in the Development of an Institution', *British Journal of Psychiatry*, vol. CLIX (July 1991), pp. 69–77.

55 *Report of the Metropolitan Commissioners in Lunacy to the Lord Chancellor* (1844), pp. 85–93; Scull, *Most Solitary of Afflictions*, p. 163; Mellett, *Prerogative of Asylumdom*, pp. 28–33.

56 BCRO, LB/2/3, 14 September 1836; WRCRO, C85/107, West Riding Asylum, 11th Report (31 December 1829), 13th Report (31 December 1831).

57 Knight, *Observations on Derangement of the Mind* (London, 1827), p. 25.

58 See chapter 8 for the employment of restraint.

59 NCRO, SO/HO/1/9/1, nos. 668, 679, 707, 722; Knight, *Observations on Derangement of the Mind*, p. 120; R.G. Hill, *A Concise History of the Entire Abolition of Mechanical Restraint in the Treatment of the Insane and of the Introduction, Success and Final Triumph of the Non-Restraint System* (London, 1857), pp. 82–3; C. Crommelinck, *Rapport sur les Hospices d'Aliénés de l'Angleterre, de la France et de l'Allemagne* (Courtrai, 1842), p. 71.

60 *Lonsdale Magazine*, February 1821, p. 44.

61 NCRO, SO/HO/1/9/1, nos. 658, 669, 730.

62 NkCRO, SAH 123, 6 May 1814–27 November 1815.

63 LPL, *Report of the Medical Officers* (1841), pp. 9–10.

64 W.H. Gilbey, 'On the Dysentery Which Occurred in the Wakefield Lunatic Asylum in the Years 1826, 1827, 1828, and 1829', *North of England Medical and Surgical Journal*, vol. I (1830–1), pp. 91–101; LAO, LAWN 1/2/3, 'Governors' Memorandum Book', 10 April 1839; LPL, *Report of the Medical Officers* (1841), p. 4; Crommelinck, *Rapport sur les Hospices*, p. 148; *Journal of Mental Science*, vol. II (1855), no. 17, p. 268.

65 *Lonsdale Magazine*, February 1821, pp. 44–6; BCRO, LB/2/3, 14 September 1836; LAO, LAWN 3/1, West Riding Asylum, 6th Report (31 December 1824); Pliny Earle, *A Visit to Thirteen Asylums for the Insane in Europe* (Philadelphia, 1841), p. 12.

66 GLRO, MA/A/J/2, 6 January 1831; LAO, LAWN 1/1/4, 2 March 1840–21 June 1841; NkCRO, SAH 123.

67 Knight, *Observations on the Derangement of the Mind*, p. 91; NkCRO, SAH 123, 27 September 1815; NCRO, SO/HO/1/9/1, no. 703; LAO, LAWN 1/1/4, 25 May, 15 June, 8 July 1840, 4, 18 October 1841.

68 LAO, LAWN 1/2/1, 29 October 1824, LAWN 1/1/4, 26 October, 14, 21 December 1840, 4, 25 January, 1 March, 17 May, 21 June 1841, LAWN 1/1/5, 11 April, 26 September 1842; NkCRO, SAH 3, 27 April 1818, SAH 123, 29 October 1815; NCRO, SO/HO/1/3/1, 26 December 1816, 2 January 1817.

69 NkCRO, SAH 123, 24 September, 23 December 1814, 1, 3 January, 24 February, 6, 26 March 1815.

70 NCRO, SO/HO/1/9/1, nos. 600, 768; NRL, qL3648, Nottingham Asylum, 8th Report (1818); LAO, LAWN 1/1/1, 27 August, 3 September 1821; NkCRO, SAH 123, 19 September 1815, SAH 126, 5 January 1821, 5, 20 October 1823, 5 February 1824.

71 LPL, *Report of the Medical Officers* (1842), pp. 8–12; WRCRO, C85/107, West Riding Asylum, 23rd Report (31 December 1841).

72 NkCRO, SAH 127, 18 January–12 December 1841; Crommelinck, *Rapport sur les Hospices*, p. 137; Hill, *Entire Abolition of Mechanical Restraint*; J. Conolly, *The Treatment of the Insane Without Mechanical Restraints* (London, 1856).

73 NkCRO, SAH 123, 22 February, 20 May 1815, SAH 126, 18 November 1821, 15, 17 September 1822, SAH 127, 24, 25 February 1840; NCRO, SO/HO/1/3/2, 30 July 1832 (quote), 14 July 1836, SO/HO/1/3/3, 14 December 1842; SCRO, D550/3, 19 February 1823, D550/4, 9 July 1830, D550/5, 27 July 1836; GCRO, HO22/1/1, 29 January 1823, HO22/3/1, 30 January 1827, 27 March 1829, 28 May, 24 September, 31 December 1830, HO22/3/2, 12 August 1839, 23 February, 25 October 1841, 20 October, 19 November 1843, 27 May 1845, D3848/1/1, no. 79, 18 July 1839, 25 May 1843 (quote); LAO, LAWN 1/1/1, 23 September 1822, 12 May 1823, LAWN 1/1/2, 26 May 1828, LAWN 1/1/3, 14 May 1832, 10 February 1834, 16 January, 15 May 1837, LAWN 1/1/4, 16, 21 April 1838, 11 March 1839.

4

'The Most Essential Instruments': From Keepers to Attendants

Whether the orientation of an asylum veered more toward custody or toward cure, the role of the staff who attended directly to the patients was central. They formed the crucial link between the regime and the individual patient, mediating and implementing the policy and practice decisions of the visitors and the superintendent. Yet their situation was by nature paradoxical. Within the institutional hierarchy, they were considered 'menials', markedly subordinate to the superintendent. At the same time, however, they exercised considerable authority and control over the patients, individually and collectively, their position and influence enhanced by their relatively small numbers.

The lowly status of asylum staff was reflected and reinforced by the nomenclature. Generically, in the eighteenth and early nineteenth centuries they were referred to as 'servants'. Their custodial role was emphasized by the increasingly common usage of the description of 'keeper', with its associations of prison. There was also a significant domestic service element, directly expressed in the terms 'porter' and 'maidservant', employed at the Norfolk Asylum. As asylum regimes were reformed and attained greater sophistication from the 1830s onwards, older terminology acquired unwelcome connotations. With a stronger emphasis on the asylum's curative intent, the staff role acquired a more caring aspect. The male keeper now became an 'attendant' and the female keeper a 'nurse'.

For Anne Digby, in her study of the York Retreat, staff formed the 'hidden dimension' that historians of the nineteenth-century asylum had tended to overlook. There have now been attempts to begin to redress the omission. Most historiography has tended to stress the limitations of those placed in the responsible position of providing direct care to patients, as indeed did some contemporaries. Keepers and attendants have been widely characterized as being recruited from the lowest strata of society, as being intellectually limited and as being unsophisticated in their approach to caring. Their shortcomings could provide contemporaries with a convenient explanation for the asylum's low recovery rates. Their deficiencies were reflected in poor pay and low status. However, like all generalizations, although having some foundation, they are open to challenge. There is enough evidence of humane practice and of positive relationships between patients and staff to render such conclusions unsafe. For John Conolly, the attendants were 'the most essential instruments' of the non-restraint system. This pivotal role was as applicable under the old regime as it was in the post-1845 asylum.[1]

'LIMBS OF BRITISH OAK, AND NERVES OF WIRE'

> It must. . .be of the first importance that (with allowance for the difficult and painful nature of their duties,) the attendants should possess experience and integrity, and be themselves, by their character and conduct, able to command the respect and confidence of the patients entrusted to their care.[2]

The significance of the keepers to the asylum's workings was partly determined by their scarcity. Norms as to the staff–patient ratio had become established before the era of county asylums, with one keeper usually being responsible for a whole ward or gallery. Liverpool Asylum, in 1812, employed two male and two female 'servants' for its 70 patients. At its counterpart in Manchester in 1818, there were three men and two women assistants for over 90 patients. These ratios were initially bettered in the county asylums. Nottingham Asylum began with four keepers, two of each sex, which was increased to six by 1815, although a fatal incident there in late 1816 ensured the reluctant acceptance of the principle of one keeper to each gallery. This meant that new asylums would open with a relatively high staff–patient ratio, until their numbers began to build up. At Stafford, within a few months of opening, there was a keeper for each of the six galleries, though there were fewer than 60 patients in the asylum. Such relatively generous ratios did not continue, however, as patient numbers grew and cells and galleries filled.[3]

The basic standard of one keeper per gallery remained established practice. By 1830, in some larger asylums, each keeper was looking after upwards of twenty patients. At Lancaster, fifteen keepers were in charge of over 330 patients. Elsewhere, arrangements were more generous. At Stafford, there were thirteen for 190 patients, and at Gloucester eleven for about 100, whilst at Bodmin there were six for 82 patients, and at Bedford seven for only 52. Staffing levels had to take account of the growing numbers of patients whose levels of dependence or disturbance presented greater call on the keeper's time, and of the need to ensure adequate security. It became increasingly common for an assistant keeper to be employed on wards for refractory or 'dirty' patients, a need taken into account by the Middlesex justices in planning their Hanwell showpiece. They calculated that most patients would require a ratio of one keeper to 24; however, those who were 'dangerous, wet, or noisy' needed a ratio of one to twelve.[4]

For justices and superintendents, thrift and economy were serious concerns to be balanced against provision of a proper level of care and supervision, which accounted for wide differentials in staffing levels. The notoriously parsimonious Norfolk justices were, in 1840, employing only six keepers and nurses for their 180 patients, a ratio of 1:30. At the other end of the scale, proportions at Stafford (seventeen keepers), Gloucester (fourteen) and Maidstone in the same year were 1:15. In between, Hanwell's 48 keepers (and 870 patients) made for a ratio of 1:18. The other two very large asylums, Wakefield and Lancaster, were both managing with ratios of approximately 1:24. The dissemination of the non-restraint system had some effect on staffing levels, with the recognition that it required more staff to manage difficult patients, but this did not materially alter the significant differences that persisted.[5]

Asylum managers largely recognized the importance of recruiting staff of sufficient calibre, in order both to enable the asylum to function and to convince parish officers that the institution was a safe option for their unpredictable clientele. For example, on opening in 1818, the Stafford visitors advised the public that they had appointed 'skilful Officers and Servants', who would provide for the 'care and protection' of the unfortunate patients, and implement medical and moral treatment with 'kindness, attention, and humanity'. Each class of patients would have the benefit of 'Experienced Keepers'. In reality, this was little more than a statement of hope, for there was rarely a ready source of staff with direct experience of care of the insane. Most superintendents had to recruit as best they could, according to the dictates of their local labour market. This usually meant bringing in people from a variety of backgrounds, who appeared to possess suitable physical and personal characteristics.[6]

Where possible, staff who had some direct experience were recruited. William Ellis at Wakefield was able to use his personal connections to appoint a keeper who had worked at the Retreat for several years. Later, when he moved to Hanwell in 1831, he took three of his trusted Wakefield staff with him, though two could not settle and returned to their previous posts. The assistance received by George Poynder from Stafford's John Garrett in setting up Gloucester Asylum included the recommendation of the keepers John Hart and Edward Day, who had worked at Stafford for two years and a year respectively. A third, Joseph Carter, came with a recommendation from Nottingham, and a fourth experienced man came recommended by William Ricketts, the proprietor of the private Droitwich Asylum. Desirable as it was perceived to be, however, previous experience did not guarantee suitability. Poynder's successor Samuel Hitch in 1838 recruited Lawrence Flinn, earlier employed at two private asylums (William Conolly's at Castleton House, Cheltenham, and Bompas's at Fishponds near Bristol). Only after appointing Flinn was Hitch advised that at Fishponds his conduct had been of 'an immoral and improper nature', and at Castleton House the 'duplicity and falsehood' in his character had led to his early departure. The precipitate employment of an apparently experienced man demonstrated some lack of liaison between asylum managers and proprietors.[7]

Other asylums were not as successful as Gloucester in attracting staff who had learned the role elsewhere. One alternative to the recruitment of experienced people was internal promotion, an arrangement that had been common in eighteenth-century Bethlem. This was most feasible for female staff, where young women appointed as domestic servants could gain some knowledge and understanding of other aspects of asylum work. At Stafford, a chain of promotion developed, whereby staff were gradually advanced to the role of keeper. In July 1824, when Frances Uppendine, assistant keeper in the female lower basement, gave notice, Sarah Devole, the kitchen maid, was appointed in her place. The following year, when Devole herself left, she was replaced by Prudence Harding, 'errand girl and housemaid'. In March 1834, with the departure of Jane Price, the keeper of the 'Chamber Story', a series of promotions followed: Jane Toy was advanced from the lower paid 'Attic Gallery', and her place taken by Elizabeth Dodd, the upper housemaid; Dodd was succeed by Jane Johnson, the kitchen maid, who was replaced by Ann Hodgson, the laundry girl (who subsequently progressed to upper housemaid and then keeper). Elsewhere, domestic work was also used as a preparation, though to a lesser extent than at Stafford. At Lincoln in the 1830s, the porter was promoted to keeper, and 'charwomen' were advanced to nurses, though more as a response to a desperate staffing situation than as a planned process of promotion.[8]

Where recruitment or internal promotion did not produce experienced staff, there was little pattern to the type of people engaged. In an advertisement for 'Servants' in 1831, the Lincoln governors advised that 'Persons from the Country will be preferred'; it was unclear whether this was because of their likely attitudes or attributes, or because of their expectation of lower wages. Certainly, agricultural workers formed one of the main sources of keepers for private asylums. The perceived nature of the work led some superintendents to favour people with an institutional or a disciplinary background, like the army or the prison service, which appeared to have provided the bulk of the male staff at Middlesex Asylum. Joseph Tindall, a London policeman, was engaged as a keeper at Lincoln in August 1831. Most commonly, male keepers were recruited from among the semi-skilled or skilled artisan class. When Suffolk Asylum opened in 1829, the first three men appointed were Thomas Warne (24), a bricklayer and plasterer, George Durrent (25), a carpenter, and Joseph Joss (23), a smith. Their deficiencies in knowledge and skills were compensated by the expensive recruitment for three months of William Webster, an experienced keeper from London, to instruct them.[9]

The employment of artisan tradesmen had direct practical advantages in the economical running of an asylum where basic staffing levels were kept low. At Cornwall Asylum in the early 1820s, of the three male keepers, the head keeper was also the baker, and another doubled as shoemaker. At Stafford, it was the practice to employ a brewer/keeper; in 1836, John Gripton was engaged as 'Keeper & Brewer, & to Milk the Cows &c'. At Nottingham in 1832, Thomas Powell, the superintendent, was ordered to enquire for 'an efficient Gardner to act also as a Keeper'. At Wakefield, where the supervision of working patients was a key aspect of the keeper's role, the early recruits included a shoemaker, a gardener and a 'cloth manufacturer'. A similar practice followed elsewhere, at Gloucester for example, as employment schemes were developed. Even where specialist tradesmen, such as carpenters, joiners, engineers or bakers, were employed primarily to conduct their trade, it was expected that their role would include some direct work with patients.[10]

A significant element of the keeper's role comprised routine domestic work. Consequently, domestic servants – butlers, grooms and maids – provided a fertile source of asylum staff. At Hanwell, most female nurses came from a domestic service background. They could bring the advantages of proven reliability and loyalty, backed by a reference from a respectable source. At Stafford in 1829, John Garrett appointed as assistant keeper Richard Wiggin, who had previously 'lived in the service of Mr Beech', a 'gentleman', from whom he received a 'good character'. The appointment evidently proved successful, for Wiggin was still working in the asylum fifteen years later. John Conolly's experience led him to conclude that 'the class of persons who are qualified to be upper servants' proved to be the best attendants, whether male or female.[11]

One group who knew all about the realities of asylum life was the patients. A few were deemed sufficiently responsible and capable on recovery to be employed as staff, either as domestics or as keepers. Some recovered patients made the transition at Hanwell; four were taken on as nurses between 1834 and 1839, and all these remained in post for at least five years. At Stafford, particularly in its early years, ex-patients were employed on several occasions. During 1819, a convalescent man named Redfern was briefly given responsibility for eight patients, and Sarah Hatton was put in charge of a gallery, a post she retained for five months. Both, however, suffered relapses and resumed patient status. In February 1821, the newly discharged Luke Statham was retained as keeper, but lasted only three months. Despite the limited success of these arrangements, John Garrett persevered. During 1822, three patients, John Ford, Frances Tucker and Frances Uppendine, were made up to keepers on discharge. Ford lasted six months, and Tucker four months before she became a patient again, but Frances Uppendine continued as a keeper for over two years. The employment of former patients begs questions as to whether they were viewed as conveniently accessible labour by unparticular managers, or whether their retention indicated an enlightened use of their unique experience.[12]

Out of the unlikely material from which asylum staff were drawn, exemplary qualities and attributes were expected. Ideals associated with 'moral treatment' influenced expectations, even in institutions where practices were essentially custodial. Paul Slade Knight of Lancaster Asylum suggested in 1821 that it was 'of the utmost consequence' that keepers should be 'of good moral and religious characters, minutely clean, mild, firm, and intelligent'. Prescribed in the rules of Suffolk Asylum were certain standards of conduct, which prefaced the keepers' practical responsibilities; their first duty was to observe 'the utmost patience, mildness, and forbearance' toward the patients. An expectation of unexceptionable conduct became the norm, as in C.C. Corsellis's call for 'constant vigilance, forbearance, and kindness'. Tuke, in 1841, went further and contended that the attendant was required to 'counteract some of the strongest principles of our common nature'. Samuel Gaskell and Edmund de Vitrie, having considered the recruitment requirements for reform of Lancaster Asylum's regime, noted that, although the role was essentially 'menial', something more than a 'mere servant' was wanted; attendants should be well educated and have principles and 'moral character' to withstand close investigation. Above all, they needed 'great forbearance' and an ability to control temper under 'the most exasperating circumstances'. The welfare of the patient, with all his imperfections, was to be the attendant's primary consideration. These sorts of requirements allowed little place for human frailty.[13]

The reality frequently departed from the ideal, as several commentators lamented. The influential Scottish alienist W.A.F. Browne observed that asylum servants were often 'of the very worst caste', and 'coarse and uneducated'. His opinion of their general character was particularly poor: 'Keepers are the unemployed of other professions. If they possess physical strength, and a tolerable reputation of sobriety, it is enough, and the latter quality is frequently dispensed with.' Tuke had been slightly more charitable, suggesting that in large asylums staff rarely possessed the necessary qualities, 'unless we consider as such: "Limbs of British oak, and nerves of wire"'. In practice, certain physical attributes were always considered necessary. Even where cure was the main object, keepers required an imposing presence for reasons of security and control. It was not only a question of size and strength, but also of general deportment, as Knight explained:

> It is of importance that all who have the charge of ministering to the insane, should have prepossessing persons and manners; and nothing in either, that could easily be ridiculed, much less excite ridicule, because all lunatics are physiognomists, and many of them very acute and sarcastic observers.

Advertisements for keepers or attendants frequently emphasized youth, vigour and height. Like at Lincoln in the 1830s, they would be chosen for their 'strength, activity, and possession of temper'. As Peter Nolan has shown, the nature of the work was seen to require 'stout men'.[14]

The personal qualities of staff were bound to fall short of the expressed hopes and expectations. Andrew Scull was unduly blunt in characterizing keepers and attendants as drawn from the 'dregs of society'. However, their deficiencies were widely recognized by contemporaries. Harriet Martineau, after her visits to Hanwell, acknowledged the difficulties that the Ellises experienced in selecting suitable staff from 'the multitude of ignorant mercenaries' who applied. Their illustrious successor, John Conolly, later stigmatized most keepers in the unreformed asylums as 'merely persons unfit for any other employment', fierce and 'utterly untrustworthy'. Patients might be subjected to the control of 'discharged servants, idle and dissipated mechanics, and other objectionable characters, to whom [one] would not have entrusted the care of valuable dogs'. Conolly perhaps had a point to drive home, boldly contrasting the practices of the model 'non-restraint' asylum with the abuses of earlier years. He had highlighted the shortcomings of a proportion of asylum employees, to judge by the steady stream of dismissals that occurred. However, there were many to whom Conolly's strictures could not fairly be applied, who were committed to the service of the patients and who put up with the unwholesome aspects of the work, despite the disadvantageous pay, status and conditions.[15]

THE TASK

> Never take a fancy to one patient more than another; have no favourites; treat them all alike, and always with care and circumspection; be all eye to their looks and movements, and all ear to their expressions; their ways are to be closely and constantly watched: for it is thus that their disorders are to be found out, and the best modes of treating them.[16]

The task of keeper, nurse or attendant was always complex and many-faceted. Nolan has identified four main aspects – rule keeper and enforcer; servant to the patients; spiritual guide; and intermediary between doctor and patient.[17] There were other elements too, like protection of the vulnerable, and a therapeutic role which included observation and encouragement. On a practical level, the keeper provided occupation and amusement to his charges. In addition, he (or she) was there to offer an example, even a role model of proper, respectable and normal behaviour. The balance of emphasis between these roles would vary according to places and situations. They were all, however, somehow to be carried out by one unremarkable person of relatively humble station, who was much of the time in sole charge of upwards of twenty patients.

The keepers' arduous duties began at the point of admission, when they were required to examine each person and their clothing, removing any potentially dangerous items. A more personal physical examination might be prescribed, as at Dorset Asylum, where the keepers had to check for swelling, spots and vermin, and then cut and cleanse the hair. The upkeep of hygiene and cleanliness was an ongoing responsibility. At Gloucester, the keepers were to wash their patients and comb their hair daily, wash their feet weekly, and shave the men twice weekly. At Forston (Dorset), they were expected to give 'strict attention' to 'a high degree of cleanliness in every particular', and daily examine the skin for soreness and discoloration. The table of attendants' duties introduced at Lancaster in 1841 was even more prescriptive and specific. The attendants had to cut patients' hair each month, bath them fortnightly, change their clothes and put dubbin on their shoes weekly, and shave them and change their linen twice weekly, as well as provide a daily wash and hair brush.[18]

It was important for staff to ensure that patients retained at least the vestiges of respectable appearance. The image of the wild, unkempt madman had to be dispelled. Consequently, shaving was a closely regulated activity, perhaps with specified days; at Middlesex and Dorset, Wednesdays and Saturdays. Keepers might earn additional pay for shaving; at Bedford they were given one penny per patient, up to twice per week. At Lincoln, they received an annual addition of half a guinea. As late as 1846, payments of one penny per head were implemented at Norfolk Asylum. The job could be given to a particular keeper; at Bodmin, one man combined the roles of 'Head keeper, Baker and Shaver'. At Stafford, in 1819, Thomas Barnes was granted an additional £5 on his salary for shaving the patients. Clearly, this was a duty regarded with some distaste, which required additional inducements.[19]

The emphasis on cleanliness and neatness applied also to the physical surroundings. In the mornings, after attending to patients' hygiene and taking them to breakfast, the keeper's attention moved to the cells and galleries. The actual duties would usually be stated explicitly in the rules, as at Lincoln:

> That they shall wash all the apartments in the respective Wards, as often as the Director shall appoint; and that they shall sweep them every morning, conveying away all foul straw and dirt, so that every part of the house and premises may be preserved clean, neat, and wholesome.

The Nottingham rules had the added requirement to convey 'foul straw, dirt, and filth' to the garden before nine. The maintenance of cleanliness remained central to the keeper's role. This was made clear in the detailed directions issued at Lancaster in 1841, which underlined the attendants' duty to preserve 'the utmost neatness, order, and cleanliness', as ordered surroundings would help to soothe the mind and provide an example to the recovering patient. Although Gaskell and de Vitrie had construed much of the work as 'menial', they did not minimize its importance in the curative process.[20]

Practical duties continued from morning until night. Waking times for staff and patients were usually laid down. The less able or motivated inmates would have to be helped from bed and then assisted to dress.

Beds had to be made each morning. At meal times, the keepers supervised the patients in the dining area, and distributed, maintained and cleaned the utensils and implements. Responsibilities also included the care of other equipment, such as bedding, chamber pots and furniture. In asylums like Wakefield, where employment was established extensively, the oversight of working patients was a principal aspect of the keeper's task. Where patients were less fully occupied, they had to be overseen in the day-room or directed in the airing court. Finally, in the evening, the staff had to ensure that they were put to bed, and in some instances secured there. Even then, the duties had not ended, for the keeper remained in charge whilst asleep, as before the early 1840s there were no serious moves to employ night-watch staff.[21]

The work of the staff was directed largely toward creating and perpetuating an ordered and regulated institution. Central to this, the asylum had to provide protection and security for patients, staff and the wider public. To minimize the chances of escape, keepers were expected to lock and unlock the cell, gallery and day-room doors at the relevant times. The keys would be attached to their clothing, or to a belt, to ensure safe-keeping. They were required to maintain order within their galleries, and to ensure that patients were not put at risk by their own actions or by those of others. Suicidal attempts, and outbreaks of violence, had occasionally to be prevented. These responsibilities required both continual vigilance and a readiness to intervene actively on occasions. Until the reforms of the late 1830s, the brief to preserve order and security was backed by ready access to the implements of mechanical restraint.[22]

Although the custodial and the menial aspects of the role predominated, there were also definite therapeutic and caring elements. However restrictive or austere the regime, some part of the keeper's efforts was directed toward maintaining patients' physical health and contributing toward their mental recovery. The common injunction to exercise 'patience, mildness, and forbearance', and the checks that were in place, emphasized the interpersonal component. The manner in which staff were to relate to patients might be laid out in some detail. The Gloucester rules of 1823 were fairly specific:

> No Keeper shall at any time attempt to deceive or to terrify a patient; nor to irritate the patient by mockery, by mimicry, or by wanton allusions to any thing ludicrous in the present appearance or ridiculous in the past conduct of the patient.

They were not to 'indulge or express vindictive feelings', but forgive 'all petulance and sarcasms', treating the least and the most troublesome with equal consideration. If adhered to, such exhortations denoted an important therapeutic dimension.[23]

The content of later guidance and instructions to staff became increasingly sophisticated. At the Oxford Asylum, the keepers were to regard themselves as performing a sacred duty:

> ALWAYS bear in mind that you are in your senses, and that those who are under your care are not: this is your health and happiness; that is their affliction and disease: and you cannot better shew your gratitude to God for his mercy and goodness to yourself, than by shewing kindness and consideration to these your afflicted brethren.

The tone here was unusually religiose. Like their near neighbours at Gloucester, the Radcliffe's keepers were expected to exercise exemplary self-control under provocation. They could not allow themselves to be angered by 'scoffs, taunts, or mockery', for these were 'words without meaning in the mouths of those who utter them'. Although less overtly religious in orientation, the post-1832 expectations on the Lincoln 'attendants' displayed similar concern for the patient's dignity and individuality. Staff should not try to 'deceive or terrify' any patient, or violate promises. They were not to show 'incivility, disrespect, contempt, mockery, mimicry, or sarcasm', not to allude to anything 'ridiculous or degrading', nor swear at or address them in a raised voice or 'imperious tone'. The problem, however, with these sorts of entreaties was that the standards were hard to enforce. The experience at Lincoln over the next decade showed that practical reality could fall far short of what was anticipated.[24]

The publication of detailed instructions for staff appears to have begun in the 1840s, and was certainly more an attempt to raise poor standards than an illustration of current practice. Those produced at Lancaster in 1841 were part of a wide-ranging attempt to counteract more than two decades of sterility and repression. Attendants' duties were set out, comprising the daily routine, and responsibilities in the areas of domestic work, administration, security and direct patient care. Perhaps more significant than the recitation of duties, however, were the supplementary directions to regulate conduct. The preamble set the new tone:

> It is the duty of every attendant to endeavour to acquire an interest in the cases under his care. He should try to bring himself to feel a strong desire to promote their recovery, and should make a determination to use every means in his power to accomplish that end. He should also be active in devising means to render them comfortable and happy as circumstances may admit.

The standards of behaviour emphasized the importance of self-restraint, of understanding and appreciating the basis of the patients' unpredictable presentations, and of kind and fair treatment. Where violence occurred, guidance was given on how to deal with it carefully and cautiously, or by the rapid presence of sufficient numbers of staff, rather than by direct physical intervention.[25]

The Lancaster instructions called for the highest individual qualities from attendants, in both the caring and the supervisory aspects of their work:

> The personal services which are rendered to the sufferers must be characterised by an untiring patience, a constant exercise of gentleness, and be combined with the utmost vigilance. At no time must the attendant allow his mind to relax, nor must he ever display the least irritability, but strive to conduct everything with the greatest calmness.

Other establishments gradually followed in formulating detailed regulations, coupled with similar injunctions on standards of performance. At Hanwell, they were laid out in a 'Manual' of the attendant's duties in 1846. Such regulations formed the basis of later more sophisticated staff handbooks. Their precepts were an essential accompaniment of the reforms in asylum management associated with the 'non-restraint' movement. They underlined the transition of the role of 'keeper' to the far more complex and sophisticated one of 'attendant'. This was an important stage in the emergence of an incipient specialism, eventually to become that of the psychiatric nurse.[26]

WORKING CONDITIONS, WORKING REALITY

> There is scarcely a reflecting person who would engage in a service attended with considerable personal hazard, and where the emoluments are scanty, and little more than sufficient for the day which is passing over him: and for which employment he must be disqualified as he advances in years: – a bootless drudgery, where knowledge and experience are profitless, when bodily vigour has declined.[27]

John Haslam, the long-serving apothecary of Bethlem, recognized the importance of employing the right calibre of people as keepers in a public asylum. Like many contemporaries trying to achieve something in the world of the madhouse and the asylum, he was well aware of the difficulties faced by staff in their unenviable task. Even John Conolly, whose hopes for what attendants could achieve were as pious as any, conceded that their duties were 'fatiguing, depressing, often repulsive'.[28] Yet there were always people prepared to undertake the work, and to remain in the same post for many years until they were no longer capable. For some, the disagreeable elements of the work and the conditions were countered by the attractions of a predictable income, food and lodging, a degree of status or power, and the personal rewards associated with the care and protection of the disadvantaged and stigmatized.

The earnings levels of keepers and attendants, relative to their superintendents, reflected the gulf in status and perceived levels of responsibility. County asylum staff pay structures were adapted from those established at Bethlem, St Luke's and the provincial subscription asylums. Other bases for comparability were salaries in private madhouses, in other public institutions like prisons, hospitals and workhouses, and in domestic service. Like most of their counterparts, keepers' pay was set on an annual basis, and included full board and lodging. Although there were variations between asylums, associated with local labour markets, it is clear that a notional rate for the job developed. The view of contemporaries like Haslam and W.A.F. Browne was that they were poorly paid. According to Browne, keepers received 'a pittance', which was not only below what was allowed to 'cooks and coachmen', but also less than the 'common artizan' and many engaged in 'the most servile employments'. Historians have largely accepted this argument. However, it may be an oversimplification, not taking proper account of payments in kind received as part of residence in the asylum.[29]

Table 2 Keepers' salaries, 1830 (£s)[30]

	Males	*Females*
Bedford	12–20	10–15
Lincoln	15–20	10.10
Nottingham	20	10.10
Stafford	20–25	13.10–15
Cornwall	25	15
Wakefield	23–27	10–13
Gloucester	27	17
Lancaster	30	15

By the 1820s, the norm for male keepers' wages in public asylums had generally settled at between £20 and £25 per annum, and for females at £10 to £15, levels somewhat in excess of pay in private asylums. An 1830 survey by the Middlesex justices, in determining what to pay staff in their new asylum, showed the range of rates paid (see Table 2). Local influences were apparent in fixing pay rates. The similarity between neighbouring Nottingham and Lincoln, as in other aspects of their operation, is striking; the discrepancy on male rates was only because of one lower paid junior keeper at Lincoln. The higher rates, particularly for male staff, at Gloucester, Wakefield and Lancaster may have reflected the need to compete in the labour market for people of a calibre otherwise attracted into the skilled textile trades. John Walton, in his study of Lancaster Asylum, noted that recruitment was from strata well above the 'dregs' of the labour market (a conclusion rather at variance with Scull's). At the other extreme was Norfolk Asylum, whose justices omitted to respond to the Middlesex call for information. They steadfastly continued to pay the bare minimum to their 'porters' and 'maidservants'. In 1835, the men were receiving 16 guineas per annum and the women 10 guineas. Apart from this dissent from the norm, justices elsewhere accepted the emerging conventions. At the new asylums opened in Suffolk (1829), Middlesex (1831) and Kent (1833), initial rates were set at £25 for male keepers, although ranging from £12 to £18 for females.[31]

Visitors and superintendents were well aware of the need to pay acceptable salaries if they were to attract and retain anything like the quality of staff they claimed to seek. This meant resisting pressures to reduce expenditure by economizing on staff costs. As a Suffolk justice pointed out in 1835, in seeking to defend their keepers against just such an attempt:

> The sad nature of their duties demand liberality in wages and diet. The chief indeed the only considerations that can induce such sacrifices as are required of them. Those who know most of what those duties and sacrifices are will be the more surprized that respectable individuals can be found to perform and suffer them.

By this time, most larger asylums were setting up a career structure. The Middlesex survey in 1830 had shown that at two asylums, Cornwall and Lancashire, the post of head keeper had been established, with additional pay of £5 to £10 per annum. Others, such as Lincoln and Stafford, eventually followed suit. Incremental wage scales were also introduced. At Stafford, from 1825 onwards, keepers were appointed at £20, with annual additions of £1 up to £25. Gloucester later adopted a similar arrangement, with a range from £21 to £27. The market, however, continued as a key local determinant; wages at Lincoln and Suffolk were periodically lowered and raised, to adjust the balance between economy and ability to recruit.[32]

There were some opportunities for staff to earn additional money. Wages might be supplemented for additional duties, like shaving the males, work in the gardens or fields, supervision and training of working patients, or night-watch. At some asylums there was scope for *ad hoc* payments. At Norfolk, generous long service gratuities provided some compensation for the low wages. In 1826, three staff were awarded sums between 3 and 5 guineas for 'having conducted themselves properly in their respective Situation, and having received excellent Characters from the master'. In 1835, a surplus in the accounts led to still more generous payments, with John Ellis receiving a reward of £12 for sixteen years' service, and Susan Clarke 10 guineas for fourteen years. At Stafford, long service payments were made periodically, and salaries were further augmented by Christmas bonuses. Sometimes there were one-off rewards, like when Samuel Brogdale at Nottingham received a sovereign in June 1836 for preventing a serious accident to a patient, and again two years later for his action in averting a suicide. In 1840 another Nottingham keeper was given a sovereign for intervening to protect Thomas Powell, the superintendent, from a violent attack.[33]

The keeper's standard of living was much enhanced by not having to pay basic living expenses. The provision of lodging and food were important considerations in the attractiveness of asylum employment. The generosity of the dietary was influenced by a prevailing idea that keepers required plenty of meat to keep their strength up. At Gloucester, for example, when it opened in 1823, the keepers were initially allowed eight ounces of best quality meat daily. However, after they complained that this was inadequate, it was increased to twelve ounces. Indeed, certain quantities and quality of food would become established as an entitlement; attempts at alteration could become the focus of staff dissent and protest.[34]

As well as relatively generous food provision, male and female asylum staff were allowed ale and beer, sometimes in substantial quantities. It became an expected condition of service that an ample supply of beer should be readily available. In the circumstances, staff would naturally take advantage of the opportunities. At Lincoln in 1830, after a period of excessive indulgence, limits were imposed, with male staff restricted to two pints of beer daily and females to one pint, in addition to an ale allowance. However, this was seen as too strict, and the following year it was altered to three pints of malt liquor for the men, and one and a half for the women. At Thorpe (Norfolk) in 1844, male staff were being allowed two and a half pints of small beer and one pint of strong beer daily. The perennial problem of alcohol abuse among asylum staff, which resulted in numerous dismissals, could not have been unrelated to this apparent largesse.[35]

The provision of full board and lodging gave the keepers a strong sense of security. However, there were considerable disadvantages. Accommodation was normally in a single room, adjoining or even contained within the gallery for which they were responsible, subjected constantly to all the sounds and smells of the asylum. The long working hours, the limited leisure time, as well as the nature of the work and its all-embracing commitment, meant that the keeper was liable to become as tied to the institution as were his patients. This relationship of dependency was furthered by the restrictions and sanctions to which staff were subjected, exemplified in the rules and regulations, hung up in the wards, in their room, perhaps issued to them personally, or even read aloud to them by the superintendent when they took up their employment.[36]

In several asylums, particularly the larger ones, the relationship between keepers, institution and patients was physically represented by the wearing of uniform. This was another practice adopted from Bethlem, whose 'basketmen' wore blue uniforms with silver badges, and from the subscription asylums. At Exeter Asylum in 1812, the head keeper and two under-keepers wore 'a plain livery & have the appearance of footmen'. At Wakefield, male staff were each given a new suit of livery annually. Across the Pennines at Lancaster, both male and female staff wore a livery; the females' gowns were designed to match the coats of the male keepers. Elsewhere, the uniforms were perhaps less striking. At Oxford Asylum, male keepers were issued with a 'drab-cloth jacket and waistcoat' once a year, to promote a tidy and orderly appearance. The imposing outfits of keepers were likely to offer a striking contrast to the plain uniform dress of patients, enforced at Wakefield, Hanwell and elsewhere.[37]

The keepers' dependent status was underlined by restrictions imposed over most aspects of their lives. Working life was constrained by the details of conduct within house rules. These covered not only the expected exemplary treatment of patients, and the avoidance of improper force, but also defined aspects of personal responsibility. Keepers were normally not permitted to leave their wards, other than on urgent business. If they did leave, they had to ensure safety and security, which meant locking doors, and possibly arranging the restraint of potentially violent patients. Other aspects of relations with patients were controlled to prevent exploitation, for example by strict rules against the receipt of perquisites or payments from patients or relatives for any services.[38]

Tight limits were placed on social and personal lives. Time off was strictly limited, usually to only a few hours a week. Problems of recruitment and retention, and difficulties of proper enforcement, led to a gradual easing of restrictions and a more permissive policy. However, abuses inevitably followed, which would lead to a reimposition of controls. At Gloucester, in the mid-1830s, staff were permitted to stay out on alternate nights. However, Samuel Hitch sought to curb the practice because of the 'Evils connected with it', in the form of 'peculation and drunkenness'. In 1842, after William Flowers stayed away a day and a night without permission, leaving his patients 'totally unprovided for', the privilege of overnight absence without express approval was abolished. However, by the early 1840s asylum managers were accepting that staff had to be allowed opportunities for leisure and a social life away from the institution. At Lancaster, attendants were allowed out every other evening, the unmarried from 7 p.m. to 9.30 p.m., and those who were married overnight. In addition, they could go out every third Sunday as well as for a half day every three weeks. These liberalizing measures aimed to improve relations between staff and management, and promote greater loyalty. They signalled a growing acceptance of the need for more favourable conditions for hard-pressed attendant staff.[39]

Relations between the sexes were tightly controlled, with prohibitions against visits to each other's quarters. For a long time it was widely the case that staff were not permitted to marry, and were required to leave if they did so. The rules at Dorset Asylum made the position quite clear: the 'Inferior Officers and Servants' should be 'unmarried, and free from the care and charge of children'. At Stafford in January 1825, the experienced keeper Joseph Swannick wished to get married and sought permission to continue in post; his application was refused on the grounds that it was 'incompatible with his duties as keeper'. At times these limitations might be revoked or eased, according to local circumstances, but they continued at some asylums. The case was starkly put by the Gloucester visitors at the end of 1836, who resolved that 'no Sub-officer nor servant of either sex, to be hereafter engaged, shall be married. . . & that any who shall marry shall be dismiss'd'. As late as 1843, two attendants at Stafford, Henry Wood and James Hall, were sacked for having married. An exception was made for Samuel Poole, the attendant to the private patients, who admitted to having been married for a year and a half but was unaware of the prohibition; he was allowed to remain 'in consequence of his general good conduct'. However, a strict policy was by now becoming outmoded and unrealistic, as Gaskell and de Vitrie at Lancaster had clearly recognized.[40]

The subordination of staff was reinforced by a series of sanctions. As part of the objective of 'safe custody', the 1808 Act gave scope for hefty fines on officers or servants who allowed anyone to escape, through neglect or connivance. Fines normally consisted at least of the expense involved in pursuit and recapture. A repetition could lead to dismissal. Other misdemeanours might be met with a reprimand, a fine or discharge. The acceptance of gratuities, the incidence of drunkenness or the act of striking a patient were all offences liable to dismissal. Normally, though, a first and even a second offence would be dealt with by a reprimand or a fine, with removal only resulting from further transgression. Similar discretion was used for absence without leave, staying out overnight without permission or lateness. However, in stricter regimes, like Wakefield, where Higgins and Ellis sought to impose a religious morality, discipline was more summary and other offences could bring dismissal, such as a male being found in the female quarters without satisfactory reason. Penalties could be imposed for a whole series of other errors and omissions. At Dorset Asylum, there were fines for not locking up cutlery, tools or instruments after use, for a door or fire-guard left unlocked, for leaving the ward without notice, and for allowing patients to rise in the morning before staff were ready to take charge of them. In practice, the extent to which sanctions were imposed differed considerably, according to the relative laxity or strictness of the regime, and also according to local issues of staff recruitment and retention.[41]

Dismissals were not uncommon, sometimes for unspecified misconduct or repeated rule-breaking, occasionally for theft or embezzlement, but more usually for drunkenness or ill-treatment of patients. In many cases these misdemeanours emanated from a response to the undoubted pressures associated with the job and the conditions under which it was carried out. Untrained staff were rarely prepared for the daily realities of the gallery. W.A.F. Browne stressed how the 'peculiar situation' of the keeper meant he was invested with 'great and but ill defined power'. The belief that they were expected to impose authority led to a tendency to 'punish, domineer, and restrain' to an extent that could easily become cruel and tyrannical.[42]

Evidence confirms that the use of force toward patients was a regular, even expected, occurrence in some institutions. The unique surviving 'Master's Journals' from Norfolk Asylum provide ample testimony to an unfortunate state of affairs. A not untypical instance occurred in November 1827: the patient Chas Woodhouse complained that he had lost the sight of an eye after a blow from the long-serving porter John Ellis. Though Ellis denied striking the blow, he did admit to having 'kicked Cooper and other patients on the breach [i.e. bottom] to compel them to go into the Room', an offence earning only a severe reprimand and a request by the visitors that 'all violence should be avoided'. Elsewhere, outbreaks of violent conduct toward patients occurred periodically, perhaps connected to particular circumstances. Most notably, the abolition of mechanical restraint at Lincoln, Hanwell, Lancaster, and elsewhere tended to lead to an upsurge of violence by staff whose vulnerability had become suddenly exposed.[43]

Physical ill-treatment was usually with fists or feet, but there were weapons to hand in the form of leather straps or other restraint instruments. The imposition of restraint on a reluctant patient was a situation open to escalation. Two Stafford keepers, Andrew Calley and Thomas Jones, were threatened in March 1825 with dismissal for beating a patient with the restraint straps, though on appeal they were merely fined £1 each. Of course, staff often had to protect themselves, and there was a fine line between firm handling and excess. John Emerson, a Lincoln keeper, had a severe reprimand in January 1837 for having 'thrown down' a patient; he avoided dismissal because of 'his excellent previous character for humanity and forbearance'. Keepers could find other irregular ways of imposing their authority, such as an enforced shower bath. Joseph Swannick, an apparently indispensable keeper at Stafford, was reported in August 1824 for immersing a patient's head in a bucket of water; his punishment consisted only of a reprimand, even though he had beaten another patient not long before. The keepers at Stafford may well have been especially unruly. A colourful former patient, there in the 1830s, later recalled 'manifold horrors' and 'atrocious cruelty' committed by 'miscreants of the deepest dye'. On its own, this was dubious evidence, until linked with James Wilkes's description of the demoralization and brutalization of the keepers he encountered when he took up post in 1841.[44]

Staff were at times subjected to considerable provocation. Norfolk Asylum's porters and maidservants perhaps administered summary punishment more frequently than most, but they could be on the receiving end almost incessantly. Between the opening of the asylum in 1814 and the end of 1815, they had stones and chamber pots thrown at them, and were punched, kicked, bitten and scratched; matters did not greatly improve over the following years. Violence to staff also became a serious problem at Lincoln during its upheavals in the late 1830s and early 1840s.

John Emerson, in defending his own actions before a Governors' inquiry, described his experiences:

I have received injury myself in the struggles. I had my two front teeth loosened once and at another time had my skin broken. At another time a patient struck me on the hand with an iron bar which he had forced from the Window. My hand was laid open by the blow. I once received a blow on my nose and once on my lip. I have received many blows at different times which I cannot now recollect.[45]

Whilst the experience of staff at the more tightly controlled asylums might have been less fraught, all were likely to experience periodically the painful consequences of patients' disordered perceptions and behaviour. Arguably, violence and injury were among the anticipated hazards of the job.

The pressures on keepers came not only from the threat and actuality of violence. The unpredictable, disinhibited and destructive behaviour of patients brought particular stresses on staff required to remain with them for extended periods. Certainly there was some recognition of what the Nottingham visitors described in 1823 as their 'harassing and anxious life'. Even the critical W.A.F. Browne acknowledged that:

the labour of the conscientious keeper never terminates, that he has neither nights nor days of rest, that anxieties, provocations, disappointments, and disgusts follow each other in constant succession. . .

Corsellis at Wakefield drew attention to the 'great suffering' induced by duties 'so oppressively arduous to the mind, as well as body'. Enforced 'wakeful nights and anxious days' could, he emphasized, insidiously undermine health. Much stress was attached to the onerous responsibilities of prevention. The possibility of self-harm by the suicidal, and the consequent necessity for vigilance was, as George Button at Dorset suggested, a cause of 'great anxiety'. These sorts of pressures were perhaps at least as great as those emanating from threat and injury.[46]

It might be expected that a job that combined modest wages, restrictive employment conditions and debilitating strain from the actual work would see a high staff turnover. Although every asylum at times did have problems of retention, available records do not suggest noticeably rapid changes. There were exceptions at certain places during critical periods, such as Lincoln during the transition to 'non-restraint', when the stream of staff quickly leaving matched the numbers dismissed for misconduct. More generally, there was an observable tendency for a significant proportion of keepers and attendants to remain for long periods, sometimes until they became incapable. Every asylum had its long-serving

1. Nottinghamshire General Lunatic Asylum. From Annual Report, 1818, engraver John Wilkins. (Courtesy of Nottingham Local Studies Library)

2. Bedfordshire County Lunatic Asylum. From J. Matthiason, *Bedford and its Environs* (Bedford, 1831), engraver R. Havell. (Courtesy of Bedfordshire and Luton Archives).

3. Staffordshire General Lunatic Asylum. From W. White, *History, Gazetteer, and Directory of Staffordshire* (Sheffield, 1834), engraver T. Radcliffe.

4. Norfolk County Lunatic Asylum (1825). Engraver T. Barber. (Courtesy of Norwich Local Studies Library).

5. Lincoln Lunatic Asylum. From First Report (1822), engraver O. Jewitt. (Courtesy of Lincolnshire Archives).

6. Oxford (Radcliffe) Lunatic Asylum. From *Useful Information Concerning the Origin, Nature, and Purpose of the Radcliffe Lunatic Asylum* (Oxford, 1840).

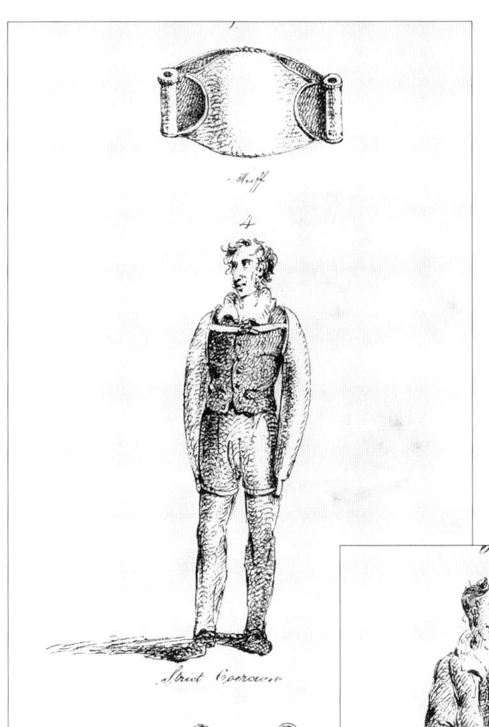

7. Mechanical Restraint (1). From P. Slade Knight, *Observations on the Causes, Symptoms and Treatment of Derangement of the Mind* (London, 1827). Captions:– 1 – 'Muff'; 2 – 'Sleeves'; 4 – 'Strict Coercion'. (Courtesy of Wellcome Institute Library, London).

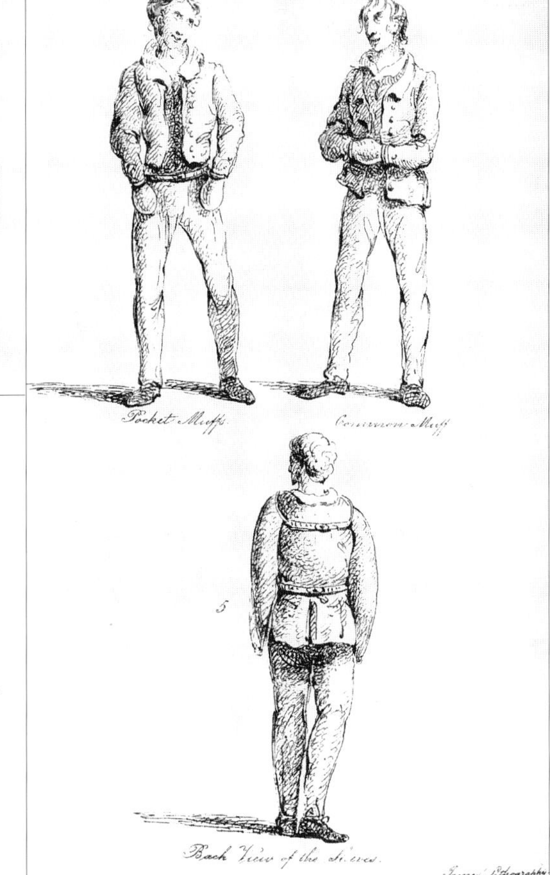

8. Mechanical Restraint (2). From P. Slade Knight, *Observations on the Causes, Symptoms and Treatment of Derangement of the Mind* (London, 1827). Captions:– 3 – 'Common Muff'; 5 – 'Back view of the Sleeves'; 6 – 'Pocket Muffs'. (Courtesy of Wellcome Institute Library, London).

9. Mechanical Restraint (3). Caption:– 'Strong leather belt & braces consisting of iron chain sewn up in leather: chains from the belt to the wrist allowing limited motion. Weight 7 lbs. In use at the Lancaster Asylum until about 1840.' Drawn by Dr Pritchard of Lancaster. (Courtesy of Lancaster Reference Library).

10. Mechanical Restraint (4). Caption:– 'Showing back view of the same with padlock fastening.' Drawn by Dr Pritchard. (Courtesy of Lancaster Reference Library).

staff, like Edward Hart and Mary Peters at Gloucester who, in January 1844, were rewarded for twenty years' service conducted 'in the most faithful and zealous manner'. Wakefield's dependence on 'old servants' was noted by Dr Cookson from Lincoln in 1841, and Dr Crommelinck also observed that several staff had been there for more than twenty years. In 1844 the contribution of an ailing attendant on the epileptic and idiotic patients was acknowledged; for 22 years he had carried out his arduous duties with 'mildness, cheerfulness, and diligence'. Even at Norfolk Asylum, where staff were subjected to persistent physical assault, some remained long-term.[47]

At Stafford Asylum, where comprehensive records on the staffing establishment have survived, the trends are clear. Although there were keepers and nurses who did not remain for long, they were the exception. The norm was to stay between two and five years, but some remained for much longer. The aforementioned Joseph Swannick, appointed in September 1820, continued until 1841 when he had to leave due to his own derangement. His brother Thomas had joined him in 1824, and also stayed nearly twenty years; they were among several groups of brothers employed at different times. Jane Tickell, appointed two months after Joseph Swannick, remained for 26 years, finally resigning in October 1846 due to 'age and infirmity'. Others, like James Wood, Richard Wiggin and Sarah Eccleston, worked in the asylum for upwards of ten years. The reforms in its regime conducted by James Wilkes from 1841 onwards, however, led to major upheavals in the composition of the staff, as those who could not adapt to more liberal patient management methods were eased out.[48]

Various reasons could be advanced to explain why staff remained so long, despite all the shortcomings, disagreeable aspects and hazards of the work. Not least, there is the Goffmanesque characterization that they became as institutionalized as their chronic patients. After all, the asylum environment catered for all their basic needs whilst providing clear and predictable boundaries and routines to order their lives. The evident abuses that occurred were symptomatic of the power that could be wielded in a closed institution by people of limited skill and ability, but with considerable delegated authority. This, for some, was an undoubted additional attraction of the work.[49]

There is, however, a danger of too negative a reading of how keepers and attendants performed their duties. For some the work was a vocation, which provided an opportunity to care for and benefit people in great need. Records tend to highlight poor practices; diligent performance was not often considered worthy of record. It is apparent, though, that the ideals expressed in asylum rules were often pursued, despite all the pressures and influences tending in other directions. C.C. Corsellis's contention in 1841 that the 'character and conduct' of some attendants was 'beyond praise' did not merely represent a West Riding phenomenon. John Kirkman at Suffolk Asylum paid tribute to the 'unwearied kindness' of its attendants over their many years of service. Dr Crommelinck, from the evidence of his visits to several asylums, was struck by the warmth of the feeling of patients toward the staff who looked after them:

> This attachment, which manifests itself sometimes by the most extraordinary proofs, is met with in the lunatic who has become incurable, as with he who has become convalescent: one knows not whether to say it is stronger with the one than the other.

These relationships could only be a reflection of the quality of care provided by individual staff members.[50]

Even where abuses were occurring, they did not necessarily represent the full picture. At Lincoln in 1841, in the wake of a succession of dismissals, Sir Edward Bromhead paid sincere tribute to the 'forbearance and humanity' with which most attendants had conducted themselves in the difficult conditions following the abolition of restraint. A patient recently discharged from Stafford in 1829, John Ryland of Birmingham, wrote to thank the physician and superintendent for the attention he had received. He particularly acknowledged his obligation to the keepers:

> James Wood for his friendly treatments – Joseph Swannick was consoling to me; indeed all the Keepers behaved well to me.

The singling out of Swannick is particularly significant, as he had previously been disciplined on at least two occasions for assaults on patients.[51] It illustrates the complications involved in assessing the manner in which staff performed their task. The complex interaction between the nature and requirements of the institution, the conditions under which they worked, the spectrum of patient behaviours, and the human characteristics of fallible individuals, could never produce a straightforward or predictable outcome.

The multiple roles of keepers and attendants, as carers, therapists, domestic servants, security officers and enforcers of order and discipline, would pose a severe challenge to the most capable individuals. The expectations placed on the people employed to carry out these roles were bound to be disappointed. In practice, the characterizations of asylum staff as being from the lower social strata, poorly educated and ill-equipped for their responsible duties were not without foundation. Salary levels were never likely to attract people of a calibre commensurate with the aspirations expressed in rule-books. Partly this was dictated by considerations of economy in asylum management. However, the conclusion is almost inescapable that, despite frequent platitudinous statements about the essential role of attendant staff, low remuneration reflected a lack of regard for the value of their work, as compared to the higher profile contributions of superintendents and medical officers.

NOTES

1 A. Digby, *Madness, Morality and Medicine: A Study of the York Retreat, 1796–1914* (Cambridge, 1985), pp. 141–70; Peter Nolan, *A History of Mental Health Nursing* (London, 1993); R. Russell, *Mental Physicians and Their Patients: Psychological Medicine in the English Pauper Lunatic Asylums of the Later Nineteenth Century* (PhD, University of Sheffield, 1983), pp. 124, 305–16; R. Russell, 'The Lunacy Profession and its Staff in the Second Half of the Nineteenth Century, with Special Reference to the West Riding Lunatic Asylum', in W.F. Bynum, R. Porter and M. Shepherd, *The Anatomy of Madness: Essays in the History of Psychiatry* (3 vols, London, 1985–8), vol. III, *The Asylum and its Psychiatry*, pp. 291–315; L.D. Smith, 'Behind Closed Doors: Lunatic Asylum Keepers, 1800–60', *Social History of Medicine*, vol. I, no. 3 (December 1988), pp. 301–27; J. Andrews, A. Briggs, R. Porter, P. Tucker and K. Waddington, *The History of Bethlem* (London, 1997), pp. 288–306; D.J. Mellett, *The Prerogative of Asylumdom: Social, Cultural and Administrative Aspects of the Institutional Treatment of the Insane in Nineteenth Century Britain* (London, 1982), pp. 41–4; J. Walton, 'The Treatment of Pauper Lunatics in Victorian England, 1816–1870' in A. Scull (ed.), *Madhouses, Mad-Doctors and Madmen* (London, 1981), pp. 179–82; A. Scull, *The Most Solitary of Afflictions: Madness and Society in Britain, 1700–1900* (London, 1993), p. 173; J. Conolly, *The Treatment of the Insane Without Mechanical Restraints* (London, 1856), p. 98.

2 WRCRO, C85/114, West Riding Asylum, 25th Report (1844), pp. 19–20.

3 SCRO, Q/AIc, Box I, letter 11 March 1812 from J. Squires, Governor of Liverpool Asylum; Warneford Hospital Archives, W.P.5, xv, letter 7 April 1818 from M. Taylor, Manchester Infirmary; NCRO, SO/HO/1/3/1, 4 December 1811, 26 December 1816; *Select Committee on Madhouses* (1814–15), p. 180, evidence of Reverend J. Becher; SCRO, D550/62, 2 January 1819.

4 GLRO, MA/A/J/1, 29 November 1827, MA/A/J/2, 29 November 1830; SCRO, D550/62, 17 February 1821, 10 May 1822, D550/63, 5 August 1826, 7 July 1832; BPP 1836, vol. XLI, *County Lunatic Asylums, Returns*, pp. 3, 7, 8, 11, 20, 21, 24, 29, 31.

5 CKS, U1515/OQ/L1, Serjeant Adams to Lord Marsham, 22 December 1840.
6 *Staffordshire Advertiser*, 26 September 1818; Smith, 'Behind Closed Doors', pp. 305–8.
7 University of York, Borthwick Institute, C/1, 18 May 1818, Ellis to Jepson; WRCRO, C85/107, 13th Report (1832), p. 3; SCRO, D550/62, 4 November 1820, 5 January 1822; GCRO, HO22/1/1, 26 January, 10 July 1823, D3848/1/1, 7 July 1838, W. Conolly to Hitch.
8 Andrews *et al.*, *History of Bethlem*, p. 292; SCRO, D550/4, 24 July 1824, 26 March, 23 April 1825, 24 March 1834; LAO, LAWN 1/1/3, 9 July 1832, 6 July 1835, LAWN 1/1/4, 25 May, 29 June 1840; Walton, 'The Treatment of Pauper Lunatics', p. 181; Camilla Haw, 'John Conolly's Attendants at the Hanwell Asylum, 1839–52', *History of Nursing Journal*, vol. III, no. 1 (1990), pp. 26–58.
9 LAO, 1/1/3, 29 August, 17 October 1831; Smith, 'Behind Closed Doors', p. 107; Haw, 'John Conolly's Attendants', pp. 30–1; SuCRO, Acc 2697, 9 September 1828.
10 CCRO, DDX 97/1, 31 August 1824; DCRO, *Report of Visiting Justices* (Epiphany 1838), p. 4; SCRO, D550/4, 21 December 1833, D550/5, 13 March 1835, 26 November 1836; GCRO, HO22/1/1, 1 August 1823 (letter 5 April 1823, Ellis to Poynder), 11 October 1841, HO22/8/1, *Annual Reports*, 1842; NCRO, SO/HO/1/3/2, 30 July 1832, 28 February 1833; CKS, Q/GCL/1, 2 June 1832; BPP 1836, vol. XLI, *County Lunatic Asylums, Returns*, pp. 5–6 – at Cheshire Asylum, where there were only two designated keepers of each sex, the gardener acted as 'superintending keeper for such patients as work without the walls', and the inner porter for those working 'within the walls'; the cook/baker also assisted 'when needful'.
11 Nolan, *A History of Mental Health Nursing*, pp. 48–9; Haw, 'John Conolly's Attendants', p. 29; J. Conolly, *The Construction and Government of Lunatic Asylums* (London, 1847), p. 86; SCRO, D550/4, 14 April 1829, D550/63, 9 May 1829, D550/64, 28 December 1844.
12 Haw, 'John Conolly's Attendants', p. 30; SCRO, D550/3, 26 January 1822, D550/62, 11 June, 2 October 1819, 25 March 1820, 17 February, 5 May 1821, 2 February, 10 May, 12 July, 30 August, 28 December 1822, 9 October 1824.
13 WRCRO, C85/115, 25th Report (1844), p. 20; Tuke, 'Introductory Observations' in M. Jacobi, *On the Construction and Management of Hospitals for the Insane* (London, 1841), p. xxxi; *Lonsdale Magazine*, February 1821, p. 46; SuCRO, B106/10/4.2, Suffolk Asylum, Rules, p. 13; LPL, Lancaster Asylum, *Report of the Medical Officers* (1841), p. 12; Harriet Martineau, 'The Hanwell Lunatic Asylum', p. 310, in *Tait's Edinburgh Magazine* (1834), pp. 305–10.
14 W.A.F. Browne, *What Asylums Were, Are, and Ought to Be: Being the Substance of Five Lectures Delivered Before the Managers of the Montrose Royal Lunatic Asylum* (Edinburgh, 1837; reprinted London 1991), pp. 150–1; S. Tuke, *Description of the Retreat* (York, 1813), pp. 117–18; Paul Slade

Knight, *Observations on the Causes, Symptoms and Treatment of Derangement of the Mind* (London, 1827), p. 124; *Nottingham Journal*, 30 November 1811; LAO, 1/1/4, 21 April 1838; *Lincoln, Rutland and Stamford Mercury*, 13 October 1837; Nolan, *History of Mental Health Nursing*, p. 48.

15 A. Scull, 'Mad-Doctors and Magistrates: English Psychiatry's Struggle for Professional Autonomy in the Nineteenth Century', *Archives Européennes de Sociologie*, vol. XVII (1976), p. 298; Scull, *Most Solitary of Afflictions*, p. 173; Martineau, 'The Hanwell Lunatic Asylum', p. 310; Conolly, *Treatment of the Insane*, p. 97; Nolan, *History of Mental Health Nursing*, pp. 46–52.

16 Warneford Hospital Archives, W.P.3 (viii), Radcliffe Asylum, Instructions to the Keepers, Male and Female.

17 Nolan, *History of Mental Health Nursing*, pp. 53–4.

18 GRL, J7.26, Gloucester Asylum, Rules, pp. 19–20; LPL, *Report of the Medical Officers* (1841), p. 16.

19 DCRO, Dorset Asylum, Rules, p. 20; BPP 1836, vol. XLI, *Returns*, p. 18; BCRO, LB/1/8, 3 October 1812; LAO, LAWN 1/1/1, 18 February 1820; NkCRO, SAH 6, 31 March 1846; SCRO, D550/1, 13 February 1819; CCRO, DDX 97/1, 31 August 1824; GRL, J7.26, Gloucester Asylum, Rules, p. 20.

20 LLSL, Lincoln Asylum, Rules (1819), p. 14; NRL, Nottingham Asylum, Rules, pp. 60–1; Gloucester Asylum, Rules, p. 20; Dorset Asylum, Rules, p. 20; LPL, *Report of the Medical Officers* (1841), pp. 12, 19–20; Warneford Archives, W.P.68 (x), Radcliffe Asylum, *Rules* (1836), p. 32.

21 Dorset Asylum, Rules, pp. 19–20; Gloucester Asylum, Rules, pp. 19–21; Lincoln Asylum, *Rules* (1819), p. 14, *Rules* (1832), pp. 20–1; Nottingham Asylum, Rules, p. 59; BPP 1836, vol. XLI, *Returns*, pp. 18–19; GCRO, HO22/1/1, 1 August 1823; WRCRO, C85/114, 24th Report (1843), p. 10; SCRO, D550/1, 3 July 1844.

22 Conolly, *Treatment of the Insane*, pp. 102–3; Dorset Asylum, Rules, pp. 20–1; Gloucester Asylum, Rules, p. 20; Lincoln Asylum, *Rules* (1832), p. 22; SCRO, D550/4, 3 January 1824.

23 SuCRO, B106/10/4.2, Suffolk Asylum, Rules, p. 13; Gloucester Asylum, Rules, pp. 21–2; LPL, *Report of the Medical Officers* (1841), pp. 20–1. (There are interesting parallels here with the earlier quotation from Knight about the importance of keepers' appearance not being open to ridicule.)

24 Warneford Archives, W.P.3 (viii); Lincoln Asylum, *Rules* (1832), p. 24.

25 LPL, *Report of the Medical Officers* (1841), pp. 16–21 (main quotation, p. 19).

26 Ibid., p. 20; Haw, 'John Conolly's Attendants', pp. 35–7; Nolan, *History of Mental Health Nursing*.

27 J. Haslam, *Considerations on the Moral Management of Insane Persons* (London, 1817), p. 34.

28 Conolly, *Treatment of the Insane*, p. 103.

29 Andrews *et al.*, *History of Bethlem*, pp. 293–4; C.N. French, *The Story of St Luke's Hospital* (London, 1951), p. 45; M.A. Crowther, *The Workhouse System, 1834–1929* (London, 1981), pp. 121–31; Browne, *What Asylums Were, Are, and Ought to Be*, p. 166; Smith, 'Behind Closed Doors', pp. 310–12; SCRO,

Q/AIc, Box I, letter 10 March 1812 from Reverend Joseph Manning, Exeter; Mellett, *Prerogative of Asylumdom*, pp. 42–3.

30 GLRO, MA/A/J/2, 29 November 1830.

31 Walton, 'Treatment of Pauper Lunatics', p. 182; GLRO, MA/A/J/2, 6 January, 9 May 1831; NkCRO, SAH 5, 27 March 1835; SuCRO, Acc 2697, 9 September 1828; CKS, Q/GCL/1, 2 June 1832, 9 March 1833.

32 SuCRO, Acc 2697, 23 June, 13 October 1835, 19 June 1840. At Bodmin, the post of head keeper had been established by 1824 – CCRO, DDX 97/1, 21 August 1824; GLRO, MA/A/J/2, 29 November 1830; SCRO, D550/4, 23 July 1825, 21 December 1833, D550/5, 13, 27 March 1835; GCRO, HO22/3/1, 25, 30 April 1834; LAO, LAWN 1/1/3, 28 December 1829, 17 October 1831, 19 March, 2 April, 28 May, 11 June, 9 July 1832, 17 June 1833, LAWN 1/1/5, 20 November, 4 December 1843.

33 NkCRO, SAH 4, 30 January 1826, SAH 5, 17 March 1835; SCRO, D550/1, 4 July 1832, D550/4, 25 June 1825, 19 August 1826, 27 January 1827, 3 May 1828, 16 November 1833, D550/5, 7 March 1840; NCRO, SO/HO/1/3/2, 9 June 1836, 11 June 1838, 12 March 1840; GLRO, MA/A/J/2, 6 January 1831.

34 SuCRO, B106/10/4.4 (1), Suffolk Asylum, 1st Report (1839), p. 10; GCRO, HO22/1/1, 10 July, 13 August 1823, HO22/3/1, 5 February 1830; LAO, LAWN 1/1/3, 11 July 1831, 29 July 1833, LAWN 1/1/4, 21 April 1838; BPP 1836, vol. XLI, *Returns*, pp. 8, 11 – at Kent Asylum, male keepers were allowed one pound of cooked meat per day, and females half a pound.

35 LAO, LAWN 1/1/3, 22 February, 1, 8 March 1830, 14 February 1831; NkCRO, SAH 6, 26 November 1844; BPP 1836, vol. XLI, *Returns*, pp. 8, 11 – at Kent, male keepers were allowed four pints of small beer daily, and females two pints; at Lancaster the men had two gallons per week.

36 Warneford Archives, W.P.68 (x), p. 32; Suffolk Asylum, Rules, p. 12; GLRO, MA/A/J/2, 2 March 1831; SCRO, D550/4, 20 December 1823; GCRO, HO22/1/1, 17 July 1823; *Select Committee on Madhouses* (1814–15), p. 179, evidence of Reverend J.T. Becher; BPP 1836, vol. XLI, *Returns*, pp. 18–19.

37 Andrews *et al.*, *History of Bethlem*, p. 295; SCRO, Q/AIc, Box I, 10 March 1812; GLRO, MA/A/J/2, 29 December 1830, 2 March 1831; B. Parry-Jones, *The Warneford Hospital, Oxford 1826–1976* (Oxford, 1976), p. 13; Walton, 'Treatment of Pauper Lunatics', p. 179; Higgins, *Rules for the Management of the Pauper Lunatic Asylum for the West Riding of the County of York*, p. 22.

38 Dorset Asylum, Rules, pp. 20–2; LPL, *Report of the Medical Officers* (1841), pp. 16–18; Warneford Archives, W.P.68 (x), p. 32; Suffolk Asylum, Rules, pp. 13–15; Gloucester Asylum, Rules, pp. 19–20; Nottingham Asylum, Rules, pp. 59– 60; Lincoln Asylum, Rules, p. 14; BPP 1836, vol. XLI, *Returns*, p. 19.

39 GCRO, HO22/3/1, 25 April 1834, HO22/3/2, 25 October 1842; LPL, *Report of the Medical Officers* (1841), p. 16; C. Crommelinck, *Rapport sur les Hospices d'Aliénés de l'Angleterre, de la France et de l'Allemagne* (Courtrai, 1842), p. 141; LAO, LAWN 1/1/4, 10 September 1838.

40 Suffolk Asylum, Rules, p. 14; Dorset Asylum, Rules, p. 18; SCRO, D550/4, 29 January 1825, D550/5, 22 May 1843; GCRO, HO22/1/1, 26 December 1836; LPL, *Report of the Medical Officers* (1841), p. 16.

41 48 Geo. III, Cap. 96, Section XXIII; Dorset Asylum, Rules, pp. 21–2; Suffolk Asylum, Rules, p. 14; Gloucester Asylum, Rules, p. 19; Higgins, *West Riding Asylum, Rules*, pp. 18–19; LPL, *Report of the Medical Officers* (1841), pp. 16, 18; SCRO, D550/4, 27 March, 28 August 1824, 1 October 1825, 21 December 1833; GLRO, MA/A/J/2, 2 March 1831; WRCRO, C85/114, 25th Report (1844), p. 21; CCRO, DDX 97/2, 27 April 1841, 31 October 1843; LAO, LAWN 1/1/3, 20 January 1834.

42 SuCRO, Acc 2697, 2 October 1832; SCRO, D550/5, 13 March 1827; NCRO, SO/HO/1/3/3, 31 March 1843; LAO, LAWN 1/1/2, 10 October 1823, 14 May 1827, 10 March 1828, LAWN 1/1/3, 6 August, 3 September 1832, 4 August 1834, 30 March 1835, 15 August 1836, LAWN 1/1/4, 3 June 1839, 25 May 1840, 19 July 1841, LAWN 1/1/5, 20 October 1837, 1 January 1838, 5 May 1840; GCRO, HO 22/3/1, 10 August 1832, 25 April 1834, HO 22/3/2, 1 July 1839, 2 August 1841 – three nurses and a keeper were dismissed in order to show a 'fit example to the other Servants', following a series of incidents involving men being entertained by the females; two years earlier, four of the six nurses had been sacked at once (HO22/1/1, 24 June 1839); Browne, *What Asylums Were, Are, and Ought to Be*, pp. 151, 167.

43 NkCRO, SAH 4, 28 November 1827, SAH 123–7. (Some of these volumes are not available for research, due to the effects of water damage after a fire at Norwich Central Library in 1994.) For violence associated with non-restraint, see chapter 8.

44 SCRO, D550/4, 27 March, 28 August 1824, 12 March 1825; GCRO, HO22/1/1, 13 October 1823, HO22/3/2, 15 March 1841, 14 March 1842, 11 November 1844; NCRO, SO/HO/1/3/2, 9 December 1831, 17 February 1841; LAO, LAWN 1/1/3, 9 December 1833, 16 February 1835, 5 December 1836, 16 January 1837; NkCRO, SAH 4, 27 July 1829, SAH 6, 28 November 1843, 29 October 1844, 20 September 1845; T. Mulock, *British Lunatic Asylums: Public and Private* (Stafford, 1858), p. 16.

45 NkCRO, SAH 123, 126, 127; LAO, LAWN 1/1/4, 6 April (quote), 15 June 1840, LAWN 1/1/5, 22 August, 5 September 1842.

46 DCRO, *Report of Visiting Justices* (Epiphany 1844), pp. 12– 13; *Nottingham Journal*, 18 October 1823; Browne, *What Asylums Were, Are, and Ought to Be*, p. 166; WRCRO, C85/107, 23rd Report (31 December 1841).

47 LAO, LAWN 1/1/4; SuCRO, B106/10/4.4 (3), 3rd Report (1841), p. 12; GCRO, HO22/3/1, 5 February 1830, HO22/3/2, 2 August 1841, 29 January 1844; NkCRO, SAH 5, 27 March 1835; WRCRO, C85/114, 25th Report (1844), p. 21, C85/588, Visitors' Book, 29 May 1841 (W. Cookson); Crommelinck, *Rapport sur les Hospices*, p. 141.

48 SCRO, D550/62, 23 September, 4 November 1820, 2 February 1822, 27 March 1824, 26 November 1825, D550/63, 9 May 1829, 18 April 1835, 10 February 1838, D550/64, 28 December 1844, D550/5, 19 April 1841.

49 E. Goffman, *Asylums* (New York, 1961), pp. 74–112.

50 WRCRO, C85/107, 23rd Report (31 December 1841); Crommelinck, *Rapport sur les Hospices*, p. 141; SuCRO, B106/10/4.4, 3rd Report (1841), p. 12, 6th Report (1844), p. 14.

51 LLSL, Lincoln Asylum, 17th Report (1841), p. 4; SCRO, D550/4, 27 March, 28 August 1824, 14 April 1829.

5

Inside the Asylum

Under the County Asylum law, if a poor man be afflicted with mental derangement, he is taken to a large prison, where scarcely any sound can reach his ears, but the heart-appalling cries of others in a like state with himself, and most likely excluded entirely from the sight of any pleasing object.[1]

The conflicting ideological strands of custody and cure each contributed to the evolution of the asylum environment. The 1808 Act (as amended in 1811), with its directives of 'cure, comfort, and safe custody', had perpetuated the tensions in the objectives of public asylums. An administration based round the county justices, with their experience of establishing and operating prisons and their concern for local public order, was likely to lean toward the more custodial manifestations in determining asylum ethos. The philanthropic influences of the voluntary hospital movement, the ameliorating aspirations of lunacy reformers, the exposures of the 1815 Select Committee, and the example of the York Retreat, did serve to temper some potential excesses. The early county asylums consequently developed as complex institutions providing active medical and 'moral' treatment with a curative intent, in an environment designed for control and containment, if not intimidation. Thomas Bakewell's crude characterization of them as 'mighty prisons' carried more than an element of truth. From an architectural perspective, Thomas Markus has noted the carceral connotations of passages, tunnels, segregated stairs, inspection holes, walled courts and classification by space. The asylum's place between prison and hospital was exemplified by the adjoining features of cell and gallery. The strength of these features exercised a pervasive influence in determining the conditions experienced by the inmates.[2]

Apart from Jonathan Andrews's detailed study of eighteenth-century Bethlem, conditions within early public asylums have received limited attention from historians. The studies of private asylums by Parry-Jones and Charlotte Mackenzie, as well as Anne Digby's work on the York

Retreat, have all made important contributions to an understanding of the asylum experience in the early nineteenth century. Where there has been reference to conditions inside public asylums, it has concentrated on aspects like classification, the promotion of an ordered community and the detrimental consequences of having to contain growing numbers of mainly chronic patients in buildings which were hardly designed to accommodate them.[3] The generalized descriptions are not without foundation, but closer examination reveals a more varied and layered picture.

THE CUSTODIAL INSTITUTION

The external architecture of early nineteenth-century asylums superficially bore more resemblance to hospital than prison. Their siting in ample grounds, with views over open countryside, confirmed the therapeutic intent of their founders. However, closer inspection of the buildings' external detail would reveal the marks of security and control, clearly demonstrated in outer walls, constructed of thick solid brick and 10, 12 or even 15 feet high. In several instances, as at Bedford, Wakefield and Lincoln, early estimates of the required wall height proved inadequate to prevent escapes, and the walls had to be raised; at Thorpe (Norfolk), they were raised twice by the end of 1817. The perimeter wall served as a strong barrier to those inside and a deterrent symbol to those outside.[4]

The walls not only protected the surrounding community from the dangers of escaping lunatics, but also shielded patients from the voyeurism and insulting merriment of the curious observer. The Gloucester visitors had to act in 1823 to deal with the 'great number of idle people' loitering outside the building, especially on Sundays. The Sunday outing also proved a problem at Stafford, where in 1825 John Garrett complained about crowds of people gathered on the public road opposite, 'who gaze at & frequently call to converse with the patients'. He also had to request the commanding officers of the local militia to prevent their soldiers climbing onto the walls. Lincoln Asylum's prominent location led to perennial difficulties in protecting the patients from abuse. As late as June 1840, one of the physicians, Dr William Cookson, was protesting that 'There was the usual indecent scene upon the walls of this Institution this afternoon, boys & half grown men staring & hooting at the male & female patients in the front grounds.' Clearly a high wall was not of itself sufficient protection. It did, however, perpetuate the separation and stigma of the asylum inmates.[5]

The outer windows conveyed an impression to the onlooker perhaps even starker than the walls. They were mostly small, often little more than apertures, set high up, and usually protected with iron bars, iron shutters or wire gratings. In several asylums, the windows were unglazed, as at Bedford where a local observer described the building's contrasts:

> The entrance is handsome, and the facade of the building might be considered as particularly light and beautiful but for the upper segments of the blank and arched windows, which alone are open; and which, being furnished with iron bars, present the revolting idea of confinement, notwithstanding the general air of grandeur which is reflected from the whole.

Bedford, as one of the prototype county asylums, perhaps manifested the most explicit prison-like qualities. Similar architectural principles were adopted at most of its successors. Only at Wakefield, prompted by Samuel Tuke's design proposals, was there a serious attempt to provide windows that sought not to convey a coercive intent. Here they were of an ordinary design and at normal height, with security provided by cast iron frames.[6]

Although several asylums boasted extensive grounds, their use for recreation was limited, other than where they catered for private patients. Paupers normally exercised in stone-flagged or gravel airing courts, similar in design and lay-out to those of the new model prisons. If not enclosed on all sides by the building, they were rendered dull and gloomy by high walls designed to prevent escape. John Conolly graphically described the 'dismal yards' with:

> monotonous gravel courts, surrounded by walls from ten to fifteen feet high; without a tree; without a shrub; without a blade of grass; without shade in the heat of summer, or shelter from the rains of winter. . .

The Nottingham visitors in 1831 acknowledged the disinclination of patients to exercise in courts which 'cannot be divested of their prison features', and which contained no 'subjects of the vegetable kingdom'. A consequence of high-walled yards was the lack of view of the surrounding area. Again, only at Wakefield were efforts made to overcome this, by raising the centre of the airing courts for 'convalescent' patients, so that they could see out over the wall into the countryside. As much as any other aspect of asylum design, the yards and courts reinforced an impression of punishment and deterrence.[7]

Inside the building, the design principles also resembled those of the penitentiaries. Patients were accommodated in single cells, with a small window, normally at a height to receive light and air but to see little more than the sky. Security was not the only consideration. The intent was also to seclude, to minimize harmful stimulation for the agitated lunatic. The case was powerfully put by several Lancashire physicians in 1810, who contended that the accommodation needs of patients 'labouring under the most dismal and gloomy depression' were similar to those 'under the most furious madness'. To assuage their 'dreadful paroxysms' required:

> stillness, solitude, *darkness*, the exclusion, as much as possible, of all external impressions on the organs of sense, and of every source of corporeal or mental irritation.

For those suffering 'the gloom of deep melancholy', there was little point in providing a pleasant prospect or interesting scenery, as it would not affect their train of thought. The therapeutic benefits of solitude and darkness did not, however, impress later critics like Conolly who, in his critique of the older asylums, particularly condemned the windows:

> placed so high that no one can look out of them; windows of small and scarcely transparent panes of glass, set in thick and heavy frames of wood, and guarded on the outside of the building.

The occupants of the more central cells of Bodmin Asylum, with its radial design, suffered particularly due to their proximity to other wings. At Gloucester, whose back-to-back cells opened into the galleries, the only light was that admitted through the cell door from windows several feet away; Dr Crommelinck described them in 1841 as 'dark and miserable'. Where basement cells were used, as at Nottingham, Stafford, Gloucester and Chester, they were especially gloomy.[8]

Cells were frequently deficient in ventilation and heating; it was a problem for designers and engineers to provide warmth and air simultaneously. Open apertures admitted cold air, but closed glass window panes restricted fresh air supply. The main night ventilation might be the impure air of the galleries, admitted through small holes in the cell doors. Floors were either of wooden boards or stone flags. Stone accentuated the cold, particularly in basements where the 'noisy' or 'dirty' patients were congregated. Much time and money was expended by visitors and superintendents in the attempt to provide efficient heating systems. Under-floor flues, stoves and fires in grates were all tried together or separately. The much-admired steam pipe system developed at Derby Infirmary was widely copied. Nevertheless, most ventures had scant success. At Norfolk Asylum, an expensive steam pipe system proved so inadequate, with the January temperature similar inside to that outside, that it had to be abandoned; the problem of cold remained unsolved there for another 30 years. Even where systems functioned, the heat would be concentrated in the galleries and day-rooms, with little permeation through to individual sleeping cells.[9]

Within the cells, the bedding varied according to continence and nocturnal behaviour. 'Dirty' patients were frequently accommodated on straw, usually contained within a crib or trough bedstead. These were easy to fit with leather straps, to restrain patients inclined to get out of bed during the night. People whose bladders and sphincters were under control, and who were more inclined to remain in bed, might be provided with an iron bedstead, a horse-hair mattress and sheets. However, straw continued to be extensively used in several asylums until the 1840s and beyond. Generally patients slept one to a bed, though in rural counties like Cornwall and Dorset it was considered acceptable for some female patients to share a double bed.[10]

The cell's aura of imprisonment, conveyed by high barred window and cold stone floor, was reinforced by its door, made from heavy wood or, in some instances, partly or entirely of cast iron. It might be secured from outside by a large heavy bolt, as well as by a lock. Cell doors were normally locked at night and unlocked in the morning, and contained an inspection plate which the keeper could open to observe the patient when he chose. The door opened into a gallery, either a roomy area well equipped with windows on the other wall, or otherwise merely a narrow, gloomy and airless corridor with a line of cells on each side.[11]

The gallery system of construction was notoriously noisy. Sounds were conducted and magnified through floors, doors and walls, particularly at night. Thomas Bakewell depicted, after a visit to Wakefield Asylum, how distressing to new patients was the transmission of cries and moans. Captain Chapman, an assistant poor law commissioner, was caustic about the defects of the otherwise 'admirably regulated' Bodmin Asylum:

> Its vaulted roofs, like bomb proofs, appear destined rather to stand a siege than for the confinement of unarmed and generally harmless human beings: and instead of being calculated to promote quiet and repose, so necessary to recovery, become rather conductors of every sound, and make every cry reverberate in the ears of the unfortunate inmates.

An articulate Liverpool Asylum patient described in 1826 the sleepless nights spent in his cell due to the 'screams of murder, loud knockings, and pitiable cries' of the more violent patients. These noise problems were common. At Stafford, attempts were made to lessen the disturbance from the noisiest patients by fitting double doors on their cells, but generally the difficulties were not tackled until architects addressed them when designing extensions or new buildings.[12]

In most asylums, galleries served as day-rooms as well as passages. Day-rooms provided for recreation, particularly in inclement weather. They were normally well secured, with iron doors or gates, and bars or wire guards on the windows. Where open fires provided warmth, they were surrounded by heavy iron fireguards. Furniture was initially sparse, and likely to consist of forms fixed to the walls, and box seats adaptable as restraining chairs. At Wakefield, where the objective was a model asylum on Samuel Tuke's principles, rooms were specifically designed and constructed as day-rooms, and furnished according to domestic standards, but this was not the norm elsewhere.[13]

Meals were normally taken in the day-room. In several asylums, there were no tables and patients ate from their laps. At Norfolk Asylum, as late as 1843, one of the visitors commented disapprovingly:

> I observe both in the mens & womens rooms there is a sadd [*sic*] want of accommodation at the dinner hour, in neither of the rooms are there tables to support their platters, whilst eating, some are sitting, others standing, walking, or lying down, no requisite accommodation, of course no regularity.

At Nottingham, tables fixed to the floor were first installed in 1831. Knives and forks were not usually provided, because of the perceived risk. The 1791 version of Manchester Asylum's rules had proscribed their use, and others followed suit. One alternative to cutlery was the all-purpose 'trencher'. Food would be cut into small pieces by the kitchen staff. Crommelinck noted at Wakefield that 'the potatoes are always reduced to a paste and the meat is minced', to ensure that patients could digest their food without chewing. The use of crockery was unusual, with tin cans or what Pliny Earle described as 'a small wooden dish, similar to a pail', provided for eating. These could serve for liquids or solids, illustrated by a decision of the Lincoln governors in 1831:

> Ordered, That a tin be provided for the Breakfast and another for the Supper of every Patient, the latter tin also to serve for beer at Dinner.

Gardiner Hill later recalled the consequence for patients' eating habits; they would swallow their food 'after the fashion of wild animals'.[14]

Asylum food exemplified the interface between principles of economic management and those of curative treatment. With improvement of physical health deemed an essential element in the restoration of mental health, patients' diet was a central part of the treatment armoury. The normal breakfast was oatmeal porridge, gruel or milk broth, and supper was usually bread and cheese, or perhaps bread, treacle and milk. The main meal, dinner, varied widely between asylums as to quality and quantity, with meat content the general yardstick for determining standards. Bedford Asylum established a dietary regime in 1812 that became fairly common, with a meat dinner on four days, and a broth made from the previous day's boiled meat on the other three. Nottingham improved on this slightly with a roast meat dinner on Sundays, and three other meat days, with boiled beef, boiled mutton and Irish stew respectively. A similar menu was adopted at Wakefield, Lincoln and Gloucester, and was probably fairly general. Ale or beer was frequently provided, for nutritional purposes.[15]

There were differences between the sexes, to take account of perceived differing physical needs. At Nottingham and Lincoln, the men had 'good milk pottage' for breakfast, whilst the women received coffee and dry toast. In the evening, the men were given bread, cheese and beer (changed in 1830 to broth with bread and vegetables), and the women tea with bread and butter. There was also differentiation according to social class (and funding). At Gloucester, in 1823, paupers were generously provided with meat on four days (roast meat, boiled beef, boiled mutton and Irish stew), comprising eight ounces each time of the best quality, with broth on two days and rice pudding on the other. Charity patients had the same, but private patients were given roast or boiled meat daily. Subsequently, the visitors realized they might have been over-generous and meat allowances were periodically reduced, with exemptions only for those employed. At Lincoln, when the dietary arrangements were revised in 1830, the first- and second-rank patients were given meat with puddings and vegetables daily. The paupers, on the other hand, suffered a deterioration in their fare, with rice pudding now the main course three days a week.[16]

Pauper patients in rural counties received the least generous diets, though probably deemed more than ample for impoverished agricultural labourers. At Bodmin, the dinner in 1820 consisted of meat on three days, and soup broth or rice milk on the other days. One of the poorest dietary lists was at Dorset Asylum, where in 1838 the dinner contained meat only twice per week; the other days' main meal consisted of suet or rice pudding on two days, soup and bread on two days, and bread and cheese on the other. Patients 'actively employed' in the asylum or its grounds received extra diet. A few years later the superintendent, Dr George

Button, was contending that the poverty of the dietary had been a cause of 'general debility' which had impeded patients' recovery.[17]

The competition between the visitors of the Norfolk and Suffolk asylums to achieve the more swingeing ecomomies took its toll in both institutions. In 1839, pauper patients at Melton were receiving less than one pound of meat per week. John Kirkman openly protested in his first annual report:

> this is the least possible quantity that should be tolerated, with due reference to the health and cure of persons whose unhappy condition frequently arises from, and is constantly dependent on, an exhausted state of brain, and nervous energy. Of all economy an ill regulated dietetic economy is the very worst.

Insanity, he exhorted, 'requires and demands' a liberal diet. He reiterated his protests the following year, suggesting that economy on food was 'unquestionably a disadvantage'. The Norfolk dietary contained meat three days per week, with suet pudding, rice pudding or dumplings on the other days. Hunger was evidently a problem, for in March 1841 the staff were called on to protect the older and more infirm patients from having their food taken by younger ones.[18]

Dietary shortcomings attracted increasing attention as attempts were made to identify reasons for the asylums' poor performance in achieving cures. John Thurnam, the former superintendent of the York Retreat, in a survey of seven county asylums in 1845, noted the wide disparities. The dietaries in the asylums of Nottingham, Stafford and Gloucester were among the more generous; those of Lancaster, Wakefield, Middlesex and Suffolk were far less liberal, providing less than half the amount of meat offered in the first group. He pointed to a significant statistical correlation between liberality of diet, death-rates and recovery-rates.[19]

Apart from seasonal adjustments for breakfast, meal-times were rigidly fixed. Order and regularity pervaded most aspects of asylum life, as far as was possible with congregations of disordered people. Cleanliness and neatness, of property and people, became essential measures by which observers judged an asylum and its quality of care. A comment in 1836 by a Lancaster Asylum visitor could have been taken from any visitors' book and typified what they were looking for: 'Visited the whole of the Institution & found the greatest order & cleanliness in each gallery.' A group of Leeds Guardians going round Wakefield Asylum in 1839 found it 'very clean & comfortable and every thing wearing the appearance of order and propriety'. Similar observations were repeated almost endlessly. The Metropolitan Commissioners, conducting their first national tours in 1842 and 1843, made sure to comment favourably on each county asylum's neatness and cleanliness, whatever other shortcomings they noted. Their comments reflected to an extent what they had seen, but more importantly served to reinforce the standards expected in a well-conducted institution.[20]

The greatest obstacles to order and cleanliness were many of the patients whom the asylum was designed to serve. The 'refractory' or 'dirty' patients posed a threat to fixtures and fittings. Their noise and behaviour also upset other patients' tranquillity. The Nottingham governors, in the early 1820s, called for action to alleviate the problems caused by 'the more clamorous patients when they labour under the violent paroxysms of maniacal excitement'. They exerted a 'baneful influence' on the minds of the calmer patients, as well as interrupting staff's nocturnal rest. The disorderly patients would normally be separated out, as part of the process of 'classification', into separate cells, galleries and day-rooms. In some asylums, the problem had been underestimated in the planning and construction, and managers had to improvise. The usual solution was to place the least socially acceptable in the basement. However, in some asylums, like Dorset, there was not even unsatisfactory separate provision, due to lack of will or lack of funds. Even the ostensibly progressive governors of Lincoln Asylum were unable to properly separate 'quiet' and 'noisy' patients before 1838.[21]

After gender, the most important basis for separation and classification was social class. In joint asylums with sophisticated arrangements, like Gloucester, distinct portions of the building were allocated to first (private), second (charitable) and third (pauper) class patients. The arrangement persisted generally that private patients were housed in the front centre of the building and the paupers in the wings. Accommodation standards, day-rooms and exercise facilities varied accordingly. At Chester and elsewhere, private patients had access to the extensive landscaped grounds for recreation, whilst the paupers were confined to the small enclosed courtyards. The services offered were determined largely by the level of payment. At Stafford and Gloucester, for example, private patients could pay a supplement to have a separate sitting-room, a room for a personal servant and wine served with meals.[22]

As far as possible, the more refined private patients were protected from contact with the undesirable excesses of the paupers. The differences between conditions for private and pauper patients could be extremely marked. Dr Crommelinck, after visiting Gloucester, contrasted the 'opulence, luxury, the most prodigious comfort, the most refined stylishness' of the first-class quarters in the crescent with the 'den of misery and grief' inhabited by the paupers. The principle of separation might be sacrificed, though, where a private patient became dirty or refractory, leading to placement with paupers of similar habits, as at Lincoln in 1828, where 'insensible' or disorderly first-class patients were considered to be no longer conscious of the significance of class differentials. A point came where the niceties of social status were superseded.[23]

DECAY AND RENEWAL

During the 1820s and 1830s, managers and medical officers were faced with a growing range of difficulties which challenged the asylum's justification as the model for statutory provision of care and treatment of the insane. The philosophical dichotomy between custody and cure became more stark, precipitating the great debate over mechanical restraint. Shortcomings in the original siting, design and equipment of the buildings caused increasingly serious problems. The inadequacies of the staff, both numerical and in quality, became ever more apparent. Management inertia, fuelled by the dispersal of power and the quest for economy, produced a slow response to changing circumstances. Most significantly, the inexorable growth in numbers of patients and the size of the institution brought new problems which had not been anticipated, as the asylum was transformed from a relatively small and compact facility to a large and rambling one providing for a conglomeration of differing and often contradictory needs. The consequence, widely replicated, was a general and steady deterioration in conditions, occurring at a time of emerging awareness of the delicate interrelationship between physical surroundings, crowding, cleanliness, health and disease.

One perennial difficulty was the provision of adequate water to meet the institution's needs; according to Chris Philo the issue became an 'obsession'. Supplies normally came either from a reservoir on top of the building, or from underground springs or wells. Surveyors had consistently underestimated the required quantity of water, particularly if the building was later expanded. At Gloucester, where there were deficiencies from the beginning, special measures had to be taken to fetch water from elsewhere. Samuel Hitch protested to the visitors in October 1835 that:

> there is again a total failure of Water, & that he is oblig'd to haul water by the hogshead from a considerable distance & under very disagreeable circumstances for all the purposes of the Establishment.

Attempts to find a solution failed and Gloucester's problems persisted. Kent Asylum, opened in 1833 and built with the benefit of experience gained from elsewhere, was soon in trouble. In the summer of 1835, 64,000 gallons had to be brought up from the river, at a cost of £45. Eventually, the visitors were forced to invest heavily in a steam engine to raise water from the valley below; the annual outlay helped account for the asylum's high charges. Particular problems were also encountered at Middlesex, Lancashire and Cornwall Asylums. At Hanwell, for several years, water was brought at great expense from the Grand Junction Canal, until the canal company refused to continue this and an artesian well had to be sunk at a cost of nearly £1500. The Metropolitan Commissioners noted at Bodmin, in 1843, that it was frequently short of water; when they visited the resulting 'discomfort and evils' were 'very perceptible'.[24]

Water shortages proved most serious of all at Wakefield where, despite choice of a site with the prospect of 'there always being an abundant supply of water', the springs were exhausted during the summer of 1819, and further wells had to be sunk. In 1824, the wells failed and water had to be brought from the river. During 1828 a long borehole was sunk, which Ellis expected to secure a sufficient supply. However, by 1834, the optimism proved unfounded, with serious shortages occurring because of the hot summer. During 1837 matters became more critical than ever; Corsellis voiced his concerns:

> The want of water has been a serious inconvenience; during the summer months, the wells, the tank, and every other receptacle were dry; the water used for brewing and other domestic purposes, was carried from the river; the bathing of the patients was suspended for many months, and could not be renewed till within the last fortnight.

A further well was built; nevertheless in 1843 there was another crisis, baths were suspended, and water was fetched in carts from the river. By this time, the connection between deficiencies in water supply and the high incidence of disease and epidemic in the asylum had become apparent.[25]

Shortcomings in water supply accentuated the problems of adequate sanitary provision. In most asylums water closets were installed, with some contrivance to flush them through. The arrangements frequently proved defective, resulting in pervasive stenches through parts of the building. At Wakefield, the closets were frequently reported blocked by patients throwing articles of clothing down them. Thomas Powell at Nottingham developed an ingenious self-flushing water closet designed both to minimize unpleasant odours and to prevent the problem of patients eating their own excrement. Even where proper facilities were provided, however, less scrupulous patients might prefer to make more convenient arrangements, as the Gloucester visitors heard in 1841:

> The ventilating grates, which are now placed upon the surface of the ground in the corners of the male airing grounds, being used by some of the Patients as urinary conduits, and thereby occasioning a noisome effluvia, it will be advisable to fix them higher in the wall.

At Norfolk Asylum there were no water closets attached to the wards; as late as 1854, all the patients were having to use open air privies, 'whatever might be their own condition, or the state of the weather'. Facilities for bathing also varied considerably, with large communal baths for each sex having been provided at Wakefield.[26]

Sanitation problems were common to many early nineteenth-century public buildings, their solution beyond most engineers' abilities. Sewage systems remained crude and unsophisticated. Those in asylums were developed locally, with little apparent reference to elsewhere. In late 1824 a serious nuisance arose at Gloucester from 'the filth issuing from the common sewers'. Sewage was likely to be drained into a cess pool, which could prove both a nuisance and a health hazard if not sited at an appropriate distance. At Lincoln Asylum, cess pools adjoined the patients' outdoor walk areas until 1844. The problem of 'noxious effluvia', however, was accepted as a normal concomitant of concentrating people in a large building, and was not seriously confronted until its link with disease became clear.[27]

The 1808 Act had called for asylums to be sited in an 'airy and healthy' situation. Although in most cases, justices sought sites which met the criteria, others were less discerning. Norfolk Asylum's promoters paid little heed and built on a low site near the river. Stagnant water would accumulate nearby, and a 'damp foggy air' sometimes filled the building. Pervasive dampness proved to be a continuing hazard, the problems worsening over the years. At Dorset Asylum, where cost considerations also led the justices to by-pass the Act's recommendations, a serious and ongoing problem of dampness in the lower wards developed due to the asylum's location:

> After heavy rains, or an extensive thaw, the water flows down from the hills behind the house into the valley, and the bricks being laid immediately on the earth, absorb and retain the moisture, creating a humidity, which is highly injurious to the health and comfort of the patients.

Eventually, in 1842, the floors had to be taken up and re-laid. Elsewhere, as at Bodmin and Gloucester, dampness presented a consistent problem.[28]

The effects of a damp atmosphere could be tackled partly by ventilation. The difficulty remained to reconcile the conflicting requirements for fresh air and warmth, particularly in winter. Attempts to raise the temperature could make rooms 'overpoweringly offensive for want of sufficient ventilation', as at Gloucester in late 1824. The problem was most acute in basement accommodation, housing refractory or 'dirty' patients. Samuel Hitch protested in 1834 that his existing male noisy ward was 'cold – unventilated – & scarcely fit for human habitation'. John Conolly drew attention to the ramifications of basement-rooms in the first generation of county asylums: 'From subterranean dormitories insidious streams of corrupted air are for ever rising, pervading every room above ground, ascending every staircase, and infecting every corner. . .' Sickness, Conolly contended, was the frequent result. At Lincoln, ventilation was given precedence over warmth, with severe consequences, as the critical Dr William Cookson claimed in November 1842:

> In our establishment owing to the absence of warming apparatus we have a severe climate to contend with – our temperatures varying with the external atmosphere insomuch that during the last month our Patients have frequently slept in temperatures from two to three degrees above the freezing point.

The main heating method at Lincoln continued to be an open coal fire at the end of each gallery.[29]

Inadequate heating systems were a persistent problem. At Stafford in February 1819, soon after opening, John Garrett temporarily moved the male patients from the lower gallery because of the cold, an option no longer available once the building became fully occupied. In several asylums it remained unresolved, cold becoming the accepted norm. Rooms and cells with stone floors proved the most difficult to warm, without a large outlay. Eventually, some visitors succumbed and found the money, as at Suffolk in the 1840s after a series of protests by John Kirkman about the effects of the severe cold on the health of patients in the basement; a combination of flues and open fireplaces brought some relief. The overall lack of urgency demonstrated in tackling heating deficiencies suggests some lingering adherence to beliefs about insane people's lack of sensitivity to cold.[30]

The search for the most appropriate flooring was also subject to conflicting considerations. The disadvantages of stone floors, particularly in basements, were increasingly apparent. At Stafford, 'footboards' had to be put down in 1827 to protect the feet of females in the basement from the cold and damp. Samuel Hitch objected particularly to stone floors, 'upon the ground of their distracting so much heat from the Bodies of Patients who when excited are with great difficulty kept clothed'. Wooden floors, however, had the marked disadvantage of being liable to infusion with wet and pungent substances. One of the Stafford visitors in April 1841 noted a 'very offensive smell' in the basement day-room, due to the defective state of the floor; the soil underneath was 'completely saturated with urine'. The same problem became apparent at Lancaster, where the original sleeping-room floors were boarded. Those in the dirty patients' rooms 'became so much saturated with urine &c as to be rendered incapable of being made dry or free from unsavoury smells'. They were replaced with stone-flagged floors, heated by under-floor flues, which alleviated concern over the many patients who discarded their socks and shoes. Generally, however, stone floors became regarded as the greater evil and were gradually dispensed with in most asylums. They were not replaced at Nottingham until the mid-1840s, and at Norfolk Asylum, consistently the worst managed of all, cold stone floors persisted into the 1850s.[31]

The main threat to the sanitary state of the institution stemmed from patients' incontinence, disinhibition or lack of interest in cleanliness. Classification tended to lead to a congregation of the worst-affected patients in the basement. At Lancaster, with its under-floor heating, the results of poor ventilation in the basement struck several of the visitors, who found themselves overpowered by the stench, 'arising it is said from the Hot Air acting upon the Wet of the dirty patients in this Gallery'. An unusual and later notorious solution was adopted, in the form of two 'warm rooms', the name deriving from their heated stone floors. Along the inner wall were fourteen stalls or boxed seats, to which unruly or dirty patients were kept constantly chained, clothed in a 'short petticoat', to give them unlimited use of the facilities. They drained into a long leaden trough, 'immediately below these seats and communicating with a common drain or sewer', which was regularly flushed out during the day, by means of a water tap. These 'warm rooms' remained in operation at Lancaster until 1841.[32]

The multiplicity of problems which visitors and medical officers had to contend with in trying to provide a healthy and comfortable environment were greatly accentuated by the overcrowding which accompanied the inexorable rise in patient numbers. One of the asylums worst affected was Lancaster; a visiting magistrate pointed out in 1839 that 'the building is by no means adequate to the number of its inmates', and that parts never so intended were being used as sleeping-rooms. In the early 1840s, it was 'crowded to excess', 90 people being crammed into airing courts designed for 30. At Gloucester in 1840, the pauper day-rooms contained more than double the numbers they were intended for; in July 1842, the asylum contained 272 patients, but there was only 'proper accommodation' for 194. The situation became so acute by early 1845 that Mrs Hitch, the matron, lodged a written protest with the visitors, alleging 'crowded and dangerous' accommodation in the female pauper wing, where 'very constricted room' for 85 patients was occupied by 113. The resulting mix of all types of patients had, she claimed, proved almost fatal when an old woman was badly beaten by a younger patient.[33]

Some of the worst problems were at Dorset Asylum, where George Button repeatedly called for improvements. He pointed out to the justices in 1844 that attic rooms designed for three patients were having to contain six. He protested that 'the results of animal exhalations in close & over-crowded apartments are highly injurious', leading to diseases; the breathing of 'such contaminated air' was inducing 'languor and depression of spirit' and loss of appetite. At Norfolk Asylum, concerns about health were also articulated by the medical officers. Due in part to its particularly poor recovery-rate, the asylum's accommodation became insufficient within a few years of opening. By 1829, the visiting surgeon, Mr Dalrymple, expressed the fear that 'sickness & death may hereafter be produced by the extraordinary number of patients & the difficulty of proper accommodation for them'.[34]

The severe and recurring problems of West Riding Asylum were particularly well documented. Opened in 1818 for 150 people, the asylum's population had reached 230 by 1823, though William Ellis argued conveniently that the generous original design made up to 250 manageable. His arch-critic Caleb Crowther accepted no such rationalizations: 'You cannot cram into an Asylum, built to accommodate only one hundred and fifty patients, two hundred and fifty-six, without rendering it unwholesome.' By 1829 even Ellis was having to acknowledge that several rooms were much too crowded. Repeated building programmes over the next two decades only brought temporary respite between periods of discomfort. Samuel Tuke, writing in 1841, was clearly shocked and distressed at what had happened to his brainchild. He found 296 people occupying 'day-rooms, galleries, and lodging-rooms' designed for 150:

By this increase, however, the whole system originally laid down has been interrupted; and the eye is struck with the want of accommodation for the number who occupy the wards; and it deserves most serious consideration, whether the space allotted to the number of human beings, enclosed within the walls, is really sufficient for health.

As he pointed out, architects needed to plan accordingly if the number of inmates was to be twice as many as intended.[35]

The passage of time and the benefit of experience did not ease the situation at Wakefield. In January 1844, with the number of patients having reached 433, Corsellis devoted four pages of his report to the problem, arguing that the increase in numbers was reducing the therapeutic benefits of asylum care. At the end of the year, with little relief, he pointed out that the bustle created by crowding patients into the day-rooms was the reverse of beneficial; sleeping in crowded rooms was still worse, and neutralized the 'soothing tranquillizing treatment' of the asylum. Even the Metropolitan Commissioners in 1844, who were fairly effusive in their general praise of Wakefield, referred to its 'too crowded state' and registered a strong protest at the consequent 'highly objectionable' practice of placing two men together in single rooms. A few months later, there were still eleven rooms in which men were sharing, and the angry Commissioners successfully pressurized Corsellis to abandon the practice. The corollary was that over 150 patients were refused admission during 1845 owing to lack of accommodation.[36]

The steadily deteriorating overall conditions within the asylums, worsened by overcrowding, raised growing concerns about disease and mortality. At the same time, debate about the state of public health in towns and cities was raising general awareness on the relationship between crowding, water supply, refuse disposal, ventilation and disease.[37] John Conolly summarized the problem, as it affected the asylum:

By the accumulation of so many persons, day and night, in a lofty building, many of whom can seldom leave the wards, and no one of whom is in perfect health, the asylum becomes subject to every atmospheric and terrestrial influence unfavourable to life.

After a visit in 1841, John Thurnam voiced concern about the relationship between overcrowding and a high mortality rate at Stafford Asylum, particularly in view of its relatively high standard of patient diet. He concluded that the problem must be related to the particular arrangements that had been made to deal with the crowded state of the building:

The ventilation appeared to me to be defective; as it could hardly fail to be, when the exercising galleries, which flank the sleeping rooms of the patients, were every evening divided by folding partitions and fitted up with beds, so as to afford sleeping accommodation for nearly double the number of that for which each gallery so divided was orginally intended.

Elsewhere, there was growing anxiety about the possible consequences. Reverend Charles Crawley, chairman of the Gloucester visitors, was clearly aware of the potential for a scandal in late 1840 when bad weather confined the patients indoors:

my attention has been powerfully directed by the very offensive and hot effluvia generated in the Basement Day Rooms for the Male and Female Paupers by their very crowded occupation. . .I do believe that every thing, that the utmost care can take, both as to cleanliness and ventilation, as far as possible has been done to counteract this – but certainly without that effect, which I should imagine to be absolutely requisite to the prevention of the most dangerous fevers. . .

Although his asylum escaped some of the worst consequences, Crawley's fears were realized elsewhere.[38]

Disease, often of an epidemic nature, became prevalent in several asylums, most commonly in the form of dysentery or related complaints. It was endemic at Stafford before a new heating and ventilation system was introduced in 1842. Dorset Asylum was subject to several outbreaks of dysentery, some fatal, before the sodden floors in the lower wards were replaced in the same year. An outbreak at Gloucester in 1844, attributed to problems with the drains, claimed at least two lives. At Lancaster, bowel diseases were a perennial problem. Paul Slade Knight had to contend with 70 cases during the year to June 1824, which he attributed to the water and the asylum's 'contiguity to boggy ground'. These ailments continued to recur, with 'diarrhoea' claiming the lives of many patients within a few weeks of admission, before Gaskell and de Vitrie in 1841 instituted an effective programme of measures to combat it. Even the new Kent Asylum suffered a fatal outbreak of dysentery in January 1834, only a year after opening, with the loss of six male patients.[39]

Dysentery proved a particular scourge at Wakefield. During the 1820s, a series of epidemics claimed many lives, and the poor state of health in the asylum became notorious. In the autumn of 1828, at least 54 patients were attacked with the disease and fourteen died. A ward had to be cleared in order to set up a separate infirmary for the victims, and a special laundry built in one of the airing courts. Four years of continuous outbreaks caused a growing alarm, particularly as nurses, keepers and domestic staff were succumbing. At least eight people died in a virulent episode in 1830, and more died the following year, including the 3-year-old son of Dr and Mrs Corsellis. According to the later researches of the physician Thomas

Giordani Wright, dysentery persisted into the mid-1830s and the number of deaths due to it had been greatly underestimated.[40]

Various explanations were advanced for Wakefield Asylum's susceptibility to dysentery. William Ellis demonstrated a link with the 'offensive and unwholesome effluvia' arising from the badly-constructed privies. However, their replacement with water-closets in 1828 brought no immediate improvement, and the disease returned the next year. Caleb Crowther derided the attempts to improve toilet facilities: 'On walking over the house a disagreeable fetid odour, a malaria might be perceived which could easily be traced to the privies.' The basic problem, he suggested, lay with the chronically poor water supply, which rendered the water-closets ineffective. An attempt by Dr Gilbey, another physician, to analyse the problem in 1830 was hampered by difficulties in obtaining valid information from lunatic patients whose senses were 'so much deadened, by the weakening of the cerebral influence', and whose 'common feelings of human nature' were 'almost extinct'. Basing his conclusions largely on an examination of the stools, Gilbey had no doubt that the root cause of the contagion was the overcrowded state of the building, which aggravated the problems associated with its design and construction. The 'miserably small' wash-house, which adjoined the kitchen, contributed to the 'malaria'; the 'stench and abomination' from the large quantity of filthy linen affected not only the patients employed in 'this loathsome office', but the whole house. Then there was the drainage – 'nothing can be conceived more infamously contrived'; all of the 'scourings and ordure' flowed into four tanks, placed within three or four yards of the wards. Gilbey's comprehensive assessment led to some new sanitary measures, but several years elapsed before dysentery was brought under control at Wakefield.[41]

Contagious fevers, of one form or another, afflicted patients and staff of most asylums. An influenza epidemic, complicated by consumption, brought 'considerable havoc' to Wakefield Asylum in 1837, leaving more than 30 patients dead. In the same year at Lancaster, 46 perished due to 'pthisis after influenza'. At Lincoln, an outbreak of fever in late 1843 carried off seven patients, as well as affecting the staff, the county press alleging that the number of fatalities was actually greater. Its origin was traced to the cess pool; at Dr Charlesworth's behest a drainage tunnel was then built, and the problem abated. The cholera epidemics of 1832 and 1849 also took their toll. Lancaster Asylum disastrously caught the tail-end of the earlier outbreak, sustaining 94 deaths. At Wakefield, Corsellis and the visitors congratulated themselves on how their sanitary precautions had fended off the 1832 outbreak, despite a serious problem in the surrounding districts. The epidemic of 1849, however, proved devastating, despite the inevitable clean-up and sanitary measures. It claimed more than 100 lives in the asylum, with much of the blame again attributed to 'wretched drainage', more than twenty years after its effects were first exposed.[42]

An unavoidable picture emerges of public asylums as unwholesome and disease-ridden places, resulting from increasingly overcrowded conditions in buildings that were damp, cold, cramped and ill-ventilated. This is perhaps too stark and simplistic an image, as some attempts were being made to improve the asylum environment, particularly from the mid-1830s onwards. The movements to bring about reform in methods of care and treatment, at Lincoln and elsewhere, which culminated in the 'non-restraint' system, brought other improvements in their train. Indeed, Robert Gardiner Hill, the architect and publicist of the new approach, stressed that the abolition of restraint was only part of a wider philosophy. There had also to be suitable and comfortable internal arrangements within the house, regard to personal hygiene and cleanliness, an ample water supply, effective ventilation and heating, and attention to the occupation and amusement of the patients. Whilst Hill and Charlesworth worked to improve the general conditions at Lincoln, and Conolly followed at Hanwell, others embarked on a similar process, like Gaskell and de Vitrie at Lancaster, Samuel Hitch at Gloucester, John Kirkman at Melton and James Wilkes at Stafford.[43]

At Lincoln, where the contrast between the elegance of the exterior and the grimness of much of the interior had been so marked, Charlesworth started to implement improvements in amenities and comforts, along with building adaptations and changes in patient management methods, from 1828 onwards. Over the next few years, some of the custodial trappings were withdrawn. Sash windows replaced those covered with wire mesh, and glass panes replaced wood and iron in the entrance doors to the wards. Ventilation was improved, and the installation of coal fires gave a more comfortable feel to the house (though with limited effect on its temperature). During 1834, sofas and couches were placed in the wards. Externally, grass replaced gravel on its recreation grounds, walkways were widened and flower gardens were created. Elsewhere, amid mounting criticism of the prison-like environment of the asylums, serious attempts were initiated to improve physical conditions. In the early 1840s, in the wake of the new thinking on restraint, iron bars, wire mesh, iron fire surrounds and other obvious custodial features were removed or reduced, and walls were lowered at several places. There were noticeable effects on people's demeanour. At Lancaster, the changes brought about 'an increased degree of cheerfulness' and less destructiveness amongst the patients, and similar results were recorded at Stafford.[44]

The incidence of disease and high mortality rates brought an increasing awareness of the need for measures to improve health. Along with the installation of new heating systems, attention was being paid to effective ventilation. At Dorset Asylum, which had been particularly unhealthy, windows hitherto secured for years were opened in 1843. At Nottingham measures were taken to ventilate the 'worst parts' of the building. More consideration was given to the nutrition of people whose poor, often debilitated, physical condition rendered them vulnerable to illness. Principles of rigidly economical management were set aside as dietary improvements were widely implemented. At Dorset, the weekly menu was completely revised and the meat allowance almost doubled; according to Dr George Button the better diet brought a 'manifest improvement' in the condition of the patients: 'They appeared as if restored to new life, they became active and stout; and the increased contentment which prevailed, added in no small degree, to the general comfort of the asylum.' At Lancaster, where 'abject want' had been identified as the strongest 'exciting cause' of patients' insanity, a more varied and plentiful diet was initiated, with immediate effects on patients' physical well-being. The example had been set at Hanwell by John Conolly, who had introduced a far more liberal dietary after several years of strict economy under the Ellises.[45]

Other means were adopted to improve patients' quality of life, in measures which became extremely familiar in the post-1845 asylums. Various recreation facilities were developed. Airing grounds were enhanced at Nottingham, Lancaster, Dorset and Wakefield, by planting trees and shrubs and laying out walks. At Gloucester, Samuel Hitch had by 1841 encouraged the visitors to take things still further, and they discovered that better surroundings induced better behaviour:

> The exercising grounds, formerly scenes of occasional riot and confusion, with indications of mischief and destruction scattered on all sides, are now laid out as vegetable and flower gardens, and planted with fruit trees. To these, all the patients of each class and sex respectively, have constant access, and yet the productions of each are permitted to flourish, and their fruits to attain maturity.

New furniture was provided to make wards and day-rooms more 'domestic' in outlook. The spirit of improvement even reached Norfolk Asylum, where in 1843 the visitors yielded to outside criticism and invested in tables for patients previously forced to eat from their laps. Elsewhere, flowers began to appear on wards, as well as prints on walls and reading material on tables, to accompany the upsurge in leisure pursuits and entertainments which characterized the new asylum regimes of the 1840s.[46]

Where new wings were added, like at Lancaster, Melton, Bodmin and Wakefield, these were designed and equipped very differently to the building's older portions. At Wakefield, after being shown the new wing in 1841, patients clamoured for a transfer. However, although such improvements benefited those in the new accommodation, the contrast with conditions in the existing areas was stark. Nowhere was this more apparent than at Lancaster, where Dr Crommelinck was dismayed at what he found in 1841. He advised his government that the asylum presented 'a kind of panorama of the old and the new system'; no other he had visited presented greater contrasts. The new wings were built with 'an elegance and a stylishness' not comparable with any other pauper establishment, whilst the old part was completely different. Sanitary conditions were 'the most diametrically opposed':

> There, the patient is full of health and vigour; here he grows sickly, the decline often draws him to the tomb. On one side they recover while on the other they fall into dementia, if death does not come to deliver them. . .

Crommelinck had expressed similar concerns about Gloucester Asylum, comparing not new and old sections, but those allotted to private patients and paupers. The visitor fell 'from the Eden into hell'; the contrast was 'revolting' between the opulent crescent and the confined cells, narrow corridors and airless darkness of the pauper sections. He had perhaps gone to Gloucester before the programme of improvements, but his criticisms demonstrated that, even in the best regarded of asylums, there was much work to be done to bring conditions into line with the early ideals.[47]

Certainly, by the time the Metropolitan Commissioners in Lunacy published their great survey in 1844, the process of improvement and reform in the public asylums had gained a momentum. Ideals of cure were in the ascendant over those of custody. Although the Commissioners' report acknowledged shortcomings and did not disguise most of the worst deficiencies, it was written with the clear intention of showing the superiority of the county asylum over the abuse-ridden private asylum system. They produced sufficient evidence of acceptable standards and conditions to justify advocacy of the compulsory dissemination of the model. Their observations highlighted the order, regularity and cleanliness of the institutions, whilst playing down the complex issues associated with the accumulation of growing numbers of chronic, hopeless and 'incurable' patients. The argument was that it was not the principle of county asylums that was wrong, but rather that mistakes had been made in their construction and management, and had been magnified by their continual growth. The central role of the state in the provision of care for the insane had been confirmed; the lessons of the pilot group of public asylums were there so that mistakes might not be repeated.

NOTES

1 Thomas Bakewell, 'Remarks on County Asylums', *Imperial Magazine*, vol. XI (November 1829), col. 1086.

2 L.D. Smith, 'Close Confinement in a Mighty Prison: Thomas Bakewell and his Campaign Against Public Asylums, 1815–1830', *History of Psychiatry*, vol. V (1994), pp. 191–214; T.A. Markus, *Buildings and Power: Freedom and Control in the Origins of Modern Building Types* (London, 1993), pp. 130– 40.

3 J. Andrews, *Bedlam Revisited: A History of Bethlem Hospital c.1634–1770* (PhD, University of London, 1991), pp. 134–238; J. Andrews, A. Briggs, R. Porter, P. Tucker and K. Waddington, *The History of Bethlem* (London, 1997), pp. 200–21; W.L. Parry-Jones, *The Trade in Lunacy* (London, 1972); C. MacKenzie, *Psychiatry for the Rich: A History of Ticehurst Asylum, 1792–1917* (London, 1992); A. Digby, *Madness, Morality and Medicine: A Study of the York Retreat 1796–1914* (Cambridge, 1985); A. Scull, *The Most Solitary of Afflictions: Madness and Society in Britain, 1700–1900* (London, 1993), pp. 167–72; T.A. Markus, *Buildings and Power*, p. 40.

4 J.H. Matthiason, *Bedford and its Environs; or an Historical and Topographical Sketch of the Town of Bedford* (Bedford, 1831), p. 117; BCRO, LB/1/8, 5 September 1812; J. Conolly, *The Construction and Government of Lunatic Asylums* (London, 1847), pp. 7, 49; WRCRO, C85/107, West Riding Asylum, 1st Report (31 December 1819); LAO, LAWN 1/1/1, 29 October 1821, 28 January, 10 April, 28 October 1822; NkCRO, SAH 2, 28 April 1814, SAH 3, 5 July 1817.

5 SCRO, D550/4, 8 January, 6 May 1825; GCRO, HO22/1/1, 8 May 1823; LAO, LAWN 1/2/3, 14 June 1840.

6 Matthiason, *Bedford*, pp. 117–18; Conolly, *Construction and Government*, p. 7; S. Tuke, *Practical Hints on the Construction and Economy of Pauper Lunatic Asylums* (York, 1815), pp. 36–9; *Wakefield and Halifax Journal*, 15 December 1815; *Journal of Mental Science*, vol. II, no. 17 (1855), pp. 276–7; B. Cashman, *A Proper House: Bedford Lunatic Asylum, 1812–1860* (North Bedfordshire Health Authority, 1992), pp. 25, 74.

7 *Report of the Metropolitan Commissioners in Lunacy to the Lord Chancellor* (1844), pp. 23, 31; J. Hemingway, *History of the City of Chester* (Chester,

1831), p. 228; Conolly, *Construction and Government*, pp. 49–50; C. Crommelinck, *Rapport sur les Hospices d'Aliénés de l'Angleterre, de la France et de l'Allemagne* (Courtrai, 1842), pp. 109–10; Watson and Pritchett, *Plans, Elevations, Sections and Description of the Pauper Lunatic Asylum Lately Erected at Wakefield* (York, 1819), p. 25; *Nottingham Journal*, 5 November 1831.

8 *An Address to the Magistrates of the County of Lancaster on the Situation Proposed for the Intended County Lunatic Asylum* (Liverpool, 1810), pp. 29–30; Conolly, *Construction and Government*, p. 35; *Metropolitan Commissioners in Lunacy* (1844), pp. 13, 22; *The Builder*, 25 July 1846, p. 349; J.E. Huxley, 'History and Description of the Kent Asylum', *Journal of Mental Science*, vol. I, no. 3, 15 February 1854, p. 41; Crommelinck, *Rapport sur les Hospices*, pp. 109–10.

9 J. Taylor, *Hospital and Asylum Architecture in England, 1840–1914* (London, 1991), pp. 1–3; *Lonsdale Magazine*, February 1821, p. 44; SCRO, D550/1, 12 July 1827; GCRO, HO22/1/1, 31 March 1813, 29 May 1823, 18 October 1824; Crommelinck, *Rapport sur les Hospices*, pp. 109–10, 152; *Metropolitan Commissioners in Lunacy* (1844), pp. 17–20; Watson and Pritchett, *Plans. . .of the Pauper Lunatic Asylum at Wakefield*, pp. 27–8; NkCRO, SAH 2, 27 November 1813, 1, 29 January, 26 February, 26 March 1814, SAH 137, 9 September 1842. For the problems associated with cold at eighteenth-century Bethlem, see Andrews, *Bedlam Revisited*, pp. 176–80.

10 CCRO, DDX 97/1, 16 March, 18 June 1819, DDX 654/246, 11 December 1844; SCRO, D550/5, 24 June 1834; NCRO, SO/HO/1/3/3, 17 March 1841; GCRO, HO22/8/1, Annual Report 1837/8; DCRO, Forston House (4), Michaelmas 1841; LLSL, Lincoln Asylum, 21st Report (1845), p. 6; WRCRO, C85/107, West Riding Asylum, 10th Report (31 December 1828) – the annual expenditure table shows £66 spent on straw; NkCRO, SAH 137, 19 July 1843. Straw continued to be widely used at Norfolk Asylum into the 1850s – *Journal of Mental Science* (7), 15 August 1854, p. 100. At Manchester Asylum, there was a group known as 'Straw Patients', who were kept out of sight of the others 'on account of being unclean' – Warneford Hospital Archives, WP 5, xv, letter dated 7 April 1818.

11 R.G. Hill, *Total Abolition of Personal Restraint in the Treatment of the Insane* (London, 1839), Appendix A, pp. 59–60 – at the Lincoln Asylum, some of the original cell doors were clad in iron in 1821 after a patient had succeeded in smashing three of them; Paul Slade Knight, *Observations on the Causes, Symptoms and Treatment of Derangement of the Mind* (London, 1827), Appendix, 'An Account of the Various Sensations Felt by a Person Deprived of Reason by a Fever' – 'The noise made by the shutting and locking of the doors appeared very strange to me; and that occasioned by the opening of them, had a no less striking effect on my mind.' Knight commented that 'All the room doors, about fifty in each gallery, were locked every night, and unlocked in the morning.'; Conolly, *Construction and Government*, pp. 14– 15; Huxley, 'History of the Kent Asylum', pp. 41–2;

J. Foulston, *The Public Buildings Erected in the West of England by John Foulston, F.R.I.B.A.* (London, 1838), pp. 68–70.

12 *Imperial Magazine*, vol. V (October 1823), cols. 892–3; BPP 1834, vol. XXVIII, *Report from Her Majesty's Commissioners on the Administration and Practical Operation of the Poor Laws*, p. 429; *Morning Herald*, 12 January 1826; SCRO, D550/4, 3 April 1824, 26 March 1831; GCRO, D2593/2/3, 'Explanation of Plan for Proposed Additions to the Gloucester Lunatic Asylum', 25 March 1831.

13 Taylor, *Hospital and Asylum Architecture*, p. 135; *Metropolitan Commissioners in Lunacy* (1844), pp. 22–3; GCRO, HO22/1/1, 27 February, 29 May 1823; Tuke, *Practical Hints*, pp. 24–5; Watson and Pritchett, pp. 1–2, 28–9; R.G. Hill, *A Concise History of the Entire Abolition of Mechanical Restraint in the Treatment of the Insane* (London, 1857), p. 81; *Eighth Report of the Commissioners in Lunacy* (1854), p. 137, evidence of James Wilkes.

14 NkCRO, SAH 137, 23 May 1843; *Nottingham Journal*, 5 November 1831; SCRO, Q/AIc, Box I, 'Rules for the Government of the Lunatic Asylum in Manchester' (1791); Crommelinck, *Rapport sur les Hospices*, pp. 71–2; R.G. Hill, *Concise History*, pp. 82–3; LLSL, Lincoln Asylum, *Rules* (1819), p. 9, *Rules* (1832), p. 22; Pliny Earle, *A Visit to Thirteen Asylums for the Insane in Europe* (Philadelphia, 1841), p. 13.

15 BCRO, LB/1/8, 17 July 1812, 3 September 1814 – the meat allowance was reduced to three days per week in 1814; LAO, LAWN 1/1/1, 18 December 1820; E.P. Charlesworth, *Remarks on the Treatment of the Insane and the Management of Lunatic Asylums* (London, 1828), pp. 11–12; G. Higgins, *Rules for the Management of the Pauper Lunatic Asylum for the West Riding of the County of York, Erected at Wakefield* (Wakefield, 1821), pp. 14–15; BPP 1836, vol. XLI, *County Lunatic Asylums, Returns*, pp. 3, 5, 8, 9, 10, 18, 21, 24 – by 1836, Bedford Asylum offered meat for dinner three days a week, bread in a tin filled with broth three days, and suet pudding on Saturdays (p. 3); at Lancaster, there was meat daily, but in the form of pies one day, soup one day and 'scouse' five days per week. Dietary lists had not altered greatly from those provided at earlier asylums. A Bethlem dietary sheet dating from 1692 showed dinner to contain meat on three days, bread and cheese on three days and pease pottage on Saturdays (Andrews, *Bedlam Revisited*, p. 192).

16 GCRO, HO22/1/1, 10 July 1823, 11 April 1832, 25 April 1837, 24 June 1839; LAO, LAWN 1/1/1, 18 December 1820, LAWN 1/1/3, 18 January 1830; BPP 1836, vol. XLI, *County Lunatic Asylums, Returns*, pp. 8, 10, 21, 24 – social class differentiation in diet at Gloucester was still in place in 1836; similar distinctions operated at Stafford.

17 DCRO, Reports of Visiting Justices (Epiphany 1838), p. 9, (Epiphany 1844), p. 18; CCRO, DDX 97/1, 18 August 1820; BPP 1836, vol. XLI, *Returns*, pp. 6, 8.

18 SuCRO, B106/10/4.4, Reports of Suffolk Lunatic Asylum (1), p. 9, (2), pp. 4–6; NkCRO, SAH 5, 25 April 1836, 29 March 1841; BPP 1836, vol. XLI, *Returns*, pp. 20, 28 – at Suffolk, dinner comprised meat two days per week,

soup twice, dumplings with sweet sauce twice and 1lb of shortcake with beer on Saturdays.

19 J. Thurnam, *Observations and Essays on the Statistics of Insanity* (London, 1845), pp. 95–7; *The Lancet*, 12 December 1840, p. 409.

20 LCRO, QAM/1/33/11, 12 August, 16 October 1836, 25 October 1842; SuCRO, ID407/B16/1, Suffolk Asylum Visitors' Book, 2 December 1829 – 'It is impossible to speak in too high terms of the excellent order cleanliness & kind & good management which strikingly pervades the whole of this valuable institution', 5 May 1837 – 'most highly gratified with the perfect order & cleanliness which I have observed throughout. Nothing in fact can surpass it. . .', 4 September 1843; GCRO, HO22/50/1, Gloucester Asylum Visitors' Book, 7 October 1830 – Dr James Monro of Bethlem commented 'The cleanliness of the apartments must strike every person who visits the house. . .I have been very much pleased with the order kept.'; Stanley Royd Hospital, West Riding Asylum Visitors' Book, 29 August 1839, 26 February 1840, J.F. Geary, a Leeds missionary – 'Much pleased with the cleanliness, order and regularity of the patients, and grateful with the manner in which they have replied to some questions on the goodness and Love of God.'; NkCRO, SAH 137, 22 October 1819, 11 October 1827, 13 December 1834, 9 September 1842.

21 Hemingway, *History of the City of Chester*, p. 228; *Metropolitan Commissioners in Lunacy* (1844), p. 22; SCRO, D550/4, 28 February, 3 April 1824, 26 March 1831, D550/5, 18 October 1837 – 'I regret to observe so many very bad cases in the female basement gallery'; NCRO, SO/HO/1/3/1, 21 March, 17 October 1816; *Nottingham Journal*, 13 October 1821, 18 October 1823; LLSL, Lincoln Asylum, *Rules* (1832), p. 19 – the revised rules stated 'The Violent, the Noisy, the Unclean, and the Refractory Patients shall be kept apart from the others as much as possible, especially in the night.'; Hill, *Total Abolition*, pp. 44, 104; DCRO, *Report of Visiting Justices* (Epiphany 1844), p. 42.

22 L.D. Smith, '"Levelled to the Same Common Standard": Social Class in the Lunatic Asylum, 1780–1860'in D. Ashton, R. Fyson and S. Roberts (eds), *The Duty of Discontent: Essays for Dorothy Thompson* (London, 1995), pp. 142–66; *Metropolitan Commissioners in Lunacy* (1844), p. 31; Hemingway, *History of the City of Chester*, p. 228; SCRO, D550/1, 13 July 1820; GCRO, HO 22/1/1, 8 July 1833.

23 Crommelinck, *Rapport sur les Hospices*, p. 109; Hill, *Total Abolition*, p. 40; LLSL, Lincoln Asylum, 4th Report (1828), p. 2, pamphlet, 'At A General Board of Governors', 13 October 1828.

24 Christopher P. Philo, *The Space Reserved for Insanity: Studies in the Historical Geography of the Mad-Business in England and Wales* (PhD, St David's University College, Lampeter, 1992), p. 195; *Metropolitan Commissioners in Lunacy* (1844), pp. 14, 16; *Lonsdale Magazine*, February 1821, p. 44; CCRO, DDX 97/1, 9 November 1840; GCRO, HO22/1/1, 19 October 1835; HO22/3/2, 20 May, 4 October 1845; KCRO, Q/GCL/1, 27 October 1835, 25 October 1836, 16 April 1839.

25 WRCRO, C85/107, 31 December 1819, 31 December 1828, 31 December 1834, 31 December 1837, C85/114, 20th Report (1839), p. 9, 24th Report (1843), p. 11; LAO, LAWN 3/1, West Riding Asylum, 6th Report (1824); C. Crowther, *Some Observations Respecting the Management of the Pauper Lunatic Asylum at Wakefield* (Wakefield, 1830), p. 9.

26 CCRO, DDX 654/246, 21 July 1828, 21 October 1843; GCRO, HO22/1/1, 12 May 1832, HO22/3/2, 20 September 1841, 4 September 1843; WRCRO, C85/107, 31 December 1828, 31 December 1830, 2 January 1833, 31 December 1841; Crowther, *Management of the Pauper Lunatic Asylum at Wakefield*, p. 9; C. Crowther, *Observations on the Management of Madhouses* (London, 1838), p. 20; *Journal of Mental Science*, 12 August 1854, pp. 100–1; Crommelinck, *Rapport sur les Hospices*, pp. 148–9.

27 Edwin Chadwick, *Report on the Sanitary Conditions of the Labouring Population of Great Britain* (1842, Edinburgh: 1965 edn), pp. 99–109, 135–50; GCRO, HO22/1/1, 18 October 1824; LLSL, Lincoln Asylum, 20th Report (1844), p. 4; LAO, LAWN 1/1/4, 26 August 1839.

28 Cambridge University Library, Hunter Collection, *Report of the Visiting Justices of the Norfolk Lunatic Asylum* (1844), pp. 6–7; NkCRO, SAH 2, 27 November 1813, SAH 6, 30 October 1843, 5, 26 September 1844; DCRO, *Reports of Visiting Justices* (Epiphany 1842), pp. 3, 11, (Epiphany 1843), p. 4, Forston House (4), Easter 1841, Michaelmas 1841, Michaelmas 1842; CCRO, DDX 97/1, 12 June 1821, DDX 654/246, 21 July 1828; GCRO, HO22/3/2, 4 September 1843.

29 *Metropolitan Commissioners in Lunacy* (1844), p. 17; CCRO, DDX 654/246, 19 September 1839, 10 February 1841, 5 October 1843; GCRO, HO22/1/1, 18 October 1824, 17 October 1834, HO22/3/2, 16 May 1842; Conolly, *Construction and Government*, p. 30; LLSL, Lincoln Asylum, 7th Report (1831), p. 3, 16th Report (1840), p. 4, 20th Report (1844), p. 6; LAO, LAWN 1/1/5, 28 November 1842, 5 February 1844, LAWN 1/2/5, 9 July 1834, 14 January 1835, 10 October 1838; Hill, *Total Abolition*, p. 43; W. White, *History and Directory of the County of Lincoln* (Leeds, 1826), p. 42.

30 SCRO, D550/2, 27 February 1819; SuCRO, B106/10/4, Suffolk Asylum, 3rd Report (1841), p. 8, 4th Report (1842), p. 6, 8th Report (1846), pp. 5–6; Andrews, *Bedlam Revisited*, p. 176–8.

31 SCRO, D550/1, 11 July 1827, D550/5, 31 May 1841; *Lonsdale Magazine*, February 1821, p. 44; GLRO, MA/A/J/1, 14 January 1828, letter from Dr D. Campbell and William Davidson to Middlesex Justices; CCRO, DDX 654/246, 21 October 1843; GCRO, HO22/8/1, Gloucester Asylum, Annual Report (1843), D2593/2/3, 5 April 1832; LLSL, Lincoln Asylum, 15th Report (1839), p. 7, 16th Report (1840), p. 4; Crommelinck, *Rapport sur les Hospices*, p. 152; *Journal of Mental Science*, 12 August 1854, p. 100.

32 W.H. Gilbey, 'On the Dysentery Which Occurred in the Wakefield Lunatic Asylum in the Years 1826, 1827, 1828, and 1829', p. 93, *North of England Medical and Surgical Journal*, vol. I (1830–1), pp. 91–101; LPL, *Report of the Medical Officers of the Lancaster Lunatic Asylum* (1841), pp. 4–5. At Stafford in

October 1829, out of 25 males in the basement only six were 'cleanly in their habits'; of the females there were seven out of nineteen (SCRO, D550/63, 17 October 1819); LCRO, QAM/1/33/11, 12, 18 October, 7 November, 15 December 1836, 8 September 1837, 17 January 1838.

33 LPL, *Reports of the Medical Officers* (1841), pp. 5, 14, (1842), pp. 4, 6; LCRO, QAM/1/33/11, 16 August, 1 September 1839, 13 September 1843; GCRO, HO22/1/1, 12 October 1840, HO22/3/2, 28 September 1840, 25 July 1842, 13 January 1845; *Metropolitan Commissioners in Lunacy* (1844), pp. 83–5.

34 DCRO, Forston House (4), Easter 1844; NkCRO, SAH 4, 1 January 1827, 24 November 1828, 29 June, 31 August, 30 November, 28 December 1829, SAH 6, 26 October 1840, 25 February 1841.

35 LAO, LAWN 3/1, West Riding Asylum, 5th Report, LAWN 1/1/5, 25 September 1843; WRCRO, C85/107, 31 December 1825, 31 December 1826, 31 December 1829, 31 December 1834, 31 December 1835, 31 December 1836, 31 December 1840; Crowther, *Management of the Pauper Lunatic Asylum at Wakefield*, p. 9; Tuke, 'Introductory Observations' to M. Jacobi, *On the Construction and Management of Hospitals for the Insane* (London, 1841), pp. iii–iv.

36 WRCRO, C85/114, West Riding Asylum, 25th Report (1844), pp. 3–6, 26th Report (1845), pp. 3, 7; John Goodchild Collection, Wakefield, *Report of the Visiting Justices of the West Riding Pauper Lunatic Asylum* (1844, 1845).

37 M.W. Flinn, Introduction to Chadwick, *Sanitary Condition of the Labouring Classes*; F.B. Smith, *The People's Health 1830–1910* (London, 1979), pp. 195–248; R. Hodgkinson (ed.), *Public Health in the Victorian Age*, vols. I & II (Farnborough, 1973).

38 Conolly, *Construction and Government*, p. 10; Thurnam, *Observations and Essays on the Statistics of Insanity*, p. 88; GCRO, HO22/3/2, 28 September 1840.

39 *Metropolitan Commissioners in Lunacy* (1844), p. 17; GCRO, HO22/3/2, 28 September 1840; DCRO, *Report of Visiting Justices* (Epiphany 1842), pp. 3, 11, Forston House (4), Easter 1841, Michaelmas 1842; LPL, *Report of the Medical Officers* (1841), p. 4; Knight, *Observations on Derangement of the Mind*, p. 119; CKS, Q/GCL/1, 10 March 1834.

40 WRCRO, C85/107, 31 December 1828, 31 December 1829; Crowther, *Management of the Pauper Lunatic Asylum at Wakefield*, pp. 8–9; Crowther, *Observations on the Management of Madhouses*, pp. 19–22; T. Giordani Wright, *Cholera in the Asylum: Reports on the Origins and Progress of the Pestilential Cholera in the West Yorkshire Lunatic Asylum During the Autumn of 1849, and on the Previous State of the Institution* (London, Wakefield, 1850), pp. 13–14, 37.

41 WRCRO, C85/107, 31 December 1830, 31 December 1831, 31 December 1834, 31 December 1836, C85/108, 15th Report (1834), p. 5; Crowther, *Management of the Pauper Lunatic Asylum at Wakefield*, p. 9; Gilbey, 'On the Dysentery Which Occurred in the Wakefield Lunatic Asylum', pp. 92–4.

42 LLSL, Lincoln Asylum, 20th Report (1844), p. 3; LAO, LAWN 1/1/5, 22 January, 5 February 1844; J. Todd and L. Ashworth, *The House: Wakefield Asylum 1818...* (Wakefield Health Authority, 1993), pp. 60–1; WRCRO, C85/107, 2 January 1833 – 'These measures were successful, for while Cholera seized victims in almost every situation and class of society, the cell of the maniac escaped.', 31 December 1837, C85/108, 15th Report (1834), p. 4; *London Medical Gazette*, vol. IX (1849), p. 865, cited in H. Marland, *Medicine and Industrial Society in Wakefield and Huddersfield, 1780–1870* (Cambridge, 1987), pp. 44–5; GLRO, H11/HLL/A7/1, 7th Report of William Ellis (Epiphany 1838), pp. 35–6.

43 Hill, *Total Abolition*, pp. 38–46. For Samuel Hitch, see Smith, '"A Worthy Feeling Gentleman": Samuel Hitch at Gloucester Asylum, 1828–1847' in H. Freeman and G.E. Berrios, *150 Years of British Psychiatry*, vol. II, *The Aftermath* (London, 1996); for Gaskell and de Vitrie, see Walton, 'The Treatment of Pauper Lunatics in Victorian England, 1816–1870' in A. Scull (ed.), *Madhouses, Mad-Doctors and Madmen: The Social History of Psychiatry in the Victorian Era* (London, 1981), pp. 173–7, and A. Scull, C. Mackenzie and N. Hervey, *Masters of Bedlam* (Princetown, 1996), pp. 165–74; for Kirkman, see R. Hunter and I. Macalpine, *Three Hundred Years of Psychiatry, 1535–1860* (Oxford, 1963), pp. 882–4.

44 Charlesworth, *Remarks on the Treatment of the Insane*, pp. 6–14, 37–9; LLSL, 'At A General Board of Governors', 13 October 1828, Lincoln Asylum, 4th Report (1828), pp. 1–4, 7th Report (1831), p. 3, 8th Report (1832), pp. 3–4, 16th Report (1840), p. 4, 20th Report (1844), p. 6; Hill, *Total Abolition*, pp. 43, 89–90; LAO, LAWN 1/1/2, 5 October 1827, LAWN 1/1/3, 6 December 1830, 23 January, 23 April, 29 October 1832, 7 April, 21 July 1834, 23 February, 20 April 1835, LAWN 1/1/4, 15 October 1838, LAWN 1/2/3, 9 July 1834, 8 July 1835, 9 October 1839; LPL, *Report of the Medical Officers* (1842), pp. 4–5; *Eighth Report of the Commissioners in Lunacy* (1854), Appendix G, pp. 137–8, evidence of James Wilkes; GCRO, HO22/3/2, 21 February 1843; *The Lancet*, 13 November 1841, p. 230.

45 DCRO, *Reports of Visiting Justices* (Epiphany 1843), pp. 4, 18, (Epiphany 1844), p. 18; *The Lancet*, 13 November 1841, p. 230; *The Times*, 4 December 1839; A. Suzuki, 'The Politics and Ideology of Non-Restraint: the Case of Hanwell Asylum', *Medical History*, vol. XXXIX, no. 1 (1995), p. 9; LPL, *Report of the Medical Officers* (1841), p. 10.

46 LPL, *Reports of the Medical Officers* (1841), p. 13, (1842), p. 5; *The Lancet*, 13 November 1841, p. 230; WRCRO, C85/107, 31 December 1841; GCRO, HO22/8/1, *Annual Reports*, 1841, 1842, HO22/3/2, 20 January, 2 August 1841, 28 February 1842; NkCRO, SAH 6, 30 October 1843, SAH 137, 23 May, 29 August 1843; DCRO, *Reports of Visiting Justices* (Epiphany 1844), pp. 18–19, 21; LAO, LAWN 1/1/3, 9 May, 12 September 1836, LAWN 1/1/5, 29 August 1842.

47 SuCRO, B106/10/4/4.4 (8), Suffolk Asylum, 8th Report, pp. 5– 6; WRCRO, C85/107, 31 December 1841; CCRO, DDX 654/246, 8 October 1843; Crommelinck, *Rapport sur les Hospices*, pp. 108–10, 131, 137.

6

Treatment and Care

It should be remembered that whatever may be the results of humane and scientific treatment, and to whatever degree of excellence, the best arrangements may have brought them, these Institutions are receptacles into which society pours off its refuse ingredients. What would be the condition of society without such provisions for public security?[1]

By the early 1840s, the thoughtful Charles Caesar Corsellis had become philosophic, if not resigned, about the limitations on what could be achieved in his much-praised Wakefield Asylum. His words illustrate the paradox of asylum treatment. There had been, at Wakefield and elsewhere, genuine attempts to approach patient management in ways that were both 'humane' and 'scientific', to effect the largest possible number of recoveries. At the same time, there had to be an acceptance of the role and responsibility of the asylum as a place of custody to protect the public. Disappointed expectations of cure brought a growing tendency to blame the patients, or the many 'hopeless' cases, and the authorities who sent them to the asylum long after any prospect of cure had disappeared.

The therapeutic sterility of the later nineteenth-century county asylums, which accompanied their expansion to massive proportions and their containment of large numbers of the chronically deteriorated, has been well documented.[2] There has perhaps, as a consequence, been a tendency to assume a similar lack of endeavour to actively treat patients in the earlier asylums. In fact, the evidence points in the contrary direction. Many asylum superintendents and physicians utilized a range of techniques, both medical and 'moral', in an attempt to bring about recoveries. If success in achieving the desired goal was limited, it was in many instances not for the want of trying. The early practitioners were largely motivated by curative ideals. Their limited success served to chasten optimism, and to contribute to the resignation, or realism, which Corsellis and others increasingly expressed.

PRINCIPLES OF ASYLUM TREATMENT

The rhetoric of reforming justices, asylum managers and medical officers was strongly influenced by ideals of cure and alleviation. Although custodial and protective functions were acknowledged, these were accorded a secondary place in the public representation of the asylum. The preoccupation with cure was not new, but followed from the professed orientation of treatment at Bethlem and the subscription asylums.[3] Although county asylums were required to accept many with apparently hopeless conditions, there was to be an attempt to bring about recovery. At Wakefield, the objective was enshrined in the Rules: 'no practice, which experience may dictate, or modern discovery suggest' was to be left untried. The Dorset justices, in planning their asylum, argued that 'every possible attention should be paid to the cure of the Patients', as some 'may, by a curative process, be restored to perfect health & Sanity', leading to a diminution of 'the Disease of Lunacy' and a reduced burden on the poor-rates. The Gloucester visitors, with the highest recovery-rates of the early county asylums, still held to the conviction after nearly twenty years' operation that the asylum's 'sole objects' were the cure of the patients and the kind treatment of the incurable.[4]

The process of cure was seen to begin with the act of committal. If the lunatic's disorder was to be tackled, he or she had to be removed from its 'exciting cause'. The ideal of separation from family, friends and neighbourhood had become an orthodoxy in the care of the insane well before 1800. As early as 1758, William Battie of St Luke's had declared:

> Madness. . .requires the patient's being removed from all objects that act forcibly on the nerves, and excite too lively a perception of things, more especially from such objects as are the known causes of his disorder; for the same reason as rest is recommended to bodies fatigued, and the not attempting to walk when the ancles are strained.

His rival John Monro of Bethlem, though dismissive of many of Battie's ideas, concurred in the necessity of confinement, which might on its own bring about restoration. The perceived benefit of removal became the primary theoretical basis for institutionalization, whether in private madhouse or public asylum. Respected practitioners like Leicester's Thomas Arnold reinforced the therapeutic imperative of separation in their writings.[5]

The doctrine was employed in seeking public support for implementing the 1808 Act. Dr John Storer, Nottingham Asylum's great advocate, contended in 1811 that 'entire separation' from family and friends was 'indispensable', for even their 'tender assiduities' could aggravate the disease of a suspicious and deluded patient. The patient also had to be removed from the irritation caused by the 'contumelious gaze of vulgar curiosity'. The new generation of writers on insanity stressed the importance of confinement. According to George Man Burrows, practitioners unanimously held to the necessity for separation from 'all customary associations, his family, and his home'. Ralph Fletcher, consulting surgeon to Gloucester Asylum, argued the necessity of removal from the 'original causes of the malady', to avoid 'ruinous consequences'. The asylum's visitors expressed the argument with a degree of certainty in 1838:

> Separation. . .from the ordinary way of life and from ordinary companions, and the breaking into the habits and associations which existed when the disease of mind commenced, is known to be one of the very first and most important steps to cure.

The importance of separation and removal had now become axiomatic, a solid and incontrovertible justification for the existence of the asylum.[6]

The corollary to the requirement for removal was early treatment. If committal were to be effective in bringing about cure, it had to happen as soon as possible after the disorder appeared. This depended on early recognition of the symptoms. According to William Ellis, detection required not only much care and attention, but also the experience of a trained practitioner, for 'common observers' were unlikely to notice the insidious signs of a diseased action of the brain. The 'prospect of affording relief' depended upon early attention to the disease. Dr Francis Willis's contention in 1815 that nine out of ten lunatics could recover, if brought to an asylum and treated within three months of the disorder's commencement, was widely quoted and supported. Paul Slade Knight of Lancaster Asylum argued it forcefully to his visiting justices in 1822. Robert Gardiner Hill, in his celebrated 1838 lecture, accepted the improbability that an insane person would regain his reason 'except by removing him early to some institution for that purpose'. If too much time elapsed before tackling the disease, so the argument ran, the danger of incurability set in; the longer the disorder was neglected, the greater the certainty of its permanence. This core principle became both a rationale for asylum treatment and an explanation for its frequent failure.[7]

Treatment regimes had to deal with conditions whose origins were identified as both physical and 'moral' or psychological. Physical treatments to tackle organic ailments were therefore supplemented by moral treatments. 'Moral treatment' was not, as frequently characterized, a new system developed at the York Retreat. Practitioners in those madhouses and asylums which pursued objectives of cure rather than containment were employing moral treatment techniques before the Retreat's advent, and the term had begun to come into general use. The Tukes in reality adopted the best existing practice. Samuel Tuke, in his celebrated *Description of the Retreat*, codified the various aspects of moral treatment and emphasized their efficacy in the treatment and management of mental disorder. He did not, however, claim to have been the originator of the techniques. The tendency of more recent writers to misuse the terminology has served both to cloud the proper interpretation of moral treatment methods and to underestimate their prevalence.[8]

Moral treatment ideals figured prominently in the publicity statements and literature emanating from early nineteenth-century asylums. In particular, the aim of a gentle approach to patient management was reiterated constantly. The 1815 Select Committee, in seeking to highlight good practice, heard from Reverend J.T. Becher, one of Nottingham Asylum's leading figures, that 'ours is a system of great tenderness and indulgence'. The reformers dominating the Committee intended the dissemination of the approach. Another of its key witnesses, the magistrate Godfrey Higgins, intent on providing something very different to the abuses of York Asylum, wrote into the rules of the new West Riding Asylum that 'the unhappy objects of the institution will be treated with the greatest humanity and kindness, – that every comfort, which they are capable of receiving, will be administered to them. . .'. Lincoln Asylum's governors promised a 'sedulous attention' to the patients' comfort. Their physician, Dr Charlesworth, wrote in 1828 of the great importance of maintaining a 'uniformly kind demeanour, and a cheerful and familiar manner' toward the patients. Such ideas gained general currency. For John Kirkman, the devout superintendent of Suffolk Asylum, 'soothing kindness' was 'the great secret of moral management'; the essence of treatment was 'a uniform system of kindness by every means and in every way'.[9]

Mildness and gentleness were not pursued just for their own sake. Such methods were also advocated in order to reassure the public and gain their moral and financial support. Asylum visitors, as at Gloucester, sought to convey that treatment in their institution was conducted on 'humane principles', as the most effective means of achieving recovery. The espousal of humanitarian ideals as the basis of successful treatment permeated the writings of asylum doctors throughout the period. As Dr George Button expressed it:

the exercise of the purest and most enlightened humanity, is not merely eventually the most economical, but also the most effectual means which can be resorted to, to ameliorate the condition of mankind, whether sane or insane.

The rhetoric of kindness and humanity became a *sine qua non*. The reality experienced by patients, however, did not always equate with ideals which were hard to uphold in institutions whose physical reality was often custodial and spartan.[10]

Moral treatment comprised more than a gentle, considerate approach. There were also aspects which sought to alter inappropriate behaviour. By 1800, the conception was widely accepted that the doctor had to gain ascendancy over the madman, as a precursor to curative treatment. Monro in 1758 pointed out its importance in breaking bad habits – the patient had to be brought to obey the person treating him. William Cullen in 1784 argued the need to employ 'a very constant impression of fear' and to inspire the patient with the 'awe and dread' of particular people. William Pargeter in 1792 wrote of the importance of the '*government* of maniacs', to be achieved by 'mildness or menaces'. Like others, he advocated the intimidatory use of the eye in gaining the patient's submission. Experienced practitioners, like Thomas Arnold and Joseph Mason Cox, also upheld a firm approach and the achievement of domination over the lunatic, albeit tempered by more gentle measures to gain his confidence. John Haslam stressed the need to instil respect and obedience as a basis of that confidence. Although a gentle, dignified manner and a restrained temper were the most effective means, certain boundaries had to be established:

the superintendent must first obtain an ascendancy over them. When this is once effected, he will be enabled, on future occasions, to direct and regulate their conduct, according as his better judgment may suggest. He should possess firmness, and, when occasion may require, should exercise his authority in a peremptory manner.

Even Samuel Tuke acknowledged that the 'principle of fear' had an important place. These ideas informed the treatment principles of the managers of the new asylums. As John Kirkby, vice president of Nottingham Asylum, aptly put it in 1814, the system of tenderness and gentleness was united with a 'firm and powerful resistance' against maniacal paroxysms.[11]

For a regime where the avowed purpose was 'cure' and restoration to sanity and social competence, it became important to acknowledge and appeal to the patient's underlying rationality. Tuke had emphasized the importance of treating patients as far as possible as rational. Their 'superior motives' were to be encouraged, and their 'desire of esteem' stimulated; correct behaviour would be reinforced by receiving esteem and respect. His ideas directly influenced Thomas Morris at Nottingham and William Ellis at Wakefield. Other influential practitioners like Thomas Bakewell, the great critic of public asylums, and E.P. Charlesworth of Lincoln, though approaching the matter from different perspectives, laid similar stress on the centrality of treating the patient as a rational being. The 'lucid intervals' were to be encouraged, and behaviour or conversation based on erroneous perceptions ignored or minimized. This approach was followed by the more reflective asylum doctors such as John Kirkman, who was keenly aware of the need to deflect attendants from their natural temptation to indulge patients' fantasies. The principle remained intact, though adherence to it proved more problematic as superintendents increasingly lost direct control of the routine running of their asylums.[12]

The reinforcement of rational behaviour required treatment tailored to the characteristics and needs of individual patients. According to Dr John Storer of Nottingham, treatment of the insane was 'an art of itself'; it had to follow 'correct observation and persevering reflection on the moral and physical temperament of the afflicted'. The individualization of care may have been a rather pious aspiration, particularly in large pauper-dominated institutions, but its pursuit was still being claimed. The journalist Edward Baines, visiting Lancaster Asylum in 1825, commented that no 'general and undiscriminating' modes of treatment were adopted, but 'every patient is treated as the peculiarity of his or her own case may require'. John Kirkman, describing the intentions at Melton in 1845, insisted that: 'for any effective treatment of the insane, their several dispositions must be studied, their characters ascertained, and their feelings treated'. Although ever more difficult to fulfil as asylums grew more populous, idealism continued to motivate superintendents such as C.C. Corsellis. He considered that there could be no general rules on treatment; with the 'ever varying form of their malady' and the 'infinite number of concomitant circumstances', each case remained a study in itself.[13]

One important means of attempting to match treatment to individual circumstances was a system of classification. The principle, established in the subscription asylums, was taken into account in planning the first county asylums. Initially, the arrangements were crude. At Nottingham, the plans only stipulated the separation of convalescents and incurables. In the early Stafford plans, proper classification meant not to 'mix the outrageous with the quiet, nor the dirty with the cleanly'. At Bodmin, the six spokes of its distinctive panopticon were divided to provide for ordinary, convalescent and incurable patients of each sex. At Lincoln, the intention was to keep the convalescent patients 'as much as possible, separate from others labouring under greater degrees of malady'. Such elementary classification was supplemented by social-class separation. In relatively small asylums, it was hardly practical to implement anything more sophisticated at this stage of their development.[14]

A greater attention to classification followed Samuel Tuke's *Practical Hints* for the construction of the West Riding Asylum. These formed the clearest link between the practice of the York Retreat and of the more progressive county asylums. Tuke sought to offset the disadvantages of placing large numbers together in a single institution. His idea was to group patients into a 'little family', whereby they might form supportive relationships, and enabling attention to be given to individuals and their particular disease patterns and needs. Tuke recognized the practical difficulties of implementing classification in a large institution like Wakefield. He proposed separation according to the degree of the disorder, rather than its 'species' or duration. As far as possible, the intention was to ensure that 'the comforts of one class, are not, in degree, sacrificed to the wants and comforts of another'. His plan was for three classes:

> 1st class, Those who are disposed to incoherent laughing and singing; and generally, all those who are capable of very little rational enjoyment.
>
> 2nd class, To consist of those who are capable of a considerable degree of rational enjoyment. In this class, most of the melancholics and hypochondriacs will be included. Several of this class will be able to assist in the house, or be engaged in some useful labour.
>
> 3rd class, The convalescents, and those patients whose derangement leaves them fully capable of common enjoyment. A few of the best melancholics should also be admitted into this class.

Provision had to be made also for the 'worst patients', but not in a separate annex, because of the danger of their being exposed to 'filth, starvation, and cruelty', as had occurred at York Asylum. Instead, Tuke argued, they should be placed in single rooms, within the main building.[15]

As far as possible, Wakefield's architects implemented plans based on Tuke's principles. There were initially five wards for each sex, described in 1823 by William Ellis in a letter to George Poynder at Gloucester:

> Two of the Wards for the males are set apart for the Maniacal, the fatuous and Epileptic: the other three are occupied by those who vary in their approaches to perfect sanity.

The classification arrangements at Wakefield influenced much of what came after. Charlesworth's programme of reform at Lincoln in 1828 was based around a new system with a minimum of three classes, according to their state – the 'insensible', the 'ordinary' and the 'convalescent'. The violent, noisy, unclean and 'refractory' were to be kept apart, especially at night, with particular attention paid to separating the convalescents. As expectations became greater and buildings were further developed, arrangements in most asylums became more sophisticated. Distinct parts of the building and grounds would be allocated to people according to constellations of behaviour, levels of competence or stages of recovery.[16]

By 1840, classification had attained a pivotal place in the theory and practice of treatment. Superintendents who sought to make an imprint developed their own models. At Wakefield, Corsellis laid down a system based on five diagnostic divisions – mania, monomania, melancholia, dementia and idiotcy. The maniacs and idiots were to be kept entirely apart from the others; the melancholics were not allowed to associate together, but were mixed with those 'most likely to divert and cheer them'. Samuel Hitch at Gloucester also divided patients into five categories – the quiet and approaching convalescence; epileptics; the fatuous; the dirty and noisy; and the 'working class', consisting of convalescents and 'incurables' capable of employment. At the large Lancaster Asylum, there were ten distinct classifications, matching the number of wards for each sex. The epitome of the system was achieved at Hanwell, where in 1843 there were 27 wards, each designated for patients of particular ability levels or behaviour patterns. Although unhappy about Hanwell's excesses, the Metropolitan Commissioners in 1844 gave full endorsement to the essential place of classification in the county asylum. By this time, it was as much a vehicle for organizing and running the institution as it was an agent of treatment.[17]

MEDICAL AND PHYSICAL TREATMENT

> I have very little doubt that there is in nature some medicine, with which I am at present unacquainted, that would operate as a specific in these cases. What it is I know not. . .[18]

Contemporary psychiatry retains a convenient view of the nineteenth century as a therapeutic desert, represented by hordes of chronic patients warehoused in great asylums, whose 'treatment' consisted largely of food, warmth, work and regimentation. In reality, by 1800 the range of treatments available to asylum medical men was considerable. By 1850, there was a veritable array. The extent of intervention in individual cases, however, varied markedly. At one extreme, Ebenezer Owen, the master of Norfolk Asylum, told the stunned Metropolitan Commissioners in August 1843 that:

> he would not venture upon the responsibility of acting or applying remedies, that he could not bleed, and had no knowledge or experience, medical or surgical.

When asked what he would do if such treatment were required, he responded that he would send to Norwich (three miles away) for one of the medical officers:

> He subsequently directed our attention to a pony on the lawn, which he informed us was constantly ready to be saddled as occasion required.[19]

At the other extreme was an energetic figure like William Ellis, whose practice comprised various treatments, tailored to individual presentation, in addition to his meticulous attention to the detailed direction of the asylum's operations.

Ellis became an adherent of the principles of phrenology, as did several other asylum medical men. Whether or not accepting its tenets, most alienists were convinced of the essential contribution of bodily ailments to mental illness, and of the physical imbalances which accompanied the symptoms of distress, agitation and mood disorder. Even where the identified aetiology was 'moral', a physical component was to be anticipated. Paul Slade Knight, the former Lancaster superintendent, was more definite:

> I have no hesitation to declare my firm conviction, that in every case of deranged intellect the disease proceeds immediately from corporeal disorder, and at the same time I am equally well satisfied, that the structures of various human frames differ greatly in the susceptibility of this influence on the intellect.

Though not all went as far as Knight in ascribing a physical basis, it was generally accepted that much treatment effort should be directed toward restoration of a bodily equilibrium, on the premise that an improvement in physical health would bring alleviation of the mental ailment. This would be attempted by diagnosis and treatment of the underlying physical problem, and by measures to strengthen the constitution.[20]

The Lunacy Commissioners' remarkable survey of 1847 into medical treatments in asylums, public and private, showed a wide range of medicines and other physical remedies being employed. Intended to disseminate good practice, it demonstrated that some practitioners were quite sophisticated in their treatment approaches. However, it was evident that similar drugs were being used to contend with quite disparate symptomatology, and that there was little consistency of practice between asylums. Diagnosis and prescription were made on an individualistic and *ad hoc* basis. Treatment regimes continued to be dominated by the empiricism characteristic of many eighteenth-century practitioners. There was still nothing resembling an agreed set of remedies to be implemented for particular mental conditions.[21]

The bodily disorders associated with insanity were most frequently identified as connected with the nutritional and digestive systems. Initial treatment therefore focused on ensuring that the system was adequately and appropriately nourished. Dietary regulation was a continuing preoccupation of asylum doctors. For John Kirkman at Suffolk, in certain types of case, particularly those associated with exhaustion, a generous diet was more important than drugs. Puerperal mania, for example, was 'almost always cured by the judicious use of cordials, tonics, and nourishing food'. Charles Corsellis at Wakefield noted the importance of a nutritious diet for those suffering from exhaustion consequent on 'maniacal excitement', though it should not be 'too stimulating'. The prescription of a 'low diet', consisting of milk, gruel and pudding, for patients suffering from mania was common asylum practice; meat was seen as likely to increase the excitement and agitation. At Lincoln, this principle was written into the new dietary list in 1830; patients 'labouring under Fever or Maniacal Excitement' were to have no meat at dinner, but rather 'light Pudding, Broth Rice or Gruel'. Prevailing opinion accepted the contention of William Ricketts before the 1815 Select Committee that it was 'highly improper' to give a 'raving maniac' the same quantity of animal food as another patient.[22]

Although the regulation of behavioural excesses merited constant attention, it was the debilitation of a significant proportion of people admitted that most required dietary intervention. Many were in a reduced physical state, due either to poverty and deprivation or the self-neglect characteristic of some psychotic disorders. Surviving case-records also illustrate that patients suffering from mania often exhausted themselves by prolonged over-activity; their weakened physical state needed restoration. For those in a deteriorated condition, stimulating drinks, normally containing alcohol, were prescribed for medicinal purposes. Porter, in particular, was widely employed to strengthen the constitution, and physicians also utilized beer, brandy and wine (sometimes supplemented with arrowroot) for similar purpose. Easily digestible foods like sago were given to patients lacking the strength or the inclination to take proper nourishment.[23]

Anxiety to ensure sufficient food intake led to measures to force-feed those whose reluctance stemmed from severe depression or delusional beliefs about food or those providing it. The means might be drastic, according to the seriousness of the circumstances. Even Samuel Tuke had to admit that force-feeding was sometimes necessary at the Retreat, although he considered it 'the most painful duty, which the attendant has to perform'. The justification for compulsion had to be in the results. George Button reported in 1842 on the successful outcome at Dorset Asylum of three cases where suicidal patients had shown 'a most determined refusal of food'. After every other expedient attempted had failed, 'recourse was had to mechanical means' in order to preserve life; the individuals were 'subsequently restored to reason and to society'.[24]

The techniques employed were designed either to force open the mouth or to push food into the stomach. These could be crude and violent operations. At Liverpool Asylum, where dubious practices were exposed in 1826, other patients had been made to assist staff by holding and sitting on the person being fed. As late as 1851 at Norfolk Asylum, patients were 'compelled to take their food by being held by the throat'. More subtle means were generally applied. Paul Slade Knight of Lancaster Asylum, although professing doubt about the efficacy of force-feeding, used an instrument known as 'The Key' to prise open the stubborn patient's mouth; John Haslam had earlier used a similar instrument at Bethlem. Thomas Bakewell alleged in 1819 that a device was in use at Stafford Asylum for 'spouting food or medicines up the Nostrils', a claim not actually denied. The most commonly used means to force food down was a stomach pump. Charlesworth and his colleagues at Lincoln gradually concluded this to be troublesome and often dangerous, and adopted a contrivance developed by Bakewell which passed liquid through a narrow tin spout, inserted between the teeth when the patient opened them to draw breath. This was subsequently adopted elsewhere, although John Conolly concluded that whatever precautions were taken in developing devices for force-feeding, they were 'never quite devoid of evil'. With the growing ascendancy of non-restraint principles, the practice became increasingly regarded as undesirable, to be replaced by persuasion aided by fortifying liquids.[25]

Drug Treatments

Much of the asylum alienists' attention focused on the patient's digestive system, to ensure its smooth operation, its proper cleansing and the expulsion of harmful elements. The value of emetics and purgatives in the treatment of insanity had been asserted in the works of eminent practitioners from William Battie and John Monro onwards. Joseph Mason Cox, whose *Practical Observations on Insanity* (1804) went into several editions, argued that madness 'is always accompanied by corporeal disease', and was convinced that enforced vomiting 'takes the precedence of every other curative means', by relieving the stomach of impurities. Emetics were required, he suggested, in nearly every case, and purging was generally indispensable as maniacs were 'frequently and almost uniformly costive'. George Nesse Hill, who argued that the 'state of the stomach, bowels and urinary bladder demand early attention', set great store on the curative powers of emetics. Later practitioners placed less emphasis on the therapeutic centrality of emetics and purgatives, but they nevertheless continued to be significant components of the physician's armoury.[26]

Although the theoretical basis for the use of emetics was to cleanse the system, their cathartic and debilitating effects had the additional advantage of calming agitated patients suffering from mania or other disorder characterized by over-activity or excitable behaviour. The twin rationales were summed up in 1847 by Dr Tyerman of Cornwall Asylum – emetics 'often assisted in subduing excitement and in promoting the functions of the abdominal viscera'. The one most favoured in asylum treatment was tartrate of antimony. John Ferriar had been employing it at Manchester Asylum in the 1790s, and observed that it acted 'briskly' and 'had an instantaneous effect in restoring a degree of rationality'. The surviving Nottingham case-book for the years 1824 to 1829 illustrates its frequent use, particularly where patients exhibited disturbed behaviour. For example, Hannah Carp (25) was in a state of 'high excitement' after admission in January 1827; three days later she had worsened and had become 'noisy and raving' so she received a dose of antimony tartar. The treatment had some effect, for a few days later, though 'still greatly excited', she was reported to be more tranquil. This was the usual outcome, as the patient's reduced energy put a brake on their activity level. In some cases, this proved to be an important step toward recovery; in others it provided only temporary respite.[27]

Purgative medicines also tranquillized whilst relieving congestion in the system. A serious attempt to control a maniacal patient's behaviour might well include both emetics and purgatives. William Ellis, much of whose practice was dominated by concern with the action and product of the bowels, was certainly not averse to drastic methods:

> In cases of mania, we find the violence of the patient and the quickness of the pulse greatly reduced by doses of sulphate of magnesia, with half a grain of tartar emetic every three hours, until copious vomiting and stools have been produced.

Magnesium sulphate, popularly known as Epsom Salts, was the most widely prescribed purgative. Others in frequent use were calomel (chloride of mercury), castor oil and the highly unpleasant but effective croton oil. Purges were not only employed in mania, but also for epileptic patients, and for those suffering from melancholia, where inactive bowels were a frequent accompaniment. According to James Wilkes of Stafford:

> The employment of purgatives is rarely to be dispensed with, and these are often required in large and repeated doses to obviate the tendency to constipation which usually exists.

The symptomatic relief of congestion often aided the recovery process. Some medical men, however, remained sceptical as to the effectiveness of purgatives. Charlesworth at Lincoln had little faith in the efficacy of drugs for psychological symptoms; although he acknowledged in 1828 that 'opening medicines' were frequently required in treating patients, he observed 'no specific effects' on insanity. Some contributors to the Lunacy Commissioners' survey, like Samuel Gaskell of Lancaster, also questioned the benefit of the widespread use of purgatives. The more common approach, though, was that adopted by James Wilkes, who remained wedded to the active treatment of the 'usually defective state of the digestive and assimilative organs', as a key element in his therapeutics.[28]

Attempts were also made to tranquillize violence or other behavioural excesses by the use of sedative or narcotic drugs. Opiates were employed widely, including opium itself, henbane, morphia and especially hyoscyamus. The Lunacy Commissioners' survey showed their general use in the treatment of mania. The normally cautious John Kirkman thought them 'very valuable'. Mr Holland, superintendent of Surrey Asylum, admitted in 1847 that he 'should feel very helpless' without them. They were used also in treating other conditions, including the more agitated forms of melancholia. Preparations like aether, camphor, cannabis and Indian hemp were prescribed for similar purpose. According to James Wilkes, Indian hemp was also a 'valuable and powerful remedy' for mania; it subdued excitement and induced sleep, whereas large doses of morphia or opium had only increased the restlessness.[29]

Digitalis was found to be successful in calming disturbed patients. Paul Slade Knight was a particular enthusiast, considering it a 'most valuable medicine': 'I have uniformly found that this powerful drug exerted a beneficial effect in allaying the maniacal paroxysms, and reducing irritability.' He cited a man admitted to Lancaster in 1817, who was abusive, threatening to staff, boisterous and violently destructive; after several days of digitalis treatment he became calm and manageable. Its use, Knight suggested, enabled patients to enjoy exercise and amusement and to mingle peaceably with others; its removal had led to 'insubordinate disposition' and restlessness. It appears to have mainly been a drug of last resort, as for Susan Cox (26) of Grantham, admitted to Nottingham in 1827. Described as 'very restless and even furious', she was kept in a strait-waistcoat in a dark room and treated with antimony tartar and twice daily cold bathing of her head. Notwithstanding, she remained very violent and virtually uncontrollable. Eventually, after six weeks, digitalis was prescribed, with little initial effect, until a steadily increased dose brought her under some control. A similar progression occurred with Phoebe Biggin (23) of Heanor, admitted in early 1828. Mechanical restraint and antimony tartar did not lessen her 'frequent paroxysms of passion', but once the digitalis was given there was a fairly rapid improvement, and within eight weeks she was discharged as recovered. The obvious hesitation in its use was due to its tendency to reduce the pulse. William Ellis counselled great caution with digitalis, and avoided it as far as possible.[30]

Bodily and Mechanical Treatments

The use of drastic antiphlogistic remedies had been an established part of eighteenth-century asylum practice. Drugs which altered bodily state were augmented by depletive physical treatments, notably bleeding. The various methods of bleeding retained an important place in asylum therapeutics into the middle of the nineteenth century, and sometimes beyond. It was often a controversial treatment, with practitioners unable to agree on whether it was more harmful than effective and, if effective, how the benefits arose. William Battie had been equivocal, suggesting bleeding was 'no more the adequate and constant cure of Madness, than it is of fever'; the lancet applied to a 'feeble and convulsed Lunatic' was not 'less destructive than a sword'. Monro countered that bleeding, like purging, was 'requisite' in the cure of madness. Later writers were cautious, indicating the need for bleeding only in certain circumstances. Slade Knight, for example, did not rule it out, but suggested that it often worsened rather than reduced the excitement of someone in the 'high state'. Other alienists adopted a similar position, using various methods in particular cases, but rejecting the universal and seasonal bleeding that had characterized practice under the Monros at Bethlem.[31]

William Ellis, though expressing the view that excessive depletion was harmful, made extensive use of bleeding in his practice. He contended that mania and melancholia arose from an excess of blood, though in different parts of the brain. Local bleedings were equally applicable to both conditions; the melancholic patient, he argued, could bear as much depletion as the maniacal without injury to the constitution. He cited examples showing that he favoured application of leeches to the temples, but also employed the technique of cupping. Case-books confirm bleeding as an important element in Ellis's very active interventionist treatment methods. Examples from the Nottingham case-notes show a common practice to apply leeches on a local basis when patients' complaints included headaches. The 1847 survey on treatment methods confirmed that some asylum practitioners were still employing depletive techniques. Even John Conolly included the use of leeches among his recommended treatments for most mental conditions. By the 1840s, though, the use of bleeding was generally in decline. Charlesworth and Hill at Lincoln, and Samuel Hitch at Gloucester, had proscribed it in their asylums' practice. In an era of psychiatric 'reform', opinion increasingly coincided with the view of John Kirkman of Suffolk Asylum that the effects of depletion by the lancet were 'evil' and very hazardous, and that drug treatments were to be preferred.[32]

Different opinions also prevailed on the efficacy of blisters. John Monro 'never saw the least good effect' of them in the treatment of madness, unless it was accompanied by fever or particular symptoms. Thomas Bakewell later came to a similar conclusion: 'I never in my life heard of a blister being used either to the head, or neck, which was ever thought to do any good in this complaint.' However, another prominent madhouse keeper, Joseph Mason Cox, was of the opinion that blisters were often employed with advantage. George Nesse Hill was more equivocal, suggesting that they were sometimes of benefit, but were not to be used indiscriminately. Asylum doctors were certainly prepared to try blistering in treatment. William Ellis cited several cases where their application had contributed toward recovery. He particularly favoured applying them to the back of the neck. Dr Charles Pennington at Nottingham found blisters useful in some instances. In the interesting 1825 case of Elizabeth Dalby (33), the treatment was given to deal with a specific symptom:

> 3 Feb. Bodily health improved. The delusions continue. Says she cannot swallow, this is not correct, but probably a Blister across the Throat may be usefull and correct the Delusion.
>
> 10 Feb. Blister has been applied, and has tended to dissipate the Delusion.

Whilst far from being universally employed, blistering retained its adherents. Physicians like Sir Alexander Morison of Surrey Asylum and George Button of Dorset considered blisters to the nape of the neck beneficial in some cases of mania for their counter-irritant effects. The treatment continued in use at several asylums, for people suffering from melancholia, epilepsy or general paralysis.[33]

Other traditional invasive treatments were employed, though with less frequency. An alternative to blistering was to apply a 'seton', whereby a silken thread was drawn by a needle through a fold of skin in the nape of the neck and left for a period, the aim being to enable harmful liquids to seep away. The imperative of achieving a cleansed bowel system as a cornerstone of curative treatment led to the adoption of quicker alternatives to purgative medicines. Most common was the insertion of a 'glyster', an enema made from either tobacco or milk and flour, which could produce rapid results. Case-notes illustrate that these and other remedies were often used in combination. For example, Isabella Whiteley, admitted to Wakefield in April 1821, received a whole gamut of treatments over a three-month period, including emetics, purgatives, bleeding by leeches, shower baths and blisters. After six months in the asylum, she was discharged as being perfectly well. Although William Ellis was perhaps the most energetic and exploratory of the asylum doctors, eclecticism in treatment was also characteristic of several of his contemporaries.[34]

Ellis was also a strong proponent of techniques which aimed to control symptoms by acting on bodily temperature. The placing of ice on the shaven head was considered particularly effective in mania. Joseph Mason Cox found cold applications often advantageous to 'appease irritation and fury' and to induce sleep. Ellis was unequivocal about the benefits, arguing that 'Every public institution for the cure of the insane ought to be provided with an ice-house'. Ice was, however, not always available and similar outcomes were more generally sought by cold water and vinegar or wet cloths applied to the head. Responses to the 1847 survey by the Commissioners in Lunacy showed that the use of cold applications to quell mania remained part of the treatment regimes at several asylums, including Surrey, Dorset, Leicester, Stafford and Middlesex.[35]

Water acquired a central place in the physical treatment of insanity. Baths had been employed for therapeutic purposes in eighteenth-century Bethlem and in other public asylums. Water treatments became increasingly diverse and sophisticated, with the options of a warm or cold bath, a plunge-bath, a warm or cold shower, or a 'douche', as well as the foot-bath or 'pediluvium'. The range of intended purposes was even wider – to soothe, to arouse, to calm excitement or maniacal symptoms, to punish inappropriate behaviour, or to deter by inducing the fear of unpleasant consequences.[36] The distinction between therapy and punishment blurred as the effectiveness of the plunge-bath, or 'bath of surprise', and the cold shower-bath in dealing with aberrant behaviour became more evident. The function was clearly disciplinary, and not confined to paupers, as a member of Gloucester's house committee witnessed in 1836:

> Mr Hitch having received great complaints from the keepers of the violence and misconduct of one of the 1st class Patients Mr Millard, he considered it advisable to punish him by immersion in the Cold Bath which was performed in my presence, and from my own observation of its effect I should consider it the best punishment that could be resorted to.

A private asylum proprietor, Dr Gilliland of Hereford, visited Gloucester and found the cold bath in 'constant use'. He alleged that patients were thrown in with their hands and feet tied together. Samuel Hitch, however, insisted that the use of the bath was primarily therapeutic rather than punitive.[37]

The therapeutic origin of the cold shower (or the douche) was partly in the idea that a sudden shock might relieve the more active symptoms of the disorder, but it came to acquire ever more punitive associations. William Ellis, who regularly administered the treatment to difficult or refractory patients, admitted that its effectiveness was based on the principle of fear. Patients frequently experienced 'terror' at the prospect of the shower-bath, as case-records confirm. In 1821, a depressed patient at Wakefield, Elizabeth Coulson (28), was prescribed the shower-bath three times per week because she was 'very obstinate'. After six days it was reported: 'Has been twice in the bath which she dislikes exceedingly. On going yesterday she wept very much & promised the nurse to talk & be more cheerful if it might be omitted. It was upon those conditions. . .' Unfortunately, she failed to improve and the treatment was repeated, to little effect, before other more drastic methods were attempted. In the same year, another Wakefield patient, James Greenwood (39), was prescribed the shower-bath every other morning due to his 'very maniacal' behaviour. However, his dread of it led to a worsening of his behaviour, as was apparent from his violence and swearing toward the other patients in his ward. Ellis and his staff were not prepared to relent:

> It is correct that, by persuasion, & having learnt that resistance is in vain, he went into the shower bath this morning without force, but his dislike & dread of it are unabated. He says that he has beg'd, as for his life, that it might be omitted, that being in excellent bodily health he is at a loss to know for what purpose his medicine & the bath are ordered for him, & as he is perfectly willing to do any thing that is directed, he considers it as an undeserved & wanton punishment.

After a few days Greenwood had succumbed, and improvements in his behaviour and symptoms were being recorded.[38]

The liberalizing ideas of the late 1830s onwards brought a reaction against the use of the cold shower and the plunge-bath, and some attempts to distinguish their therapeutic from their punitive purposes. Gardiner Hill contended that the 'bath of surprise' could not have a good effect, as patients disliked it. John Conolly stopped using the douche because of the 'distress' it caused without any corresponding benefit, though he was prepared to use the cold shower-bath for violent cases. Dr Andrew Blake, physician to Nottingham Asylum, and anxious to promote its progressive credentials vis-à-vis its Lincoln neighbour, spoke disparagingly of the 'indiscriminate use' of the shower-bath in some institutions. Others were moving in the same direction, though more cautiously. Gaskell and de Vitrie at Lancaster drew the distinction between, on the one hand, the undesirable plunge-bath and douche-bath – 'remedies of questionable merit, better adapted for punishment than for cure', and the cold shower-bath which they used 'simply as a curative means'. The shower-bath was still, they claimed, particularly advantageous for 'athletic persons who are subject to periodical attacks of excitement'.[39]

The questioning of the more drastic treatments, however, led only to a temporary reduction in the use of the cold shower. Its effect in quelling manic truculence ensured its retention. Mr Holland of Surrey Asylum explained its advantages and its limitations in 1847:

> I believe a cold shower bath to be useful in mania where the patient is of robust constitution, and neither shows fear of nor offers any serious opposition to the remedy; but where such is the case, the excitement produced does away, in my opinion, with all the good likely to be effected.

It was clearly in active use at several asylums. James Wilkes employed the cold shower-bath at Stafford, albeit cautiously, to subdue the 'paroxysms', and claimed that many patients acknowledged that it alone had cured their mania. He was also prepared to utilize it for melancholic patients 'whenever there is no obvious reason for not employing it'. Others were more reluctant to prescribe the cold shower. Warm baths, however, with their inherently soothing and tranquillizing properties, remained an almost universal method of treatment throughout the whole range of mental disorders.[40]

Other physical treatments also fell into disfavour because of their unpleasant connotations. Electrification had a brief vogue, used either for stimulation or deterrence. A Wakefield patient, Elizabeth Coulson, was galvanized several times in early 1822; she told staff that 'she thinks it has done her good & that she felt afterwards more power to speak'. William Ellis, who presumably had administered her treatment, was also prepared to use electricity for more drastic purposes. There were, he suggested, patients 'so obstinate and incorrigibly perverse' that deprivation and confinement were not sufficient to subdue them. He found 'the shock of the electrifying machine' often beneficial in cases of 'determined obstinacy and bad conduct'. Terror of it could overcome the 'vicious inclination', leading the patient toward greater self-discipline in order to avoid the dreaded treatment.[41]

Ellis, whose treatment methods were a curious mixture of the gentle and the forceful, was a leading exponent of the most notorious and intimidatory of physical treatments – the circular swing chair. This contraption, originated by Erasmus Darwin in the late eighteenth century and popularized by Joseph Mason Cox, gained some prominence. The dramatic effects of 'swinging', according to Cox, provided both 'a moral and a medical mean' in treating lunatics. Alienists, frustrated at the limitations of their standard remedies, were open to persuasion on the curative benefits of an innovative and powerful method. For managers of large public asylums, the rotating chair had the considerable additional attractions of actively counteracting and deterring disturbed and excitable behaviour. It became a common feature of county asylums in the 1820s and early 1830s.[42]

Cox described a straightforward arrangement, whereby a 'common Windsor chair' was suspended from a hook in the ceiling. The patient, secured in a strait-waistcoat, was held by leather straps round the waist and legs. Variations included use of a bed instead of a chair, or placing him in a horizontal rather than a perpendicular position. The circular motion was operated by an attendant turning a lever, at a speed determined by the treatment requirements. A few circulations had 'soothing lulling effects, tranquillizing the mind and rendering the body quiescent'; this was followed by vertigo and then 'the most refreshing slumbers' of a quality to 'surpass those induced by opiates'. There were further and more dramatic effects. Patients might be deprived of their 'locomotive powers', or worse: 'One of the most constant effects of swinging is a greater or less degree of vertigo, attended by pallor, nausea, vomiting, and frequently by the evacuation of the contents of the bladder.' As with many psychiatric treatments down to the present, Cox acknowledged that the swing's effectiveness could not be accurately explained, other than the role of vertigo in often correcting the 'morbid state of the intellect'. If regulated appropriately, the swing might produce a particularly violent and high quality of vomiting, causing the expulsion of long-retained undesirable substances, which also had to beneficial in treating madness.[43]

In his case examples, Cox highlighted the treatment's psychological aspects. Fear was to be deliberately fostered. The patient's recollection of the action on his system created such an impression that 'the physician will only have to threaten its employment to secure compliance with his wishes'. The sudden cessation of swinging had similar effect to its initiation, exciting 'fear and terror' from the 'very violent shock both to mind and body'; the machine had 'amazing efficacy'. By the time of the second edition of *Practical Observations on Insanity* in 1806, Cox was even more convinced. He had experimented further, and advised practitioners that violent cases were best placed in the perpendicular position and others in the horizontal. The motion, he advised, should be begun gradually and then progressively increased to the required velocity. This apparently scientific approach evidently influenced fellow medical men.[44]

Practitioners like George Man Burrows, George Nesse Hill and Paul Slade Knight, though expressing caution about use of the swing, regarded it as an important method of treatment. For Knight, although it might further exasperate a furious patient, the machine was 'a mean in the cure of insanity, possessing immense power'. Its physical effects were even greater than those claimed by Cox; as well as giddiness and sickness, the jolt to the system led the patient not only to vomit but to pass faeces 'in rapid succession and great abundance, along with his urine'. Despite this, Knight's experience at Lancaster led him to advocate the swing's general availability. Ellis made regular use of it at Wakefield, with scarcely veiled intent to punish or modify behaviour. Thomas Cawthorne, a Leeds tailor, was bold enough to defy the central tenet of the asylum's regime in June 1821, with unpleasant consequences:

For some days he has been very high & has considered it quite beneath him to do any kind of work & kind treatment being no longer of any avail he has been in the circular swing he was very sick & vomited his breakfast.

The treatment might be given as a short-term remedy, or used repeatedly. A Nottingham patient, Mary Reddish, received regular sessions over a six-month period. A few weeks after admission in June 1827, she was being described as violent, incoherent and impetuous. In September, with 'no favourable change', the 'rotatory Chair' was prescribed, initially with no 'sensible effect'. Its use continued for three months, without apparent benefit or behavioural change. Finally, at the end of December, improvement was observed and 'ascribed to the Chair'. By late February, Mary was 'nearly convalescent' and the chair discontinued; in June she was discharged as having recovered.[45]

The Mary Reddish case highlights the inevitable question as to whether her recovery occurred despite, or because of, the treatment she received. This is apposite in regard to all the physical or 'medical' treatments employed in the early public asylums. Whether those treatments were actually efficacious, or whether 'cures' were more often the result of spontaneous remission, remains an open question, as Roy Porter has highlighted in relation to eighteenth-century practice.[46] Nevertheless, the retrospective scepticism of many of today's practitioners may be unwarranted. The extensive documentary evidence demonstrates that in most asylums the medical officers energetically attempted to 'cure' their patients. They were eclectic in their approaches and were often prepared to innovate and experiment. The roles of 'charisma' and 'placebo' in rendering treatment effective should not be underestimated, but they alone would not have achieved the steady stream of discharges. Drugs which tranquillized or caused significant physical changes, contrivances which shocked the system, and even punitive sanctions, were on occasions beneficial rather in the manner that their modern descendants demonstrate therapeutic benefits.

MORAL TREATMENT AND MORAL MANAGEMENT

I am convinced from a pretty long experience now, that it is *only* in large County Asylums that moral treatment can be carried to its proper extent, and made to produce the greatest benefit with Pauper Lunatics; and that such means not only can be carried on in large Asylums, *but have been carried on constantly* in this Asylum, from its commencement in 1818.[47]

William Ellis's confident contention in 1828 was part of a response to one of Thomas Bakewell's damaging attacks on the inadequacies of county asylums. His implementation at Wakefield of a regime incorporating moral treatment approaches had led the asylum toward the ideal of a living and working Christian community. Ellis carried the principles, as expounded by Samuel Tuke, further than most contemporaries, overtly proclaiming his intentions. He did not though retain the monopoly on this approach in a large asylum. All the new county asylums incorporated at least some methods of moral treatment into their treatment and management systems.[48]

The practices of the York Retreat had been almost equally influential on Thomas Morris, the first director of Nottingham Asylum. During his preparatory training at York in late 1811, Morris had spent time with old William Tuke, as well as Samuel Tuke and George Jepson, developing a close personal relationship with the latter. He returned to Nottingham deeply impressed with what he had learnt. In October 1812, after a few months' practice, he told Jepson that 'with us little Medicine is used, to the propriety and advantage of which, I think, you will readily subscribe'. Rather, the unpredictable character of madness meant that treatment had to accord with 'what *now* presents itself', based on being 'regular in our conduct' toward the patients.[49]

The Retreat's influence at Nottingham was steadily eroded owing to the realities and limitations of managing a disparate array of patients. The force of Ellis's zeal and commitment enabled him to maintain his regime at Wakefield and then to transport it to Hanwell. At other asylums, there was not such a clear attempt to replicate Retreat principles. Their adoption of moral treatment methods was more a practical approach to patient management, using psychological and organizational techniques already in fairly general use in both public and private asylums. Translated into operation in a large institution, 'moral treatment' became 'moral management' as these techniques became integrated into the overall systems for managing and treating patients.[50]

The practical essence of moral management was an application of means to occupy patients' thoughts and to lead them away from the distressing or irrational preoccupations that had led to incarceration. Preeminent among the methods used was the promotion of work schemes. As early as 1801, influenced by practice at the long-established Spanish asylum at Saragossa, Philippe Pinel had expounded the importance of work and occupation in treatment.[51] Pinel's influence in England was considerable, and William Ellis became the foremost proponent of work as a therapeutic tool. Other practitioners went on to implement schemes in their asylums. Not only could work be seen to have immediate therapeutic benefits, but it also constituted practical preparation for a return to society after discharge. Its place in the emergent asylum system is sufficiently crucial to merit coverage in a separate chapter.

The other central component of moral management was religion. Worship became an essential part of the programme in several asylums, reinforced by the amending County Asylums Act of 1828 which required the appointment of a chaplain, to perform divine service on Sundays and on festivals. The role of religion as a therapeutic agent became increasingly emphasized. According to the Nottingham governors in 1821, after a tentative beginning, their visiting clergyman and physician had concluded that 'religious consolation and instruction may be of great utility to the melancholic and the convalescent'. Two years later, they were emphasizing the curative value of divine service as an 'interesting occupation', tending to 'dissolve the morbid association of ideas' and diversify 'the monotony of the scene', with beneficial effects upon the mind. Religious services were also introduced at Lancaster in the early 1820s. It was reported that large numbers joined in, 'with becoming decorum in the duties of the sanctuary'. The services, by 'soothing their disordered minds', helped the restoration of reason. The asylum's then superintendent, Paul Slade Knight, was later less sanguine about the benefits of religious worship, doubting that it had any permanent effects though it did allay 'importunity and restlessness' for a short time.[52]

Organized religious practice became a standard element of asylum life. Its benefits were recognized not only as being directly therapeutic, but also as being functional by promoting order and regularity, key elements in the return to normality. George Button at Dorset Asylum noted the 'deep and earnest attention' shown by the congregation in divine worship, and the 'degree of self-control' exercised over their behaviour. Gaskell and de Vitrie, in their reform of Lancaster Asylum in the 1840s, were particularly struck by the scenes at a 'congregational assemblage' of patients:

> The quietude and seriousness, with which so large a number of maniacs conduct themselves during divine worship, forcibly exhibit the beneficial effects of moral influence and discipline; and is in itself an evidence that the religious impressions, however transitory and fleeting, with the majority, for a time at least, lead the mind to a nearer approach to reason than when not so occupied.

John Conolly emphasized both managerial and therapeutic advantages. By 'tranquillizing the excited mind', Sunday observance assisted the physician in his mission of cure.[53]

For a committed Christian superintendent like John Kirkman at Suffolk Asylum, the role of religion in treatment was yet more profound. Acknowledging the likely consequences on mental health of sectarianism, fanaticism and moral depravity, he stressed the importance of administering 'Doctrinal Truth' as an antidote. Moral and religious principles had to be 'ceaselessly inculcated' to counteract the effects of 'moral evil'. Divine intervention was a key element in recovery:

Public worship, in conjunction with those who are more favoured than themselves, does not only elevate them from the low scale of animal existence, to the feelings of their *just* (and in many instances their responsible) equality; but it leads them mutually to seek, with those who have no less need than themselves, the help of *Him*, who alone can *give* to the one, or *preserve* to the other, *'the Spirit of a sound mind.'*

Kirkman's mission was not just cure, but progression to a more Godly state of being. Asylums, he argued, ought to be 'NOBLE RELIGIOUS INSTITUTIONS', where Revelation was to be sought after.[54]

Nowhere was the place of religion in treatment nurtured more than at Wakefield. William Ellis's father had been Rector of All Hallows Steyning in the City of London. Ellis himself underwent a doctrinal conversion to Methodism. According to his daughter Harriet, when offered the Wakefield post he 'regarded the call as one from God'. He viewed each patient 'as a man and a brother', and sought to treat them as rational beings capable of receiving religious instruction. His mentor, Samuel Tuke, had argued that for many the curative benefits of chapel attendance were greater than medicine. Harriet recalled the daily services conducted at Wakefield by her father:

Those who have had the privilege of witnessing it, have often said that they can never forget the scene presented when the loud bell called the members of his afflicted household to the morning and evening prayer.

Writing to George Poynder of Gloucester Asylum in 1823, Ellis described services lasting for fifteen or twenty minutes each morning before breakfast. Sunday services, attended by about 80 patients, lasted for an hour and included a sermon. They demonstrated 'orderly and decorous behaviour', and he could 'speak with confidence as to its good effects', both on individual conduct and on the institution as a whole:

A great number of our Patients are extremely ignorant and wicked independent of their insanity. As the impression of genuine religious feelings upon the mind must produce restraint and self government, we find that in proportion as they are capable and willing to be taught, a moral change takes place for the better, they also become more manageable, and from this source they often derive comfort and consolation when shut out from any other enjoyment.

Many, he claimed, continued religious practices after they had recovered and returned home to their families.[55]

Ellis, as much as any contemporary alienist, drew attention to the role of misguided or excessive religious activity in precipitating insanity. Nevertheless, there was no perceived inconsistency in promoting a regime based around religion as a therapy. He sought to 'impress the great importance of moral and religious truths' on the patients' minds, for many were 'as ignorant of these Truths' as they were 'depraved and abandoned in their conduct'. He had little doubt that his system served to 'sooth the mind, and give consolation to the unhappy sufferers'. After his move to Hanwell, Ellis strove to continue these endeavours on a grander scale, adopting an increasingly evangelical and even missionary approach.[56]

William Ellis's departure from Wakefield did not signal any significant change in the regime. C.C. Corsellis brought an equally strong religious orientation into the asylum's management. Services continued twice daily, as well as on Sundays and festivals. The Belgian visitor Dr Crommelinck, who attended some morning services in 1841, described the scene in chapel. Corsellis read the psalms 'in an affected and touching voice', the patients responding in chorus, showing 'by their silence and their completely respectful attitude' that they joined in 'with all their soul'. A special kind of relationship developed between Corsellis and his patients:

Without any doubt, this ceremony must contribute powerfully to inspire in the patient an unlimited confidence in a doctor who they see mingling his prayers with theirs to obtain a cure from Heaven from the ills which afflict them, in a doctor, who they see implore the Creator that he will deign to restore happiness to them whom he calls his friends, his children.

Moved to tears by what he witnessed, Crommelinck found the Sunday service still more moving: 'never did religious ceremony make a more profound impression on my soul'. The attempt by both Ellis and Corsellis to transform Wakefield Asylum into a Christian therapeutic community was probably unique.[57]

The sophisticated paternalistic system at Wakefield, and later at Hanwell, was designed to influence and alter behaviour, the central objective of moral management. Although other superintendents did not aspire to the same level of behavioural intervention, there was a common intent to promote order and regularity. Rules and regulations helped maintain a system characterized by routinized meal-times, exercise periods, work and recreation times, bed-times and so on. Staff duties were carefully prescribed and timetabled to ensure preservation of routine and order. These arrangements had clear disciplinary aspects, but therapeutic advantages were also assumed to be present. Conolly concluded from his Hanwell experience that residence in a 'well-ordered asylum' was 'among the most efficacious parts of direct treatment'.[58]

Techniques to modify individual behaviour were gradually being adopted, with the planned use of rewards and punishments. William Ellis incorporated them into his practice, arguing that the medical man should ascertain a patient's likes and dislikes, and then grant or withhold indulgences according to behaviour – 'They are the lever, and frequently the only lever, by which the moral man can be moved'. At several asylums, the inducements of extra food, tea or beer were offered to encourage people to occupy themselves. A widely used deterrent to disruptive or disorderly conduct was to move the culprit to a less salubrious refractory ward or to the basement. Mechanical restraint, or the threat of it, was clearly used to modify behaviour. Physical treatments, like shower-baths and the rotating chair, were employed for their behavioural effects as well as for their perceived 'medical' properties. Although not yet operating a behavioural treatment 'system', the alienist was discovering a range of therapeutic options.[59]

Historians of psychiatry have been much exercised by considerations of the nature and purpose of moral treatment and moral management, and have tended to overstate their place in the public asylums of the first half of the nineteenth century. For Michael Fears, the county asylum movement was the 'main expression' of moral treatment, with the new asylums rooted in lunacy reform as the chief sites for putting the principles into practice. From a more critical perspective, which views moral management more as control than as therapy, Andrew Scull also accorded it a prominent role in the early county asylums. His emphasis on the 'capture' of moral treatment by medical men and its incorporation into their treatment armoury seems to correspond more closely to what happened.[60]

In the quarter century after the 1808 Act and Tuke's *Description of the Retreat*, some of the terminology and rhetoric of moral treatment became common currency in the published output of asylum superintendents and visitors. Its implementation as a coherent system of patient management, however, was problematic in institutions which originated with a more custodial intent. This is not to suggest that the principles were not influential or that aspects of moral treatment were not put into practice.

The point at which ideas and practices founded on moral treatment and moral management did gain real ascendancy in the asylum was in the dissemination of 'non-restraint' following the experiments at Lincoln and Hanwell in the 1830s. These developments were of sufficient significance to merit attention in a separate chapter.[61]

AFTERCARE

Asylum superintendents and visitors prided themselves on the 'cures' and discharges achieved. The steady stream of readmissions, however, brought growing attention to what might happen after discharge. A recognition of the common relationship between poverty, deprivation and the onset of insanity raised concerns about people returning to the circumstances which had precipitated committal. These concerns fostered the development of schemes to ease the process, by the provision of material assistance to selected patients on discharge, enabling them to tide themselves over until they could find work. Without such help, it was acknowledged that pecuniary stresses and anxieties about supporting the family could lead to relapse and readmission.[62]

The problem had been recognized in Bethlem early in the eighteenth century, and was addressed by Tyson's Gift in 1708, which provided material assistance to needy patients on discharge. The first organized aftercare scheme in a county asylum was, as with other innovations, implemented at Wakefield in the Ellis era. The problem of indigent patients returning to the community had brought isolated donations by visitors and charitable individuals, but these were not sufficient to meet the frequent need that Ellis described in early 1827:

> Patients, when they have recovered, and are about to be discharged, learn for the first time, from some relative or friend, that during their confinement, their homes have been broken up, their little furniture sold, their children sent to the Workhouse, and want and misery left them as their only portion.

To overcome these difficulties required 'an energy their weakened minds no longer possess', and they could quickly relapse. In 1825, a legacy of £1000 was left to the asylum by Joseph Harrison of Surrey, once of Wakefield. The county added £300, and two fields were purchased for the asylum's use. The rental of £36 per annum formed the central element of 'Harrison's Fund', to be supplemented by voluntary contributions. The money was used, at the visitors' discretion, to make donations to 'necessitous patients' on discharge.[63]

The operation of the Harrison Fund gained momentum during Corsellis's superintendence. A room was set aside as a 'bazaar' to sell items manufactured by the patients, and the profits added to the fund. By 1841, the bazaar was bringing in up to £100 a year and as many as 50 patients were receiving assistance on discharge. Relief became more systematized, with enquiries made into the home, family and employment circumstances of each patient and a grant made accordingly. By 1845, the bazaar profits and increased donations from the public allowed larger grants to be made to discharged patients, who could now have a 'certainty of support' before obtaining work.[64]

The idea of the Harrison Fund accompanied Ellis to Hanwell. The Adelaide Fund, initiated by a large donation from Queen Adelaide, was established in 1836. A fund to assist 'discharged indigent lunatics' was set up at Gloucester, also in 1836, and later renamed the Adelaide Charity. It provided grants as well as loans of money and tools. A similar fund was established at Dorset in 1842 at George Button's instigation, augmenting previous arrangements whereby the visitors had used profits from the sale of clogs, slippers and straw bonnets made by patients to give money on discharge. The new fund's management was sufficiently flexible to be able to provide longer-term relief to distressed former patients.[65]

One of the more sophisticated schemes was set up at Nottingham, where the Convalescent Fund was begun in 1841 after the efforts of Dr Andrew Blake, the asylum's long-serving physician. Substantial donations were received, including £300 from Lady Middleton, whose name was given to the fund. The money was invested in securities and the interest applied to relieve people exchanging the 'comfort and kindness' of the asylum for 'all the miseries & now unaccustomed privations of poverty & distress'. Over the next five years, sums from 5 shillings to more than £6 were disbursed. The most frequent purpose was to enable a person to buy new clothes or remove old ones from pawn. Others received help to buy furniture or bedding, assistance with coach fares, or even weekly maintenance payments. In several cases the fund was used to re-start someone in business. One patient, Maria Brookes, who left the asylum in 1844 after four years, received £7 for clothing, bed and bedding, as well as money to enable her to resume her former trade selling vegetables in the market. Another, Mary Barton, who recovered in the asylum from a 'mind sunk' after being left an impoverished widow with several children, was given £5 in 1844 to open a shop; she was later reported able to maintain her family. This imaginative intervention illustrated the importance that was increasingly being attached to preventative aftercare.[66]

THE PATIENT EXPERIENCE

The few published accounts of patients' experiences in asylums before 1850 are inevitably written by articulate middle-class or aristocratic writers, and relate largely to private institutions.[67] Some cameos of life in public asylums did emerge, in commentaries by visitors such as Dr Crommelinck or Harriet Martineau, or in reports of particular events or cases. Direct accounts tend to be fleeting, however, and usually written by someone with a grievance. For example, Thomas Mulock, the eccentric radical journalist and staunch campaigner against the Highland clearances, produced a polemic against asylums and mad-doctors, some years after he had been a reluctant patient in Stafford Asylum. He recalled that Stafford had been considered a model institution in the 1830s, but yet 'no thought can conceive, no tongue can tell, no pen can describe the manifold horrors, the atrocious cruelty, the fraud, the guile, the imposture that pervaded every part of that lauded asylum. . .'. Many of the abuses were, he alleged, known about but overlooked by the authorities. His charges against Stafford Asylum, though fairly unspecific, did receive some corroboration from James Wilkes, who later became the asylum's superintendent and then a Commissioner in Lunacy.[68]

Another articulate and resentful patient was the physician Dr Francis Fox of Derby, who spent more than a year in Nottingham Asylum after being admitted in October 1836. His 'insanity' had manifested itself in 'delusions concerning the treatment of the patients, and the conduct of the Governors' of the Derby Infirmary. According to Dr Andrew Blake, physician to Nottingham Asylum, Fox 'entertained many wild opinions on the subject of the happiness of the working classes, in whose welfare he took an inordinate interest'. He gained enough influence over them to bring several thousand people together to protest at the injustices perpetrated by the Derby Infirmary. His conduct eventually led him to the asylum. After leaving Nottingham, Fox sought to expose the evils he had suffered. His wrath was mainly directed against Dr Blake and Thomas Powell, the superintendent. He claimed that 'barbarous cruelties' were inflicted on body and mind in the 'Bastile', and that people slightly insane on admission had been turned into 'terrific madmen'. He published charges of violent ill-treatment, deprivation and intimidation against the asylum, though acknowledging indirectly that his own behaviour had been provocative. The allegations were strongly denied by Powell and his colleagues, who relied on the public's view that Fox was insane and his opinions untrustworthy.[69]

One unhappy public asylum patient's impressions were conveyed to the public by Thomas Bakewell, who was eager to demonstrate the superiority of small institutions for those acutely disordered. This unnamed person was distressed by the lack of 'rational society', the 'different scenes' that occurred in the asylum, and the absence of work or occupation. He particularly lamented the boredom and the company: 'I certainly am as well as I shall be in this place, having nothing to do but to wander up and down from morning to night among a set of poor objects, which I cannot help watching and noticing.' His solution would be a transfer to Bakewell's madhouse at Spring Vale. Paul Slade Knight, in reproducing the narrative through mental disorder of a former Lancaster patient, also conveyed some negative aspects of the asylum experience. This man had been chained to his bed at night because of a tendency to get out and lie on the floor. He interpreted his ordeal on more than one level:

> I lost all patience when I was chained, and was greatly agitated by anger. I concluded from this, and also from hearing some chains rattling that I must be in a land of slavery, I do not think this notion is very incorrect; for though I was in England where liberty is, and ought to be commensurate with the soil, yet I was a slave in a moral sense, for reason bowed in tame submission to the tyrant insanity.

He described graphically the noises of the shutting, locking and opening of the heavy cell doors, which magnified his impression of being in a strange and alien world.[70]

In contrast, others were only positive about their experiences. Thomas Wood of Wolverhampton, one of the first pauper patients discharged from Stafford Asylum in 1818, expressed himself 'perfectly satisfied' with the treatment received; he 'could not have been treated better, had he been a Gentleman's son'. A collection of surviving correspondence to George Poynder and Samuel Hitch, the first two superintendents at Gloucester, provides several examples of former patients and relatives expressing gratitude for the quality of the care and treatment provided. A neighbour writing in 1828 on behalf of the recently discharged John Croydon of Bridgnorth conveyed 'his grateful thanks for the kindness with which you ever treated him', and his appreciation of the care received from the keepers; if he was felt to need more treatment in future, he would not wait to be sent but 'will voluntarily place himself again under your protection'. Mary Rich of Mangotsfield, newly discharged and writing to Hitch in 1841 to advise of her safe return home, signed herself as 'your very thankful inmate'. The brother of a patient, Joseph Truebody, wrote in 1839 of the benefit his brother had received 'from your Exclent treatment as practiced in your invaluabl Instituation' (sic). The sincerity of these unsolicited testimonies was clearly apparent.[71]

Visitors and managers were particularly sensitive to the views of private and charitable patients, and keen to secure their approbation. John Ryland of Birmingham, twice a patient at Stafford, wrote in 1829 to express his gratitude to the superintendent, the physician, the visitors and the staff: 'the Asylum in its comforts and conveniences exceeds all my mind had formed of places of the kind, prior to my being an inmate of it, the privilege of walking out in the extensive grounds is invaluable. . .'. At Gloucester, where there had been difficulties in attracting sufficient lucrative private patients to support the charitable fund, the visitors were eager for respectable endorsement. The recovery of a Miss Llewellyn brought particular gratification to the chairman of the house committee, who recalled that her state of mind had been 'most lamentable'. On her discharge, she 'expressed herself with great propriety obliged by the care taken of her', and grateful to be returning home.[72]

One of the problems that Gloucester had faced in attempting to encourage private custom was the poor general image and stigma attached to public asylums. Most middle-class families still considered private care to be more acceptable. People who had been in the asylum were anxious that others should not find out. The brother of a former patient, Maria Newman of Winchcomb, wrote to Hitch of his anxieties that she was relapsing. She was blaming her family for 'letting people know that she went, and says she does not care what becomes of her now'. There was also fear and prejudice among the 'lowest classes', many of whom, according to the visitors, entertained the 'vulgar notion' that inmates were treated with inhumanity. It was this sort of prejudice (as well as other sorts) that led to the distress of Mary Williams of Cheltenham in 1841. She wrote care of 'the keepper' of the 'glouster asillum' (sic) to her husband Edward Williams, a 'Man of colour':

> I have been very much grieved by reports that have Been in circultaion I have Been told by Sivearal pepole that he is dead and that he was Stuffed wich I hop and trust is not the cause fore of all things I hope and trus the Lord will permit him to diey a Natoural Death. . .(sic)

At the same time, Mrs Williams was not fully convinced that her husband had met an unfortunate end, for she also enquired about hopes for his recovery and visiting arrangements.[73]

These impressions from former patients and relatives about the asylum and its treatment are inevitably random and diverse. For people committed and kept in the asylum against their will, and who probably did not accept their diagnosis of insanity, it would inevitably be the custodial, repressive and enforced aspects of the system and of the associated treatment that excited the strongest response. The therapeutic elements of treatment, particularly when accompanied by severe discomfort, were hardly likely to convince them otherwise. Neither were the energetic and eclectic attempts of physicians and superintendents to steer them towards 'cure' of their disorder, by 'moral' as well as medical means. Other patients, able to acknowledge the reality and depth of what had taken them into the asylum, could feel genuine appreciation for what the institution and the treatment administered had achieved for them, whether their recovery stemmed directly from the efforts of the medical men, and the benefits of the regime, or from spontaneous remission. For those outside, like Mrs Williams, public lunatic asylums remained awesome places that could inspire fear and dread, but also a certain amount of hope. The diversity of people's responses reflects both the different aspects of asylum treatment and the contrasts evident in practices between and within asylums. It must also reflect the continuing paradox of custody and cure, that within the same institution the public were to be protected whilst genuine efforts were made to promote recovery and facilitate a return to family and community.

NOTES

1 WRCRO, C85/114, West Riding Asylum, 25th Report (1844), p. 6.

2 A. Scull, *The Most Solitary of Afflictions: Madness and Society in Britain, 1700–1900* (London, 1993), chapters 6, 7; P. McCandless, '"Build! Build!", The Controversy Over the Care of the Chronically Insane in England, 1855–1870', *Bulletin of the History of Medicine*, vol. LIII (1979), pp. 553–74.

3 J. Andrews, *Bedlam Revisited: A History of Bethlem Hospital, c.1634–1770* (PhD, University of London, 1991), pp. 9, 184–6, 283–92; J. Andrews, A. Briggs, R. Porter, P. Tucker and K. Waddington, *The History of Bethlem* (London, 1997), pp. 150–1, 270–6; MRI Archives, 'An Account of the Proceedings of the Trustees of the Public Infirmary in Manchester in Regard to the Admission of Lunaticks into that Hospital' (c.1763) – this spoke of the 'great Prospect' entertained of 'frequently relieving, if not perfecting the Cure of, great Numbers. . .founded upon the Success which has constantly attended the practice at Bedlam and St Lukes'.

4 G. Higgins, *Rules for the Management of the Pauper Lunatic Asylum for the West Riding of the County of York, Erected at Wakefield* (Wakefield, 1821), p. 29; DCRO, Forston House (3), 14 October 1828; GCRO, HO22/8/1, Gloucester Asylum, Annual Report (1841).

5 R. Porter, *Mind-Forg'd Manacles: A History of Madness in England from the Restoration to the Regency* (Cambridge, 1987), pp. 155–6, 221; Scull, *Most Solitary of Afflictions*, pp. 132–8; W. Battie, *A Treatise on Madness* (London, 1758), p. 68; J. Monro, *Remarks on Dr Battie's Treatise on Madness* (London, 1758), p. 37; P. Carpenter, 'Thomas Arnold: A Provincial Psychiatrist in Georgian England', *Medical History*, vol. XXXIII (April 1989), pp. 199–216, at p. 213; George Man Burrows, *Commentary on the Causes, Forms, Symptoms and Treatment, Moral and Medical, of Insanity* (London, 1828), cited in Porter, *Mind-Forg'd Manacles*, pp. 155–6.

6 NRL, 'An Address to the Public Concerning the General Lunatic Asylum near Nottingham' (1811), pp. iii–iv, vi–vii; R. Fletcher, *Sketches from the Case Book, to Illustrate the Influence of the Mind on the Body, With the Treatment of Some of the More Important Brain and Nervous Disturbances Which Arise From This Influence* (London, 1833); GCRO, HO22/8/1, Gloucester Asylum, Annual Report (1837/8).

7 Thomas Bakewell, *A Letter Addressed to the Chairman of the Select Committee of the House of Commons Appointed to Enquire into the State of Mad-Houses* (Stafford, 1815), p. 7; Paul Slade Knight, *A Letter to the Right Honourable Lord Stanley, and the Other Visiting Justices of the Lunatic Asylum of the County of Lancaster* (Lancaster, 1822), pp. 16–18; GLRO, H11/HLL/A7/1, Third Report of William Ellis, M.D. (1834), p. 11; WRCRO, CR85/107, 31 December 1819; R.G. Hill, *Total Abolition of Personal Restraint in the Treatment of the Insane* (London, 1839), pp. 4–5.

8 K. Jones, *A History of the Mental Health Services* (London, 1972), pp. 45–54; M. Fears, *The 'Moral Treatment' of Insanity: A Study in the Social Construction of Human Nature* (PhD, University of Edinburgh, 1978); Porter, *Mind-Forg'd Manacles*, chapter 4; A. Scull, 'Moral Treatment Reconsidered', *Psychological Medicine*, vol. IX (1979), pp. 421–8. For a recent attribution of 'moral treatment' to the Retreat, see the *Guardian*, 2 October 1996, p. 15.

9 BPP 1814–15, *Select Committee on Madhouses*, pp. 178, 180; Higgins, *Rules of the Pauper Lunatic Asylum for the West Riding*, p. 29; LLSL, U.P.876, Lincoln Asylum, 3rd Report; E.P. Charlesworth, *Remarks on the Treatment of the Insane and the Management of Lunatic Asylums Being the Substance of a Return from the Lincoln Lunatic Asylum, etc.* (London, 1828), p. 20; SuCRO, B106/10/4.4, Suffolk Asylum Reports, 1839, p. 10, 1840, p. 8.

10 GCRO, HO22/8/1, Gloucester Asylum, *Annual Report* (1825); DCRO, *Report of Visiting Justices* (Epiphany 1844), p. 43.

11 Monro, *Remarks on Dr Battie's Treatise*, p. 38; W. Cullen, *First Lines on the Practice of Physic* (1784), cited in R. Hunter and I. Macalpine, *Three Hundred Years of Psychiatry* (Oxford, 1963), p. 478; A. Walk, 'Some Aspects of the "Moral Treatment" of the Insane up to 1834', *Journal of Mental Science*,

vol. C (1954), pp. 807–38; W. Pargeter, *Observations on Maniacal Disorders* (1792), pp. 49–61; J. Haslam, *Observations on Insanity* (London, 1798), pp. 122–3 (from which this quotation is taken), 128; S. Tuke, *Description of the Retreat* (London, 1813), pp. 141–2; NRL, qL3648, Nottingham Asylum, Fourth Annual Report (1814).

12 Tuke, *Description of the Retreat*, pp. 157–8; L.D. Smith, 'To Cure Those Afflicted with the Disease of Insanity: Thomas Bakewell and Spring Vale Asylum', *History of Psychiatry*, vol. IV (1993), pp. 121–4; Charlesworth, *Remarks on the Treatment of the Insane*, p. 20; SuCRO, B106/10/4 (2), Suffolk Asylum, 2nd Report (1840), p. 10. For the influence of Tuke and the Retreat, see Anne Digby, *Madness, Morality and Medicine: A Study of the York Retreat, 1796–1914* (Cambridge, 1985), chapter 10.

13 E. Baines, *History, Directory and Gazeteer of the County Palatine of Lancaster* (Liverpool, 1825), p. 17; WRCRO, C95/107, 31 December 1840; NRL, 'An Address to the Public Concerning the General Lunatic Asylum Near Nottingham' (1811), p. iv; SuCRO, B106/10/4.4 (8), Suffolk Asylum, 8th Report (1846), p. 14.

14 SCRO, Q/AIc, Box 1; J.T. Becher, *Resolutions Concerning the Intended General Lunatic Asylum Near Nottingham* (Newark, 1810), p. 5; LLSL, Lincoln Asylum, *Rules* (1819), p. 10; *Nottingham Journal*, 21 October 1826.

15 S. Tuke, *Practical Hints on the Construction and Economy of Pauper Lunatic Asylums: Including Instructions to the Architects Who Offered Plans for the Wakefield Asylum* (York, 1815), pp. 13–25 (main quotation, p. 18).

16 GCRO, HO22/1/1, 5 April 1823; Charlesworth, *Remarks on the Treatment of the Insane*, pp. 7–9; LLSL, Lincoln Asylum, 4th Report (1828), pp. 1–2, Lincoln Asylum, *Rules* (1832), p. 19; LAO, LAWN 1/1/2, 5 October 1827.

17 WRCRO, C85/114, West Riding Asylum, 21st Report (1840), pp. 3–4; *Report of the Metropolitan Commissioners in Lunacy to the Lord Chancellor* (1844), pp. 24–5, 126–7; *A Guide Through Hanwell Lunatic Asylum* (London, 1843).

18 Sir W.C. Ellis, *A Treatise on the Nature, Symptoms, Causes and Treatment of Insanity, With Practical Observations on Lunatic Asylums* (London, 1838), p. 187.

19 *Metropolitan Commissioners in Lunacy* (1844), p. 114.

20 R. Cooter, 'Phrenology and British Alienists, c.1825–1845', *Medical History*, vol. XX (1976), part 1, January, pp. 1–21 (particularly pp. 4, 17–18), part 2, April, pp. 135–51; Ellis, *Treatise on Insanity*, chapters II and III – for an earlier perspective, see W.C. Ellis, *A Letter to Thomas Thompson, M.P.* (Hull, 1815), p. 22; Paul Slade Knight, *Observations on the Causes, Symptoms and Treatment of Derangement of the Mind* (London, 1827), pp. 2 (quotation), 39–40; G.N. Hill, *An Essay on the Prevention and Cure of Insanity* (London, 1814), pp. 17–53; Fletcher, *Sketches from the Case Book, to Illustrate the Influence of the Mind on the Body*.

21 *Further Report of the Commissioners in Lunacy* (1847), Appendix L, 'Medical Treatment Now in Use in the Principal Lunatic Establishments in England'. For eighteenth-century practice, see Porter, *Mind-Forg'd Manacles*, chapter 4.

22 SuCRO, B106/10/4.4 (2), Suffolk Asylum, 2nd Report (1840), pp. 4–5; WRCRO, C85/114, West Riding Asylum, 25th Report (1844), pp. 12–13; Ellis, *Treatise on Insanity*, p. 174; LAO, LAWN 1/1/2, 18 January 1830; BPP 1816, vol. VI, *Select Committee on Madhouses*, p. 53 – William Ricketts was proprietor of the private Droitwich Lunatic Asylum.

23 Knight, *Observations on the Derangement of the Mind*, pp. 56–7; Wellcome Institute, Western MS, MS 1587, Cheshire Lunatic Asylum, Prescription Book, 1832–9; WRCRO, C85/842, C85/936; *Commissioners in Lunacy* (1847), pp. 400, 407; NCRO, SO/HO/1/9/1; LCRO, QAM 1/30/11.

24 Tuke, *Description of the Retreat*, p. 169; DCRO, *Reports of Visiting Justices* (Epiphany 1842), p. 12, (Epiphany 1844), p. 13; WRCRO, C85/936, case of Sam Winspenny; NCRO, SO/HO/1/9/1, no. 768, case of John Slack; Lancaster County Record Office, QAM 1/30/11, p. 17, case of Mary Wilcock; R.G. Hill, *A Concise History of the Entire Abolition of Mechanical Restraint in the Treatment of the Insane* (London, 1857), pp. 311–12, case of S.L.

25 Knight, *Observations on the Derangement of the Mind*, pp. 108–11; Andrews *et al.*, *History of Bethlem*, p. 276; Hill (G.N.), *Prevention and Cure of Insanity*, p. 293; *Journal of Mental Science*, vol. 7, 15 August 1854, p. 100; *Morning Herald*, 12 January 1826; *Lichfield Mercury*, 1 January 1819; CKS, Kent Asylum, CN M&F, 1833–41, p. 375, case of John Eustace, 7 October 1841 – 'He has taken very little nourishment for several days & now refuses it altogether. I administered food to him with the stomach pump.'; LLSL, Lincoln Asylum, 9th Report (1833), p. 5; Charlesworth, *Remarks on the Treatment of the Insane*, p. 13; *British and Foreign Medical Review*, vol. IX, January 1840, p. 168; GLRO, H11/HLL/ A7/1, *Second Report of John Conolly* (1840), pp. 55–6; LAO, LAWN 1/1/3, 12 October 1831; CCRO, DDX 97/1, 10 April 1826.

26 Battie, *Treatise on Madness*, pp. 74–6, 99; Monro, *Remarks on Dr Battie's Treatise*, p. 52; B. Crowther, *Practical Remarks on Insanity* (1811), cited in V. Skultans, *Madness and Morals: Ideas on Insanity in the Nineteenth Century* (London, 1975), pp. 100–2; J.M. Cox, *Practical Observations on Insanity* (London, 1804), pp. 24, 46, 76–8, 89–90; Hill (G.N.), *Prevention and Cure of Insanity*, pp. 290–1, 295; Porter, *Mind-Forg'd Manacles*, pp. 183–5.

27 *Commissioners in Lunacy* (1847), pp. 399, 406 (quotation), 429, 430; Hill (G.N.), *Prevention and Cure of Insanity*, p. 296; J. Ferriar, cited in K. Jones, *Asylums and After* (London, 1993), p. 25; NCRO, SO/HO/1/9/1, nos. 594, 598, 610–15, 621, 623, 626, 629, 632, 639, 646, 648, 657, 666, 677, 678, 694, 695, 703, 717, 725, 730; J. Todd and L. Ashworth, *The House: Wakefield Asylum 1818. . .* (Wakefield Health Authority, 1993), p. 26.

28 Ellis, *Treatise on Insanity*, pp. 107, 176, 178 (quotation), 180; Todd and Ashworth, *The House*, p. 26; Fletcher, *Sketches from the Case Book*, pp. 164–8; NCRO, SO/HO/1/9/1, nos. 584, 598, 608, 621, 631, 641, 655, 708 (case of Mary Brockupp: 1 April 1827 – 'Countenance depressed. . .Is greatly emaciated. It is very difficult to get down medicine, low grains of calomel

are to be given so insert in her food as to escape detection.' 6 April: 'The bowels have been opened by magnes. sulphate. Is on the whole less depressed and takes her food more freely. – The calomel to be repeated tonight and the salts tomorrow.' 3 May: 'Continues to improve.' 14 May: 'Dismissed on trial – apparently quite well.'); WRCRO, C85/842, cases of Isabella Whiteley, Sarah Briggs, Grace Sykes, Anne Wesley (1821), Ann Atkinson, Mary Berry (1823); C85/936, cases of George Illingworth, George Harrison, Sam Winspenny, William Greaves (1821), James Myers (1823); CKS, CN M&F, 1833–41; Charlesworth, *Remarks on the Treatment of the Insane*, p. 15; *Commissioners in Lunacy* (1847), pp. 398–9, 403, 415, 430–1, 449–50, 460 (main quotation), 462, 466–77.

29 *Commissioners in Lunacy* (1847), pp. 399–406, 415, 429–32, 437, 460, 462.

30 Knight, *Observations on the Derangement of the Mind*, pp. 49–51; LCRO, QAM 1/30/11, p. 3, case of Martha Whewell; NCRO, SO/HO/1/9/1, nos. 703, 764.

31 Andrews, *Bedlam Revisited*, pp. 283–317; Andrews *et al.*, *History of Bethlem*, pp. 270–8; Porter, *Mind-Forg'd Manacles*, pp. 184–7; Crowther, *Practical Remarks on Insanity*, cited in Skultans, *Madness and Morals*, pp. 98–9; Battie, *Treatise on Madness*, p. 94; Monro, *Remarks on Dr Battie's Treatise*, p. 52; Hill (G.N.), *Prevention and Cure of Insanity*, pp. 286–8; Knight, *Observations on the Derangement of the Mind*, pp. 41–5; SuCRO, B106/10/4.4 (2), Suffolk Asylum, 2nd Report (1840), p. 5.

32 Ellis, *Treatise on Insanity*, pp. 51, 93, 149, 168–70, 177–82; WRCRO, C85/842, case of Isabella Whiteley (1821) (4 June: 'Continues in a very high state of excitement. . .The leeches bled very freely'), Ann Atkinson (1823), C85/936, Robert Greenwood (1821); NCRO, SO/HO/1/9/1, nos. 522 (23 June 1825: 'Much relieved by the bleeding.'), 620, 635, 649, 678, 685, 695, 724, 772; *The Lancet*, 6 July 1839, p. 554; Hill (R.G.), *Total Abolition*, p. 45; L.D. Smith, '"A Worthy Feeling Gentleman": Samuel Hitch at Gloucester Asylum, 1828–1847', in H. Freeman and G.E. Berrios (eds), *150 Years of British Psychiatry, 1841–1991*, vol. II, *The Aftermath* (London, 1996), pp. 486–7; J.C. Prichard, *A Treatise on Insanity* (London, 1835), pp. 261–2; *Commissioners in Lunacy* (1847), pp. 395, 399–400, 403, 415, 429, 431, 444, 450–1, 460, 463, 483, 493–5.

33 Monro, *Remarks on Dr Battie's Treatise*, p. 47; Bakewell, *Letter Addressed to the Chairman of the Select Committee*, p. 89; Cox, *Practical Observations on Insanity* (1804), p. 94; Hill (G.N.), *Prevention and Cure of Insanity*, p. 358; Ellis, *Treatise on Insanity*, pp. 51, 93; WRCRO, C85/842, cases of Harriett Hobson, Mary Emmitt ('Blister discharged well but does not appear to have made any alteration'), Isabella Whiteley, Sarah Briggs (1821); NCRO, SO/HO/1/ 9/1, nos. 583, 599, 661, 672; *Commissioners in Lunacy* (1847), pp. 399, 403, 460, 463, 467–8, 476–9, 481–92. For Sir Alexander Morison, see A. Scull, C. Mackenzie and N. Hervey, *Masters of Bedlam: The Transformation of the Mad-Doctoring Trade* (Princeton, 1996), chapter 5.

34 Battie, *Treatise on Madness*, p. 92; Monro, *Remarks on Dr Battie's Treatise*, p. 52; Todd and Ashworth, *The House*, p. 27; NCRO, SO/HO/1/9/1, nos. 620 (Robert Clifton, 18 August 1825: 'Appears tranquil and content. Says he has had frequent pain in the head more particularly severe since he had a blow from an iron pot. Has been repeatedly bled and has had a seton on the neck.'), 649, 655 (John Brailsford, 10 April 1827: 'Mr Morris reports that the Bowels are again very slow and difficult to move. Let him have a Tobacco Glyster.'); WRCRO, C85/842, cases of Isabella Whiteley (1821), Catherine Hayley (21 November 1821, 'Had no motion after the glyster until this morning, bowels much purged again. . .'); B. Parry-Jones, *The Warneford Hospital, Oxford, 1826–1976* (Oxford, 1976), p. 19; *Commissioners in Lunacy* (1847), pp. 395, 477.

35 Ellis, *Treatise on Madness*, pp. 171, 173, 178, 180–2; NCRO, SO/HO/1/ 9/1, nos. 599, Sarah Hirst (28 September 1825: 'Has recently made no progress. Mind is frequently highly excited – The Head is to be shaved, cold application is to be made thereon four days. . .a blister is to be applied to the head and kept open.'), 703, Susan Cox (8 March 1827: 'Very restless and even furious, is not only in the Waistcoat, but in a dark room. . .Bathe the head with cold water & Vinegar night and morning.'); LCRO, QAM 1/30/11, p. 1, case of Mary Marsden (1816); WRCRO, C85/936, cases of George Illingworth (23 April 1822), Sam Winspenny (17 April 1821), William Greaves (16 July 1821 – 'Has been more maniacal for the last two days. Let him have wet clothes applied to the head.'), C85/114, 24th Report of West Riding Asylum (1843), p. 7; *Commissioners in Lunacy* (1847), pp. 395, 398, 403, 429, 433, 444.

36 Andrews, *Bedlam Revisited*, pp. 289–92; Andrews *et al.*, *History of Bethlem*, p. 272; Monro, *Remarks on Dr Battie's Treatise*, p. 52; Cox, *Practical Observations on Insanity*, pp. 91–3; Ellis, *Treatise on Madness*, pp. 108, 174; WRCRO, C85/842, cases of Harriet Hobson, Grace Sykes (1821), Harriet Thompson (1823), C85/936, George Armitage, William Holgate (1821), James Myers (1823); LPL, *Report of the Medical Officers* (1841), p. 5; Parry-Jones, *Warneford Hospital*, p. 19.

37 GCRO, HO22/1/1, 5 March 1813, 6 June 1823, D3848/1/1, no.58, 4 April 1839, Charles Bathurst to Samuel Hitch; BPP 1839, vol. IX, *Report from the Select Committee on the Hereford Lunatic Asylum*, Minutes of Evidence, p. 173; WRCRO, C85/1, 14 January 1818, C85/842, cases of Elizabeth Blackburn, Mary Emmitt (1821), C85/936, George Harrison, William Savage (1821); SuCRO, Acc 2697, 7 April 1840; NkCRO, SAH 6, 26 June 1843, 25 September, 30 October 1843.

38 Ellis, *Treatise on Madness*, p. 227; WRCRO, C85/842, cases of Elizabeth Coulson (1821), C85/936, James Greenwood (1821).

39 Hill (R.G.), *Total Abolition*, p. 47; *The Lancet*, 19 December 1840, p. 453; LPL, *Report of the Medical Officers* (1841), p. 5; *Commissioners in Lunacy* (1847), pp. 430, 445. For John Conolly's treatment practices, see Camilla Haw, 'Sketches from the History of Psychiatry: John Conolly and the Treatment

of Mental Illness in Early Victorian England', *Psychiatric Bulletin*, vol. XIII (1989), pp. 440–4.

40 *Commissioners in Lunacy* (1847), pp. 398 (quotation), 403, 405–6, 416, 429, 430, 433, 437, 444, 449, 460, 463, 468, 472, 482–3.

41 WRCRO, C85/842, case of Elizabeth Coulson, 4 April 1822; Ellis, *Treatise on Madness*, p. 227.

42 A. Scull, 'The Domestication of Madness', *Medical History*, vol. XXVII, no. 3 (July 1983), pp. 243–4; Ellis, *Treatise on Madness*, p. 227; Cox, *Practical Observations on Insanity* (1806 edn), pp. 137–76; G.M. Burrows, *Commentaries on Insanity*, cited in Skultans, *Madness and Morals*, pp. 114–7; Knight, *Observations on the Derangement of the Mind*, pp. 61–3; GCRO, HO 22/1/1, 4 July 1823; NCRO, SO/HO/1/3/2, 30 August 1827; Stanley Royd Hospital, Diary of Dr Gettings, Extracts from Minutes, February 1820.

43 Cox, *Practical Observations on Insanity* (1806 edn), pp. 137–44.

44 Ibid., pp. 140, 145, 170–1, 175–6.

45 Burrows, cited in Skultans, *Madness and Morals*, pp. 114–7; Hill (G.N.), *Prevention and Cure of Insanity*, pp. 291, 327; Knight, *Observations on the Derangement of the Mind*, pp. 61–3 (main quotation, p. 61); WRCRO, C85/936, case of Thomas Cawthorne, 10 May, 19 June 1821, also George Armitage, 24 June 1821 ('Still continues to be remarkably stupid & untractable, was put in the circular swing a fortnight ago & has been worse ever since'), C85/842, Elizabeth Coulson, 10 June 1821; NCRO, SO/HO/1/9/1, no. 730.

46 Porter, *Mind-Forg'd Manacles*, pp. 185–7.

47 Sir Andrew Halliday, *A General View of the Present State of Lunatics and Lunatic Asylums in Great Britain and Ireland* (London, 1828), Appendix III, p. 94.

48 *Imperial Magazine*, November 1827, cols. 1026–31; Halliday, *General View of the Present State of Lunatics*, p. 92.

49 S. Tuke, *Memoirs of Samuel Tuke* (London, 1840), vol. I, p. 166; Digby, *Madness, Morality and Medicine*, pp. 246–7; Borthwick Institute (University of York), C/1, Morris to Jepson, 6 December 1811, 24 October 1812.

50 A. Digby, 'Moral Treatment at the Retreat, 1796–1846', in W.F. Bynum, R. Porter and M. Shepherd, *The Anatomy of Madness, Essays in the History of Psychiatry*, vol. III, *The Asylum and its Psychiatry* (London, 1988), p. 69; A. Digby, 'The Changing Profile of a Nineteenth-Century Asylum: the York Retreat', *Psychological Medicine*, vol. XIV (1984), pp. 739–48.

51 P. Pinel, *A Treatise on Insanity* (Sheffield, 1806, translated by D.D. Davis), pp. 217–18.

52 H. Rollin, 'Religion as an Index of the Rise and Fall of "Moral Treatment" in 19th Century Lunatic Asylums in England', *Psychiatric Bulletin*, vol. XVIII (1994), pp. 627–31; 9 Geo. IV, Cap. 40, Section XXXII; *Nottingham Journal*, 13 October 1821, 18 October 1823; Baines, *History, Directory and Gazetteer of the County Palatine of Lancaster*, pp. 17–18; Knight, *Observations on the Derangement of the Mind*, pp. 92–7.

53 LPL, *Report of the Medical Officers* (1841), p. 13; DCRO, *Report of Visiting Justices* (Epiphany 1842), p. 15; J. Conolly, *The Construction and Government of Lunatic Asylums* (London, 1847), p. 124.

54 SuCRO, B106/10/4.4, Suffolk Asylum Reports, December 1839, pp. 14–15, December 1840, pp. 13–14 (main quotation), December 1842, p. 15, December 1844, p. 17.

55 H. Warner Ellis, *'Our Doctor': Memorials of Sir William Charles Ellis, M.D., of Southall Park, Middlesex* (London, 1868), pp. 2, 11–15; Suzuki, 'The Politics and Ideology of Non-Restraint: the Case of Hanwell Asylum', *Medical History*, vol. XXXIX, no. 1 (1995), p. 4; Tuke, *Practical Hints*, p. 42; GCRO, HO 22/1/1, 1 August 1823 (letter dated 5 April 1823).

56 LAO, LAWN 3/1, West Riding Asylum, 6th Report (1824); Suzuki, 'Ideology of Non-Restraint', pp. 3–4.

57 WRCRO, C85/107, West Riding Asylum, 13th Report (1832), p. 3, C85/114, 24th Report (1843), pp. 11–13; C. Crommelinck, *Rapport sur les Hospices d'Aliénés de l'Angleterre, de la France et de l'Allemagne* (Courtrai, 1842), pp. 65–6.

58 J. Conolly, *The Treatment of the Insane Without Mechanical Restraints* (London, 1856; reprinted 1973), p. 73.

59 Ellis, *Treatise on Madness*, pp. 193–4, 227–8; WRCRO, C85/114, West Riding Asylum, 25th Report (1844), pp. 13–15; DCRO, *Report of Visiting Justices* (Epiphany 1844), p. 8; GCRO, HO22/1/1, 24 June 1839; Knight, *Observations on the Derangement of the Mind*, pp. 105–6; *Journal of Mental Science*, vol. 3, 15 February 1854, p. 44; LAO, LAWN 1/1/5, 30 June 1845.

60 M. Fears, *The 'Moral Treatment' of Insanity: A Study in the Social Construction of Human Nature* (PhD, University of Edinburgh, 1978), chapter 3; Scull, *Most Solitary of Afflictions*, chapters 2–3; Scull, 'Moral Treatment Reconsidered: Some Sociological Comments on an Episode in the History of British Psychiatry', in Scull (ed.), *Madhouses, Mad-Doctors and Madmen* (London, 1981), pp. 105–18; A. Scull, 'From Madness to Mental Illness: Medical Men as Moral Entrepreneurs', *Archives Européennes de Sociologie*, vol. XVI (1975), pp. 218–51.

61 See chapter 8 for the non-restraint movement.

62 *Metropolitan Commissioners in Lunacy* (1844), pp. 27–8.

63 WRCRO, C85/107, 31 December 1825, 31 December 1826, 31 December 1828, 31 December 1841.

64 WRCRO, C85/107, 31 December 1835, 31 December 1837, 31 December 1840, 31 December 1841, C85/108, 20th Report (1839), p. 6, C85/114, 25th Report (1844), pp. 17–18, 26th Report (1845), p. 10, 27th Report (1846), pp. 5–6.

65 GLRO, H11/HLL/A7/1, *Fifth Report of William Ellis* (Epiphany 1836), p. 25; *The Times*, 4 December 1839; GCRO, HO22/3/2, 7 December 1840, 19 July 1841, HO22/37/1, HO22/37/3; *Metropolitan Commissioners in Lunacy* (1844), p. 27; DCRO, *Reports of Visiting Justices* (Epiphany 1839), p. 4,

(Epiphany 1842), p. 14, (Epiphany 1843), pp. 22–3, (Epiphany 1844), pp. 21–4.

66 NCRO, SO/HO/1/14, pp. 1–2, 11, Statements of Cases Relieved, 1841–6.

67 E.g. R. Paternoster, *The Madhouse System* (London, 1841) and J.T. Perceval, *A Narrative of the Treatment Experienced by a Gentleman During a State of Mental Derangement* (London, 1838, 1840); E. Rickman, *Madness, or the Maniac's Hall: A Poem* (London, 1841).

68 Harriet Martineau, 'The Hanwell Lunatic Asylum', *Tait's Edinburgh Magazine* (1834), pp. 305–10; Crommelinck, *Rapport sur les Hospices*; William Salt Library, Stafford, 'Remarkable Case of the Mucclestone Idiot' (1826); T. Mulock, *British Lunatic Asylums: Public and Private* (Stafford, 1858), pp. 16–17; J. Prebble, *The Highland Clearances* (London, 1963), pp. 257–66; *Eighth Report of the Commissioners in Lunacy* (1854), Appendix G, pp. 137–8; *Journal of Mental Science*, vol. II, no. 17 (1855), pp. 276–7.

69 Public Record Office, HO44/32, fos. 430–1, 28 June 1839, Andrew Blake to Lord John Russell; *The Satirist*, 25 November, 9, 16, 23, 30 December 1838, 6 January 1839. In December 1838, Fox escaped and sought admission to Lincoln Asylum where he hoped for better treatment, but was returned to Nottingham; *Nottingham Journal*, 29 November, 13 December 1838; LAO, 1/1/4, 18 December 1837.

70 *Monthly Magazine*, vol. XLIV, January 1818, p. 493; Knight, *Observations on the Derangement of the Mind*, Appendix A, 'An Account of the Various Sensations Felt by a Person Deprived of Reason by a Fever', pp. 156–7.

71 SCRO, D550/2, 5 December 1818; GCRO, D3848/1/1, 14 October 1839, Truebody to Hitch, 11 May 1841, Mary Rich to Hitch, D3848/2, Anne Lewis to George Poynder, 6 January 1827.

72 SCRO, D550/4, 14 April 1829; GCRO, HO22/3/1, 28 December 1831.

73 GCRO, HO22/8/1, Gloucester Asylum, Annual Reports (1826–30), D3848/1/1, 7 December 1840, Newman to Hitch, D3848/2, 6 June 1841, Mary Williams to Edward Williams.

7

Useful Occupation

If there was a significant advance in treatment in the early county asylums, it came with the introduction of work as a therapeutic agent. The arrangements that William Ellis implemented at Wakefield, and which others then adopted, did considerably more than provide occupation and diversion for some of the patients. They formed the basis of an organizational system which promised not only direct therapeutic benefits, but also the indirect advantages associated with the promotion and inculcation of order and routine. Perhaps equally important, for the pauper lunatic, work was to become a primary means for keeping the asylum patient in touch with the key role of a member of his class in society – that of worker. Asylum care was now to take on a distinct element of rehabilitation, in addition to the established components of custody and of cure.

The active employment of asylum inmates was certainly not a new concept. Since the seventeenth century, some of Bethlem Hospital's convalescent patients had been employed at tasks such as cleaning, burning straw or assisting the cook. In France, Philippe Pinel had in 1801 argued emphatically for the benefits of bodily labour in public asylums, as 'the only method of securing health, good order, and good manners'. He in turn had drawn on the example of the historic asylum at Saragossa in Spain, upon which he based the implementation of programmes for employing patients at the Bicetre. The York Retreat introduced useful occupation as an aspect of moral treatment, aimed at the resocialization of patients. Across the Irish sea, at Cork Asylum, William Saunders Hallaran had by 1810 established the first extensive programme of work in a British public asylum. The questioning by the Select Committee on Madhouses in 1815 showed that there was already an assumption among the lunacy reformers that the availability of means to occupy and employ patients was a yardstick for measuring how enlightened was the management of a particular institution.[1]

Historians have tended to adopt a critical stance in considering asylum work schemes, usually concluding that therapy was not the primary motive for developing them. Jonathan Andrews suggested that the early use of patients as helpers in Bethlem had more to do with understaffing. Michael Fears, whilst acknowledging the function of work as a means of stimulation and diversion, suggested that employment therapy tended to degenerate into nothing more than a means of economizing on the asylum's running costs, with an additional role in helping to maintain its social system. David Mellett accepted that work had therapeutic aspects, but contended that its importance lay more in its being a means of achieving control over patients within the asylum.[2] Such arguments are persuasive, but they may be too severe in their interpretation of the motives of those who initiated the early employment schemes.

WILLIAM ELLIS: TOWARDS A WORKING COMMUNITY

> On entering the gate, I met a patient going to his garden work with his tools in his hand, and passed three others breaking clods with their forks, and keeping near each other for the sake of being sociable. . .In a shed in this garden, sit three or four patients cutting potatoes for seed, singing and amusing each other. . .In the bakehouse, meanwhile, are a company of patients, kneading their dough; and in the wash-house and laundry, many more, equally busy. . .[3]

William Ellis was born in Lincolnshire in March 1780, the son of Reverend William Ellis, Rector of All-Hallows Steyning in the City of London. He received a classical education, and then trained as a surgeon in Hull, where he pursued his early medical career. In 1806 he married Mildred, the formidable partner in his later endeavours. Increasingly religious, Ellis embraced Methodism and became a lay preacher in Hull. As part of his work as a surgeon, he was by 1815 involved with the operation of the Sculcoates Refuge, a private madhouse which attempted to model its practices on those of the York Retreat. His *Letter to Thomas Thompson, M.P.* of that year confirms that he had gained some experience in the management and treatment of mental disorder and was developing ideas on the improvement of current practice. The *Letter* brought him to the notice of Godfrey Higgins, the magistrate embroiled in the struggle to reform York Asylum. Ellis visited the Retreat and formed a relationship with Samuel Tuke, whose ideas so influenced the planning of the West Riding Asylum. By the time he took up post at Wakefield, his professional status had been enhanced by qualification as physician.[4]

Ellis proved possibly the most effective of the early county asylum superintendents. Evidently a man whose ideological zeal was matched by prodigious energy and determination, his wide spans of control and interest comprised both the individual and the collective. He paid close attention to the assessment, diagnosis and treatment of each patient. At the same time, he was a highly able administrator and, despite his ongoing difficulties with Dr Caleb Crowther, he managed to raise the asylum to a position where it operated like an efficient mechanical system.[5] At the heart of this administrative success was the regime of work. It provided a cohesive base, both philosophical and practical, to the institution's operation. Ellis may not have been the actual originator of industrial therapy, but he was certainly the first to implement a large-scale work-based regime in a public asylum.

Ellis had stressed the importance of work as early as 1815, when ensuring consideration of his name for the forthcoming post at Wakefield. He contended that 'nothing is found so efficacious as employment' in directing the thoughts of the patient away from 'false impressions'. There needed to be a 'great variety' available, and discriminating attempts to match what was offered to individual dispositions, to include work in the open air as well as indoors. As far as possible, 'mechanics' should be encouraged to work at their own trades. Money might be earned from the produce, he suggested. The magistrates' appointment of Ellis was certainly influenced by his commitment to promote schemes of work. The building was constructed with specific provision for work rooms. The asylum's rules, drafted by Higgins, made the expectations very clear. The patients were to be employed in 'useful labour' as much as possible; the director and matron were charged to 'leave no humane and mild measures untried' to bring this into effect. They would not give satisfaction 'unless they have considerable success in this department of their duty'. Significantly, the rules also anticipated 'profits of the labour of the patients', which could be appropriated.[6]

Once in post, the Ellises quickly set about meeting the visitors' expectations. By the end of 1818, many of the patients were being employed in the grounds, mainly on digging and hoeing, or indoors where most were making clothing. Two years later, Ellis claimed that patients were manufacturing all their clothing and shoes. There were some local prejudices to be overcome, with concerns about the inherent risks involved if patients were not kept in restraint whilst working. As if to anticipate critics of the scheme, it was Ellis's proud and later repeated boast that 'notwithstanding the various tools, as well as the implements of gardening and husbandry, with which they have necessarily been entrusted, no accident of any kind has occurred'. The range of work on offer to patients was steadily extended. During 1822, more land was acquired to allow other agricultural pursuits, including dairy farming. Baking and brewing operations were established. Ellis could claim that considerable savings were being effected in the asylum's overall expenses, so permitting steady reductions in the maintenance charges to parishes.[7]

The scheme was sufficiently well established by 1823 for Ellis to describe it in detail to George Poynder, engaged in setting up Gloucester Asylum. Out of 190 patients, 112 were employed 'more or less according to their ability'. About 40, of both sexes, were making shoes and clothes. Between 30 and 40 men were employed in gardening. Many of the women were employed in domestic tasks, with the consequence that only one cook, one housemaid and one laundry maid had to be employed. The classification of patients and the staffing arrangements on the wards reflected the emphasis on work:

> The Keeper to one of these Wards is a cloth Manufacturer, another a Shoemaker, and another a Gardener. The Patients are placed under each as they are acquainted with the different employments. After the cleaning of the Wards, Bedrooms &c in which the Patients assist every morning, each of the three latter Keepers with his Patients go to work in their respective occupations.

In addition, there was a 'Farming Man' who took some patients to look after the cows and pigs. The engineer oversaw those working in the joiner's and blacksmith's shops. Similar arrangements also operated on the female side. The keepers' role was 'principally to watch over and superintend' the patients whilst they worked. Ellis did not minimize the part played by his wife and himself in the day-to-day organization. It required their personal attention and 'both great judgment and discrimination' to determine how and when the patients were to be employed, taking account of each person's mental state. He had no doubt that employment was 'the means we have found most conducive to the recovery of the Patients'.[8]

Sir Andrew Halliday, in his 1828 survey of asylums, singled out Wakefield as one of the best regulated, with its 25 acres of land, its workshops and its 'judicious system' of employment. Ellis, who corresponded with Halliday, was persuaded to lay his achievements before the public. The fundamental principle was that, for the 'lower classes', employment was 'the most salutary mode of recreation'. The whole programme was becoming increasingly sophisticated, in pursuit of the goal of 'constant and regular employment':

> for that purpose, not only farming and gardening, but all trades have been forced into the service; we have spinners, weavers, tailors, shoemakers, bakers, brewers, blacksmiths, joiners, painters, bricklayers, and stonemasons, all employed. All the clothing for the patients is manufactured and made by themselves; we bake our own bread, brew our own beer, and nearly one half of both male and female patients are constantly engaged in some kind of labour.

Again Ellis stressed the absence of serious accidents. More significantly, he emphasized the considerable financial savings to the running of the asylum.[9]

The employment project was not free from problems. Patients were not always as committed as the Ellises and their staff. William Ellis found some reluctant to exert themselves, with perseverance needed to gain their co-operation. Their likes and dislikes had to be ascertained, and indulgences had to be granted or withheld 'according to their behaviour'. These were frequently 'the only lever, by which the moral man can be moved'. Mildred Ellis, who took responsibility for employment of the females, was well aware of the need to offer them more than just the idea that work was beneficial:

> It requires all the exertion I am capable of, with the aids I now have, to get the laborious and dirty work of the wash house and the Kitchen, done by the patients; for it must be remembered, that this work, in itself, affords no pleasure in the performing, and it is by kindness only, they are bribed to do it.

The 'kindness' she referred to included granting dietary and other inducements. The distaste for laundry work was no doubt increased by its hazardous and unhealthy nature; some working there succumbed to dysentery in the outbreaks of the late 1820s. Case-notes show that patients did not always willingly accept their productive role. Refusal to work might be interpreted as a symptom of relapse or even misbehaviour. Dissent could result in punishment, as Thomas Cawthorne found in 1821; his continued obstinacy and lack of response to 'kind treatment' brought a few doses of the circular swing.[10]

Ellis's undoubted success at Wakefield in creating a regime that appeared to be ordered, therapeutically effective and economical attracted envious attention. Inevitably, he was courted for the most prestigious and lucrative of all public asylum posts – the new Middlesex County Asylum. The appointment in 1831 gave Ellis the opportunity to translate his schemes of large-scale patient employment from industrial West

Yorkshire to the less promising but more challenging environs of teeming late-Hanoverian London. Undaunted, he set about implementing his plan with determination. As he claimed in his first report, the 'great principle' of employment had been constantly acted upon in the eight months since the asylum opened. Its sheer magnitude offered the opportunity for 'every variety of interesting occupation' within its walls. Significantly, too, there already were savings of 'great expense' to the county.[11]

Despite the 'great difficulty' experienced in inducing some reluctant Middlesex paupers to work, due to their expectation of payment, the scheme was pursued relentlessly. By the autumn of 1834, more than 320 out of 560 patients were regularly employed. The range of trades and occupations varied slightly from Wakefield. There was a higher emphasis on agriculture and gardening, in the absence of clothing manufacture. A larger number of women were employed than men, with many engaged in knitting and needlework, as well as the local trades of straw-hat and basket-making. Other crafts were added, including twine-spinning, mop manufacture, shoemaking and brick-laying. Work was even found for the 'imbecile and fatuous'. Ellis's convictions as to its value continued to strengthen. He contrasted other asylums where the inmates wandered up and down the galleries and courts all day in 'listless indolence' with the scene at busy Hanwell. His 'experience of twenty years' had confirmed his view that 'constant, energetic employment' was the 'sole remedy' to be relied upon to dissipate the delusional and erroneous wanderings of the mind.[12]

Harriet Martineau's eulogistic portrayal of Hanwell in 1834 served to bring the Ellises and their system before a wider liberal public. Her picture of something approaching a communal idyll, where patients worked contentedly, conversed animatedly, responded eagerly to the dinner-bell, and flocked to the chapel, all under the benign superintendence of Dr and Mrs Ellis, appeared to point the way toward the quelling, if not the actual conquest, of insanity itself. Her only regret was that this model regime was not available for the disadvantaged middle-class casualties of mental disorder. Visitors came to view the asylum in increasing numbers. The interest even of Royalty was aroused, bringing the patronage of Queen Adelaide to establish the fund for discharged patients, and more significantly, the first such accolade for a mad-doctor, a knighthood in 1836 for William Ellis.[13]

Notwithstanding the relentless growth in the numbers of patients and the consequent expansions of the building, further elaborations were made to the employment arrangements. New trades were added, like brush-making. The 'mischievous', or refractory, patients were brought into the system; their work in picking cocoa-nut fibres not only earned income but had the further advantage of reducing the destruction of their clothes, thus rendering restraint less necessary. Sir William Ellis was proud of what had been achieved: 'The Establishment of itself thus presents rather the appearance of a little independent colony, than of a sick hospital; each one taking a share in promoting the general welfare.' This apparent attainment of the communitarian vision, however, was not to everyone's liking. Criticism was growing from within the Middlesex magistracy of Ellis's all-embracing autocratic approach, of some of his administrative shortcomings, and of his preoccupation with reducing the charges to parishes and poor law unions as low as possible, by policies of rigid economy. Confrontations led to his resignation and replacement during 1838. He did not survive long to enjoy the move into private asylum management.[14]

The significance of Sir William's achievements was not lost on contemporaries or successors. His practical application of 'moral treatment', with its ensuing therapeutic gains, was recognized as a key stage in the development and liberalization of the asylum. Ellis's early mentor, Samuel Tuke, paid tribute in 1841 to the 'skill, vigour, and kindliness towards the patients' of his recently deceased pupil, who had pioneered the systematic introduction of labour into British public asylums. An anonymous asylum superintendent acknowledged that Ellis had 'eminently distinguished himself' with his plan. Even critics had to grudgingly accept his achievement. The most prominent, John Conolly, had some difficulty in coming to terms with his predecessor's legacy and reputation. He initially characterized Sir William and Lady Ellis's exhibition of the 'spectacle of tranquil and useful occupation' as a 'vainglorious display'. Subsequently, Conolly was forced to retract. Whilst castigating the prevalence of restraint under Ellis, he conceded that his predecessor's employment scheme was a 'step of extreme importance' in the management of the insane; the principle of employing the patients in a wide range of work 'cannot be too highly spoken of'. Its place in the mainstream treatment armoury was now secured.[15]

THERAPY AND THRIFT

The advantages of the employment scheme at Wakefield, and later at Hanwell, were evident enough. Here was something practical and specific which magistrates and managers could implement, that brought expectations of therapeutic benefits for the patients, greater order for the asylum and financial savings in its administration. The first significant recruit to the Ellis plan was Gloucester Asylum, where there was a clear attempt, from its opening in 1823, to replicate a system with work as its core element. After receiving detailed advice from Ellis, George Poynder had additional rules and regulations framed, which anticipated that as many pauper patients as possible would be employed on their wards, with an emphasis on making and repairing clothing and linen. Convalescent females were to be employed in the laundry. Garden work was to be established. For the patients, these measures would be 'to their very great advantage in body and mind'. At least as significantly, the work done would be 'to the profit of the Institution'. By the end of 1825, a 'great proportion' of the male patients were being employed in the gardens and grounds, and the women in sewing, knitting 'and other avocations'.[16]

Under Samuel Hitch's superintendence, employment arrangements at Gloucester were developed considerably. Additional land was acquired in 1833 and 1837. Initially, outdoor work was for male patients only, but in 1838 females were also offered the opportunity, subject to considerations of 'propriety'. Over the next few years the range of work was expanded, with patients engaged in bricklaying, demolition, digging, pipe-laying, painting, window-cleaning and carpentry, as well as shoe-making and tailoring, for which resident tradesmen were employed as instructors during 1842. A private patient was even appointed as a paid accountant to the asylum. Pauper women were deployed to clean the chambers of the 'first-class' male patients. Hitch also promoted agricultural work outside the asylum boundaries, in order to widen opportunities. This was a risk he felt worth taking, though escapes inevitably occurred. A further problem with the employment scheme, as Ellis had found at Wakefield, was that patients were not always willing to work; in June 1839, the meat and beer allowances had to be reduced for 'those patients who do not or will not employ themselves'. Nevertheless, the overall success of the scheme contributed to the widely held perception of Gloucester as one of the best-managed county asylums.[17]

The personal influence of William Ellis was clearly apparent at Dorset Asylum. Its second superintendent, Thomas Quick, appointed in 1836, had served as apothecary at Hanwell for four years. Work was generally introduced over the following two years, and by the middle of 1838 it was claimed that 80 out of 99 patients were employed – a higher proportion than at any other asylum. The males were engaged outside in gardening, water pumping, digging and ground clearance, and inside in shoe- and clog-making, picking flock and coir, and tailoring. The females made straw hats and bonnets and knitted stockings, as well as the more usual clothes-mending, cleaning and laundry. Quick was succeeded during 1842 by George Button, another Ellis alumnus, who had left Hanwell after finding himself at odds with the Conolly regime. Button paid glowing tribute to his late mentor, who had carried out his system of labour 'to an extent never before deemed practicable'. He sought to emulate Ellis's methods, albeit on a scale consistent with a much smaller institution. The range of agricultural and other outdoor tasks undertaken was extended, as was the indoor production of a range of goods for sale. Diversification did bring its problems, however, as when the mangel-wurzel crop failed in 1844![18]

Even after Ellis had departed to Hanwell, Wakefield remained a model of how an asylum could be managed with work as its centrepiece. His successor C.C. Corsellis made clear from the beginning his intention to maintain the status quo. In practice he did rather more, developing the arrangements to a point where in 1841 Dr Crommelinck considered Wakefield pre-eminent over all other asylums in England. In the preceding ten years, Corsellis had built steadily on the efforts of his predecessor. Employment on the land, in the house, and in specific trades were all extended. In 1836 two additional fields were bought, with one being converted into a garden specifically for cultivation by female patients. By 1841, 41 acres were under cultivation, rising to 50 in 1845. Indoor work was also developed; additional looms were acquired for woollen- and linen-weaving by women. The manufacture of fancy goods for sale was promoted, with the profits being channelled into the Harrison Fund to assist patients leaving the asylum. The profits of the other employment ventures were applied to lower the asylum's running costs and to reduce charges to the poor-law unions.[19]

If Corsellis was to be believed, the patients were highly sensible of the benefits gained from working. He poignantly described in 1837 the 'tears of gratitude' shed by hundreds restored to health. The acquisition of new looms for the women during 1840 brought forth some pleasing scenes of industry:

> A.H. a noisy, mischievous patient, now chatters to herself, and winds bobbins with the utmost diligence. F.G. who has several times attempted self-destruction by hanging, and used to sit in a corner silent and gloomy, now plies the shuttle with a smiling face, and laughs with delight at the admiration bestowed by visitors on her dexterity.

Nevertheless, inducements other than persuasion, in the form of food and drink, were needed to get some to work. This rather galled Corsellis, for whom the therapeutic gains were self-evident. These could hardly be doubted when patients were 'taught to feel that happiness is surely found in the path of duty', by employing those faculties still available. As well as a means to raise the spirits, work was also a tranquillizing agent. By inducing fatigue more effectively than a narcotic drug, it brought the benefit of refreshing sleep. It served to calm 'excited feelings' by the 'gentle and firm' system of moral discipline, and by the diversion of the mind from morbid thoughts. Perhaps more importantly, as Corsellis conceded, labour prevented the monotony of life in a lunatic asylum from becoming an 'intolerable burden'.[20]

Elsewhere, the dissemination of Ellis's programme was more patchy. At most public asylums, aspects were gradually adopted in a piecemeal fashion, but without any evident intent that work should be more than a means to constructively occupy a limited number of patients, or to raise some produce for home consumption. Sir Andrew Halliday's survey in 1828 gave the issue a greater prominence and raised an expectation that work should be provided, with implied criticism of those asylums where lack of land rendered any extensive scheme impractical. Some at least were spurred to more energetic measures, but these tended to be relatively limited in scope.[21]

In general, it was outdoor work that tended to be the most favoured, with its connotations of healthy physical exercise. Halliday showed that the land attached to asylums, available for agriculture, horticulture and recreation, ranged from almost none at Norfolk and a mere three acres at Bedford to 30 acres at Stafford, which was better placed even than Wakefield. A similar survey in 1844 by the Metropolitan Commissioners illustrated a 'comparable' spread. They noted the worst deficiencies at the older asylums – Nottingham, Bedford and Norfolk, where the encroachments of the surrounding town or other geographical problems restricted the scope for acquiring land. Apart from the well-endowed West Riding Asylum, the more recently established Surrey and Kent Asylums (the latter with 37 acres) were the best situated, having been located with space as a consideration. The amount of land in itself, however, was not always a measure of the extent of employment. At well-managed asylums like Nottingham, there were attempts to maximize opportunities for work, despite a lack of space. At Suffolk Asylum, although 30 acres had been available, 22 of them were leased out to earn an income.[22]

The development of land-based employment schemes necessarily involved an expensive initial outlay. County justices and visiting governors would have to be convinced not only that work was of recuperative value but also that there would be economic benefits to the institution. At Nottingham, the decision to spend £700 in 1818 for a small portion of land seemed to have more to do with the 'considerable benefit' to the asylum by its cultivation than with the opportunity to employ those male patients 'to whom bodily labour may be deemed serviceable'. The eight acres retained by Suffolk Asylum as 'garden and potatoe ground' were intended not only to provide employment, but also to supply the house with vegetables and fruit. The aim of self-sufficiency in ground produce remained a strong motivation for the development of patient participation in garden cultivation. By the late 1830s, at even the more backward asylums, like Cornwall and Bedford, convalescent patients were engaged in this work.[23]

Economic motives also underlay the organization of some non-agricultural outdoor work, particularly that associated with building. Savings were achieved by the unpaid labour of patients. At several asylums, including Chester, Cornwall, Dorset, Stafford and Lincoln, water pumps operated by capstan wheel were installed. These were cheap, labour-intensive means of augmenting the institution's water supply. At Chester, in 1836, upwards of ten men were employed on pumping daily, whilst at Stafford as many as 28 were involved. Patients were widely engaged to assist in laying out airing courts and exercise grounds, breaking stones or moving earth. At Lancaster, where major building works took place in the early 1840s, patients excavated and removed 'to a considerable distance' 15,000 square yards of earth. At Suffolk Asylum, up to 40 patients were 'actively and unceasingly' involved in assisting the paid contractors in all the tasks associated with constructing the new buildings, like excavation, brick-making, brick-laying and carpentry. John Kirkman proudly informed the justices of a saving to the county funds of all of £200.[24]

Indoor work was also actuated to an extent by economic motives. Although there was an undeniable therapeutic and rehabilitative element to laundry work, cleaning wards, bed-making, sewing, knitting and so on, there was also a saving to the running costs. As early as 1815, Reverend J.T. Becher told the Select Committee that the employment of able patients on domestic work at Nottingham Asylum was a means of 'reducing the number of servants' as well as advancing recovery. Although not always expressed so overtly, this remained an underlying consideration. Sometimes it was a question of unavoidable expediency. At Gloucester in June 1839, the dismissal of four female nurses for misconduct left a depleted staff. A week later, however, the remaining two nurses were reportedly managing so well with patients' assistance that the decision to proceed with new appointments was deferred. At Lincoln Asylum in 1841, beset as it was by financial problems as well as difficulties in maintaining order and control, patients were enlisted to help the staff with the routine chores on the wards and a kitchen maid post was dropped with the idea that patients would take over. These were largely *ad hoc* arrangements, though William Ellis had recognized from the beginning that, with proper organization, there were considerable savings to be made by reducing the prospective staffing levels.[25]

Considering the observable and measurable achievements at Wakefield by the mid-1820s, however, the dissemination of Ellis's programme through asylumdom was not as rapid as might have been expected. This had much to do with conceptions about the capabilities of the insane, or about the risks they posed. Despite Ellis's claims that he had encountered few accidents, even though patients were entrusted with potentially dangerous implements, others were less willing to take the risk. When John Kirkman sought to develop employment at Suffolk Asylum in early 1837, the visitors were agreeable to female patients mending clothes, but they baulked at the suggestion that male patients should work as tailors or shoemakers, as this would be 'the means of introducing amongst them instruments of a dangerous nature'. Nowhere was this position articulated more strongly than at Lincoln where, though Charlesworth and Gardiner Hill prided themselves on the asylum's progressive achievements, there was strong resistance against most proposals for employment. Hill expressed himself 'decidedly opposed to all Employment of Lunatics by which dangerous implements are put in their hands', and advocated fresh air and exercise as being more curative. Although some work was introduced at Lincoln, it was never on any significant scale.[26]

Ellis himself considered that the lack of development of patient employment was because 'so strong a prejudice exists against it' on the part of many 'professional gentlemen'. The dilatoriness of many justices and some superintendents was clearly associated with lingering conceptions that the asylum's function was primarily custodial and its inmates beyond the reach of useful or productive occupation. Thus, for example, the repeated pleas of Norfolk Asylum's visiting medical officers that work would be beneficial and curative for the patients, continued to fall upon deaf ears. Returns to Parliament in 1836 highlighted the absence of activity:

> As to modes of occupation. There are none particularly but when convalescent Female Patients are employed in cleaning and washing & the Male Patients in assisting the Porters on the premises in gardening.

The managing justices remained unmoved, evidently viewing the provision of therapeutic activity as beyond their remit, until the Metropolitan Commissioners cast their critical eyes on the situation in 1843. Reluctantly, Norfolk Asylum's officers took steps to come into line.[27]

By this time, however, some sort of plan for the occupation of patients in public asylums had become regarded as an essential element of best practice. W.A.F. Browne, in his 1837 elaboration of a vision for the asylum, had extolled the virtues of patient labour. Clearly influenced by Ellis's achievements, he advocated a regime which encouraged patients to utilize their full abilities, and be meaningfully rewarded by payments in kind. His ideal comprised a 'hive of industry', in surroundings resembling 'some vast emporium of manufacture'. Droves of merry, contented inmates would be busily engaged in a whole range of outdoor and indoor tasks, unskilled, skilled and supervisory, according to their abilities. There would be something for everyone to do:

> In one part of the edifice are companies of straw-plaiters, basket-makers, knitters, spinners, among the women; in another, weavers, tailors, saddlers, and shoemakers, among the men. For those who are ignorant of these gentle crafts, but are strong and steady, there are loads to carry, water to draw, wood to cut, and for those who are both ignorant and weakly, there is oakum to tease and yarn to wind.

In this idyll, the difficulty was not in getting the reluctant to work, but rather in 'restraining their eagerness, and moderating their exertions'. Browne's imagery of work at the heart of what Scull has styled 'the Asylum as Utopia' formed, significantly, the culmination of 'What Asylums Ought to Be'.[28]

RATIONAL AMUSEMENTS

An important aspect of the liberalization of asylum regimes from the late 1830s onwards was the attempt to relieve the monotony of institutional life and to provide greater stimulation. It had long been established that active diversion of the thoughts was a key element in the therapy that an asylum could offer. Work was one important part of this. However, not all patients were capable of work or motivated to engage in it. There were also practical difficulties which restricted the availability of sufficient work to fill long days. Asylum managers increasingly promoted leisure and recreational pursuits as an alternative or supplement to work. By the early 1840s, there was a certain amount of vying between asylums as to which could offer the most imaginative activities for patients. This was to form the basis for the elaborate recreational arrangements which characterized some of the large post-1845 institutions.

In the best-run private madhouses, a range of leisure pursuits would be made available to the patients, including musical instruments, reading material, games, sports and supervised walks or rides in the country.[29] In most public asylums, until at least the 1820s, there was only a limited provision of activities, with patients left largely to their own introspective devices. The chief regular pastime was supervised exercise, either in the airing courts or, if the weather was inclement, in the galleries. Where other leisure pursuits were offered these tended to be rather basic and crude. The superintendent of Stafford Asylum was ordered in 1818, soon after opening, to provide draught and cribbage boards, packs of cards and 'odd volumes of entertaining books'. At Lancaster, the outdoor quadrangle was arranged so that patients could play games in one part of it. At Norfolk in early 1818, boards for drawing and wooden bricks were provided. At Nottingham in the winter of 1826, a bagatelle board was a means of alternative amusement when patients could not take outdoor exercise in bad weather. The general level of provision appears to have been very limited at this stage.[30]

During the 1830s, as part of the gathering preoccupation with liberalizing and reforming the asylum, more attention was given to the constructive use of patients' time and the promotion of 'rational amusements'. As W.A.F. Browne recognized, some were not capable of work, or their social backgrounds inclined them toward other types of occupation. Asylum managers responded by providing various forms of recreation, including opportunities to read and to participate in music, sports and games. Where previously it had been assumed that most patients were beyond such indulgences, opinion had shifted to embrace the idea that not only might they gain some harmless enjoyment but there might also be some therapeutic benefits from stimulating the faculties.[31]

Encouragement of reading became a growing preoccupation, with libraries being set up in several asylums. At Lincoln, the library was established in 1834, in the Board Room, with an emphasis on works of natural history; in 1836, bookcases were placed in the day-rooms. At Lancaster, by 1841, the library had 296 volumes, read with 'apparent pleasure and interest'. At Wakefield in 1844, there were 140 volumes of 'interesting and instructive works', selected with consideration as to their 'probable influence' on the readers. Corsellis clearly had reservations, however, and was concerned that some patients were unable to sleep after prolonged attention to a book, and that 'maniacal paroxysms' might ensue. Button at Dorset had no such qualms, believing the asylum's library, with books of a 'moral and religious character' or that were 'instructive and entertaining', played an important part in moral treatment. Indeed, there could be even more significant gains:

> An amusing volume often arrests the attention, and withdraws the mind from its morbid train of ideas, to others of a more healthful character, and thus proves a powerful auxiliary in tranquillizing the feelings.

The provision of lighter reading, in the form of periodicals and newspapers, became common. Journals such as the *Penny Magazine*, the *Saturday Magazine*, *Chambers Edinburgh Journal* and the *Illustrated London News* were made available, to ensure an adequate and 'improving' educational content.[32]

After a successful concert in Lincoln Asylum's grounds by the local Blue Coat school band in January 1840, Robert Gardiner Hill commented that 'Lunatics are fond of music'. They were still more fond of participating in it. Instruments were acquired at several asylums, the most popular being a hand organ, but there were also violins, flutes and accordions. At Nottingham in 1842, singing lessons were introduced. At Gloucester, communal singing sessions had been instituted on a weekly basis, with patients of all classes participating; to the paupers it was 'the greatest treat' and the highlight of the week. Various types of musical entertainment emerged. At Lancaster, a custom developed on special occasions of groups of patients dancing to the music of a fiddler, dressed in garish fancy costume. Samuel Gaskell, the superintendent, considered that such events were 'important agents in the treatment of insanity'; they could avert 'excitement'. However, his Belgian guest Dr Crommelinck was not convinced, finding the uninhibited scene rather 'barbaric'. He urged Gaskell to proscribe the practice, after he had endured the sight of patients dressing up in the garb of the opposite sex and performing scenes of 'true bacchanal', their wandering imaginations causing them to 'lose all control on their words as on their gestures'.[33]

The celebrated asylum balls developed out of these sorts of gatherings, made possible by the less restrictive climate accompanying the non-restraint movement. Samuel Hitch claimed in 1841 that Gloucester had been the first to introduce balls; 'large parties for Dancing' had always been promoted. In fact, these were events largely geared toward the private patients of his asylum. Initially viewed as a curious novelty, the asylum ball attained widespread popularity over the next few years. At Lincoln, where Charlesworth and Hill sought to keep the asylum in the limelight of progressive practice, balls were established on a monthly basis, encompassing all classes of patients. They lasted from 6.30 p.m. until 10 p.m., with refreshments of lemonade, fruit and buns being provided. Propriety was ensured by the practice of ensuring that males and females participated in separate parts of the house. Respectable visitors from the city were invited to join in. One initially bemused convert described the scene in October 1841:

> There was a commingling of every grade and shade of lunacy, from those approaching convalescence to the most violent; from the harmless to the occasionally most dangerous; from the humorous and amusingly eccentric to the hypochondriacal, all joining merrily and happily in the dance, or looking on in quiet enjoyment.

The monthly entertainment became a fixed part of Lincoln's programme. It was found that people who were 'on other occasions gross in their conduct or conversation' would exercise an increasing degree of self-control at such events. Balls and concerts were, however, more than just a safety valve; they were also an important element in the process of resocialization.[34]

By the early 1840s, activities had become increasingly diverse, as superintendents tried to find new ways to occupy, amuse and stimulate their patients. There was a greater range of indoor games, including skittles, chess, draughts, dominoes, bagatelle, backgammon and cards, as well as entertainments like magic lantern shows. Outdoors, there were sports, like bowls, tennis, shuttlecock and football. There were garden parties in the summer. Outings beyond the asylum walls became a feature, either in organized walks, visits to local churches on Sundays, or to places of interest like zoos and concert halls. At Lincoln, Dr Charlesworth had introduced birds and animals, including guinea pigs and a monkey, for patients to look after. Ever intent on innovation, in 1839 he and Gardiner Hill went further and introduced two young children into the house, for the female patients to play with and to instruct, an idea adopted from Dundee Asylum. Hill noted in his journal how the children seemed 'very happy and cheerful', were not at all 'alarmed', and 'would rather remain here than return to their own homes'. The therapeutic effect was palpable:

> The children amuse the patients very much – some find employment in teaching them to read, others in teaching them to knit, &c. It is quite pleasing to see the children with their arms round the patients waists taking exercise in the Galleries, &c.

Despite the apparent enthusiasm of all parties, however, this unusual experiment was fairly short-lived. Anxieties about risk loomed larger than any consideration of the therapeutic possibilities, leading to the abandonment of the idea.[35]

The fate of this one particular Lincoln experiment perhaps exemplified how far things had progressed in the management of asylums since the turn of the century, as well as being indicative of the caution that still remained. The uneven progress of schemes of work and of recreation also reflected the continuing dual approach to the insane within the institution. However, ideas of the asylum as being orientated to cure rather than custody were clearly in the ascendant. The 'moral' or non-medical aspects of treatment were becoming dominated by the deliberate construction of a complete environment that sought to promote therapeutic improvement by means of active participation. The individual lunatic patient was being required to make a practical contribution in return for care, comfort and pleasant pastimes. Increasingly, he or she was being asked to play an active part in the institutional community, rather than simply being a passive recipient or reluctant prisoner. This move toward a new asylum order both contributed to and gained impetus from the emergent movement for non-restraint.

NOTES

1 J. Andrews, *Bedlam Revisited: A History of Bethlem Hospital c.1634–1770* (PhD, University of London, 1991), pp. 201–2; P. Pinel, *A Treatise on Insanity* (Sheffield, translated by D. Davis, 1806), p. 216; S. Tuke, *Description of the Retreat* (London, 1813), pp. 155–6; A. Digby, *Madness, Morality and Medicine: A Study of the York Retreat 1796–1914* (Cambridge, 1985), chapter 4; R. Hunter and I. Macalpine, *Three Hundred Years of Psychiatry, 1535–1860* (Oxford, 1963), pp. 648–52; *Report of the Select Committee on Madhouses, with Minutes of Evidence* (1814–15), pp. 125–6, 180, (1816), p. 52.

2 J. Andrews, 'Hardly A Hospital, But a Charity for Pauper Lunatics?', in J. Barry and C. Jones (eds), *Medicine and Charity Before the Welfare State* (London, 1991), p. 75; M. Fears, *The 'Moral Treatment' of Insanity: A Study in the Social Construction of Human Nature* (PhD, University of Edinburgh, 1978), pp. 230–46; D. Mellett, *The Prerogative of Asylumdom: Social, Cultural and Administrative Aspects of the Institutional Treatment of the Insane in Nineteenth Century Britain* (London, 1982), pp. 26–7.

3 Harriet Martineau, 'The Hanwell Lunatic Asylum', *Tait's Edinburgh Magazine* (1834), pp. 305–10.

4 H. Warner Ellis, *'Our Doctor': Memorials of Sir William Charles Ellis, M.D., of Southall Park, Middlesex* (London, 1868), pp. 2–10; W.C. Ellis, *A Letter to*

Thomas Thompson, M.P. (Hull, 1815); C. Crowther, *Some Observations on the Management of Madhouses* (London, 1838), p. 55; Digby, *Madness, Morality, and Medicine*, pp. 243–5.

5 See chapter 2 for the disputes with Crowther.

6 Ellis, *Letter to Thomas Thompson*, pp. 11–15; G. Higgins, *Rules for the Management of the Pauper Lunatic Asylum for the West Riding of the County of York, Erected at Wakefield* (Wakefield, 1821), pp. 24–5; Watson and Pritchett, *Plans, Elevations, Sections and Description of the Pauper Lunatic Asylum Lately Erected at Wakefield* (York, 1819), pp. 2, 28–9.

7 WRCRO, C85/107, Annual Reports, 31 December 1819, 31 December 1820, 31 December 1821; LAO, LAWN 3/1, West Riding Asylum, 4th Report (1822), 5th Report (1823); Sir W.C. Ellis, *A Treatise on the Nature, Symptoms, Causes and Treatment of Insanity, With Practical Observations on Lunatic Asylums* (London, 1838), p. 8.

8 GCRO, HO22/1/1, 1 August 1823 (letter dated 5 April 1823); Warner Ellis, *'Our Doctor'*, pp. 42–3.

9 Sir A. Halliday, *A General View of the Present State of Lunatics, and Lunatic Asylums in Great Britain and Ireland* (London, 1828), pp. 17, 19, Appendix III, p. 93 – letter dated 30 November 1827.

10 Ellis, *Treatise*, p. 194; letter from Mrs Ellis, cited in D. Alexander, *An Impartial Statement of the Question Recently Agitated Between Dr Crowther and Dr Alexander Respecting the Visiting Department of the Pauper Lunatic Asylum* (Wakefield, 1825), pp. 14–15; W.H. Gilbey, 'On The Dysentery Which Occurred in the Wakefield Lunatic Asylum in the Years 1826, 1827, 1828, and 1829', *North of England Medical and Surgical Journal*, vol. I (1830–1), p. 93; WRCRO, C85/936 – cases of Joseph Senior, 30 May 1821 and Thomas Cawthorne, 25 March, 19 June 1821.

11 GLRO, H11/HLL/A7/1, 1st Report of William Ellis (Epiphany 1832), p. 4.

12 GLRO, H11/HLL/A7/1, 2nd Report (1833), 4th Report (1835); *The Times*, 30 October 1834.

13 Martineau, 'The Hanwell Lunatic Asylum', pp. 305–10; A. Suzuki, 'The Politics and Ideology of Non-Restraint: the Case of the Hanwell Asylum', *Medical History*, vol. XXXIX, no. 1 (1995), p. 3; GLRO, H11/HLL/A7/1, 5th Report (1836), p. 25.

14 GLRO, H11/HLL/A7/1, 6th Report (1837), pp. 30–1, 7th Report (1838), p. 37; Suzuki, 'Politics and Ideology of Non-Restraint', pp. 3–5, 9.

15 *Familiar Views of Lunacy and Lunatic Life* (London, 1850), pp. 141–2; GLRO, H11/HLL/A7/1, Reports of John Conolly, 2nd Report (1841), p. 65; S. Tuke, 'Introductory Observations' to M. Jacobi, *On the Construction and Management of Hospitals for the Insane* (London, 1841), p. xxvii; *British and Foreign Medical Review*, vol. XIV, April 1839, pp. 47–50, vol. XVII, January 1840, pp. 157, 183–6.

16 GCRO, HO22/1/1, 13 August 1823.

17 GCRO, HO22/8/1, *Annual Report* (1825), HO22/1/1, 2 January 1833, 2 April 1838, 24 June 1839, 6 April 1840, 21 June, 11 October, 27 December

1841, 5 April 1843, 4 March 1844, HO22/3/1, 28 May 1830, 15 May 1833, HO22/3/2, 11 January 1836, 12 August 1839, 27 April 1840, 23 February 1841; L.D. Smith, '"A Worthy Feeling Gentleman": Samuel Hitch at Gloucester Asylum, 1828–47', in H. Freeman and G.E. Berrios (eds), *150 Years of British Psychiatry, 1841–1991*, vol. II, *The Aftermath*, pp. 479–99 (London, 1996); BPP 1836, vol. XLI, *County Lunatic Asylums, Returns*, p. 8.

18 DCRO, Forston House (4), 4 January, Michaelmas 1836, *Reports of Visiting Justices* (Epiphany 1838), pp. 4–5, (Epiphany 1839), p. 3, (Epiphany 1840), p. 6, (Epiphany 1842), p. 14, (Epiphany 1843), pp. 18–20, (Epiphany 1844), pp. 19–20; BPP 1836, vol. XLI, *County Lunatic Asylums, Returns*, p. 7.

19 C. Crommelinck, *Rapport sur les Hospices d'Aliénés de l'Angleterre, de la France et de l'Allemagne* (Courtrai, 1842), pp. 66; WRCRO, C85/108, 13th Report (1832), p. 3, C85/107, 31 December 1836, 31 December 1837, 31 December 1840; C85/114, 25th Report (1844), p. 17, 27th Report (1846), p. 6; BPP 1836, vol. XLI, *Returns*, p. 31.

20 WRCRO, C85/107, 31 December 1837, 31 December 1840, C85/114, 25th Report (1844), pp. 13–15, 27th Report (1846), p. 6.

21 Halliday, *General View*, pp. 19–24; BPP 1836, vol. XLI, *Returns*, pp. 3, 5, 6, 9, 11, 25, 29.

22 Halliday, *General View*, pp. 21–4; *Report of the Metropolitan Commissioners in Lunacy to the Lord Chancellor* (1844), pp. 14–16, 128–33; SuCRO, B106/10/4.4 (1), Suffolk Asylum, 1st Report (1839), p. 5; NkCRO, SAH 137, 9 September 1842, 29 August 1843.

23 NRL, qL 3648, Nottingham Asylum, 8th Report (1818); Suffolk Asylum, 1st Report, p. 5; Pliny Earle, *A Visit to Thirteen Asylums for the Insane in Europe* (Philadelphia, 1841), pp. 62–4; BPP 1836, vol. XLI, *Returns*, pp. 3, 6.

24 J. Hemingway, *History of the City of Chester* (Chester, 1831), vol. II, p. 228; Earle, *Visit to Thirteen Asylums*, p. 64; DCRO, Forston House (4), Easter 1842; SCRO, D550/4, 26 December 1829, 30 February 1830; LPL, *Report of the Medical Officers* (1842), p. 5; Crommelinck, *Rapport sur les Hospices*, p. 148; NCRO, SO/HO/1/3/3, 17 August 1842, 20 December 1843, 6 March 1844; LAO, LAWN 1/1/3, 22 June 1835, LAWN 1/1/4, 19 February 1838; BCRO, LB/1/1, 5 September 1812; SuCRO, B106/10/4/4 (7), Suffolk Asylum, 7th Report (1840), pp. 4, 10–12.

25 *Report of the Select Committee on Madhouses, with Minutes of Evidence* (1815), p. 180; LAO, LAWN 1/1/4, 14 April 1841; GCRO, HO22/1/1, 1 August 1823, 24 June 1839.

26 *The Times*, 30 October 1834; SuCRO, Acc2697, 19 January 1837; R.G. Hill, *Total Abolition of Personal Restraint in the Treatment of the Insane* (London, 1839), pp. 10, 86–7, 102–3.

27 *The Times*, 30 October 1834; NkCRO, SAH 3, 25 October 1819, 28 March 1821, SAH 4, 25 October, 29 November 1824, 26 September 1825, SAH 5, 29 February 1836, SAH 128, 31 July 1843, SAH 137, 9, 15 September 1842, 19, 23 May, 29 August 1843, SAH 141, 22 August 1844, 22 January 1846.

28 W.A.F. Browne, *What Asylums Were, Are, and Ought to Be* (Edinburgh, 1837; reprinted London, 1991), pp. 191–7, 229–31 (main quotation, p. 229); A. Scull (ed.), *The Asylum as Utopia: W.A.F. Browne and the Mid-Nineteenth Century Consolidation of Psychiatry* (London, 1991).

29 W.L. Parry-Jones, *The Trade in Lunacy* (London, 1972); C. Mackenzie, *Psychiatry for the Rich: A History of Ticehurst Asylum, 1792–1917* (London, 1992), pp. 41–4, 67–70, 140–1; L.D. Smith, 'To Cure Those Afflicted with the Disease of Insanity: Thomas Bakewell and Spring Vale Asylum', *History of Psychiatry*, vol. IV (1993), pp. 121–4.

30 SCRO, D550/2, 5 December 1818; *Lonsdale Magazine*, February 1821, p. 43; NkCRO, SAH 3, 26 January 1818; NCRO, SO/HO/1/3/2, 30 November 1826.

31 W. White, *History, Gazetteer, and Directory of Staffordshire* (Sheffield, 1834), p. 136; Browne, *What Asylums Were, Are, and Ought to Be*, pp. 230–1.

32 LAO, LAWN 1/1/3, 14 May 1832, 1 September 1834, 19 January 1835, 21 March 1836, 12 June 1837, LAWN 1/1/5, 29 August 1842; LPL, *Report of the Medical Officers* (1841), pp. 11–12; WRCRO, C85/114, 25th Report (1844), p. 17; DCRO, *Annual Reports* (Epiphany 1843), p. 20, (Epiphany 1844), p. 18 (quotation); CCRO, DDX 97/2, 27 February 1844; NCRO, SO/HO/1/3/3, 5 August 1839.

33 LAO, LAWN 1/1/4, 8 July 1840, Appendix B (29 January 1840), LAWN 1/2/3, 29 May, 23 September 1841; Stanley Royd Hospital, Diary of Dr Gettings, Extracts from Minutes, July 1825; BCRO, LB/1/8, 28 April 1829; SuCRO, Acc 2697, 19 January 1837, B106/10/4.4 (5), 5th Report (1843), p. 10; GCRO, HO22/8/1, *Annual Report* (1842); NCRO, SO/HO/1/3/3, 29 June 1842; LLSL, Lincoln Asylum, 18th Report (1842), pp. 7–8, 21st Report (1845), p. 4; LPL, *Report of the Medical Officers* (1841), p. 11.

34 GCRO, HO22/8/1, *Annual Report* (1841); Crommelinck, *Rapport sur les Hospices*, p. 114; LLSL, Lincoln Asylum, 18th Report (1842), pp. 7–8, 21st Report (1845), p. 4; LAO, LAWN 1/1/4, 25 October 1841; *The Lancet*, 20 November 1841, p. 276, 15 January 1842, p. 545.

35 LPL, *Report of the Medical Officers* (1841), p. 11; SuCRO, B106/10/4.4 (5), 5th Report (1843), p. 10; WRCRO, C85/114, 25th Report, p. 15; LLSL, Lincoln Asylum, 18th Report (1842), pp. 8–9; LAO, LAWN 1/1/3, 6 December 1830, LAWN 1/1/4, 14 October 1839, 30 March 1840, 8 February, 8 July 1841, LAWN 1/1/5, 5 May, 27 October 1845, LAWN 1/2/3, 9 October 1839, 12 July 1842; DCRO, *Report of Visiting Justices* (Epiphany 1843), pp. 21–2; GCRO, HO22/8/1, *Annual Report* (1841); Crommelinck, *Rapport sur les Hospices*, pp. 112–15.

8

With Due Restraint

I assert then in plain and distinct terms, that in a properly constructed building, with a sufficient number of suitable attendants, restraint is never necessary, never justifiable, and always injurious, in all cases of Lunacy whatever.[1]

Nothing in the history of the asylum in the first half of the nineteenth century epitomizes the ongoing dynamic between custody and cure like the use, misuse and disuse of mechanical restraint. The first county asylums were established at a time when restraint was an integral element of treatment and management, accepted and regarded as indispensable. By the time that asylum provision was made compulsory in 1845, restraint and its proponents had been vilified as inhumane and oppressive. The practice was being driven out of public asylums, and those who continued to adhere to it were construed as reactionary and forced onto the defensive. The treatment of insanity had been brought into the arena of reform of perceived social abuses, and a new orthodoxy established whose tenets were to remain unchallengeable for several decades.

The ideological triumph of the non-restraint movement, and its success in shaping psychiatric and public opinion, has greatly affected the perception of the pre-abolition asylum, down to the present day. A whole mythology has developed about the evils and cruelties routinely and systematically practised in the public and private asylums of the eighteenth and early nineteenth centuries, alongside received ideas about the physical and material conditions within them.[2] The perceptions have been perpetuated by those who came later and sought to contrast the achievements of a supposedly more progressive age with the dark days that preceded it. This is not to contend that the mythology is unfounded, for there were indeed numerous examples which could support it. However, there is a serious risk of oversimplification, associated with the tendency to interpret earlier circumstances by current standards rather than in their historical context.

THE ERA OF COERCION

In the charitable asylums of the eighteenth century, the use of mechanical restraint had been commonplace. Its legitimacy was recognized in house rules which required staff regularly to inspect and rub with flannel the hands and feet of patients chained or otherwise confined. Writers on insanity prescribed restraint as an essential tool in the mad-doctor's repertoire and a necessary element in the regimen of the madhouse. The system of 'mild discipline' advocated by Dr John Ferriar of the Manchester Lunatic Hospital included confinement of the legs and arms of the 'furious' and shutting in a darkened cell. Where there was dissent on humanitarian grounds, it would be more about the means of restraint than a questioning of the essential premise. John Haslam, for example, pointed out the deficiencies and discomforts of the strait waistcoat, but advocated instead the use of manacles to the wrists.[3]

At the archetypal public asylum, Bethlem, various forms of restraint were in common usage, particularly at night-time, and were the basis of the critical notoriety which followed the exposures of the 1815 Select Committee. At the ostensibly more progressive St Luke's the situation differed only in degree. The earliest provincial public asylum, the Norwich Bethel, was actively employing a range of implements by the 1750s, including hand-cuffs, padlocks, chains, strait waistcoats and restraint chairs. Although constitutions spoke of mildness and gentleness, practice was similar at the subscription asylums, like York, Manchester and Liverpool. When the small Leicester Asylum, which Thomas Arnold had worked so hard to promote, opened in 1794, it was equipped with a whole panoply of restraint instruments which included strait waistcoats, straps, locks and restraint chairs. There was no perceived dissonance between liberal ideals and custodial practice.[4]

The Rationales for Restraint

The legislators of 1808 and the policy-makers who developed the new generation of asylums had few qualms as to the prospective place of restraint within them. The investigations of the 1815 Select Committee did not question restraint itself, but rather the context in which it occurred and its misuse. Restraint had several rationales, portrayed not only as an essential means of maintaining control, but also as a prerequisite for curative treatment. The excited patient's behavioural excesses had to be checked before medical and moral treatments could be brought to bear. As Haslam expressed it:

> Abundant experience teaches us that restraint is not only necessary as a protection to the patient and to those about him, but that it also contributes to the cure of insanity.

Three decades later, in 1843, George Button of Dorset Asylum put it more emphatically. To achieve a cure, it was necessary to subdue and shorten the 'violence of the paroxysm'; the habit of ungovernable 'involuntary impulses' had to be broken, and restraint was the quickest and most effective means of doing this. With the whole basis of restraint under question in the early 1840s, its apologists offered a therapeutic defence. The argument was stated succinctly by Samuel Hadwen, a former house surgeon of Lincoln Asylum. For the 'rational and experienced practitioner', restraint implements formed one of his 'best and most important remedies'; if used with discrimination, the instrument was 'a moral agent of incalculable benefit'.[5]

The perception of restraint as a 'moral agent' was bound up with its punitive properties. It could serve a directly behavioural function for the recipient, acting as a check and deterrent to anti-social acts. It might also deter others who witnessed the discomfort and humiliation. Paul Slade Knight, former superintendent of Lancaster Asylum, suggested in 1827 that all coercion was punishment; to be effective it had to be imposed 'firmly and mildly'. Patients had to be taught 'by the powerful means used' that resistance was useless. Case-notes from several asylums illustrate clearly the administration of restraint as a direct response to bad behaviour, whether or not considered consequential on the mental disorder.[6]

In the most repressive regimes, there was no attempt to camouflage punitive intent. At Liverpool Asylum in the mid-1820s, patients who had expressed dissent or criticized the management or medical staff were subjected to being strapped tight in the restraint chair, strait jacket or both. At Norfolk Asylum, punitive coercion was systematically employed over many years. The tone was set early, in November 1814, when the physician and the surgeon called for more restraint 'to prevent them from tearing their cloathes breaking windows and committing other irregularities'. Mr Caryl, the master, did as instructed and daily had people leg-locked, chained, strait-jacketed, locked in restraint chairs in the yard or strapped in bed. Sharp punishment was the norm, as for James Betts in March 1815:

Broke one of the Iron Bars out of the Fire Guard belonging to the approbation Day room – for which I ordered him to be put to bed and there chained down till he behave better.

The response did not discriminate between the sexes, which Celia Howes found out two months later:

Become very violent and distroyed her own Cap and Two of the other Patients. Therefore orderd her to Bed, and afterwards Lockd her down by one wrist and and one Leg, and orderd her to be keep so till she behavd better.

In countless instances Caryl's patients were dealt with in a similar fashion, for offences which included escape attempts, breaking furniture, destroying clothes or bedding, verbal abuse and assaults on staff or other patients.[7]

The main basis of justification for restraint, though, was preventive, in particular to restrict chances for the patient to harm himself, other patients or those caring for him. Even in the most liberal and progressive institutions, like the York Retreat, restraint would be imposed without question for these reasons, as Samuel Tuke readily acknowledged. In a county pauper asylum, the authorities were not prepared to tolerate behaviour that might pose a risk. For Paul Slade Knight, the purpose of the restraint instruments he employed was that 'the patient is effectively prevented from tearing or destroying things, or taking off his clothes, nor can he strike so as to effect any injury. . .'. Under Knight's superintendence at Lancaster, determined restraint was frequently imposed to quell violent behaviour. In the case of Martha Whewell (53), her unruliness after admission in October 1817 led to several days' confinement in 'the Chair'. Two months later, after some improvement when she was 'sometimes calm & reasonable', there were still times when:

she becomes violent – abusive, spitting at every one, striking them &c, so as to render it necessary to be put in a state of Coercion – in which state she continues, for the most part, several days; when the paroxysm abates, and she is gradually more calm.

Also in 1817, Elizabeth Roberts (36) was 'so violent as to require almost constant Coercion in the Strait Waistcoat'. Their cases could be replicated many times over.[8]

Suicide was always a sensitive issue for superintendents. Coroners' inquests were far from welcome, even though asylum staff were usually exonerated. Failed attempts were likely to be followed by restraint. William Greaves (45), a Sheffield silversmith confined in Wakefield

Asylum, tried twice in one day to hang himself using a handkerchief in August 1821 and was then 'secured'. Restraint was the routine response at Norfolk Asylum to acts of self-injury. One patient, Phoebe Land, caused real concerns in July 1815. She made several suicide attempts, for which she was first put in hand locks and then the strait waistcoat. After more attempts whilst in restraint, there were further measures:

> Ordered Mrs Land to be very closely locked in the day and both hands and legs to be locked at night, and to have someone sleep in the room with her.

Some self-harming behaviours left little scope for inaction. In July 1820, at Norfolk, John Long tried to cut his throat several times, and then attempted to pick his eye out with a pin. Even after his hands were locked to the bed, he still managed to remove one eye and damage the other during the night. In 1823, Sarah Fenton's hands were confined night and day after she cut her tongue with an old pair of scissors, her third suicidal act in a few days. Other perceived harmful acts might also be curtailed by mechanical coercion. George Button at Dorset Asylum referred in 1843 to cases 'unfit for publication' because of the 'disgustful practices' to which the patients had become addicted; only restraint could prevent a descent into 'the lowest state of human degradation'.[9]

Considerations of risk and unpredictability led some asylum managers to impose restraint automatically on newly admitted patients. This occurred at Nottingham after the incident in December 1816 when two patients were killed by two others. Although the inquest attached no blame to the director Thomas Morris or the keepers, the governors wanted no more chances taken and ordered Morris in future to place every new patient under 'proper restraint' until 'their temper and disposition can be sufficiently ascertained'. At Lancaster, it was for many years the 'established custom' to put each new patient under restraint at night; they were only released when, 'from familiarity with their symptoms', it was thought they could be trusted without it. Restraint would also be employed to prevent escapes, or as a response to patients' attempts to abscond. As Kathleen Jones has pointed out, the 1808 Act actively encouraged the practice of restraint, by imposing heavy fines on keepers who failed to prevent escapes.[10]

Nocturnal restraint permeated much wider than the precaution of securing untried new patients. Apprehension of night-time danger or disorder led to the widespread chaining or strapping of people into bed. At Norfolk Asylum in 1818, the master admitted he was 'under the necessity' of keeping two-thirds of the patients in wrist locks fixed to the bed at night. Considerable numbers were secured in their beds in Stafford and Lancaster Asylums. At Lancaster these included all those considered violent or who suffered from epilepsy. Epilepsy posed a particular problem, because of the risk of accident during a fit, which continued to provide a strong defensive argument for advocates of selective restraint. Safety and security were not the only motives, however. Staff convenience and administrative economy were significant influences. With a normal complement of only one keeper to a ward, it had to be ensured that his or her night-time rest was not affected by patients wandering or getting into other mischief.[11]

Patients, however, were not necessarily unwilling recipients of restraint. Some, particularly among those with recurrent complaints, developed a degree of insight into their condition. They might even express gratitude for having been restrained. Certainly there were instances when patients actually requested it for their own safety, as Samuel Tuke pointed out in 1842. Slade Knight had earlier argued that 'strict coercion' in some cases contributed to the patient's tranquillity and comfort, and frequently they would 'earnestly. . .solicit coercion'. An illustration of this earnestness, and of a suitably prompt response, was recorded at Norfolk Asylum in 1843:

> William Thurston is again today much excited and demanded in great rage to have the Hand Muffs put on himself ('to prevent mischief') to which he was indulged – and had it not been complied with he would have fulfilled his promise.

Some sought confinement to prevent self-injury. At Lincoln in 1824, the 'very melancholy' Elizabeth Rust asked to be restrained 'or she should do some mischief to herself – for she was tired of living'. According to C.C. Corsellis, immersed in the battle to defend restraint in 1839, there were often instances where patients realized their symptoms were returning and requested restraint, proof that when their judgement was clear they could recognize 'how beneficial it had been to them'. Allowing for the exaggeration of a debating point, it is nonetheless clear that some patients did accept restraint as an appropriate response to their excesses.[12]

The Implements of Restraint

The contrivances employed to restrain patients varied greatly in the extent to which they constricted movement. The coercion chair was probably the most effective means of achieving this. It came into common use at most public asylums, and attracted particular notoriety when the specifics of restraint came under scrutiny. The chair could be adapted to increase or reduce the extent of confinement, by altering the number and distribution of straps or locks. One of its main advocates, William Ellis, considered it a 'very convenient and easy mode of confinement'. Early in his reign at Wakefield, twelve were acquired to confine refractory patients. He took the chair to Hanwell; by the time he left, 28 were available. According to his son in 1840, Ellis had mainly used them for epileptic or 'imbecile' patients, likely to sustain sores if confined to bed. This contention, however, was part of an attempt to rescue his father's name from tarnish by the non-restraint zealots. Under Ellis's successor at Hanwell, James Millingen, their use multiplied and 40 were later dismantled. Corsellis, who followed Ellis at Wakefield, had also continued and extended the use of the chair for containing the more intractable patients, well after others had abandoned it.[13]

Chains or manacles could offer an equally tight control on the person's movements, particularly when joined to the wall or immovable furniture. The more liberal-minded superintendents or visitors had qualms about chains, because of their prison connotations, but this did not preclude their use at Stafford, Nottingham and in the notorious 'warm rooms' at Lancaster. Chains were particularly prevalent in the more custodial rural county asylums. At Bedford, patients were still being chained to the wall in the 1840s. At Norfolk, in its early years, people were frequently chained in or onto the bed, and to indoor or outdoor furniture. The visiting surgeon, Dalrymple, reported with satisfaction in July 1814 that 'no patient was chained except when in bed'. A typical recipient was Thomas Cook, who on New Year's Day in 1815 threw his chamber pot at the 'porter' trying to give him his supper; Caryl 'ordered him to be keep to is bed chained for two days'. One persistent offender, Robert Russell, received a double punishment in April 1815 for destroying his jacket and waistcoat; Caryl ordered that he be 'Keep Lockd into the day chair of day time and cross lockd to his bed'. Numerous patients, whose deviant actions were usually construed as misdemeanours rather than symptoms, were dealt with in similar fashion. Only in 1843 were the chains grudgingly removed from the beds and the seats in the day-rooms and yards at Thorpe, at the behest of the Metropolitan Commissioners.[14]

Leather straps were frequently used to secure patients to chairs or beds. Straps, belts or chains, sometimes in conjunction, could also provide less restrictive localized restraint. Use of the hands might be constrained by wrist locks or hand-cuffs, still leaving the person free to walk around. Alternatively, locomotion could be restricted by ankle or leg locks, or 'hobbles', leaving the hands free. Other contrivances which offered partial prevention included hand-muffs and long leather sleeves, particularly advocated by Slade Knight – 'by far the best mode of securing a violent lunatic I can imagine'. The sleeves would be attached to a belt across his chest, fastened across the shoulders by a strap with a lock, and across his back by straps between the elbows. If accompanied by leg locks, 'the patient will be rendered almost powerless'; they could wear the sleeves 'for months' without sustaining any injury. Each superintendent tended to have his preferred means. Some, like Slade Knight and Ellis, invented new items or adapted old ones to meet their requirements. Ellis's preference was for wide canvas sleeves, the 'most simple and least objectionable mode of confinement', with leather used only to cover the hands.[15]

The strait waistcoat had the advantage of only confining the upper part of the body, leaving the person free to move around. To its advocates, it was the most effective and also the most humane means of restraint; to others it was too constricting and uncomfortable. Joseph Mason Cox concluded in 1804 that every other means 'must yield' to the improved strait waistcoat. For George Nesse Hill, in 1814, it was an 'admirable contrivance'. Samuel Tuke, conceding that coercion was at times a 'necessary evil', considered the waistcoat less irritating and degrading than other means, because those confined in it could walk about the room or lie on their bed 'at pleasure'. Others were far from convinced. John Haslam argued that its disadvantages outweighed any advantages. In particular, he pointed out, the patient was unable to feed himself, was likely to accumulate nasal mucus, and 'cannot assist himself in his evacuations', thus becoming dirty. Of the county asylum practitioners, Slade Knight's experience led him to conclude that the strait waistcoat had many powerful objections, not least that 'in hot weather particularly it is very oppressive to the patient, it cramps him exceedingly, and is at all times peculiarly offensive'. William Ellis adopted an equivocal position. When laying out his principles, in 1815, in support of his interest in the Wakefield post, he related its efficacy to timescales. The waistcoat was 'better than any other mode' for short periods of confinement, but long periods were distressing for very powerful or violent patients because of the heat and constriction of the arms.[16]

The strait waistcoat was probably the most widely employed instrument in public asylums, and increasingly was seen to symbolize restraint itself. Its use became challenged, however, after problems arose. A 'severe accident' happened at Norfolk Asylum in December 1820 to a patient confined in a strait waistcoat; questions were asked, and its use there abandoned in favour of chains and belts. A significant event occurred at Lincoln in February 1829, when a pauper patient, William Scrivinger, was found dead from strangulation after being strapped to the bed during the night in a strait waistcoat and left unattended. Although the waistcoat was not abandoned after the investigation, tight limitations were imposed on its use. The circumstance proved highly influential in shaping events leading to the abolition of restraint at Lincoln.[17]

The Prevalence of Restraint

One of the more imponderable questions is how extensive was the employment of mechanical restraint in the pre-reform asylum. With one or two exceptions, records have not survived and probably were not kept. There certainly was considerable variation between asylums, and changes over time within the same institution. The indications are that the persistent use of restraint permeated the asylum regimes in rural counties like Norfolk, Bedfordshire, Kent and Cornwall.[18] There is also strong evidence that those in industrial Staffordshire and Lancashire were among the leading exponents. Then, of course, the reformers at Lincoln and Hanwell were able to highlight the previous prevalence of restraint in their establishments. The inevitable conclusion is that its practice was virtually universal, differing only in degree.

Thomas Prichard, the first superintendent of the Northampton subscription asylum when it opened in 1838, travelled about to form his ideas before commencing in post. He noted the amount of restraint employed at Leicester and particularly Bedford Asylum, where he found the patients 'in so horrid and deplorable a State' that the 'strenuous. . .asseverations' of its governor alleging this to be unavoidable almost led him to resign before he started. Thirty patients were subsequently transferred from Bedford to Northampton, most coming in 'under restraint of every description and many ironed arms & legs'. An inventory taken at Bedford Asylum in June 1834 provides ample evidence to support Prichard's impressions. In the women's gallery, there were:

2 pair of belts and Gloves; 6 Muffs and Straps; 2 Collars;
6 New Strait Waistcoats; 12 Old ones;
3 pair of list shoes; 12 wrist locks;
11 pair of Police handcuffs.

In one of the men's galleries, there were:

5 pair of Hobbles or confinements for the feet; 2 Collars;
7 pair of Hand Cuffs; 7 wrist locks; 3 Leg locks;
4 pair of belt and Gloves; 4 pair of Straps; A long Chain.

Even if exhaustive, this was a formidable array for a small asylum.[19]

Bedford, though exhibiting one of the most austere regimes, was not unique. When Gaskell and de Vitrie took up appointment at Lancaster in 1841, they found 30 people confined in handcuffs, leg locks or strait waistcoats, 30 or 40 chained down in the 'warm rooms', and a larger number secured in bed at night. The extent of Lancaster's coercive system was well illustrated by a remarkable collection of implements, retained for exhibition after abolition, comprising more than 200 items which included: large quantities of leather straps and body belts; numerous pairs of hand-cuffs; leg locks; leather sleeves, gloves and muffs; body fastenings made of heavy chains covered with leather; and two leather face muzzles. A very similar situation faced James Wilkes when he took over at Stafford, also in 1841. His predecessor, John Garrett, had kept weekly lists of the names and numbers of patients under restraint. In the mid-1830s, between 20 and 30 at a time had been recorded, though Wilkes was sure the figures were a considerable under-representation. In addition, individual keepers had habitually placed patients in restraint without express sanction, in order to assert control and maintain order in their galleries.[20]

The theoretical premise was that, if employed appropriately, restraint would continue only as long as the patient remained agitated or violent, then be removed as he became calmer. The surviving detailed records for Stafford Asylum, even with their limitations, demonstrate how far practice fell below this ideal. Between 1818 and the end of 1841, when restraint was effectively abolished, 350 patients (out of a total of almost 2700 admitted) were recorded as being restrained at some point. However, many of these experienced more than one period of confinement; for some there were multiple episodes. The records also indicate a significant number of people kept constantly restrained for long periods, as shown in Table 3. Despite their under-representation, the Stafford records were remarkably frank. By any criteria, it would be difficult to provide therapeutic justification for so many instances of prolonged restraint, and particularly for the twenty confined for more than a year. Of those restrained for more than five years, it is striking that all were women. Dorothy Myatt was in constant restraint between 1823 and 1839, and then intermittently until abolition in March 1842 when she was the last woman liberated. Sarah Mason was held for thirteen years, between 1821 and 1834, as was Frances Tunnicliffe, who remained in restraint from 1825 until she died in June 1838.[21]

Table 3 The employment of continual mechanical restraint, Staffordshire General Lunatic Asylum, 1818–1841

Time period	*Numbers of patients*
4–12 weeks	98
12–26 weeks	32
6–12 months	19
1–5 years	13
5+ years	7

The Stafford evidence of repeated and enduring confinement highlights the reality that restraint affected more people than those directly subjected to it. Its role as a deterrent, an example and an indicator of the nature of power relations within the institution could not fail to be influential right through the asylum population. What eventually led to the movement for abolition was not just the intrinsic nature of restraint, but what it signified and the difficulties and abuses that accompanied it. These produced a growing climate of doubts, not only about its morality, but also about its therapeutic value and its efficacy as an agent of behavioural management.

The Limitations of Restraint

Mechanical restraint sometimes failed to prevent the evils it was intended to confront. Successful suicides showed its limitations. A male patient at Nottingham in 1818, with one hand secured to the bed, managed to tear his sheet and strangle himself. At Wakefield in 1822, a man held in a refractory cell, tightly restrained with leather straps and belts, his hands locked into leather pouches, successfully hanged himself after gnawing through one of the pouches to get his fingers out and then unbuckle a strap. At Norfolk Asylum, widespread restraint only partially curbed tendencies toward self-harm. It also did not prevent patients from causing damage to furniture and equipment or one another. On the contrary, in many instances it increased the victim's anger and provoked him into violence.[22]

As critics like Conolly and Hill later pointed out, resentment of restraint often occasioned the disorders it was supposed to curb. The actual process of placing a patient in restraint might lead to violence on both sides, or what Hill called a 'ruffianly and exciting struggle'. He referred, in 1840, to earlier days at Lincoln Asylum when there were: 'standing fights between patients and Attendants of attendants first giving the Patient a good licking and then chaining him up and of the attendants stating such practice to be necessary'. In a different context, William Ellis acknowledged the inherent violence in the situation. He argued that, although mildness and forbearance were desirable in applying 'coercive measures', it was sometimes necessary to 'assemble such a force that the appearance of the persons alone may prevent all opposition'. The problem with this approach was that the boundary between threat and action was always liable to be crossed in the heat of a confrontation.[23]

Ellis's concept of a show of strength was rather more subtle than the way things could operate in practice. At Norfolk Asylum, the use of force was for a long time overt rather than covert. In early 1815, the master's patience was severely tested by several of his reluctant inmates. Jemima Dobby had already succeeded in breaking a leg lock; two nights later, Caryl was driven to drastic action:

> Proved so violent in going to Bed that the Patients maid could do nothing with her – she forst two of the chaines of the Bedstead – I was under the necessity of going and locking her down by both Hand and one of her Leg with a box of the face in to bargin.

Caryl would not tell his staff to do anything he would not do himself, as Susanna Page discovered later in the same year:

> became very violent and abusive, I was under the Necessity of forseing her to bed in which she gave battle – I took her by the Neck and forsed.

The 1826 exposures of the regime at Liverpool Asylum showed how easily the application of restraint could degenerate into a violent incident. Patients were manhandled into strait waistcoats or restraint chairs, and the straps deliberately drawn so tight as to cause severe pain. They were beaten with the straps, and even subjected to indecent humiliation. Similar problems were occurring at Stafford around the same time; two keepers were disciplined for beating a patient with restraint straps and another for dipping a man's head into a bucket of water whilst putting him under restraint. These detected instances were indicative of a much wider problem at Stafford. Whilst such examples do not prove widespread abuse, they give a fair indication of how matters could degenerate.[24]

Under the old coercive regime, there is little doubt that the scope for abuses was considerable. To a large extent this was related to poor staffing levels. It was normal to have one keeper in charge of a ward, containing up to 30 patients; on a 'refractory' ward, they might sometimes have an assistant. The keeper was effectively responsible day and night, seven days a week. The pressures were immense in looking after a disparate group of disturbed, noisy, incoherent and often agitatated patients, whose symptoms were barely controlled by medication. Left largely to their own devices, with limited outside supervision, keepers might have little choice but to resort to selective restraint in order to retain control and protect themselves.[25]

Ultimately, the upsurge of opinion against the restraint-based regime was related almost as much to its effects on the staff and the management who imposed it as on the unwilling recipients. Critics were able to speak of how the continuing 'oppression' of patients led to the demoralization and even the brutalization of the staff. As James Wilkes pointed out, the evil of the system was related not only to the extensive coercion of the patients, but to the whole character and image of the asylum. Extensive restraint was taking place in dark, drab insitutions, with high barred windows, iron doors, strongly guarded fireplaces and staples in the walls for confinement to the furniture. Thomas Bakewell's predictive imagery of the 'mighty prison' in which helpless lunatics would be closely confined had been fulfilled. The coercive system and its surroundings had come to dominate the people within. With the remorseless accumulation of chronic, 'incurable', and 'hopeless' patients, there came an increasing concern that the asylum regime had become sterile and anti-therapeutic. Thus, not only was the public asylum falling short of its key objectives, but it had become patently an illiberal institution needing re-evaluation in a consciously reforming age.[26]

THE STRUGGLE FOR ABOLITION

Mechanical restraint and coercion increasingly came to symbolize the old system of managing the insane. The theoretical basis for the abandonment of restraint stemmed directly from the new orientation toward a milder approach to patient management, which had been exemplified by the work of the York Retreat and expounded by Samuel Tuke. Several historians have, like John Walton and Nancy Tomes, identified non-restraint as an integral element of moral treatment. Most recently, Asa Briggs in *The History of Bethlem* has conflated the two terms and used them interchangeably. However, although there was a clear linkage, it took several decades to coalesce fully. Mechanical restraint remained in use at the Retreat long after Tuke's *Description*, and at other institutions considered to operate a mild system, without their humanitarian credentials being challenged. The growing emphasis on the techniques of moral treatment, though, did bring an inevitable questioning of the benefits of physical coercion.[27]

The misgivings of lunacy reformers about mechanical restraint had been heightened by evidence to the Select Committee of 1815, particularly the revelations as to practices at Bethlem. The visitors and superintendents of the new county asylums would consequently proclaim their policies of kind and humane treatment, which included the minimization of what William Ellis in 1822 referred to as 'those coercive measures formerly used in other Asylums, but which have been so justly reprobated'.[28] However, the difficulty was that superintendents and staff could see no viable alternative means to control aberrant behaviour. Restraint therefore remained in general use through the 1820s and 1830s, whilst concerns were growing about both its efficacy and its moral justification.

The abolition of mechanical restraint, the events surrounding it, the controversies it engendered, the consequences for patients and staff, and its place in the history of psychiatry, have all received a good deal of attention from historians and from psychiatrists interested in the development of their specialty. Mythologies have developed, particularly around the key protagonists and their achievements. One of them, John Conolly, has been elevated to quasi-heroic status by his successors.[29] Whilst not seeking to detract from Conolly's well-documented achievements at Hanwell, the following sequence will concentrate more on the train of events at Lincoln Asylum and subsequent responses at the provincial county asylums.

The Lincoln Saga

It is significant that the movement for the reduction and later the abolition of restraint originated, not in a county asylum, but at Lincoln Asylum, founded and funded by public charitable subscription. Its clientele was not dissimilar to that of joint asylums like Nottingham, with a mixture of private, charitable and pauper patients. Lincoln's management arrangements, however, allowed more scope for innovation. Independent of control by the county magistracy, the governors could determine their own policies. By 1830, the asylum was graced with a large number of governors, in excess of 150. Most took little more than a passing interest in asylum affairs, however, and a small group of men was able to dominate key areas of policy formation. The most prominent was Dr Edward Parker Charlesworth, one of the asylum's three physicians. An assiduous attender of weekly Board meetings, he was prepared to spend much of his time dealing with the routine minutiae of asylum management. A prominent local radical political activist, Charlesworth became for many years the driving force behind the process of reform at Lincoln Asylum.[30]

Charlesworth's preoccupation with improving conditions in the asylum, and amelioration of the harsher coercive techniques, began early on. His initial concerns centred around the lack of means to classify patients, resulting from a shortage of funds. In December 1821, he protested that the consequence was that patients were 'on many occasions confined with chains'. In early 1823, he complained:

> The Association of the men has now become so insupportably inconvenient, that some are kept almost constantly in manacles, or apart in the maniacal cells, to protect the weak and quiet from the outrages of the strong. . .

By 1827, his position and influence within the Board had advanced to a point where he was able to carry through a detailed scheme of classification, accompanied by a complete reorganization and expansion of the asylum's accommodation. With this achieved, and the improvements published in his 1828 book *Remarks on the Treatment of the Insane and the Management of Lunatic Asylums*, Charlesworth had staked his claim to a position as an authority on mental disorder and on progressive approaches to its management and treatment.[31]

In the book, Charlesworth promoted himself and Lincoln Asylum as adherents to the principles of moral treatment. Attention was to be given to healthy exercise, pleasant surroundings and useful occupation. Patients were to be addressed as if they were rational. It was essential, he said, to maintain a 'uniformly kind demeanour' toward them. At the same time, he described candidly the means of restraint and coercion in use at Lincoln – leather belts, wrist locks, muffs, hobbles and the strait waistcoat. Charlesworth suggested, however, that their employment was in decline, and advocated safeguards to limit improper use. His writings betrayed a growing concern about the obvious inconsistencies between a liberal intent and a custodial reality.[32]

Charlesworth's implementation of piecemeal practical reforms had gained a clear momentum by 1830. He promoted more open access to the asylum, to guard against inappropriate practices behind closed doors. Weekly inspections by Board members were initiated, along with a more open visiting policy. It was restraint, though, which increasingly engaged Charlesworth's attention. He obtained agreement to have the instruments kept in a central place, where their use could be monitored. He led the governors to begin to question the use of the strait waistcoat. His campaign received a fortuitous boost with the death of William Scrivinger in 1829 from strangulation in a strait waistcoat. This proved a watershed event in the march toward abolition, with regulations immediately being instituted to restrict use of the waistcoat.[33]

Charlesworth was an energetic and determined advocate for any chosen cause. His outspoken and forthright approach attracted opponents, and enemies. One of these was the asylum's first director, Thomas Fisher. Charlesworth managed to have him ousted during 1830 after a long-running and bitter row, partly fuelled by accusations that Fisher had made excessive use of restraint. After his departure, a succession of young, recently qualified men were appointed as director, or 'house surgeon' as the post was re-named. They all fell under Charlesworth's influence, as he continued to make the running in determining asylum policy. Expectations on them were made explicit in the Annual Report for 1831: 'the fair measure of a Superintendent's ability in the treatment of such patients, will be found in the small number of restraints which are imposed'. During 1832, the asylum's rules were revised, confirming stricter control on the use of restraint and the requirement to record all instances. Charlesworth's position, at this point, was essentially to seek a mitigation of restraint by the elimination or replacement of the harsher instruments.[34]

The issue of restraint was now becoming the yardstick by which the success of the asylum and its officers was judged. The 1833 report declared it 'unceasingly an object' to dispense with or improve the instruments. During Samuel Hadwen's fifteen months as house surgeon, after his appointment in April 1834, there was a marked reduction in their use. By August, periods of several days were passing without any patients in restraint. On his departure the Board expressed 'high approbation' of the 'very small proportion of instances of restraint' during his time in post. When Robert Gardiner Hill, aged 24, replaced Hadwen in July 1835, his path had virtually been mapped out. A Lincolnshire man, qualified in London the previous year, Hill had been appointed house surgeon to the

Dispensary in Lincoln. His potential was spotted by Charlesworth, who encouraged him to apply for the vacancy at the asylum, despite (or maybe because of) his inexperience. Hill was clearly ambitious and saw the opportunity to make an impression and a name for himself.[35]

Whilst Hill's role in what followed cannot be minimized, it has to be said that he was presented with favourable circumstances, and given ongoing guidance and support by Charlesworth. Conscious of his own limited knowledge and experience in the field of mental disorder, Hill initially spent several hours each day in the role of attendant in order to obtain a clear picture of the asylum's operation. As he later recalled, he saw enough to conclude that restraint could be dispensed with. Within a short time after he took up office, periods of several weeks were passing without the use of restraint. By early 1836, the 'regularity and order' in the house was visible, and visitors were impressed with the near-elimination of coercion.[36]

Hill proceeded cautiously over the ensuing months. An earlier achievement of complete cessation was hampered by a delay in opening a new gallery for disturbed female patients. On the male side, sixteen months elapsed down to April 1837 without any restraint being employed, apart from a brief period of a few hours when Hill was absent. He tentatively suggested that it 'may be possible' to conduct an asylum without recourse to any instruments whatever, with these being replaced with 'undivided personal attention' toward the patient. The Board showed appreciation for what Hill already had achieved by adding £20 to his annual salary. Matters were now moving steadily toward a climax. In the next Annual Report in March 1838, Charlesworth, as chairman of the Governors, spoke of the imminence of the 'bold conception' of going beyond mitigation to a formal abolition of restraint. The benefits were, he considered, beyond question:

> This striking process of amelioration affords good encouragement for persevering in a system so successfully commenced; and the more so, as a corresponding decrease of violence, accidents, and revolting habits have accompanied the change.

Any possible reservations or sources for dissent were being laid aside.[37]

The final declaration of the unique achievement came in the middle of 1838 at a public lecture in the Lincoln Mechanics' Institute, whose president Sir Edward Bromhead was also a vice-president of the asylum and a close friend of Charlesworth. On June 21st, Robert Gardiner Hill proudly proclaimed his achievement at the nearby asylum:

Turn your eyes to that noble Edifice, which is at once one of the greatest ornaments of modern date, which this City can boast, and a lasting memorial of your charity and benevolence. Thence are derived all my materials: there I have not only matured the plans, but have also witnessed and rejoiced in their complete success. There at this moment they are in full operation; and, I may be allowed to state, that they have already produced results beyond my most sanguine expectations.

He contrasted the former cruel treatment of lunatics with the enlightened methods exemplified by the York Retreat, now expanded upon at Lincoln. Without false modesty and with due sense of history, he declared: 'I wish to complete what Pinel began.' Hill boldly crowned his argument with the assertion that would echo down the years, that restraint was 'never necessary, never justifiable, and always injurious'. It was, he insisted, possible to achieve the 'total banishment' of restraint instruments and 'all other cruelties whatsoever'.[38]

Publication of the lecture brought the Lincoln experiment to the notice of the wider public and particularly the medical profession. Hill supplemented the lecture with a preface, statistical tables and extensive appendices illustrating the steady diminution of restraint since the asylum's inception. The book attracted considerable attention, following the publication of extracts in *The Lancet* and an enthusiastic review in the *British and Foreign Medical Review*, whose editor, Dr John Conolly of Hanwell Asylum, gave fulsome praise:

In this particular there is apparently no asylum in England which presents so remarkable a model as that of Lincoln. Of all the works that have appeared on the subject of lunatic houses since the publication of Mr Tuke's account of the Retreat, there is none which contains matter more deserving of attention. . .

He anticipated, not without foundation, that Hill's statements 'will be received in many asylums with surprise and even with incredulity'. Conolly had by this time visited Lincoln and had set about replicating its system at Hanwell. He credited his fellow physician Dr Charlesworth with services to 'the cause of humanity and in behalf of the insane', second only to those of 'him who first released them from their chains'. He evidently regarded Hill as little more than an able assistant, though perhaps not going as far as other established alienists who considered him an opportunist upstart.[39]

The declaration of abolition and the ensuing publicity, far from heralding the new dawn, ushered in a period of bitter conflict, both within Lincoln Asylum and in wider asylum and medical circles. The enthusiasm that carried through the reform was not itself sufficient to deal with the consequences. Hill's youthful zeal led him to strive energetically to justify non-restraint and disseminate it through asylumdom, but with a degree of naivety and impetuosity. His mentor Charlesworth was apparently content for Hill to both accept the limelight and deal with the difficulties and the abuse which emanated from those who either felt under personal attack or sought to defend a more conservative ideological position.

The alternative to restraint advocated by Charlesworth and Hill was a higher staff–patient ratio, accompanied by close observation and watchfulness, whereby patients could be prevented from harmful or destructive behaviours before they escalated. If restraint were needed, it was to be by firm and skilful holding by attendants, who were expected to possess an imposing physical presence serving as both a deterrent and a security for agitated and disturbed patients. In reality, the changed role of staff and the expectations on them to manage without their former means brought an increasing vulnerability and feeling of powerlessness. There were distinct signs of a breakdown in order in parts of the asylum, notably in the female refractory North Gallery. The consequence was an upsurge in reported instances of ill-treatment of patients by attendants. During 1839 and early 1840, a veritable procession of staff came and went, some leaving voluntarily, but most dismissed for misconduct. A picture emerged of an institution where controls had lapsed, and staff were increasingly engaged in indisciplined and brutal behaviour.[40]

The very real problems present in Lincoln Asylum drew out the opponents of abolition. Chief among these was another of the asylum's three physicians, Dr William Cookson, whose uncle Dr Alfred Cookson had been a strident opponent of Charlesworth in the 1820s. The asylum's medical supervision arrangements, whereby the three physicians acted a month at a time in rotation, restricted Charlesworth's powers, even though he was designated the senior physician. Cookson recruited as his lieutenant Samuel Hadwen, Hill's predecessor as house surgeon, who nursed a grievance for not having received credit for his own contribution to the reduction of restraint, and was now a member of the Board of Governors. Cookson considered the whole non-restraint experiment dangerous and unproven and set about making matters as difficult as possible for Charlesworth and Hill. He was not averse to encouraging dissent among the staff and also enlisted the powerful matron, Anne Vessey, to the anti-abolition cause. He collected and presented evidence from former patients and staff to demonstrate that non-restraint was failing, and that mechanical coercion had been replaced by physical coercion and abuse. Hill found himself cornered, convinced not without reason that there was 'an organised attempt to break up the humane system of treating the patients' and to discredit him by forcing a return to restraint. Unable to cope with this level of stress and hostility, and in increasing desperation, he resigned during April 1840.[41]

Hill's departure did not quell the arguments raging among the deeply factionalized Lincoln governors. He ensured his own continuing involvement by paying the subscription to become a governor. Over the next two years the quarrels as to whether mechanical restraint or manual control constituted the greater oppression or cruelty were fought out in the boardroom and in the local press. In July 1840, Hill and Charlesworth achieved a partial victory when the Board of Governors, after a detailed submission from Hill, confirmed non-restraint to be 'founded on the soundest principles' and that the policy would continue. This failed to stem the opposition of Cookson and Hadwen. Verbal feuding between them and Charlesworth and Hill escalated dangerously in 1841 to encompass threats and even challenges to duel, accompanied by accusations and counter-accusations of cowardice. By 1843, the Hill–Charlesworth faction had gained the ascendancy, and the opposition gradually petered out, confirmed by Cookson's resignation as physician to the asylum in February 1844. The depth and vehemence of the quarrel had represented much more than a clash of strong and stubborn personalities. Above and beyond that, it exposed the profound tensions between the proponents of radical and progressive change and those wary of the consequences of the abandonment of tried and trusted practices.[42]

A Wider Conflict

Similar ideological tensions were all too evident in the fierce controversy that developed away from the Lincoln hothouse. The stakes had been raised by the accession of John Conolly to the non-restraint cause after visiting Lincoln in May 1839. His rapid implementation at the huge Hanwell Asylum, and his eloquent progress reports, took the whole profile of the movement into a different dimension. The issue permeated the public domain and all the arguments for and against the use of mechanical restraint – rational, moral, philosophical and therapeutic – were rehearsed several times over. Physicians, superintendents and visiting magistrates of public asylums, proprietors of private asylums, and sundry lay people all became embroiled, and of course Hill and the other Lincoln protagonists could not remain aloof. Thomas Wakley, editor of *The Lancet*, played his part in stirring up a heady brew.[43]

The opening salvo had been fired, fairly innocently, by C.C. Corsellis of West Riding Asylum. In his Annual Report for 1839, he had argued that there were always circumstances which required restraint; to rely on surveillance was an 'absurdity' to anyone having 'practical acquaintance' with the care of the insane. *The Lancet* reproduced selected parts of the report in February 1840, highlighting Corsellis's obvious dissent from the principles disseminated at Lincoln and Hanwell. Gardiner Hill accepted the bait and responded with a cogent argument for the essential humanity of non-restraint. It was, he insisted, 'the system which must and will ultimately prevail in every asylum in our land'. Corsellis then joined the debate with enthusiasm. Claiming that restraint was hardly in evidence at Wakefield, he contended that its selective use was actually more humane than the struggles that must accompany surveillance and manual control. Having been in correspondence with other asylum superintendents to canvass support, he felt confident in asserting that non-restraint was a 'wild scheme'. Its proponents were, he suggested, guilty of 'arrogant dictation' and a lack of professional respect toward colleagues 'labouring with us in the same great cause'.[44]

A rather patronizing response by Hill, in which he acknowledged Corsellis's 'humane management' but expected him soon to 'emancipate himself' from the 'mischievous and insidious principle', only served to provoke a more adversarial confrontation. Corsellis in May scornfully dismissed Hill as a man of little talent, and pointed to the rapid turnover of staff and dismissals for maltreatment at Lincoln as evidence of the system's failure. Non-restraint was nothing more than 'a piece of contemptible quackery – a mere bait for the public ear'. This proved too much for the temperamental Dr Charlesworth, who was roused to challenge Corsellis to a duel. Having not received satisfaction, Charlesworth sought to publicly embarrass his adversary. He passed information about the use of restraint at Wakefield to Serjeant John Adams, the campaigning Middlesex magistrate who had initially despatched Conolly to Lincoln. Adams's correspondence with his West Riding colleagues led to an investigation which ascertained the continuing use of restraint chairs and strait waistcoats in the asylum, but accepted Corsellis's justifications. This unsatisfactory outcome extracted one of Charlesworth's own very rare published contributions to the debate.[45]

Serjeant Adams became one of the main participants in the exchanges, taking particular issue with Samuel Hadwen and William Cookson who both weighed in with their attacks on the state of Lincoln Asylum. Gardiner Hill, by now having vacated his post, also continued to battle it out in print with them. With the increasing coverage, both in *The Lancet* and in *The Times*, of Conolly's progress at Hanwell, several asylum managers and medical officers felt obliged to declare a position on the issue. The proximity of Nottingham Asylum to Lincoln placed its physician Dr Andrew Blake and superintendent Thomas Powell under particular pressure. In the well-publicized thirtieth Annual Report in 1840, they claimed that it had for some time been 'our most most anxious wish' to use 'the least possible personal restraint'; however, total abolition remained an 'Utopian proposal'.[46]

The Nottingham intervention in the discourse proved particularly telling. If Blake and Powell were to be believed, they had been steadily implementing a policy of restraint minimization, accompanied by a steady elimination of the prison-like features of the old asylum, since the early 1830s. This had been carried out, however, without a clear declaration of abolition. Like Corsellis, Dr Blake had been particularly stung by Hill's categorical assertions that restraint was 'never justifiable' and 'always injurious', characterizing him as an impetuous young man vainly hoping to share Pinel's immortality. Essentially though, Blake and Powell sought to define a middle road in the dispute, by giving examples of cases where principles of humanity indicated that people at least needed to be prevented from hurting themselves. Their concern was that partisanship based around the idea of 'never' was obscuring patients' best interests. With the assertion in Nottingham's 1841 Annual Report that they had 'virtually' abolished restraint in treating 'ordinary cases', Serjeant Adams ('A Looker-On') was able to trumpet another key accession to the cause.[47]

The Dissemination of Non-Restraint

Despite the vehement attacks on Hill and Conolly and their principles, non-restraint had attracted influential recruits by the end of 1840. At the recently established Northampton Asylum, Thomas Prichard had effectively implemented a non-restraint policy from its opening in 1838, apparently unaware of events at Lincoln. John Kirkman of Suffolk Asylum, having read Hill's book, declared for the 'NO-RESTRAINT PRINCIPLE' in 1839. He affected surprise at all the fuss, claiming that 'personal restraint has been almost unknown to us' for several years. He was not prepared, however, to subscribe to its complete proscription, as there was always the possibility of its being required on humanitarian grounds. Clearly irritated that his contribution to emancipation had been overlooked, Kirkman accused others of 'self-aggrandizement' and exaggeration to secure their argument.[48]

Several of the older county asylums were, like Nottingham, among the earliest to adopt non-restraint methods. The evils arising from long exposure to the previous regime were clearly apparent to the more enlightened superintendents and medical officers. Samuel Hitch at Gloucester was the first significant convert. In March 1840, he visited Hanwell and returned enthused, to report that the absence of restraint there 'is stated to conduce greatly to the cure' and was effected by having more day-rooms and a higher proportion of keepers than at Gloucester. He persuaded the visitors to immediately take on two additional staff to begin the process. The policy was steadily implemented over the following months, though the visitors continued to reject the view that restraint was prejudicial in all circumstances. By the end of 1841, without a formal declaration, the transformation was complete, and the chairman was impressed with the consequences: 'Though restraint of every kind is wholly abolished, not a sound of disturbance or noise is heard even in cases of patients who were formerly most refractory and violent.' The general improvements within the asylum were confirmed in the Annual Report, with a recognition that patients were 'as securely managed' and 'governed with much less difficulty and disturbance' than had formerly been the case.[49]

Gloucester was regarded as a key recruit to the cause. Serjeant Adams complimented Samuel Hitch on his 'admirably regulated asylum', and Gardiner Hill expressed 'particular pleasure' at the contents of the 1841 report. Hitch, recently qualified as a physician, had by now acquired a good deal of personal prestige among his peers. The high level of public interest in the whole abolition debate had considerably raised the professional profile of asylum medical men. After corresponding with other like-minded superintendents and physicians, Hitch convened the first meeting of the Association of Medical Officers of Hospitals for the Insane in November 1841, which was to form the basis of their professional association. With representatives from Nottingham, Lincoln, Lancaster and Northampton Asylums, as well as the York Retreat, the hegemony of the progressives was ensured.[50]

Concurrent with Hitch's innovations at Gloucester, Gaskell and de Vitrie, newly appointed at Lancaster, were introducing drastic changes. With more than 500 patients, Lancaster was the largest county asylum after Hanwell, and their inspiration came largely from what Conolly had rapidly achieved. Their task was plain enough; in the asylum's overtly custodial surroundings, mechanical coercion had been 'uniformly adopted as a means of allaying violence'. By the end of 1840, several months had passed without recourse to restraint, though Gaskell and de Vitrie were careful like their Nottingham counterparts not to assert that it would never be needed again. They followed up by dismantling much of the prison-like infrastructure, and removing the iron bars from the windows: over nineteen tons of iron were allegedly taken out. Other improvements were introduced to brighten the surroundings and provide more activities for the patients. Faced with a similar situation when he took over at Stafford in late 1841, James Wilkes implemented comparable measures. Like at Lincoln, Gloucester and elsewhere, a marked improvement in patients' demeanour and a decline in destructive behaviour was reported at both Lancaster and Stafford.[51]

The adherents of non-restraint did not, however, have matters all their own way, particularly in the asylums of the more rural counties. At Dorset Asylum, Dr George Button arrived from Hanwell during 1842, after having been house surgeon under Ellis and then Conolly, from whose approach he had clearly dissented. Although he instituted measures to improve practices, he claimed general support for his view that the 'judicious application' of restraint was 'necessary, humane, and curative'. The most he was prepared to concede, two years on, was that its use was kept to the necessary minimum. At the Bedford and Norfolk Asylums, where unqualified laymen continued to hold the posts of governor or master, the whole debate appears to have passed them by. Although the extent of restraint employed at both declined from a particularly high incidence, this was due more to the representations of Lunacy Commissioners than to any ideological conviction.[52]

An unusual situation developed at Kent Asylum, where the visitors adopted a more adventurous approach than the cautious superintendent, George Poynder. John Adams visited in the summer of 1838; after attempting unsuccessfully to persuade Poynder of the benefits of the Lincoln experiment, he turned his attention to Lord Marsham, the leading county magistrate, supplying him with descriptions of progress at Hanwell and copies of Lincoln's Annual Reports. The visitors were partially converted, and in January 1840 accepted the principle that lunatics could be controlled without 'irksome confinement or irritating restraint'; they anticipated the time when there would be no instance of 'a wretched Patient bearing the appearance of a fettered or manacled prisoner'. However, they remained apprehensive of 'fearful results' and a lack of action led Adams publicly to cite Kent as an example of continued cruel and excessive restraint. Poynder was forced to defend his own and his institution's reputations. The persistent Adams prevailed on Lord Marsham and by early 1841 the visiting justices had embraced non-restraint; Poynder had been outflanked.[53]

By 1842, when the Metropolitan Commissioners in Lunacy undertook their journeys around the county asylums, the adherence to non-restraint, or at least to near-elimination, had been widely signalled. It was being practised in large measure, with the exceptions mentioned and also of Wakefield, where Corsellis had shown little inclination to back down in the face of external criticism.[54] Within a comparatively short space of time, Hill, Charlesworth, Conolly and their supporters had achieved a remarkable triumph. The force of their argument, backed by practical application, had attained such a dominance in the management of insanity that the onus was clearly on opponents to demonstrate that non-restraint was flawed. By employing arguments which contrasted oppression, cruelty and injustice, with humanity, liberty and justice, they had outmanoeuvred even those practitioners who had been implementing a gradual liberalization of asylum regimes.

Hill must claim some particular credit. The very certainty of his youthful idealism and impetuosity, which so enraged those who felt their professional integrity to be questioned, could not do other than bring out a forceful response from those he challenged. The fortuitous arrival on the scene of someone like John Conolly, determined to enhance his reputation by demonstrable success in the unlikely territory of a giant pauper lunatic asylum, was a timely boost. The accession to the cause of someone of his professional stature and impeccably respectable credentials ensured that his conclusions, however rapidly arrived at, were taken seriously.[55] Of course, both were operating on fertile ground, for the sterility of the public asylum system was all too evident. Any cohesive proposal that offered material improvement and the prospect of 'cure' would be an attractive option. In the non-restraint system, the answer appeared to have been found to the problem of how to reconcile the need for control with the aspiration of cure. The system, with its accompaniments of improved surroundings, more purposeful activity for patients, higher staff ratios, surveillance and watchfulness, and alternative methods of control of destructive behaviour, seemed to offer the prospect of a revolution in treatment. The whole essence of asylum care and patient management had apparently undergone a fundamental metamorphosis.

A NEW ERA

Such a profound upheaval in systems of management and treatment brought difficulties as well as benefits. The problems that occurred within Lincoln Asylum in the aftermath of abolition indicated that non-restraint was not of itself a panacea. To succeed, the new system required change in various ways and on several levels. Hill insisted on the requisites of 'a properly constructed building' and 'a sufficient number of suitable attendants'. Though fundamental, these requirements were easily overlooked or minimized due to practical and financial constraints. The early county asylums would need extensive modification to be 'properly constructed'. Attendants were likely to need attitudinal change, training and, in many cases, replacement and re-selection in order to function in a different environment, if they were to be 'suitable'.[56]

Without the ready availability of restraint implements, the alternative methods advocated by Hill and Conolly were put to the test. For Conolly, the 'real character' of non-restraint was 'watchful, preventive, almost parental superintendence'. This was similar to Hill's emphasis on constant surveillance. At both Lincoln and Hanwell, however, it soon became apparent that some more active means of control were still needed. Conolly's chosen method, adopted by others, was seclusion. This was no new remedy, for isolation of an agitated patient in a dark cell had been common practice in the old regime. Its therapeutic rationale was to limit external stimulation, as well as to reduce the scope for destructive behaviour. In the post-abolition asylum, seclusion was more likely to mean removal to a padded room for a prescribed period.[57]

Several padded rooms were fitted out at Hanwell, attached to the refractory wards. Their declared purpose was the 'temporary seclusion of Patients while labouring under maniacal paroxysms'. Samuel Hitch had some equipped at Gloucester 'for the worst cases of refractory patients'. This was despite his implicit criticism of Conolly in 1840, when he pointed out that solitary confinement was an 'obvious personal restraint'. The Metropolitan Commissioners found seclusion coming into general use, with solitary cells and padded rooms being fitted up in many public asylums. They noted its efficacy:

> Seclusion (or solitary confinement) is found to have a very powerful effect in tranquillising, and subduing those who are under temporary excitement or paroxysms of violent insanity.

Indeed, the Commissioners were clearly uneasy about the trend, suggesting that solitary confinement without safeguards was even more open to abuse than visible 'bodily coercion'. At Lincoln, where the process of reform had not ended with the abolition of restraint, Hill's successor William Smith went on to abolish seclusion in 1842, having concluded it to be scarcely less oppressive than mechanical restraint. Others, however, did not follow the Lincoln example.[58]

Where Conolly and his followers had adopted seclusion as their reserve method of curbing disruptive behaviour, Hill and Charlesworth had clearly advocated the use of an imposing physical aspect. Hill stipulated that attendants should be 'strong, tall, and active'; their presence was to act as a deterrent and also to inspire a feeling of security. Despite the scope for accusations of replacing mechanical restraint with physical restraint, both remained unrepentant. Charlesworth declared his position unequivocally in July 1842:

> I state as a matter of principle, admitting of exceptions, that Lunatic Patients cannot be managed by attendants who are not tall and powerful, unless recourse be had either to Mechanical restraint, or to blows in self defence.

The problem at Lincoln, however, had been that many attendants clearly did not meet Hill's basic requirement of suitability. They had not the experience or understanding to avoid the many provocations and temptations arising as a consequence of some patients' behaviour; 'blows' and excessive force were the frequent response. The succession of dismissals during 1839 and 1840 illustrated how far things had gone wrong.[59]

The adjustments required by staff used to the ready availability of restraint instruments were considerable. Inevitably, staffing problems accompanied the implementation of non-restraint. At Stafford, Wilkes found 'deep-rooted prejudices' to contend with. Gaskell and de Vitrie were also confronted with a far from easy task at Lancaster. Attendants who had previously only considered their duty finished 'when they had chained down the patients' had some difficulty in developing the necessary 'watchfulness, care, and ingenuity' that was to substitute for coercion. It would take some time for them to learn the skills of 'circumspection and readiness in allaying excitement'. John Conolly, in his impatience to achieve a rapid transition at Hanwell, also experienced resistance from staff who perceived their authority and their personal security threatened.[60]

A great deal depended on the staff, whose role was central in making the new system function properly, which was recognized in Conolly's description of attendants as the 'most essential instruments' of the non-restraint system. He acknowledged that much was expected from people of 'humble rank'. These disparate, poorly trained and ungenerously paid people had to be moulded into a new kind of attendant. According to one of the Lincoln governors:

> It must require some dignity of mind and superior moral feeling in an uneducated person, to enter into the idea that moral control should, with some little addition of trouble to themselves, supersede the ready, handy, and direct recourse to brute force and mechanical power, which they had previously used.

To meet the expectations of the new system, keepers and nurses had to develop the ability to ignore or withstand the frequent provocation and irritation to which they were exposed.[61]

One method of seeking to influence staff behaviour was through detailed written instructions. In the Lancaster regulations of 1841, staff were exhorted to maintain patience and self-control in the face of all provocations. Another significant innovation at Lancaster, with similar intent, was the creation of a supervisory hierarchy. The post of 'Chief Attendant' was established, responsible for the direction and supervision of the other attendants. Promoted from the ranks, he reported directly to the superintendent and took on some of his more routine duties. A similar scheme was instituted at Lincoln during 1840 and 1841 and proved a major step in bringing the asylum's disorders under control. Its head keeper and head nurse were to be selected from 'the same Class' as the other staff, and were expected to inform the house surgeon of any wrongdoing by their colleagues. It took some time, however, for the arrangement to work properly, for the first head nurse, Sarah Cawston, was herself dismissed for ill-treatment a few weeks following appointment, after being injured in a struggle with an unusually violent female patient.[62]

The propagandists for non-restraint, even allowing for exaggeration and selectivity, could mobilize ample evidence to demonstrate its significance and effectiveness. Charlesworth's claim in 1838 that abolition had brought a decrease of violence, accidents and 'revolting habits' was reinforced by events in the asylums that followed the Lincoln example. Gaskell and de Vitrie at Lancaster observed that, after the removal of the instruments and the consequent freedom of movement of patients, 'their condition was nearly in every instance considerably improved'. In some cases their change in habits and appearance was so striking 'that in a little while they were with difficulty recognised'. Wilkes's experience at Stafford was equally remarkable:

> The excitement of the patients generally was decidedly diminished: they were less noisy and restless at night, and destructive propensities and objectionable habits were, in many instances, gradually overcome.

A visitor to Gloucester in November 1842 noted that the 'most decided improvement' had taken place; the absence of restraint was accompanied by 'almost universal quietude and orderly conduct'. The new freedoms which brought these favourable changes in patients' behaviour and demeanour reflected an apparent rejuvenation of the institutions' hitherto sterile management regimes.[63]

At Lincoln the benefits had proved short-term, and gave way to a period of turmoil. A similar pattern occurred elsewhere, and the Metropolitan Commissioners were seriously concerned about some of what they saw. At Suffolk Asylum they witnessed serious disturbances in the female refractory ward and airing court – a scene of 'distressing turbulence and confusion', as a 'great number' of 'violently excited' patients abused and attacked one another. On visiting again, the Commissioners ignored the matron's advice not to go into the female refractory yard and saw patients half naked after destroying their clothes, one struggling constantly with a nurse, and others in a state of 'fury'. Even at the Hanwell showpiece in June 1843, they observed some disturbing occurrences. A female who was trying to bite others as well as herself had to be violently manhandled into a cell by several nurses. There were instances of serious attempts at self-harm, and of fighting among the patients; one patient was actually killed by another during the period of the visit.[64]

Most of these difficulties, however, proved largely transitory. Eventually, as the non-restraint system became established and officers and staff learnt new methods for the management and control of patients, the problems were overcome. The threats to the progress of the system were set aside, and confidence grew that this really was, as the German observer Dr Granville described, the dawn of a 'new era' in the treatment of the insane. Such was the growing strength of the non-restraint movement that it was bound to be profoundly influential in the formation of public policy. Although the Metropolitan Commissioners had expressed some reservations, the movement played its part in the coalescence of ideas which produced the two parliamentary Acts of 1845, arguably the most significant mental health legislation of the century. The mandatory requirement for county magistrates to establish, either alone or in conjunction with other counties, a pauper lunatic asylum laid the basis for an institutional system that dominated the management of mental disorder for almost 150 years. These new asylums were expected to develop with the principles Conolly had expounded as the perceived basis of their philosophy of care and treatment.[65]

Despite the transitional problems, it is hard to dispute the portrayal of non-restraint by its promoters and supporters as a reform of profound significance. It was seen to symbolize an entirely different and more enlightened approach to the care and treatment of mentally disordered people. In this altered scheme, abolition was only a part of a wider approach which included an overhaul of all aspects of the asylum's physical environment and its regime. It marked a watershed in the development of provision for the insane, and appeared to represent a permanent shift along the the custody–cure axis.

Historians, however, have not been uniformly kind to non-restraint and its advocates. In the same way that Foucault questioned whether the 'moral treatment' of The Retreat signified what was in reality a more subtle system of oppressive control, scholars like Andrew Scull have laid out a similar case for non-restraint.[66] The paraphernalia of mechanical restraint and the concomitant prison-like surroundings were being replaced by a more aesthetically pleasing environment and means of control that were less overt but at least equally powerful. As the management techniques of the post-restraint asylum became more sophisticated, a new order was gradually imposed in which uniformity, routine, regularity and regimentation became paramount. This is a more than tenable argument with the benefit of hindsight. It tends, though, to attribute to those who steered through the changes some motives which may not have been present. They perceived it to be a humanitarian crusade, resulting in a great advance which reduced the misery and suffering of the most disadvantaged people and offered clear therapeutic benefits. If the new system did have to comprise some new and subtle means of control of patients, this was partly to ensure it did not collapse.

The questionable elements in the longer-term influence of non-restraint were perhaps other than abstract politico-philosophical considerations about the replacement of overt by covert control mechanisms. As Nancy Tomes has argued, English asylum doctors developed a degree of complacency, based on the moral superiority which their successful embrace of non-restraint signified. A case could be made to contend that the advance of the art of treatment of mental illness was effectively halted for at least a generation.[67] The euphoria among lunacy reformers and progressive alienists about the potential therapeutic benefits of the non-restraint asylum created raised expectations as to cure rates and the reduction of the incidence of madness. Having achieved this major advance, there seemed to be less need to pursue other treatment options. Everything associated with the old regime had become discredited. The use of medicines and physical treatments declined, as 'moral' means of treatment began to be viewed as paramount. In effect, non-restraint and its accompaniments increasingly became a substitute for active treatment. This undoubtedly contributed to the developing therapeutic sterility of the great late Victorian asylums, which many would argue continued well into the twentieth century.

NOTES

1 R.G. Hill, *Total Abolition of Personal Restraint in the Treatment of the Insane* (London, 1839), p. 22.

2 Hill, *Total Abolition*; J. Conolly, *The Treatment of the Insane Without Mechanical Restraints* (London, 1856); D. Hack Tuke, *Chapters in the History of the Insane* (London, 1882); K. Jones, *A History of the Mental Health Services* (London, 1972). For the wider context of the non-restraint movement, see Nancy Tomes, 'The Great Restraint Controversy: A Comparative Perspective on Anglo-American Psychiatry in the Nineteenth Century', in W.F. Bynum, R. Porter and M. Shepherd (eds), *The Anatomy of Madness: Essays in the History of Psychiatry*, vol. III, *The Asylum and its Psychiatry* (London, 1988), pp. 190–225.

3 SCRO, Q/AIc, Box I, 'Statutes, Laws, and Rules for the Government of the Leicester Lunatic Asylum' (1794), Rules for the Government of the Lunatic Hospital and Asylum in Manchester (1791); J. Ferriar, *Medical Histories and Reflections* (1795), cited in R. Hunter and I. Macalpine, *Three Hundred Years of Psychiatry, 1535–1860* (Oxford, 1963), p. 545; J. Andrews, *Bedlam Revisited: A History of Bethlem Hospital c.1634–1770*, (PhD, University of London, 1991), p. 206; J. Haslam, *Considerations on the Moral Management of Insane Persons* (London, 1817), pp. 25–30; A. Scull, C. Mackenzie and N. Hervey, *Masters of Bedlam* (Princeton, 1996), pp. 35, 38.

4 Andrews, *Bedlam Revisited*, pp. 205–19; J. Andrews, A. Briggs, R. Porter, P. Tucker and K. Waddington, *The History of Bethlem* (London, 1997), pp. 214–17, 421–31; C.N. French, *The Story of St Luke's Hospital* (London, 1951), p. 39; M. Winston, 'The Bethel at Norwich: An Eighteenth-Century Hospital for Lunatics', *Medical History*, vol. XXXVIII, no. 1 (January 1994), pp. 27–51; N. Roberts, *Cheadle Royal Hospital: A Bicentenary History* (Altrincham, 1967), pp. 21–2; E.R. Frizelle, *The Life and Times of the Royal Infirmary at Leicester* (Leicester, 1988), p. 66.

5 Haslam, *Considerations on Moral Management*, p. 30; Scull *et al.*, *Masters of Bedlam*, p. 38; DCRO, *Report of Visiting Justices* (Epiphany 1843), p. 25; *The Lancet*, 12 September 1840, p. 907.

6 Paul Slade Knight, *Observations on the Causes, Symptoms and Treatment of Derangement of the Mind* (London, 1827), pp. 73–5; NCRO, SO/HO/1/9/1, no. 586, Catherine Mills (34), 3 February 1825: 'Has been wild and abusive – has necessarily been under restraint. Is today more composed and intelligent'; no. 678, William Bullard (49), 7 December 1826: 'Has been refractory and impatient, and altogether so ill conducted that he is confined in a dark room', 14 December: 'Is very penitent and is permitted to return to Society on trial'.

7 *Morning Herald*, 12 January 1826; NkCRO, SAH 123, 126–8.

8 S. Tuke, *Description of the Retreat* (London, 1813), pp. 172–3; A. Digby, *Madness, Morality and Medicine: A Study of the York Retreat, 1796–1914* (Cambridge, 1985), pp. 76–84; DCRO, *Report of Visiting Justices* (Epiphany 1843), pp. 24–6; E. Baines, *History, Directory and Gazetteer of the County Palatine of Lancaster* (Liverpool, 1829), vol. II, p. 17; Knight, *Observations on the Derangement of the Mind*, p. 114; LCRO, QAM, 1/30/11, pp. 3, 105.

9 WRCRO, C85/936, case of William Greaves, 5 August 1821; NkCRO, SAH 123, 24 June, 4, 6, 7 July 1815, SAH 126, 21 July 1820, 20 October 1823; DCRO, *Report of Visiting Justices* (Epiphany 1843), p. 24.

10 NCRO, SO/HO/1/3/1, 26 December 1816; LPL, *Report of the Medical Officers* (1841), p. 4; *Journal of Mental Science*, vol. II (1855), no. 17, p. 268; K. Jones, 'The Culture of the Mental Hospital', p. 20, in H. Freeman and G.E. Berrios (eds), *150 Years of British Psychiatry, 1841–1991* (London, 1991), pp. 17–28.

11 NkCRO, SAH 3, 31 August 1818; LPL, *Report of the Medical Officers* (1841), p. 4; *Eighth Report of the Commissioners in Lunacy* (1854), Appendix G, p. 137.

12 DCRO, Forston House, *Report of the Visiting Justices* (Epiphany 1843), p. 25; S. Tuke, 'Introductory Observations' to M. Jacobi, *On the Construction and Management of Hospitals for the Insane* (London, 1841), p. xxxii; Knight, *Observations on the Derangement of the Mind*, p. 75; WRCRO, C85/114, West Riding Asylum, 21st Report (1840), p. 4; LAO, LAWN 1/2/1, 29 August 1824; NkCRO, SAH 128, 8 September 1843.

13 The chair was also variously known as the 'restraint chair', the 'punishment chair' or the 'safety chair'; GCRO, HO22/1/1, 22 May 1823; *Eighth Report of Commissioners in Lunacy*, p. 137; *The Times*, 30 December 1840, 24 November 1842; GLRO, H11/HLL/A7/1, 1st Report of John Conolly (Michaelmas 1839), p. 22; Stanley Royd Hospital, Diary of Dr Gettings, Extracts from Minutes, January 1823; Sir W.C. Ellis, *A Treatise on the Nature, Symptoms, Causes, and Treatment of Insanity* (London, 1838), pp. 165–6; *Wakefield and Halifax Journal*, 22 January 1841; *Familar Views of Lunacy and Lunatic Life, by the Late Medical Superintendent of an Asylum for the Insane* (London, 1850), p. 90; NkCRO, SAH 123–8.

14 BPP 1814–15, vol. IV, *Select Committee on Madhouses*, pp. 178–9; SCRO, D550/62, 13 February 1819; CKS, U1515/OQ/L1, Adams to Marsham, 28 November 1839; B. Cashman, *A Proper House: Bedford Lunatic Asylum, 1812–1860* (North Bedfordshire Health Authority, 1992), p. 95; NkCRO, SAH 2, 25 July 1814, SAH 6, 30 October 1843, SAH 123–8, SAH 137, 29

August 1843, SAH 141, 22 August 1844; LPL, *Report of the Medical Officers* (1841), pp. 4–5.

15 Knight, *Observations on the Derangement of the Mind*, pp. 114–15; Ellis, *Treatise*, pp. 164–6; *Familiar Views of Lunacy and Lunatic Life*, pp. 88–91.

16 J.M. Cox, *Practical Observations on Insanity* (London, 1804), p. 47; Tuke, *Description of the Retreat*, pp. 164–6; Haslam, *Considerations on Moral Management*, pp. 26–8; G.N. Hill, *An Essay on the Prevention and Cure of Insanity* (London, 1814), p. 277; Knight, *Observations on the Derangement of the Mind*, p. 113; W.C. Ellis, *A Letter to Thomas Thompson M.P.* (Hull, 1815), p. 19.

17 Writing about the eighteenth century, Allan Ingram sees the strait waistcoat as the most symbolic expression of the relation between doctor and patient, rendering complete the status of the madman as an 'object' – *The Madhouse of Language: Writing and Reading Madness in the Eighteenth Century* (London, 1991), p. 35; NkCRO, SAH 3, 30 December 1820; LAO, LAWN 1/1/2, 9, 16 February, 6 April 1829; L.D. Smith, 'The "Great Experiment": The Place of Lincoln in the History of Psychiatry', *Lincolnshire History and Archaeology*, vol. 30 (1995), p. 57.

18 CKS, U1515/OQ/L1, 22 December 1840, Adams to Marsham.

19 LAO, LAWN 1/1/4, 8 July 1840, Appendix D, Prichard to Charlesworth (11 March 1840); St Andrews Hospital, Northampton, CL1, Case Books 1838/9; BCRO, LB/6/1.

20 Tuke (D. Hack), *Chapters in the History of the Insane in the British Isles*, pp. 208–9; LPL, *Report of the Medical Officers* (1841), pp. 4–5; J. Walton, 'The Treatment of Pauper Lunatics in Victorian England: The Case of Lancaster Asylum, 1816–1870', in A. Scull (ed.) *Madhouses, Mad-Doctors and Madmen: The Social History of Psychiatry in the Victorian Era* (London, 1981), pp. 170–3; Scull *et al.*, *Masters of Bedlam*, pp. 165–7; *Eighth Report of Commissioners in Lunacy* (1854), p. 137; SCRO, D550/63, 27 June 1835; L.D. Smith, 'The Pauper Lunatic Problem in the West Midlands, 1815–1850', *Midland History*, vol. XXI (1996), pp. 104–6.

21 SCRO, D550/62–4.

22 NRL, qL3648, Nottingham Asylum, 8th Report (1818); *Wakefield and Halifax Journal*, 9 August 1822; NkCRO, SAH 3, 28 March 1821, SAH 123, 11 January, 13 March, 6 July 1815, SAH 126, 20 November 1821, 17 September 1822.

23 *The Times*, 4 December 1839; LLSL, Lincoln Asylum, 17th Report (1841), pp. 7, 12–13; LAO, LAWN 1/1/4, 29 June 1840; Ellis, *Treatise*, p. 165; *The Lancet*, 22 February 1840, p. 797.

24 NkCRO, SAH 123, 5, 6 March, 15 November 1815; *Morning Herald*, 12 January 1826; SCRO, D550/4, 28 August 1824, 12, 26 March 1825.

25 L.D. Smith, 'Behind Closed Doors: Lunatic Asylum Keepers, 1800–60', pp. 318–24; LLSL, Lincoln Asylum, 9th Report (1833), pp. 4–5; Hill, *Total Abolition*, pp. 51–3.

26 LLSL, Lincoln Asylum, 15th Report (1839), p. 5, 17th Report (1841), p. 4; J. Conolly, *Treatment of the Insane Without Mechanical Restraints* (London, 1856; reprinted 1973), pp. 256–7; *Journal of Mental Science*, vol. II (1855), no. 17, p. 276; *Eighth Report of Commissioners in Lunacy*, p. 137; L.D. Smith, 'Close Confinement in a Mighty Prison: Thomas Bakewell and his Campaign Against Public Asylums, 1810–1830', *History of Psychiatry*, vol. V (1994), pp. 191–214.

27 Walton, 'The Treatment of Pauper Lunatics in Victorian England', pp. 168–9, 178–9; N. Tomes, 'The Anglo–American Asylum in Historical Perspective', in C.J. Smith and J.A. Giggs (eds), *Location and Stigma: Contemporary Perspectives on Mental Health Care* (London, 1988), p. 12; Andrews *et al.*, *History of Bethlem*, pp. 384, 390, 416, 451; R. Russell, *Mental Physicians and Their Patients* (PhD, University of Sheffield, 1983), p. 100; Digby, *Madness, Morality and Medicine*, pp. 78–84.

28 Andrews *et al.*, *The History of Bethlem*, pp. 422–7; LAO, LAWN 3/1, West Riding Asylum, 4th Report (1822).

29 Tomes, 'The Anglo-American Asylum in Historical Perspective'; R. Hunter and I. Macalpine, 'Introduction' to Conolly, *Treatment of the Insane Without Mechanical Restraints* (in the 1973 reprinting); E. Showalter, *The Female Malady: Women, Madness, and English Culture, 1830–1980* (London, 1985), chapter 1; Scull *et al.*, *Masters of Bedlam*, chapter 3.

30 Dr Edward Parker Charlesworth (1783–1853). Son of a Nottinghamshire rector, he gained his M.D. at Edinburgh in 1807; he was appointed physician to Lincoln County Hospital in 1808, and to the asylum when it opened in 1820. For the sequence of events at Lincoln, see Smith, 'The "Great Experiment"', and A. Walk, 'Lincoln and Non-Restraint', *British Journal of Psychiatry*, vol. CXVII (1970), pp. 481–96. For the Lincoln context and Charlesworth's prominent role in local affairs, see Sir F. Hill, *Georgian Lincoln* (Cambridge, 1966).

31 Hill, *Total Abolition*, Appendix A, pp. 61–70; LAO, LAWN 1/1/2, 7 April 1824, 27 March, 28 April, 5 October 1827; E.P. Charlesworth, *Remarks on the Treatment of the Insane and the Management of Lunatic Asylums* (London, 1828).

32 Charlesworth, *Remarks*, pp. 15–17, 20–1.

33 LLSL, 'At A General Board of Governors', 13 October 1828; LAO, LAWN 1/1/2, 13 October 1828, 9, 16 February, 6 April 1829; Hill, *Total Abolition*, pp. 66–71.

34 Cambridge University Library, Hunter Collection, *Proceedings of the General Board of the Lincoln Lunatic Asylum Held on October 13, 1830* (Lincoln, 1830); *Lincoln Herald*, 16, 23, 30 October 1829; LAO, LAWN 1/1/3, 31 May, 21 June, 28 July, 2 August, 13 October 1830; LLSL, Lincoln Asylum, 7th Report (1831), p. 2; Lincoln Asylum, *Rules* (1832), p. 23; Hill, *Total Abolition*, pp. 71–82.

35 Hill, *Total Abolition*, pp. 88–9; LLSL, Lincoln Asylum, 9th Report (1833), pp. 4–5; LAO, 1/1/3, 9 April 1834, 8 July 1835; DNB, entry for Robert Gardiner Hill; Walk, 'Lincoln and Non-Restraint', p. 484.

36 R.G. Hill, *A Concise History of the Entire Abolition of Mechanical Restraint in the Treatment of the Insane* (London, 1857), p. 12; Hill, *Total Abolition*, pp. 95–101; LLSL, Lincoln Asylum, 14th Report (1838), p. 4.

37 *Stamford Mercury*, 13 October 1837; LAO, LAWN 1/1/4, 11 October, 6 November 1837; LLSL, Lincoln Asylum, 14th Report (1838), pp. 4–6.

38 Hill, *Total Abolition*, pp. 2–4, 20–2; *Lincoln and Stamford Mercury*, 29 June 1838; Walk, 'Lincoln and Non- Restraint', pp. 484–5.

39 *British and Foreign Medical Review*, vol. IX (January 1840), pp. 153–5; Scull *et al.*, *Masters of Bedlam*, pp. 70–1.

40 LLSL, Lincoln Asylum, 17th Report (1841), pp. 4–9; LAO, LAWN 1/1/4, 11 March, 22 April, 6, 12, 27 May, 1 July, 5 August, 23 September, 21 October, 18 November 1839, 27 January, 2, 9, 16, 30 March, 13 April, 8 July 1840.

41 Hill, *Concise History*, pp. 35–6; LAO, LAWN 1/1/4, 2, 9, 23 March, 6, 8, 13 April, 11, 18 May, 8 July 1840, LAWN 1/2/3, 10 April 1841.

42 LAO, LAWN 1/1/4, 11 May 1840–12 January 1842, LAWN 1/1/5, 22 August 1842–19 February 1844, LAWN 1/2/3, 1 June 1840–12 July 1842; *Lincoln and Stamford Mercury*, 10 July 1840; *Lincoln Gazette*, 10, 24, 31 March, 5, 12, 26 May, 16 June, 14, 21, 28 July, 13, 27 October 1840; *The Times*, 13 July 1840. The battles that took place in Lincoln have left a huge written legacy; for a fuller resumé of the exchanges, see Smith, 'The "Great Experiment"'.

43 Hill, *Concise History*, p. 17; *The Lancet*, 8 February 1840–22 August 1842; *The Times*, 4 December 1839, 18 November 1840; GLRO, H11/HLL/A7/1, The Reports of John Conolly, M.D.; Scull *et al.*, *Masters of Bedlam*, pp. 65–8.

44 WRCRO, C85/114, West Riding Asylum, 21st Report (1840), pp. 4–5; *The Lancet*, 8, 22 February, 21 March 1840.

45 *The Lancet*, 11 April, 9 May 1840; Hill, *Concise History*, p. 17; C. Crommelinck, *Rapport sur les Hospices d'Aliénés de l'Angleterre, de la France et de l'Allemagne* (Courtrai, 1842), p. 102 – when asked for his choice of weapons, Corsellis is reputed to have responded 'I choose *The Lancet*'. Charlesworth was not new to duelling, having fought a duel in 1824 with Colonel Sibthorp, the high Tory Lincoln M.P. (Hill, *Georgian Lincoln*, p. 278); Scull *et al.*, *Masters of Bedlam*, pp. 150–2; A. Suzuki, 'The Politics and Ideology of Non-Restraint', *Medical History*, vol. XXXIX, no. 1 (1995), pp. 1–17, pp. 8–11; *Wakefield and Halifax Journal*, 22 January 1841.

46 *The Lancet*, 12 September, 24, 31 October, 7, 21, 28 November 1840; *The Times*, 4 December 1839, 18 November, 30 December 1840; Scull *et al.*, *Masters of Bedlam*, pp. 66–9. Thomas Powell's sister was Matron at Hanwell.

47 *The Lancet*, 12, 19 December 1840, 9 January, 6 February, 24 April, 13 November 1841.

48 Hunter and Macalpine, *Three Hundred Years of Psychiatry*, pp. 897–9; Hill, *Concise History*, pp. 14–16; A. Foss and K. Trick, *St Andrew's Hospital, Northampton: The First One Hundred and Fifty Years 1838–1988* (Cambridge, 1989), pp. 30–3; SuCRO, B106/10/4.4, Suffolk Asylum, 2nd Report (1840), p. 3, 3rd Report (1841), pp. 3–5, 4th Report (1842), pp. 13–15, 5th Report (1843), pp. 7–8.

49 GCRO, HO22/1/1, 6 April 1840, HO22/3/2, 16 March 1840, HO22/8/1, *Annual Reports*, 1840, 1841; *The Lancet*, 31 July 1841.

50 *The Lancet*, 14, 21 May 1842; L.D. Smith, '"A Worthy Feeling Gentleman": Samuel Hitch at Gloucester Asylum' in Freeman and Berrios (eds), *150 Years of British Psychiatry*, vol. II, pp. 489–92; T. Outterson Wood, 'The Early History of the Medico-Psychological Association', *Journal of Mental Science*, vol. XLII, no. 177 (April 1896), pp. 241–60; A. Walk and D.L. Walker, 'Gloucester and the Beginnings of the R.M.P.A.', *Journal of Mental Science*, vol. CVII, no. 449 (July 1961), pp. 603–32; Crommelinck, *Rapport sur les Hospices*, pp. 150–5.

51 Scull *et al.*, *Masters of Bedlam*, pp. 164–9; Walton, 'The Treatment of Pauper Lunatics', pp. 171–80; LPL, *Reports of the Medical Officers* (1841), pp. 7–8, (1842), pp. 4–8.

52 DCRO, *Reports of Visiting Justices* (Epiphany 1840), p. 6, (Epiphany 1842), p. 16, (Epiphany 1843), pp. 23–6. It would appear that Button had effectively been dismissed by the pro-Conolly Middlesex magistrates (Scull *et al.*, *Masters of Bedlam*, pp. 151, 315). BCRO, LB/6/4, Inventories – 1843, 1846; NkCRO, SAH 127, 128 – the Masters' Report Books contain numerous entries re the use of restraint during the 1840s.

53 CKS, Q/GCL/1, 7 January 1840, U1515/OQ/L1, Adams to Marsham, 28 November, 7 December 1839, 22 December 1840, Poynder to Adams, 6 November 1840, 5 January 1841, Adams to Poynder, 16 November 1840, 6 January 1841.

54 *Report of the Metropolitan Commissioners in Lunacy to the Lord Chancellor* (1844), pp. 140–6.

55 For Conolly's professional ambitions, see Scull *et al.*, *Masters of Bedlam*, chapter 3.

56 Hill, *Total Abolition*, p. 27.

57 Ibid., pp. 37, 47; Conolly, *Treatment of the Insane*, pp. 35, 42–3.

58 *A Guide Through Hanwell Asylum* (London, 1843), pp. 6–10; GCRO, HO22/3/1, 18 October 1841, 10 January, 25 October 1842, HO22/8/1, *Annual Reports*, 1840, 1842; *Metropolitan Commissioners in Lunacy*, p. 146; LAO, LAWN 1/1/4, 12 January 1842; LLSL, Lincoln Asylum, 18th Report, pp. 5, 28 – Smith anticipated that the abolition of seclusion would be disseminated 'as an accompaniment and part of the humane system of the disuse of instruments'.

59 Hill, *Total Abolition*, pp. 38, 44; LAO, LAWN 1/2/3, 12 July 1842, LAWN 1/1/4, 22 April, 6 May, 1 July 1839, 2 March, 4 May 1840; Crommelinck, *Rapport sur les Hospices*, pp. 100–2; *The Lancet*, 7, 28 November 1840, 9 January 1841, 9 April 1842.

60 *Eighth Report of Commissioners in Lunacy* (1854), p. 137; LPL, *Report of the Medical Oficers* (1841), p. 7; Conolly, *Treatment of the Insane*, pp. 95–9.

61 Conolly, *Treatment of the Insane*, p. 98; LLSL, Lincoln Asylum, 17th Report (1841), p. 9; *British and Foreign Medical Review*, vol. IX (January 1840), p. 163.

62 LPL, *Report of the Medical Officers* (1841), pp. 15–21; LLSL, Lincoln Asylum, 17th Report (1841), pp. 5–6; LAO, LAWN 1/1/4, 8 April, 18, 25 May, 22 June 1840.

63 LPL, *Report of the Medical Officers* (1841), pp. 6–7; *Journal of Mental Science*, vol. II (1855), no. 17, p. 276; GCRO, HO22/3/2, 22 November 1842; LLSL, Lincoln Asylum, 14th Report (1838), p. 6.

64 *Metropolitan Commissioners in Lunacy*, pp. 141–3.

65 A.B. Granville, *The Spas of England and Provincial Sea Bathing Places: Midland Spas* (London, 1841), p. 87; A. Scull, *The Most Solitary of Afflictions: Madness and Society in Britain, 1700–1900* (London, 1993), chapters 6–8; Jones, *History of the Mental Health Services*, pp. 141–55; P. Bartlett, *The Poor Law of Lunacy* (PhD, University of London, 1993), chapter 3.

66 M. Foucault, *Madness and Civilization* (London, 1971); Scull, *Most Solitary of Afflictions*, chapters 4, 6.

67 Tomes, 'The Anglo-American Asylum in Historical Perspective'; Scull, *Most Solitary of Afflictions*, chapter 6; P. McCandless, '"Build! Build!" The Controversy Over the Care of the Chronically Insane in England, 1855–1870', *Bulletin of the History of Medicine*, vol. 53 (1979), pp. 533–74.

Conclusions: In Pursuit of Cure

The new county asylums that were established after the Act of 1808 embodied both continuity and innovation. Their genesis can be clearly traced to the public subscription asylums of the eighteenth century. More than that, their construction, their administrative arrangements, their organizational structure, their medical supervision and their treatment methods all derived directly from their predecessor institutions.[1] The main innovation was the very realization of the ideal of a county pauper asylum, whether or not combined with a charitable undertaking. The legislation may have been permissive, but its practical result was that the state had intervened directly in a significant area of health care and had laid down some basic standards of practice. An important principle had, perhaps inadvertently, been established. The provision of 'cure, comfort and safe custody' in publicly funded institutions was from now on a legitimate public concern.

The practical significance of the 1808 Act has tended to be underestimated, with some historians stressing how few counties adopted the legislation rather than how many actually did build an asylum.[2] By 1825, the existing county asylums were an important part of the fabric of institutional management of the insane. Along with the charitable asylums and the growing private madhouse sector, they formed an increasingly significant element in a 'mixed economy' of mental health care. Even before the passage of the mandatory legislation of 1845, the county asylums had become a central element in the provision of institutional management for the insane. Several new asylums were under construction, or in the advanced stages of planning, when the new Acts were passed.[3] If the county asylums did not yet comprise a comprehensive 'system', there had been considerable progress toward laying the basis of one.

The Act of 1808 had both recognized and prescribed the role of the public asylum in the twin aspects of custody and cure. In the first two or three decades of the new asylums' operation, the physical manifestations of custody exercised a powerful and pervasive influence over their care and treatment regimes. Custody, however, was a largely implicit motivating force. The explicit goal, most clearly expressed, was invariably 'cure'. Throughout the first half of the nineteenth century, and beyond, it permeated much of the discourse which surrounded the asylum. The promotion of cure provided the rationale for the incessant emphasis on the need for early removal to an asylum after the onset of mental disorder. Above all, it was the achievement of recovery, with its outcomes of discharge and resumption of social role, that filled reports, announcements and advertisements, as well as the written works of practitioners.[4]

The pursuit of cure had an established history. At Bethlem Hospital curability had long been placed at the heart of its admission criteria, and figures for cures achieved had been issued since the late seventeenth century. The subscription asylums had similar orientation. By the early 1770s, the Annual Reports of the Manchester Lunatic Hospital were giving a detailed breakdown of the numbers cured and relieved, both during the year and since the hospital's opening. Similar information was published for Liverpool Asylum after 1794. It was evident that the need to demonstrate cure rates of between a half and two-thirds had already become a preoccupation. It had also become a basis of competition between rival institutions. The claim on behalf of Exeter Asylum in 1807 that the proportionate number of people 'restored to reason' had 'much surpassed that of any similar establishment', typified much of the hyperbole that would continue to emanate from asylum managers.[5]

Of the first group of county asylums, only Nottingham produced Annual Reports. These provided the same sort of figures as its charitable predecessors did. In 1825 it was reported that, of 580 people admitted since the asylum opened in 1812, 224 had been discharged recovered. It was claimed, of course, that no other asylum had exceeded this proportion. By this time, other asylums were also producing their figures for public scrutiny, and offering analyses of their implications. Gloucester's Annual Reports portrayed a consistently high rate of recoveries. At the end of 1838, the visitors claimed that the asylum's cures since opening amounted to 493 out of 917 (or 54 per cent). External commentators, like James Cowles Prichard and John Thurnam, acknowledged Gloucester's achievement of the best record among the county asylums. C.C. Corsellis at Wakefield in 1839 conceded pride of place to Gloucester, but used his asylum's figures to claim leadership among the pauper-only asylums, with a cure rate of over 44 per cent, compared to 38 per cent at the Suffolk Asylum and around 20 per cent at Hanwell and Maidstone.[6]

By 1840 most of the county asylums were publishing detailed statistical tables as part of their Annual Reports. The numbers and proportions of claimed cures continued to form a central focus of these reports. Comparisons, especially if favourable, were highlighted. If unfavourable, explanations were offered which usually attributed poor results to the chronic state of patients sent off to the asylum long after the onset of their disorder. The Metropolitan Commissioners, as part of their endeavour to promote county asylums, presented statistical data which appeared to demonstrate a favourable picture.[7] There were, however, serious shortcomings inherent in the gathering and presentation of asylums' data on cure rates. The definition of 'cure' was inherently problematic. In practice, recovery might be little more than remission, to be subsequently followed by relapse. The deficiencies of the figures, however, could not diminish the continuing enthusiasm to demonstrate the effectiveness of the public asylum as an institution whose rationale was to cure people and return them to society. The shortcomings also did not serve to deflect asylum managers and Lunacy Commissioners from an evident determination to produce ever more elaborate and detailed statistics.[8]

The ascendancy of the curative ideal was expressed most clearly in the literature about treatment, and in the practical application of a growing range of therapeutic interventions. The evidence is compelling that most asylum medical men energetically strove to bring about improvement in their patients' mental conditions, adopting an eclectic approach with a preparedness to experiment. The era was characterized by the gradual adoption of the principles of moral treatment, and their translation in large institutions into moral management. The rising influence of the reform lobby encouraged a reaction against the excesses of existing custodial practices. The triumph of reform was embodied in the dissemination of the refinement of moral management which became known as the 'non-restraint' system. It constituted testimony of a profound shift along the custody–cure axis. For the future, non-restraint had provided a credible ideology to the public asylum movement.[9]

The direction and management of public asylums continued to reside in a delicate combination of both lay and medical participation. The influence of governors and justices remained strong, particularly in determining admission and charging policies. However, medical influence was clearly on the ascendant in the practical aspects of the asylum's daily operation and in the wider areas of the care and treatment of patients. The growing dominance of superintendents and other medical officers showed itself in a new assertive self-confidence, which accompanied the rise to prominence of individuals like Ellis, Hitch, Charlesworth, Hill and Conolly. The formation, under Samuel Hitch's initiative, of the Association of Medical Officers of Asylums and Hospitals for the Insane was a representation and a reinforcement of the strengthening position of asylum doctors. The general adoption of non-restraint principles, with their promise of a therapeutically-orientated institution, placed the medical men at the forefront of an apparently progressive movement.[10]

The legislation of 1845 was carried through at a time of remarkable therapeutic optimism. The existing county asylums had purportedly achieved large numbers of cures. The new ideology of non-restraint seemed to offer the prospect of building on the achievement, in a liberal institution that matched the perceived spirit of the age. The shortcomings of the system had been evident enough, but they were put to one side. The ideal of the curative asylum had been predicated on a relatively small size, with a number of patients low enough to ensure a degree of personal attention to their individual circumstances and needs. It had also assumed that a good proportion of those sent to the asylum would be in an early and curative stage of an acute disorder. The reality had been the steady accumulation of ever larger numbers of physically deteriorated, ageing people, whose chronic mental conditions were beyond redemption, in buildings becoming ever larger and more impersonal. The improved ward environment and more sophisticated moral management offered many of them only a more pleasant incarceration. Of the original three objectives of 1808, 'comfort' would now come increasingly to the fore over 'cure' and 'safe custody'.[11]

NOTES

1 Of course, the county asylums did not supersede the public subscription asylums. Subscription asylums on the earlier model continued to be opened, as at Lincoln, Oxford and Northampton.

2 K. Jones, *Lunacy, Law and Conscience, 1744–1845: The Social History of the Care of the Insane* (London, 1955), pp. 73–6; W.L. Parry-Jones, *The Trade in Lunacy* (London, 1972), p. 15.

3 See L.D. Smith, 'The County Asylum in the Mixed Economy of Care, 1808–1845', in J. Melling and B. Forsythe (eds), *Insanity, Institutions, and Society* (London, 1999); B. Forsythe, J. Melling and R. Adair, 'The New Poor

Law and the County Pauper Lunatic Asylum – The Devon Experience, 1834–1884', *Social History of Medicine*, vol. IX, no. 3 (December 1996), pp. 335–55; M.R. Olsen, 'The Founding of the Hospital for the Insane Poor, Denbigh', *Trans. Denbighshire Historical Society*, vol. XXIII (1974), pp. 193–217; Shropshire County Record Office, QS 183/4.

4 D.J. Mellett, *The Prerogative of Asylumdom* (London, 1982), pp. 28–33. Private proprietors like Thomas Bakewell and Joseph Mason Cox would proclaim their high numbers of cures, partly to promote their madhouses – T. Bakewell, *A Letter Addressed to the Chairman of the Select Committee of the House of Commons Appointed to Enquire into the State of Madhouses* (Stafford, 1815), pp. 5–10; J.M. Cox, *Practical Observations on Insanity* (London, 1804). Those county asylum superintendents who went into print also stressed curative ideals – Sir W.C. Ellis, *A Treatise on the Nature, Symptoms, Causes, and Treatment of Insanity* (London, 1838); Paul Slade Knight, *Observations on the Causes, Symptoms and Treatment of Derangement of the Mind* (London, 1827).

5 J. Andrews, *Bedlam Revisited: A History of Bethlem Hospital c.1634–1770* (PhD, University of London, 1991), pp. 489–91; N. Roberts, *Cheadle Royal Hospital* (Altrincham, 1967), pp. 29–30; MRI Archives, Annual Reports, XX (1772)–XXXVII (1791); Liverpool Record Office, 614 INF 5/2, Liverpool Infirmary, Annual Reports; Devon County Record Office, 3992 F/H13, Exeter Asylum, 6th Report (1807).

6 NCRO, QS/CA/358; *Nottingham Journal*, 15 October 1825; GCRO, HO22/8/1, *Annual Reports* 1825–38; WRCRO, C85/114, 21st Report (1839), p. 6; J.C. Prichard, *A Treatise on Insanity* (London, 1835), p. 201; J. Thurnam, *Observations and Essays on the Statistics of Insanity* (London, 1845), p. 99.

7 For examples of such reports and tables – WRCRO, C85/107, 108, 114; DCRO, *Reports of Visiting Justices of the County Lunatic Asylum*; SuCRO, B106/10/4.4; *Report of the Metropolitan Commissioners in Lunacy to the Lord Chancellor* (1844), pp. 187–9.

8 *Reports of the Commissioners in Lunacy*, 1847–90.

9 A. Scull, *The Most Solitary of Afflictions: Madness and Society in Britain, 1700–1900* (London, 1993), chapter 6.

10 Scull, *Most Solitary of Afflictions*, chapter 5; E. Renvoize, 'The Association of Medical Officers of Asylums and Hospitals for the Insane, the Medico-Psychological Association, and Their Presidents', in H. Freeman and G.E. Berrios, *150 Years of British Psychiatry*, vol. II, *The Aftermath* (London, 1996), pp. 29–78; A. Walk and D.L. Walker, 'Gloucester and the Beginnings of the R.M.P.A.', *Journal of Mental Science*, vol. CVII, no. 449 (July 1961), pp. 603–32; C. Crommelinck, *Rapport sur les Hospices d'Aliénés de l'Angleterre, de la France et de l'Allemagne* (Courtrai, 1842), pp. 150–5.

11 Scull, *Most Solitary of Afflictions*, chapters 6–7; P. McCandless, '"Build! Build!" The Controversy Over the Care of the Chronically Insane in England, 1855–70', *Bulletin of the History of Medicine*, vol. LIII (1979), pp. 553–74.

Bibliography

MANUSCRIPT SOURCES

Bedfordshire and Luton Archives: LB/1/1, Minutes of Visiting Magistrates, 1812–36; LB/1/8, Extracts of Minutes of Visitors, 1812–40; LB/6/1, 4, Bedford Asylum, inventories, 1834, 1843, 1846; OGE/1, Quarter Sessions, minutes re gaol, house of correction and asylum, 1808–12.

British Museum, Add. MSS: 40,429, Peel Papers, vol. CCXLIX, fos. 108–11, 114–15.

Centre for Kentish Studies: Q/GCL/1, Visiting Magistrates' Minutes, 1831–45; Kent Asylum, CN M&F, case-book, 1833–41; C/MD/B1, Visitors' Book, 1833–45; MH/Md 2/Ap1, Admissions Book; U1515/OQ/L1, Marsham correspondence.

Cheshire County Record Office: QJB/4/4–12, Quarter Sessions records, 1826–36.

Chester City Record Office: HW 354–8, Plans of Cheshire Asylum; HW 190, Reception Orders.

Cornwall County Record Office: DDX 97/1–2, Minutes of Subscribers and Visiting Justices, 1815–46; DDX 654/256, Cornwall Asylum, Visitors' Book, 1828–45.

Devon County Record Office: 3992 F/H6/1–2, Exeter Asylum, House Expense Books, 1801–14; 3992/F/H13, Annual Reports, 1807–23; 3992 F/H14/8, Medical Book; 3992/F/H26, Reports, 1795–1804.

Dorset County Record Office: Quarter Sessions records – Lunatic Asylums, Forston House, 1–4, 1828–44.

Gloucestershire County Record Office: HO22/1/1, Gloucester Asylum, Minutes of Visiting Justices and Subscribers, 1813–47; HO22/3/1–2, House Committee Minutes, 1823–45: HO22/50/1, Visitors' Book, 1823–30; HO22/37/1–3, Adelaide Charity, accounts; HO22/70/1, Case Book, 1823–30; D2593/2/3, plans for additions (1832); D3848/1–2, correspondence, 1826–44.

Greater London Record Office: MA/A/J/1–2, Visiting Justices' Minutes, 1827–31.

Lancashire County Record Office: QAM/1/30/11, Lancaster Asylum, Physicians' Reports; QAM/1/33/11, Magistrates' Visiting Book, 1829–46.

Lancaster Reference Library: MS 34, Lancaster Asylum, letter book, 1836–41; MS 2545, Magistrates' Minutes, 1811.

Leicestershire County Record Office: 13 D 54/3, Leicester Infirmary, Committee Book, 17 November 1815; Box 17 11A, newspaper extracts, 1833–4.

Lincolnshire Archives Office: LAWN 1/1/1–6, Governors' Minutes, 1807–53; LAWN 1/2/1, Director's Journal, 1824–8; LAWN 1/2/3, Governors' Memorandum Books, 1834–42; LAWN 2/19/1, Register of Restraint, 1829–32.

Liverpool Record Office: 614 INF 1/1–3, Minutes of Board of Trustees of Liverpool Infirmary, 1789–1826.

Manchester Royal Infirmary: Admissions Register, 1773–7.

Norfolk County Record Office: SAH 2–6, Norfolk Asylum, Visitors' Minutes, 1813–47; SAH 123–8, Master's Journals, 1814–44; SAH 137, Visitors' Book, 1814–44; SAH 141, Reports of Commissioners in Lunacy, 1844–6.

Nottinghamshire Archives: SO/HO/1/1, Nottingham Asylum, Minutes Relating to Establishment, 1803–10; SO/HO/1/2/1, Proceedings of Visiting Governors, 1810–45; SO/HO/1/2/2, Proceedings of House Committee, 1813–45; SO/HO/1/3/1–3, House Committee Minutes, 1811–45; SO/HO/1/31, Ledger, 1812; SO/HO/1/14, Lady Middleton's Fund, 1841–6; SO/HO/1/9/1, Case Book, 1824–9.

Public Record Office: MH 12/6470/18259, Report of the Insane Poor Confined in the Union Workhouse at Leicester, by Samuel Hitch (1844); MH 12/13288/18261, Report of the Insane Poor Confined in the Workhouse, Birmingham, by Samuel Hitch (1844); HO44/19, fos. 12–13; HO44/32, fos. 420–1.

Staffordshire County Record Office: Q/AIc, Box I, correspondence and miscellaneous; D550/1, Stafford Asylum, Minutes of Visitors, 1812–54; D550/2–6, House Committee Minutes, 1818–54; D550/20, Accounts for Birmingham Paupers, 1828–40; D550/62–4, Weekly Return Books, 1818–44: D550/65, Apothecaries' Day Book, 1818–19.

Stanley Royd Hospital Museum: Admission Book/Visitors' Book, 1839–41; Diary of Dr Gettings.

Suffolk County Record Office: Acc 2697, Suffolk Asylum, Proceedings of Visiting Justices, 1824–45; ID 407/B16/1, Visitors Book, 1829–46.

University of York, Borthwick Institute: C/1, Correspondence of George Jepson, 1811–20; L/3/2, Correspondence of Samuel Tuke and Godfrey Higgins, 1814–15.

Warneford Hospital, Oxford: W.P.5, correspondence, 1816–28.

Wellcome Institute: Western Manuscripts, MS 1587, Cheshire Asylum, prescription book, 1832–9; MS 7076, Robert Gardiner Hill MSS.

West Riding County Record Office: C85/1, Order Book – Pauper Lunatic Asylum, 1814–27; C85/107, Annual Reports of Director, 1819–47; C85/842, 936, Casebooks, 1821–35.

PRINTED RECORDS

Dorset County Asylum: *Reports of Visiting Justices*, 1838–44; *Rules and Regulations* (1833).
Exeter Lunatic Asylum: *Statutes and Constitution, with Rules and Orders* (1801, 1804).
Gloucestershire County Asylum: *Annual Reports*, 1824–47; *Rules and Regulations* (1823).
Hereford Lunatic Asylum: *Rules for the Government of the Lunatic Asylum in Hereford* (1799).
Lancashire County Asylum: *Reports of the Medical Officers of the Lunatic Asylum for the County of Lancaster* (1841–2).
Lincoln Lunatic Asylum: *Rules of the Lincoln Lunatic Asylum* (1819, 1832); *Reports*, 1822–46; 'At a General Board of Governors' (1828); *Instructions for Admission of Patients* (n.d.).
Liverpool Infirmary: *Annual Reports*, 1789–1831.
Manchester Royal Infirmary: *Annual Reports*, 1765–1800; *An Account of the Proceedings of Trustees of the Public Infirmary in Manchester in Regard to the Admission of Lunaticks into that Hospital* (c.1763).
Middlesex County Asylum: *Reports of the Resident Physicians*, 1832–42.
Norfolk County Asylum: *Report of the Visiting Justices of the Norfolk Lunatic Asylum* (1844).
Nottinghamshire County Asylum: *Articles of Union for the General Lunatic Asylum Near Nottingham, with the By-Laws, Rules, Orders and Regulations* (1825); *Annual Reports*, 1810–18, 1836.
Radcliffe Asylum, Oxford: *Rules and Orders of the Radcliffe Asylum* (1836); *Instructions to the Keepers*.
Staffordshire County Asylum: *Reports on Proposed Extensions and Alterations* (1847–8); *Annual Reports* (1839, 1842).
Suffolk County Asylum: *Rules and Regulations* (1828); *Annual Reports*, 1839–46.
West Riding County Asylum: *Annual Reports*, 1822–46; *Reports of Visiting Justices*, 1844–5.

ACTS OF PARLIAMENT

48 Geo. III, Cap. 96, An Act for the Better Care and Maintenance of Lunatics, Being Paupers or Criminals in England, 1808.
51 Geo. III, Cap. 79, An Act to Amend the Act for the Better Care and Maintenance of Lunatics, 1811.
55 Geo. III, Cap. 46, An Act to Amend the Act for the Better Care and Maintenance of Lunatics, 1815.
59 Geo. III, Cap. 127, An Act for Making Provision for the Better Care of Pauper Lunatics in England, 1819.
5 Geo. IV, Cap. 71, An Act to Amend Several Acts for the Better Care and Maintenance of Lunatics, Being Paupers or Criminals in England, 1824.

9 Geo. IV, Cap. 40, An Act to Amend the Laws for the Erection and Regulation of County Lunatic Asylums, 1828.
9 Geo. IV, Cap. 41, An Act to Regulate the Care and Treatment of Insane Persons in England, 1828.
4 & 5 Will. IV, Cap. 76, Poor Law Amendment Act, 1834.
5 & 6 Vic., Cap. 4, An Act to Amend the Laws Relating to Houses Licensed by the Metropolitan Commissioners and Justices of the Peace for the Reception of Insane Persons, and for the Inspection of County Asylums and Public Hospitals for the Reception of Insane Persons, 1842.
8 & 9 Vic., Cap. 100, An Act for the Regulation of the Care and Treatment of Lunatics, 1845.
8 & 9 Vic., Cap. 126, An Act to Amend the Laws for the Provision and Regulation of Lunatic Asylums for Counties and Boroughs, and for the Maintenance and Care of Pauper Lunatics, in England, 1845.

PARLIAMENTARY AND OFFICIAL REPORTS

Report of Select Committee on the State of Criminal and Pauper Lunatics (1807).
Report of Select Committee on Madhouses, with Minutes of Evidence (1814–15).
Report of Select Committee on Madhouses, with Minutes of Evidence (1816).
Returns of Lunatics Confined in Gaols, Hospitals, and Lunatic Asylums (1819).
Lunatic Asylums, Returns (1825).
Lunatic Asylums, Returns (1826).
Report from Select Committee on Pauper Lunatics in the County of Middlesex, and on Lunatic Asylums (1827).
Lunatic Asylums, Returns (1830–1).
Report from Commissioners on the Administration and Practical Operation of the Poor Laws in England and Wales (1834).
County Lunatic Asylums, Returns (1836).
Report from Select Committee on the Poor Law Amendment Act (1837–8).
Report from Select Committee on Hereford Lunatic Asylum, with Minutes of Evidence (1839).
Report of the Metropolitan Commissioners in Lunacy to the Lord Chancellor (1844).
Further Report of the Commissioners in Lunacy (1847).
Eighth Report of the Commissioners in Lunacy (1854).
Ninth Report of the Commissioners in Lunacy (1855).

CONTEMPORARY BOOKS, PAMPHLETS AND ARTICLES

Alexander, Disney, *An Impartial Statement of the Question Recently Agitated Between Dr Crowther and Dr Alexander Respecting the Visiting Department of the Pauper Lunatic Asylum* (Wakefield, 1825).

An Abstract of Proceedings Relative to the Institution of a General Lunatic Asylum in or Near the City of Gloucester (Gloucester, 1794).

An Account of the Origin, Nature and Objects of the Asylum on Headington Hill, Near Oxford (Oxford, 1827).

An Address to the Magistrates of the County of Lancaster on the Situation Proposed for the Intended County Lunatic Asylum (Liverpool, 1810).

An Address to the Public Concerning the General Lunatic Asylum Near Nottingham (Nottingham, 1811).

Arnold, T., *Observations on the Nature, Kinds, Causes and Prevention of Insanity* (Leicester, 1782–6).

Baines, Edward, *History, Directory and Gazetteer of the County of York* (Leeds, 1823).

Baines, Edward, *History, Directory and Gazetteer of the County Palatine of Lancaster* (Liverpool, 1825).

Bakewell, Thomas, *A Letter Addressed to the Chairman of the Select Committee of the House of Commons Appointed to Enquire into the State of Madhouses: to Which is Subjoined, Remarks on the Nature, Causes, and Cure of Mental Derangement* (Stafford, 1815).

Battie, William, *A Treatise on Madness* (London, 1758).

Becher, J.T., *Resolutions Concerning the Intended General Lunatic Asylum Near Nottingham* (Newark, 1810).

Blackner, John, *The History of Nottingham* (Nottingham, 1815).

Browne, W.A.F., *What Asylums Were, Are, and Ought to Be: Being the Substance of Five Lectures Delivered Before the Managers of the Montrose Royal Lunatic Asylum* (Edinburgh, 1837; reprinted London, 1991).

Burdett, Henry C., *Hospitals and Asylums of the World* (London, 1891).

Charlesworth, Edward Parker, *Remarks on the Treatment of the Insane and the Management of Lunatic Asylums Being the Substance of a Return from the Lincoln Lunatic Asylum, etc.* (London, 1828).

Conolly, John, *An Enquiry Concerning the Indications of Insanity* (London, 1830).

Conolly, John, *The Construction and Government of Lunatic Asylums* (London, 1847).

Conolly, John, *The Treatment of the Insane Without Mechanical Restraints* (London, 1856; reprinted 1973).

Cox, Joseph Mason, *Practical Observations on Insanity* (London, 1804, new edn, 1806).

Crommelinck, C., *Rapport sur les Hospices d'Aliénés de l'Angleterre, de la France et de l'Allemagne* (Courtrai, 1842).

Crowther, Caleb, *Some Observations Respecting the Management of the Pauper Lunatic Asylum at Wakefield* (Wakefield, 1830).

Crowther, Caleb, *Observations on the Management of Madhouses: Illustrated by Occurrences at the West Riding and Middlesex Asylums* (London, 1838).

Earle, Pliny, *A Visit to Thirteen Asylums for the Insane in Europe* (Philadelphia, 1841).

Ellis, William C., *A Letter to Thomas Thompson, M.P.* (Hull, 1815).

Ellis, Sir William C., *A Treatise on the Nature, Symptoms, Causes, and Treatment of Insanity, With Practical Observations on Lunatic Asylums* (London, 1838).

Familiar Views of Lunacy and Lunatic Life, by the Late Medical Superintendent of an Asylum for the Insane (London, 1850).

Fletcher, Ralph, *Sketches From the Case Book, to Illustrate the Influence of the Mind on the Body, With the Treatment of Some of the More Important Brain and Nervous Disturbances Which Arise From This Influence* (London, 1833).

Foulston, John, *The Public Buildings, Erected in the West of England by John Foulston, F.R.I.B.A.* (London, 1838).

Gilbey, W.H., 'On the Dysentery Which Occurred in the Wakefield Lunatic Asylum in the Years 1826, 1827, 1828, and 1829', *North of England Medical Journal and Surgical Journal*, vol. I (1830–1), pp. 91–101.

Granville, A.B., *The Spas of England: Midland Spas* (London, 1841).

A Guide Through Hanwell Lunatic Asylum (London, 1843).

Hallaran, W.S., *An Enquiry into the Causes Producing the Extraordinary Addition to the Numbers of the Insane, Together with extended Observations on the Cure of Insanity* (Cork, 1810).

Halliday, Sir Andrew, *A General View of the Present State of Lunatics and Lunatic Asylums in Great Britain and Ireland* (London, 1828).

Haslam, John, *Observations on Insanity* (London, 1798).

Haslam, John, *Considerations on the Moral Management of Insane Persons* (London, 1817).

Hemingway, Joseph, *History of the City of Chester* (Chester, 1831).

Higgins, Godfrey, *Rules for the Management of the Pauper Lunatic Asylum for the West Riding of the County of York, Erected at Wakefield* (Wakefield, 1821).

Hill, George Nesse, *An Essay on the Prevention and Cure of Insanity* (London, 1814).

Hill, Robert Gardiner, *Total Abolition of Personal Restraint in the Treatment of the Insane: A Lecture on the Management of Lunatic Asylums and the Treatment of the Insane, Delivered at the Mechanics Institution, Lincoln, on the 21st of June, 1838* (London, 1839).

Hill, Robert Gardiner, *A Concise History of the Entire Abolition of Mechanical Restraint in the Treatment of the Insane: and of the Introduction, Success, and Final Triumph of the Non-Restraint System* (London, 1857).

Hill, Robert Gardiner, *Lunacy: Its Past and Its Present* (London, 1870).

Huxley, J.E., 'History and Description of the Kent Asylum', *Journal of Mental Science*, vol. I, no. 3 (February 1854), pp. 39–45.

Ingleman, Richard, *A Specification Containing the Particulars of the Work to be Executed. . .in Constructing a General Lunatic Asylum Near Nottingham* (Newark, 1810).

Jacobi, M., *On the Construction and Management of Hospitals for the Insane* (London, 1841).

Knight, Paul Slade, *A Letter to the Right Honourable Lord Stanley, and the Other Visiting Justices of the Lunatic Asylum for the County of Lancaster* (Lancaster, 1822).

Knight, Paul Slade, *Observations on the Causes, Symptoms and Treatment of Derangement of the Mind* (London, 1827).

Lincoln and Lincolnshire Cabinet for 1828 (Lincoln, 1828).

Martineau, Harriet, 'The Hanwell Lunatic Asylum', *Tait's Edinburgh Magazine* (1834), pp. 305–10.

Matthiason, J.H., *Bedford and its Environs; or an Historical and Topographical Sketch of the Town of Bedford* (Bedford, 1831).

Medicus, *A Short Letter to a Noble Lord on the Present State of Lunatic Asylums in Great Britain* (Edinburgh, 1806).

Mulock, Thomas, *British Lunatic Asylums: Public and Private* (Stafford, 1858).

Outterson Wood, T., 'The Early History of the Medico-Psychological Association', *Journal of Mental Science*, vol. XLII, no. 177 (April 1896), pp. 241–60.

Pargeter, William, *Observations on Maniacal Disorders* (Reading, 1792; reprinted London, 1988).

Paul, G.O., *A Scheme of an Institution and a Description of a Plan for a General Lunatic Asylum for the Western Counties to be Built in or Near the City of Gloucester* (Gloucester, 1796).

Paul, Sir George Onesiphorus, *Observations on the Subject of Lunatic Asylums, Addressed to a General Meeting of Subscribers to a Fund for Building and Establishing a General Lunatic Asylum Near Gloucester* (Gloucester, 1812).

Paul, Sir George Onesiphorus, *Doubts Concerning the Expediency and Propriety of Immediately Proceeding to Provide a Lunatic Asylum, or, House for the Reception of Lunatics, for the County of Gloucester* (Gloucester, 1813).

Pinel, Phillippe, *A Treatise on Insanity* (Sheffield, 1806, translated by D.D. Davis).

Prichard, James Cowles, *A Treatise on Insanity* (London, 1835).

Proceedings of the General Quarterly Board of the Lincoln Lunatic Asylum, Held on October 13, 1830 (Lincoln, 1830).

Reid, Robert, *Observations on the Structure of Hospitals for the Treatment of Lunatics* (Edinburgh, 1809).

Rickman, Edwin, *Madness, or the Maniac's Hall: A Poem* (London, 1841).

Stark, William, *Remarks on Hospitals for the Cure of Mental Derangement* (Glasgow, 1810).

Thurnam, John, *Observations and Essays on the Statistics of Insanity* (London, 1845).

Tuke, Daniel Hack, *Chapters in the History of the Insane in the British Isles* (London, 1882).

Tuke, Samuel, *Description of the Retreat* (York, 1813).

Tuke, Samuel, *Practical Hints on the Construction and Economy of Pauper Lunatic Asylums; Including Instructions to the Architects Who Offered Plans for the Wakefield Asylum* (York, 1815).

Tuke, Samuel, *Memoirs of Samuel Tuke* (London, 1840).

Useful Information Concerning the Origin, Nature and Purpose of the Radcliffe Lunatic Asylum (Oxford, 1840).

Warner Ellis, H., *'Our Doctor': Memorials of Sir William Charles Ellis, M.D., of Southall Park, Middlesex* (London, 1868).

Watson and Pritchett, *Plans, Elevations, Sections and Description of the Pauper Lunatic Asylum Lately Erected at Wakefield* (York, 1819).

White, William, *History, Gazetteer, and Directory of Nottinghamshire* (Sheffield, 1832).

White, William, *History, Gazetteer, and Directory of Staffordshire* (Sheffield, 1834).

White, William, *History, Gazetteer, and Directory of Suffolk* (Sheffield, 1844).

White, William, *History, Gazetteer, and Directory of Norfolk* (Sheffield, 1845).

Wright, Thomas Giordani, *Cholera in the Asylum: Reports on the Origins and Progress of the Pestilential Cholera in the West Yorkshire Lunatic Asylum During the Autumn of 1849, and on the Previous State of the Institution* (London, Wakefield, 1850).

NEWSPAPERS AND JOURNALS

Asylum Journal of Mental Science, 1853–60.

British and Foreign Medical Review, 1838–40.

Gloucester Journal, 1793–1845.

Imperial Magazine, 1822–9.

Lichfield Mercury, 1818–19.

Lincoln Gazette, 1840.

Lincoln Herald, 1828–9.

Lincoln and Stamford Mercury, 1837–40.

Lonsdale Magazine, February 1821.

Monthly Magazine, 1816–18.

Morning Herald, 12 January 1826.

North of England Medical and Surgical Journal, 1830–1.

Nottingham Journal, 1800–35.

Staffordshire Advertiser, 1810–45.

The Builder, 1846–7.

The Lancet, 1839–51.

The Satirist, 1838–9.

The Times, 1827–45.

Wakefield and Halifax Journal, 1814–45.

SECONDARY SOURCES

Books

Andrews, C.T., *The Dark Awakening: A History of St Lawrence's Hospital, Bodmin* (Bodmin, 1978).

Andrews, Jonathan, Asa Briggs, Roy Porter, Penny Tucker and Keir Waddington, *The History of Bethlem* (London, 1997).

Ashton, O., Fyson, R. and Roberts, S. (eds), *The Duty of Discontent: Essays for Dorothy Thompson* (London, 1995), pp. 142–66.

Ashworth, A.L., *Stanley Royd Hospital Wakefield, One Hundred and Fifty Years: A History* (London, 1975).

Barry, J. and Jones, C. (eds), *Medicine and Charity Before the Welfare State* (London, 1991).

Bynum, W.F., Porter, R. and Shepherd, M. (eds), *The Anatomy of Madness: Essays in the History of Psychiatry* (3 vols, London, 1985–8).

Cashman, Bernard, *A Proper House: Bedford Lunatic Asylum, 1812–1860* (North Bedfordshire Health Authority, 1992).

Castel, Robert, *The Regulation of Madness: The Origins of Incarceration in France* (Oxford, 1988).

Chadwick, Edwin, *Report on the Sanitary Conditions of the Labouring Population of Great Britain* (1842, Edinburgh 1965 edn).

Crammer, John L., *Asylum History: Buckinghamshire County Pauper Lunatic Asylum – St John's* (London, 1990).

Crowther, M.A., *The Workhouse System 1834–1929* (London, 1981).

Davies, C. (ed.), *Rewriting Nursing History* (London, 1980).

Digby, Anne, *Madness, Morality and Medicine: A Study of the York Retreat, 1796–1914* (Cambridge, 1985).

Digby, Anne, *From York Lunatic Asylum to Bootham Park Hospital* (University of York, Borthwick Papers, 1986).

Donnelly, Michael, *Managing the Mind: A Study of Medical Psychology in Early Nineteenth Century Britain* (London, 1983).

Evans, Robin, *The Fabrication of Virtue: English Prison Architecture, 1750–1840* (Cambridge, 1982).

Finberg, H.P.R. (ed.), *Gloucestershire Studies* (Leicester, 1957), pp. 195–224.

Finnane, Mark, *Insanity and the Insane in Post-Famine Ireland* (London, 1991).

Foss, Arthur, and Trick, Kerith, *St Andrew's Hospital, Northampton: The First One Hundred and Fifty Years 1838–1988* (Cambridge, 1989).

Foucault, Michel, *Madness and Civilization: A History of Insanity in the Age of Reason* (London, 1971).

Fraser, Derek, *The Evolution of the British Welfare State* (London, 1984 edn).

Freeman, Hugh and Berrios, German E. (eds), *150 Years of British Psychiatry, 1841–1991* (London, 1991).

Freeman, Hugh and Berrios, German E. (eds), *150 Years of British Psychiatry, 1841–1991*, vol. II, *The Aftermath* (London, 1996).

French, C.N., *The Story of St Luke's Hospital* (London, 1951).
Frizelle, E.R., *The Life and Times of the Royal Infirmary at Leicester* (Leicester, 1988).
Granshaw, Lindsay and Porter, Roy (eds), *The Hospital in History* (London, 1989).
Harvey, A.D., *Britain in the Early Nineteenth Century* (London, 1978).
Hempton, D., *The Religion of the People: Methodism and Popular Religion c. 1750–1900* (London, 1996).
Henriques, Ursula, *Before the Welfare State; Social Administration in Early Industrial Britain* (London, 1979).
Hill, Sir Francis, *Georgian Lincoln* (Cambridge, 1966).
Hill, Sir Francis, *Victorian Lincoln* (Cambridge, 1974).
Hunter, David, *A History of the Coppice, Nottingham, 1788–1918* (Nottingham, 1918).
Hunter, Richard and Macalpine, Ida, *Three Hundred Years of Psychiatry, 1535–1860* (Oxford, 1963).
Hunter, Richard and Macalpine, Ida, 'Introduction' to S. Tuke, *Description of the Retreat* (London, 1964).
Hunter, Richard and Macalpine, Ida, 'Introduction' to J. Conolly, *Treatment of the Insane Without Mechanical Restraint* (London, 1973).
Hunter, Richard and Macalpine, Ida, *Psychiatry for the Poor. 1851 Colney Hatch Asylum: Friern Hospital 1973* (London, 1974).
Ignatieff, Michael, *A Just Measure of Pain: the Penitentiary in the Industrial Revolution 1750–1850* (London, 1989 edn).
Ingram, Allan, *The Madhouse of Language: Writing and Reading Madness in the Eighteenth Century* (London, 1991).
Jones, Kathleen, *Lunacy, Law and Conscience, 1744–1845: the Social History of the Care of the Insane* (London, 1955).
Jones, Kathleen, *A History of the Mental Health Services* (London, 1972).
Jones, Kathleen, *Asylums and After: A Revised History of the Mental Health Services: From the Early Eighteenth Century to the 1990s* (London, 1993).
King, Anthony D. (ed.), *Buildings and Society* (London, 1980).
Loudon, Irvine, *Medical Care and the General Practitioner, 1750–1850* (Oxford, 1986).
Macalpine, Ida and Hunter, Richard, *George III and the Mad-Business* (London, 1969).
Mackenzie, Charlotte, *Psychiatry for the Rich: A History of Ticehurst Asylum, 1792–1917* (London, 1992).
Malcolm, Elizabeth, *Swift's Hospital: A History of St. Patrick's Hospital, Dublin, 1746–1989* (Dublin, 1989).
Markus, Thomas A., (ed.), *Order in Space and Society: Architectural Form and its Context in the Scottish Enlightenment* (Edinburgh, 1982).
Markus, Thomas A., *Buildings and Power: Freedom and Control in the Origins of Modern British Building Types* (London, 1993).
Marland, Hilary, *Medicine and Industrial Society in Wakefield and Huddersfield, 1780–1870* (Cambridge, 1987).

Mellett, David J., *The Prerogative of Asylumdom: Social, Cultural and Administrative Aspects of the Institutional Treatment of the Insane in Nineteenth Century Britain* (London, 1982).

Micale, M.S. and Porter, R. (eds), *Discovering the History of Psychiatry* (Oxford, 1994).

Murray, R.M. and Turner, T.H. (eds), *Lectures on the History of Psychiatry* (London, 1990).

Nolan, Peter, *A History of Mental Health Nursing* (London, 1993).

Orme, H.G. and Brock, W.H., *Leicestershire's Lunatics: The Institutional Care of Leicestershire's Lunatics During the Nineteenth Century* (Leicester, 1987).

Parry-Jones, Brenda, *The Warneford Hospital, Oxford, 1826–1976* (Oxford, 1976).

Parry-Jones, William Lloyd, *The Trade in Lunacy* (London, 1972).

Pevsner, Nikolaus, *A History of Building Types* (London, 1976).

Pickstone, John, *Medicine and Industrial Society: A History of Hospital Development in Manchester and its Region, 1752–1946* (Manchester, 1985).

Porter, Roy, *Mind-Forg'd Manacles: A History of Madness in England from the Restoration to the Regency* (Cambridge, 1987).

Porter, Roy and Bynum, W.F. (eds), *Medical Fringe and Medical Orthodoxy* (London, 1987).

Porter, Roy and Porter, Dorothy, *In Sickness and in Health; the British Experience* (London, 1988).

Roberts, Nesta, *Cheadle Royal Hospital: A Bicentenary History* (Altrincham, 1967).

Scull, Andrew, *Museums of Madness: The Social Organisation of Insanity in Nineteenth-Century England* (London, 1979), reprinted as *The Most Solitary of Afflictions: Madness and Society in Britain 1700–1900* (London, 1993).

Scull, Andrew, *Social Order, Mental Disorder* (London, 1989).

Scull, Andrew (ed.), *Madhouses, Mad-Doctors and Madmen: The Social History of Psychiatry in the Victorian Era* (London, 1981).

Scull, Andrew (ed.), *The Asylum as Utopia: W.A.F. Browne and the Mid-Nineteenth Century Consolidation of Psychiatry* (London, 1991).

Scull, Andrew, Mackenzie, Charlotte and Hervey, Nicholas, *Masters of Bedlam: The Transformation of the Mad-Doctoring Trade* (Princeton, 1996).

Shepherd, M. and Zangwill, O.L. (eds), *Handbook of Psychiatry*, vol. I, *General Psychopathology* (Cambridge, 1983).

Showalter, Eileen, *The Female Malady: Women, Madness, and English Culture, 1830–1980* (London, 1985).

Skultans, Vida, *Madness and Morals: Ideas on Insanity in the Nineteenth Century* (London, 1975).

Smith, C.J. and Giggs, J.A. (eds), *Location and Stigma: Contemporary Perspectives on Mental Health Care* (London, 1988).

Taylor, Jeremy, *Hospital and Asylum Architecture in England 1840–1914* (London, 1991).

Thompson, F.M.L., *English Landed Society in the Nineteenth Century* (London, 1963).

Todd, John and Ashworth, Lawrence, *'The House': Wakefield Asylum 1818. . .* (Wakefield Health Authority, 1993).

Tomes, Nancy, *A Generous Confidence: Thomas Story Kirkbride and the Art of Asylum-Keeping* (Cambridge, 1984).

Waddington, Ian, *The Medical Profession in the Industrial Revolution* (Dublin, 1984).

Woodward, John, *To Do the Sick No Harm: A Study of the British Voluntary Hospital System to 1875* (London, 1974).

Wright, David and Digby, Anne (eds), *From Idiocy to Mental Deficiency* (London, 1996).

Articles

Andrews, Jonathan, 'The Lot of the "Incurably" Insane in Enlightenment England', *Eighteenth Century Life*, vol. XII (1988), pp. 1–18.

Bailey, Ann, 'The Founding of the Gloucestershire County Asylum, now Horton Road Hospital Gloucester, 1792–1823', *Trans. Bristol and Gloucestershire Archaeological Society*, vol. XC (1971), pp. 178–91.

Bolton, J.S., 'The Evolution of a Mental Hospital – Wakefield, 1818–1928', *Journal of Mental Science*, vol. LXXIV (October 1928), pp. 587–633.

Borsay, Anne, 'Cash and Conscience: Financing the General Hospital at Bath c.1738–1750', *Social History of Medicine*, vol. IV, no. 2 (August 1991), pp. 207–29.

Brown, T.E., 'The Mental Hospital and its Historians', *Bulletin of the History of Medicine*, vol. LVI (1982), pp. 109–14.

Bynum, William F., 'Rationales for Therapy in British Psychiatry: 1780–1835', *Medical History*, vol. XVIII (1974), pp. 317–34.

Carpenter, Peter, 'Thomas Arnold: A Provincial Psychiatrist in Georgian England', *Medical History*, vol. XXXIII (April 1989), pp. 199–216.

Cooter, Roger, 'Phrenology and British Alienists, c.1825–1845', *Medical History*, vol. XX (1976), part 1 (January), pp. 1–21, part 2 (April), pp. 135–51.

Digby, Anne, 'Changes in the Asylum: The Case of York, 1777–1815', *Economic History Review*, 2nd series, vol. XXXVI, no. 2 (May 1983), pp. 218–39.

Digby, Anne, 'The Changing Profile of a Nineteenth-Century Asylum: the York Retreat', *Psychological Medicine*, vol. XIV (1984), pp. 739–48.

Forsythe, Bill, Melling, Joseph and Adair, Richard, 'The New Poor Law and the County Pauper Lunatic Asylum', *Social History of Medicine*, vol. IX, no. 3 (December 1996), pp. 335–55.

Frank, J.A., 'Non-Restraint and Robert Gardiner Hill', *Bulletin of the History of Medicine*, vol. XLI (1967), pp. 140–60.

Grob, Gerald, 'Marxian Analysis and Mental Illness', *History of Psychiatry*, vol. I (1989), pp. 223–32.

Haw, Camilla, 'Sketches in the History of Psychiatry: John Conolly and the Treatment of Mental Illness in Early Victorian England', *Psychiatric Bulletin*, vol. XIII (1989), pp. 440–4.

Haw, Camilla, 'John Conolly's Attendants at the Hanwell Asylum, 1839–52', *History of Nursing Journal*, vol. III, no. 1 (1990), pp. 26–58.

Hodgkinson, R.G. 'Provision for Pauper Lunatics 1834–1871', *Medical History*, vol. X (1966), pp. 138–54.

Ignatieff, Michael, 'Total Institutions and Working Classes: A Review Essay', *History Workshop*, vol. XV (Spring 1983), pp. 167–73.

Lodge Patch, Ian, 'The Surrey County Lunatic Asylum (Springfield): Early Years in the Development of an Institution', *British Journal of Psychiatry*, vol. CLIX (July 1991), pp. 69–77.

Luckin, Bill, 'Towards a Social History of Institutionalisation', *Social History*, vol. VIII (January 1993), pp. 87–94.

McCandless, Peter, '"Build! Build!" The Controversy Over the Care of the Chronically Insane in England, 1855–70', *Bulletin of the History of Medicine*, vol. LIII (1979), pp. 553–74.

Nolan, Peter, 'The Founding of Psychiatric Nursing and its Aftermath', *British Journal of Psychiatry*, vol. CLIX (July 1991), pp. 46–52.

Philo, Chris, '"Fit Localities for an Asylum": the Historical Geography of the Nineteenth Century "Mad-business" in England as Viewed Through the Pages of the Asylum Journal', *Journal of Historical Geography*, vol. XIII (1987), pp. 398–415.

Ray, L.J., 'Models of Madness in Victorian Asylum Practice', *Archives Européennes de Sociologie*, vol. XXII (1981), pp. 229–64.

Rollin, Henry, 'Religion as an Index of the Rise and Fall of "Moral Treatment" in 19th Century Lunatic Asylums in England', *Psychiatric Bulletin*, vol. XVIII (1994), pp. 627–31.

Scull, Andrew, 'From Madness to Mental Illness: Medical Men as Moral Entrepreneurs', *Archives Européennes de Sociologie*, vol. XVI (1975), pp. 218–51.

Scull, Andrew, 'Mad-Doctors and Magistrates: English Psychiatry's Struggle for Professional Autonomy in the Nineteenth Century', *Archives Européennes de Sociologie*, vol. XVII (1976), pp. 279–305.

Scull, Andrew, 'Moral Treatment Reconsidered', *Psychological Medicine*, vol. IX (1979), pp. 421–8.

Scull, Andrew, 'The Domestication of Madness', *Medical History*, vol. XXVII, no. 3 (July 1983), pp. 233–48.

Scull, Andrew, 'Psychiatry and Social Control in the Nineteenth and Twentieth Centuries', *History of Psychiatry*, vol. II, no. 6 (June 1991), pp. 149–69.

Scull, Andrew, 'Museums of Madness Revisited', *Social History of Medicine*, vol. VI (April 1993), pp. 3–23.

Scull, Andrew, 'Somatic Treatments and the Historiography of Psychiatry', *History of Psychiatry*, vol. V, no. 1 (March 1994), pp. 1–12.

Smith, L.D., 'Behind Closed Doors: Lunatic Asylum Keepers, 1800–60', *Social History of Medicine*, vol. I, no. 3 (December 1988), pp. 301–27.

Smith, L.D., 'To Cure Those Afflicted with the Disease of Insanity: Thomas Bakewell and Spring Vale Asylum', *History of Psychiatry*, vol. IV (1993), pp. 107–27.

Smith, L.D., 'Close Confinement in a Mighty Prison: Thomas Bakewell and his Campaign Against Public Asylums, 1810–1830', *History of Psychiatry*, vol. V (1994), pp. 191–214.

Smith, L.D., 'The "Great Experiment": the Place of Lincoln in the History of Psychiatry', *Lincolnshire History and Archeaology*, vol. XXX (1995), pp. 55–62.

Smith L.D., 'The Pauper Lunatic Problem in the West Midlands, 1815–1850', *Midland History*, vol. XXI (1996), pp. 101–18.

Suzuki, Akihito, 'The Politics and Ideology of Non-Restraint: the Case of the Hanwell Asylum', *Medical History*, vol. XXXIX, no. 1 (1995), pp. 1–17.

Szasz, Thomas, 'The Origin of Psychiatry: The Alienist as Nanny for Troublesome Adults', *History of Psychiatry*, vol. VI, no. 1 (March 1995), pp. 1–19.

Walk, Alexander, 'Some Aspects of the "Moral Treatment" of the Insane up to 1854', *Journal of Mental Science*, vol. C (1954), pp. 807–38.

Walk, Alexander, 'Lincoln and Non-Restraint', *British Journal of Psychiatry*, vol. CXVII (1970), pp. 481–96.

Walk, A., and Walker, D.L., 'Gloucester and the Beginnings of the R.M.P.A.', *Journal of Mental Science*, vol. CVII, no. 449 (July 1961), pp. 603–32.

Walton, John, 'Lunacy in the Industrial Revolution: A Study of Asylum Admissions, 1848–50', *Journal of Social History*, vol. XIII, no. 1 (Fall 1979), pp. 1–22.

Winston, Mark, 'The Bethel at Norwich: An Eighteenth-Century Hospital for Lunatics', *Medical History*, vol. XXXVIII, no. 1 (January 1994), pp. 27–51.

Wright, David, 'Getting Out of the Asylum: Understanding the Confinement of the Insane in the Nineteenth Century', *Social History* of *Medicine*, vol. X (April 1997), pp. 137–55.

UNPUBLISHED THESES

Andrews, Jonathan, *Bedlam Revisited: A History of Bethlem Hospital c.1634–1770* (PhD, University of London, 1991).

Bartlett, Peter, *The Poor Law of Lunacy: The Administration of Pauper Lunatics in Mid-Nineteenth Century England with Special Emphasis on Leicestershire and Rutland* (PhD, University of London, 1993).

Doyle, A.H., *Clergy of the Church of England as Justices of the Peace 1750–1850, with Special Reference to the County of Worcester* (MA, University of Birmingham, 1986).

Fears, Michael, *The 'Moral Treatment' of Insanity: A Study in the Social Construction of Human Nature* (PhD, University of Edinburgh, 1978).

Forsyth, J.A.S., *The County Lunatic Asylums, 1808–1845: A Study of the Way in which a Building Type was Developed* (BA Architecture Dissertation, University of Newcastle, 1969).

McCandless, Peter, *Insanity and Society: A Study of the English Lunacy Reform Movement, 1815–1870* (PhD, University of Wisconsin, 1974).

Philo, Christopher P., *The Space Reserved for Insanity: Studies in the Historical Geography of the Mad-Business in England and Wales* (PhD, St David's University College, Lampeter, 1992).

Russell, Richard, *Mental Physicians and their Patients: Psychological Medicine in the English Pauper Lunatic Asylums of the Later Nineteenth Century* (PhD, University of Sheffield, 1983).

Index

Acts of Parliament
  lunatic asylums
    1808 6, 16, 20–9, 31, 33, 36, 39–40, 53, 54, 71, 94, 112, 114, 118, 125, 148, 159, 170, 188, 212, 251, 284
    1811 71, 113, 159
    1828 209
    1845 8, 275, 284, 287
  Poor Law Amendment Act (1834) 7, 115, 125
Adams, Serjeant John 267–71
Adelaide fund 214
admission(s) 24, 55, 57, 59, 70–1, 94–102, 112–17, 138, 174, 285–6
after-care 213–14
airing courts 37, 161, 172, 175, 237, 240, 275
alcohol abuse 103, 105, 108–9, 145
Alexander, Dr Disney 57–8, 67–8
alienists 4, 61, 64, 103, 112, 195, 198, 201, 205, 211–12, 264, 276
Allderidge, Patricia 2
Allis, Thomas 37
Andrews, Jonathan 5, 159, 228
antimony tartrate 198–200
apothecaries 14, 19, 35, 61–2, 67, 234
Arnold, Dr Thomas 19, 188, 191, 248
architects 32–5, 37, 164
architecture 32, 37, 159–61
Ashley, Lord 7, 81
Association of Medical Officers of Asylums and Hospitals for the Insane 117, 269, 287
asylum balls 241–2
asylums
  charitable asylums
    Bethlem 5, 14–15, 18, 19, 33–7, 103, 134, 142–3, 146, 159, 188, 197, 201, 203, 213, 227–8, 248, 260, 285
    Cork 227
    Coton Hill (Stafford) 79
    Dundee 242
    Edinburgh 40
    Exeter 6, 15–16, 18–20, 33, 35, 146, 285
    Glasgow 30, 32, 34, 40
    Guy's 14
    Hereford 15, 18
    Leicester 15, 17–18, 33, 248
    Lincoln 6, 31–2, 35–6, 53, 55–8, 61, 63, 65–6, 72, 79, 82, 96, 98, 107, 120–3, 134–5, 137, 139, 141, 143–5, 149–52, 160, 164–8, 170–1, 176–7, 190, 192–4, 196–7, 199, 201, 204, 213, 237–8, 240–3, 249, 252, 255, 258, 260–9, 272–5
    Liverpool 6, 15, 16, 29, 33, 52, 132, 163, 197, 248–9, 256, 285
    Manchester 6, 15–20, 29, 33, 35, 52, 132, 164, 198, 248, 285
    Newcastle 15, 30
    Northampton 52, 255, 268–9
    Norwich Bethel 14, 29, 52, 248
    Oxford (Radcliffe) 30–1, 35–6, 53, 75, 141, 146
    St Luke's (London) 14–16, 18–19, 33, 35, 37, 42, 53, 143, 188, 248
    York 6, 15–22, 28, 30, 32, 52, 190, 193, 228, 248
    York Retreat 3–4, 6, 28, 37–9, 42, 82, 118, 131, 133, 159–60, 166, 190, 193, 197, 208, 227–8, 250, 259–60, 264, 269
  county asylums
    Bedford 6, 26, 31–2, 38, 55, 58, 60, 61, 75–6, 82, 117, 132, 139, 143, 160–1, 165, 236–7, 253, 255–6, 270
    Cheshire (Chester) 26, 37, 52, 74–5, 82, 162, 167, 237
    Cornwall (Bodmin) 6, 26, 32, 34, 38, 55, 58–9, 62–3, 71, 74, 76, 80, 82, 114, 132, 135, 139, 143–4, 162–3, 165, 169–70, 179, 192–3, 198, 237, 255

Dorset (Forston) 26, 52, 55, 57–9, 62, 66, 72, 80, 82, 98, 101–2, 108–10, 116, 138–9, 147–8, 150, 163, 165–7, 170, 175, 178, 188, 197, 202–3, 209, 214, 234–5, 237, 240, 249, 251, 270
Gloucester 6, 16, 21, 30–2, 34–8, 40, 54–8, 60–3, 65, 70, 72, 74–5, 78–80, 82, 95–102, 106–12, 116, 124, 132–5, 138, 140–1, 143–5, 147, 151, 160, 162, 165–73, 175, 177–8, 188–94, 201, 203, 214, 216–7, 230, 234, 237–8, 241, 269–70, 275, 285
Kent (Maidstone) 26, 52, 63, 80–2, 95, 97, 133, 144, 168–9, 175, 236, 255, 270–1, 286
Lancaster 26, 29, 31–2, 36–8, 58, 60, 63, 75, 79–80, 82, 94–5, 101, 104, 107, 110, 114, 118–21, 123–4, 132–3, 136, 138–9, 141–6, 148–9, 166, 169, 172–3, 175–6, 177–9, 189, 192, 194–5, 197, 200, 204, 206, 209, 216, 240–1, 249–53, 255–6, 269–70, 273–4
Leicester 26, 64, 203, 255
Middlesex (Hanwell) 7, 26, 35, 40, 52, 58, 60, 62–5, 68–9, 74, 77, 80–2, 104–5, 109–10, 121, 133, 135–7, 139, 142–4, 146, 149, 166, 169, 177–8, 194, 203, 208, 211–13, 232–5, 253, 255, 260, 264, 266–70, 272–3, 275, 286
Norfolk (Thorpe) 26, 32, 35–6, 55, 58–9, 61, 66, 71, 73–5, 77–8, 82, 96–7, 100–1, 110–11, 119–24, 133, 139, 144–5, 148–9, 151, 160, 162–4, 166, 170, 172, 178, 195, 197, 236, 238–40, 249, 251–3, 255, 257–8, 270
Nottingham 6, 26–8, 30–3, 35–6, 38, 54–5, 58, 61–2, 70, 73–4, 78–9, 97, 101, 106–15, 119–24, 132, 134–5, 139, 143–5, 150, 161–2, 164–7, 169, 172, 178, 188–92, 200–1, 204, 207–9, 214–5, 236–7, 240–1, 251, 253, 257, 260, 268–70, 285
Stafford 26, 29–36, 38, 40–1, 54–6, 58, 61, 63, 72, 74–6, 79, 82, 95, 98, 113, 124, 132–6, 139, 143–5, 147, 149, 151–2, 160, 162–4, 166–7, 171–2, 174–5, 177, 192, 197, 199, 203, 205, 215–17, 236–7, 240, 252–3, 255–70, 273–5
Suffolk (Melton) 26, 35, 40, 52, 56–62, 66, 73–5, 77–8, 80–2, 102–3, 109, 116, 135–6, 144, 152, 166, 171, 177, 179, 190, 192, 196, 201, 210, 236–8, 268, 275, 286
Surrey 52, 63, 81, 199, 202–3, 236
West Riding (Wakefield) 4, 6, 26, 28–9, 31–3, 38–9, 42, 55, 57–8, 60–3, 65–9, 71–4, 77, 79–82, 97–8, 104–5, 108–12, 114, 118, 120–1, 123, 133, 135, 140, 143, 146, 148, 151–2, 160–1, 163–6, 169–70, 173–9, 187–94, 203–8, 210–14, 228–36, 238, 240–1, 250–1, 253, 257, 267, 271, 285
private asylums
Bethnal Green 35, 95
Bilston 95
Brislington House 33
Castleton House 134
Droitwich 76, 95, 103, 134
Fishponds 134
Haydock Lodge 72
Henley-in-Arden 95
Hereford 16, 203
Hoxton 95
Hook Norton 95
Peckham 95
Sculcoates Refuge 228
Spring Vale 41, 95, 216
West Malling 95
attendants *see* staff

Baines, Edward 94, 192
Bakewell, Thomas 40–3, 95, 103, 105, 159, 163, 192, 197, 201, 208, 216, 259
Bartlett, Peter 23, 64
basements 79, 162, 167, 171–2, 212
baths
cold 203
foot 203
plunge/surprise 203–4
warm 203–5
Bathurst, Revd Charles 65, 70
Battie, Dr William 19, 188, 198, 200
Becher, Revd J.T. 28, 38, 54, 56, 190, 237
Bedford 27
Bedford, Duke of 27
Bedfordshire 27, 29, 32
Bentham, Jeremy 34
Benthamites 22, 23
Bevans, James 34
Bicetre 227
Birmingham 76, 152, 217
Blake, Dr Andrew 204, 214, 215, 268
bleeding 101, 200–2
blisters 201–2
boards of guardians 59, 72, 96, 125, 166
boards of governors 53, 56, 70, 117, 261–3, 265–6
Bodmin 32
Bootle 29
Boston (Lincs) 72
Briggs, Asa 260
Bristol 33, 101, 124, 134

Bromhead, Sir Edward Ffrench 120, 152, 263
Browne, W.A.F., 137, 143, 148, 150, 239–40
Burrows, George Man 37, 189, 206
Button, Dr George 59, 62, 66, 73, 109–10, 116, 150, 166, 173, 178, 190, 197, 202, 209, 214, 235, 240, 249, 251, 270

calomel 199
cannabis 199
Caryl, Thomas 61, 119, 121, 249–50, 253
Castel, Robert 64
cells 24, 33, 37, 121, 132, 139, 159, 161–3, 167, 171, 179, 257, 272, 275
chains 18, 38, 120, 124, 216, 248–51, 253, 255–6, 258, 261, 273
charges 73–6
Charlesworth, Dr Edward Parker 56–7, 66, 107, 176–7, 190, 192, 194, 197, 199, 201, 238, 242, 261–7, 271, 273–4
Cheltenham 98, 100–2, 108, 112, 134, 217
Cheshire 32, 76
Chetwynd, George 36
Cirencester 72
circular swing chair 205–7, 212, 231
classification 24, 34, 42, 160, 167, 172, 192–4, 230, 261
clergymen 54–5
clerks 62
clothes
  removal of 99–100
  tearing of 99, 119–20, 233
coercion 18, 82, 118–19, 258, 260–1, 273
  see also mechanical restraint
coercion chair *see* restraint chair
cold applications 200, 202–3
Cole, W., Junior 32
Commissioners in Lunacy 195, 199, 202, 215, 270, 286
confinement, rationale for 188–9
Conolly, Dr John 60, 82, 103, 107, 109–10, 124, 132, 135–8, 142, 161–2, 171, 174, 177–8, 197, 201, 204, 209, 212, 233, 235, 258, 260, 264, 266–72, 276, 287
Conolly, William 134
Cookson, Dr Alfred 57, 265
Cookson, Dr William 151, 160, 171, 265–7
Cornwall 29, 32
Corsellis, Dr Charles Caesar 69, 72, 74, 106–12, 115, 118, 123, 136, 150, 152, 169, 174–6, 187, 192, 194, 196, 211, 214, 235–6, 240, 252–3, 267–8, 271, 285
Cox, Dr Joseph Mason 191, 198, 201, 205–6, 254
Crawley, Revd Charles 54, 65, 175
criminal lunatics 22, 94
Crommelinck, Dr C. 119–20, 124, 151–2, 162, 164, 167–8, 179, 211, 215, 235, 241
croton oil 199
Crowther, Dr Caleb 57–8, 67–9, 109, 173, 176, 229
Cullen, Dr William 191
Currie, Dr James 16, 19

Darwin, Erasmus 205
day rooms 37, 140, 163–4, 167, 173–4, 178, 240, 253, 269
delusions 99–102
Derbyshire 76, 110–11
design 28, 30–6
  see also architecture
De Vitrie, Dr Edmund 107, 120, 123, 136, 139, 147, 175, 177, 204, 209, 256, 269–70, 273–4
Devon 76, 96
Devonport 76
diet 59, 66, 77, 145, 164–6, 174, 178, 196
Digby, Anne 2, 111, 131, 159
digitalis 200
discharge(s) 24, 54–5, 59, 70–3, 213, 217, 285
disease 69, 169, 174–7, 231
Doerner, Klaus 64
douche *see* shower baths
drainage 170
drugs *see* medicines
Duck, James 60
Dunston, Thomas 33

Earle, Pliny 121, 164
economy 39, 61, 65–6, 69, 77–8, 113, 115, 133, 144, 153, 166, 168, 231–7, 252
electrification 205
Ellis, Harriet Warner 210
Ellis, Mildred 67–8, 137, 228, 230–3
Ellis, (Sir) William 28, 39, 42, 60–4, 66–9, 72, 74, 77, 81, 104–5, 108–9, 112, 114, 117–18, 121, 133, 137, 148, 169, 173, 176, 178, 189, 192–5, 200–14, 227–39, 253–4, 258, 260, 270, 287
emetics 198, 202
employment *see* work
epilepsy 114, 116, 151, 193–4, 199, 202, 252–3
Epsom salts *see* magnesium sulphate
escapes 124, 140, 148, 234, 250–1
evangelicals 22–3

Falmouth 71
fear principle 191
Fears, Michael 212, 228
Ferriar, Dr John 19, 198, 248
finances 22, 24–5, 27–31, 73–8

Fisher, Thomas 61, 66, 262
Fletcher, Ralph 189
food, refusal of 118–19, 197
force feeding 197
Foucault, Michel 13, 64, 276
Foulston, John 32, 34
Fox, Edward Long 33
Fox, Dr Francis 215

Gainsborough 98
galleries 37, 118, 122, 132, 136, 139–40, 146, 148, 159, 162–4, 167, 171–4, 240, 242, 255–6, 263
galvanization *see* electrification
games 240–2
Garrett, John 33, 35, 61, 95, 116, 133–6, 160, 171, 256
Gaskell, Samuel 107, 120, 123, 136, 139, 147, 175, 177, 199, 204, 209, 241, 256, 269–70, 273–4
Gilbey, Dr W.H. 176
Gilliland, Dr William 203
Gloucester 16, 20, 21, 97, 100, 110
Gloucester, Bishop of 55
glysters 202
governors 15, 17–19, 35, 53–4, 56–8, 66, 72–4, 78, 81, 83, 150, 164, 167, 190, 209, 261–2, 266, 274, 286
Granville, Dr A.B. 275
Grenville, Charles 22

Hadfield, James 21
Hadwen, Samuel 249, 262, 265–7
Hallaran, William Saunders 227
Halliday, Sir Andrew 102, 230, 236
Hanwell 7, 40
Harrison, Joseph 213
Harrison's Fund 213–4, 235
Harrowby, Earl of 55
Haslam, John 103, 142–3, 191, 197, 248, 254
heating 162–3, 171–2
hemp 199
Higgins, Revd Charles 118, 120, 190
Higgins, Godfrey 28–9, 33, 39, 42, 56, 66–8, 148, 228–9
Hill, George Nesse 198, 201, 206, 254
Hill, Robert Gardiner 66, 119, 122, 124, 164, 177, 189, 201, 204, 238, 241–2, 258, 262–73, 287
Hitch, Samuel 60, 62, 65, 70, 72, 79, 82, 124, 134, 147, 168, 172, 178, 194, 201, 203, 216–17, 234, 241, 269, 272, 287
hospitals
  Derby 162, 215
  Hereford 15
  Leicester 15
  Lincoln 31, 53
  Liverpool 15
  Manchester 15
  Nottingham 28
  Radcliffe Infirmary 31, 53
  Stafford 29
  voluntary 13–14, 16, 19, 53
  York 15
house committees 37, 55–6, 122, 203, 217
house stewards 62–3
house surgeons 66, 262, 265, 274
  see also superintendents
Howard, John 20
Hunter, Dr Alexander 19, 33

idiots 72, 94, 99, 112–16, 151, 194
Ignatieff, Michael 4
incurables 20, 41–2, 72, 76, 113–15, 118, 120, 152, 180, 188, 192–4, 259
infirmaries *see* hospitals
Ingleman, Richard 31–3, 35
insanity (hereditary) 106

Jepson, George 38, 208
Jones, Kathleen 23, 31, 251
justices of the peace *see* magistrates

keepers 19, 117, 122, 131–58, 216, 251–2, 256, 259
  see also staff
Keighley 106
Kent 77
Kingdon, Richard 60
Kirkman, John 60, 66, 77, 80–2, 102, 109, 116, 152, 166, 171, 177, 190, 192, 196, 199, 201, 210, 237–8, 268–9
Knight, Paul Slade 60, 104–5, 114, 118–22, 136–7,175, 189, 195, 197, 200–1, 206, 209, 216, 249–50, 252, 254

Lady Middleton's Fund 214
Lancashire 29, 32, 79, 162
Lancaster 29, 32
Lancet, The 264, 266–8
Leicestershire 76
leisure pursuits 239–42
libraries 240–1
Lincoln, Dean of 54
Liverpool 16, 29, 96
location 15, 24, 29–32, 52
London 7, 13, 232
Luckin, Bill 5
lunatic hospitals *see* asylums, charitable

Mackenzie, Charlotte 159
mad-doctors 3, 232, 248
  see also alienists

madhouses 6, 13–14, 17, 19, 23–4, 40, 73–5, 95–6, 103, 113, 143, 159, 190, 201, 240, 248, 266, 284
see also asylums, private
magistrates 23, 25–8, 31, 33, 35–9, 41–2, 53, 64–71, 77–80, 83, 95, 120, 133, 159, 229, 233, 236, 238, 267, 275, 286
magnesium sulphate 199
Maidstone 80, 95
Manchester 20, 96, 101
mania 100–1, 111, 194, 196, 198–9, 201–5
Markus, Thomas 159
Marsham, Lord 270–1
Martineau, Harriet 137, 215, 232
masturbation 105, 112
Matlock 73
matrons 57, 60–1, 65, 78, 173, 229, 275
mechanical restraint 18, 34–5, 38, 118–20, 122, 140, 149, 152, 168, 200, 212, 229, 233, 247–63, 268–74, 276
medical assistants 62
medical treatment 3, 4, 59, 194–200, 249
medicines 59, 195, 198–200
melancholia 101, 106, 112, 162, 193–4, 199, 201–2, 205, 209
Mellett, David 228
Methodism 105, 110–12, 210, 228
Metropolitan Commissioners in Lunacy 7, 52, 81, 117, 166–7, 169, 174, 179, 194–5, 236, 239, 253, 270–3, 275, 286
Middlesex 42, 64, 68–9, 232–3, 267
Middleton, Lady 214
Millingen, James 253
Monro, Dr John 188, 191, 198, 200–1
moral causes of insanity 102–12
moral management 4, 7, 34, 82–3, 190, 207–13, 286–7
moral treatment 3–4, 61, 133, 136, 159, 190–2, 207–13, 227, 233, 241, 243, 249, 260–1, 276–7, 286
Morison, Sir Alexander 202
Morris, Thomas 38, 192, 208, 251
muffs 256
Mulock, Thomas 215
music 241–2

Nash, John 15, 22
Newcastle, Duke of 54
noise 159, 163–4, 216
Nolan, Peter 137, 138
non-restraint 2, 4, 7, 82, 121, 124, 132–3, 138, 142, 150, 177, 197, 213, 241, 243, 247, 253, 259, 264–77, 286–7
Norfolk 29, 65, 76
Norwich 29, 195
Nottinghamshire 25, 27, 31
nurses *see* staff

occupations *see* work
Oldham 96
opiates 199–200
overcrowding 65, 71–2, 77, 79–82, 117, 172–4, 176–7, 180
overseers *see* parish officers
Owen, Ebenezer 195
Oxfordshire 26, 30

padded rooms 272
paralysis (general) 202
Pargeter, William 191
parish officers 25, 39, 70–2, 74, 112, 114, 133
paternalism 27, 211
patients
charity 17, 23, 58, 60, 74–5, 79, 98, 108, 111, 165, 217, 260
convalescent 136, 161, 192–4, 209, 237–8
dirty 33, 78, 120, 133, 162–3, 167–8, 171–2
numbers 63
pauper 60, 75, 79–80, 165–7, 179, 260
private 17, 23, 25, 40, 58, 62, 74–5, 79, 107, 111, 147, 161, 165, 167, 179, 217, 234, 241, 260
refractory 120–1, 133, 167–8, 171–2, 194, 232–3, 253, 272, 275
Paul, (Sir) George Onisephorus 6, 16, 20–5, 35
Peel, Sir Robert 116
Pennington, Dr Charles 38, 202
philanthropy 13–17, 28, 81
Philo, Chris 168
phrenology 195
physicians 14–15, 18–19, 31, 57–9, 65–9, 72, 78, 117, 152, 160, 162, 176, 187, 198, 209, 215, 217–18, 228, 249, 261, 266, 268–9
Pinel, Phillippe 208, 227, 264, 268
Pither, William 61
poor law 23, 76, 115–17, 163, 233, 235
Porter, Roy 3
poverty 104, 107–8, 196, 213
Powell, Thomas 120, 135, 145, 169, 215, 268
Poynder, George 35, 61–2, 133–4, 193, 210, 216, 230, 234, 270–1
Prichard, James Cowles 285
Prichard, Thomas 268
Prince Regent 29
prison(s) 20–1, 27–8, 30, 32, 34, 37, 42, 53, 131, 135, 143, 159–61, 177, 253, 268, 270, 274
protest 40–3, 123–4, 215–16
Proud, Samuel 95
puerperal disorders 99, 106–7, 196

punishment 18, 203–7, 249–51
  see also violence
purgatives 198–9, 202

Quick, Thomas 62, 234–5

radicals 23
reformers 20, 22–3, 52, 159, 190, 227, 260, 276, 286
refractory wards 133, 212, 259, 265, 275
Reid, Robert 40
religion 102, 209–11
religious insanity 102–3, 105, 109–10
religious services 79, 209–11
restraint *see* mechanical restraint
restraint chair 120, 123, 164, 249–50, 252–3, 258, 267
Richardson, Dr 67
Ricketts, William 95, 103, 134, 196
Romilly, Samuel 22
Rose, George 22
rotating chair *see* circular swing chair
rules and regulations 18–19, 28, 35, 56–7, 60, 67–8, 136, 139–41, 146–7, 152, 188, 190, 229, 234, 248, 262

salaries 61–2
sanitation 169–70, 176–7
Saragossa asylum 208, 227
Scrivinger, William 255, 262
Scull, Andrew 23, 29, 31, 59, 63–4, 93, 117, 137, 144, 212, 239, 276
seclusion 272–3
segregation *see* classification
Select Committees
  1807 6, 22–3, 27, 33
  1815 6, 28, 34, 37–8, 41, 159, 190, 196, 227, 237, 248, 260
  1827 7
servants *see* staff
setons 202
Sheffield 108, 250
shower baths 149, 202–5, 212
Shropshire 76
Shute, Dr Hardwick 57
Smith, George 99
Smith, William 273
social class 16–17, 33, 40, 75, 79, 111, 165, 167–8, 179, 193, 232
solitary confinement *see* seclusion
spectators 160
Spencer, Lord 21
sports 240–2
staff
  attributes 133–7, 141–2, 265, 272–3
  conditions 122, 142–53, 175, 259
  deficiencies 122, 137–8
  dismissals 59, 138, 146, 148, 150, 152, 265, 267, 273
  duties 57, 63, 138–42, 146, 205, 212, 230, 265, 271, 273–4
  numbers 77, 118, 122, 131–3, 259, 269
  pay 77, 122, 132, 138, 142–5, 153, 274
  promotion 134
  ratios 132–3, 265, 271
  recruitment 59–60, 133–7, 144, 148
Staffordshire 36, 40, 96, 99
Stanley, Lord 29, 55
Stark, William 30, 32, 34–5, 40
stigma 143, 160, 217
Storer, Dr John 27–8, 33, 57, 188, 192
strait waistcoats 120–1, 200, 205, 248–51, 254–6, 258, 261–2, 267
straps, leather 163, 205, 253, 256–7
straw 163
subscribers 14–16, 21, 28–31, 54, 73, 79–80
subscriptions 13–16, 29–31, 36, 53, 57, 266
Suffolk 35, 65, 76
suicide/suicide attempts 97–9, 102, 106, 123, 140, 145, 150, 197, 235, 250–1, 257
superintendents 33, 35, 37, 42, 56–63, 65, 68, 70, 81, 83, 95, 104, 107, 113–14, 116–17, 131, 133–4, 143–6, 152, 162, 166, 187, 192, 194, 199, 209–13, 215–18, 229, 233–4, 238, 240–2, 253, 260, 266–70, 274, 287
surgeons 14–16, 19, 35, 59–61, 66–7, 173, 228, 249
Suzuki, Akihito 64

Thurnam, John 166, 174, 285
Tomes, Nancy 259, 276
Tories 23
trades *see* work
trenchers 119, 164
Tuke, Daniel Hack 39
Tuke, Samuel 3, 6, 28, 33–4, 38–9, 42, 63, 81, 118, 136–7, 161, 164, 173, 190–3, 197, 208, 210, 212, 228, 233, 250, 252, 254, 259, 264
Tuke, William 208
Tyerman, Dr 198

ventilation 162, 170–2, 177–8
Vessey, Anne 265
violence
  between patients 121–3, 140, 142, 273, 275
  toward patients 148–50, 258, 265
  toward staff 121–3, 142, 149, 151, 275
visiting governors *see* visitors
visiting justices *see* visitors
visitors 27, 29, 31–3, 35, 39–40, 53–6, 58–62, 65, 69–74, 76–8, 81, 114, 117, 131, 144, 149–50, 162, 165–6, 168–73, 176, 178, 188–90, 212–14,

217, 229, 236, 238, 253, 260, 266, 269–71

wages *see* salaries
Wakefield 28, 100, 120
Wakley, Thomas 266
Wallett, George 35, 56, 61, 66
walls 32, 160–1
Walton, John 94, 144, 259
Warburton, Thomas 35
Warwickshire 76
water supplies 24, 168–70, 174, 176–7
West Riding 33, 107
Whigs 7
Whitbread, Samuel 22, 27, 33
Wilberforce, William 22
Wilkes, James 149, 151, 177, 199, 205, 215, 256, 259, 270, 273–5
Willis, Francis 189
windows 32, 162–4, 177–8
Wing, John 32
Worcestershire 76
work 57, 124, 135, 140, 194, 207–9, 214, 227–39
  agricultural 229, 232, 234
  baking 135, 230–1
  basket making 232
  brewing 135, 230–1
  bricklaying 231–2, 237
  brushmaking 232
  carpentry 135, 231, 234, 237
  cleaning 234, 237, 238
  clothing manufacture 135, 229–30, 232, 234
  digging 229, 234
  earth-moving 237
  engineering 135, 230
  framework knitting 234
  gardening 135, 230, 232, 234–5, 238
  laundry 231, 234–5, 237
  mop-making 232
  needlework 232, 234, 237
  painting 231, 234
  pipe-laying 234
  shoemaking 135, 229–32, 234
  spinning 231–2
  stone-breaking 237
  straw-plaiting 232, 234
  tailoring 231, 234
  water pumping 234, 237
  weaving 231, 235
  window cleaning 234
workhouse(s) 65, 71–4, 76, 95–6, 113–15, 143, 213
Wright, David 94
Wright, Dr Thomas Giordani 175–6
Wynn, Charles Williams 22, 24

Yarborough, Earl of 55
Yorkshire 28–9, 77